E.

Alth
move
devel
cont
playv
tions
of m
voice
hand
cultu
and
defir
of A

JULI
Inter
artic
and

Expressionism and Modernism in the American Theatre

Bodies, Voices, Words

JULIA A. WALKER

University of Illinois at Urbana – Champaign

CAMBRIDGE
UNIVERSITY PRESS

CAMBRIDGE UNIVERSITY PRESS

Cambridge, New York, Melbourne, Madrid, Cape Town, Singapore, São Paulo, Delhi

Cambridge University Press
The Edinburgh Building, Cambridge CB2 8RU, UK

Published in the United States of America by Cambridge University Press, New York

www.cambridge.org
Information on this title: www.cambridge.org/9780521108911

First published 2005
This digitally printed version 2009

A catalogue record for this publication is available from the British Library

ISBN 978-0-521-84747-6 hardback
ISBN 978-0-521-10891-1 paperback

Contents

Illustrations

Acknowledgments

When I was growing up, my grandmother, a piano teacher, took me and my sister Sarah to the Windswept Music Workshop in Berea, Kentucky every summer. There, we would take morning exercise classes, known as "body tuning," in which we would prepare our "instruments" to play for Margaret Allen, the workshop's founder and director. Margaret's philosophy, known as "creative motion musicianship," held that an artistic performance necessarily involved the whole body. Thus, after relaxing our bodies through yoga and yawning exercises in the morning, we would recondition them by moving musically to a piece of music that we had analyzed according to its rhythm and pattern of harmonic balances. In this way, we would be ready to perform the piece we had prepared for our afternoon tutorial with Margaret in an "expressive" manner.

Years later, while reading about the work of François Delsarte and his many followers in the United States, I was struck by a feeling that I was already familiar with it. Creative motion musicianship, it would seem, was simply one of many manifestations of what was once popularly known as the "expressive culture movement." My grandmother, a lifelong supporter of the workshop, was a sixth-generation Delsartian. I thus begin my acknowledgments with a "thank you" to my grandmother, Evelyn Pickett Walker (1911–1998), for introducing me to one of the subjects of this book.

Many other thanks are due, especially to those institutions and individuals who contributed directly to the book's composition. At Duke University, where this book began as my dissertation, I received crucial early feedback from my director, John Clum, as well as committee members Jane Gaines, Kristine Stiles, and Neil Blackadder. Joel Pfister also generously read and commented on an early version of my O'Neill chapter, for which I am especially grateful. At the College of William & Mary, I received two summer research grants which assisted me in the initial revisions of my dissertation research. A Mellon Foundation Grant for a one-month residency at the Harry Ransom Humanities Research Center at the University of Texas – Austin allowed me to complete my research on Elmer Rice. At the University of Illinois, I received a Humanities Released-Time Fellowship for a semester of research and writing support, along with an Arnold O. Beckman award for a research assistant as the typescript neared completion.

The preparation of this book required me to visit many archives and special collections where I was given helpful assistance by, among others: Jean-Claire Van Ryzin at the Harry Ransom Humanities Research Center; Jeremy McGraw at the New York Public Library's Billy Rose Performing Arts Collection; Raymond Wemmlinger at the Players' Club Library; the staff of the Morris Library at the University of Southern Illinois where I consulted the "John Howard Lawson Papers"; Shan Sutton and Jerry Dickey of the University of Arizona who assisted me in my research on Sophie Treadwell; the staff of the Beinecke Library at Yale University; and, at the University of Illinois, Kathleen Kluegel (English Library), Thomas Mills (Law Library), Bruce Swann (Rare Books Room), and Desiree Yamtoob (Main Stacks), all of whom helped me excavate the library's labyrinthine riches. To these names must be added Ellen McWhorter, my research assistant, Brad Campbell, Josh Eckhardt and Dan Yezbick – all graduate students in the English Department – who directed me to sources that strengthened various aspects of the book.

Here, at the University of Illinois, members of the American Literature Reading Group provided essential commentary and criticism: a special thanks to Nina Baym, Robert Dale Parker, Trish Loughran, Nancy Castro, and Mark Christian Thompson. Thanks, too, to my colleagues Cary Nelson, Joe Valente, Ramona Curry, Jed Esty, and Zack Lesser, who served as critical interlocutors and/or provided valuable advice.

Special thanks go to Jeff and Susan Lawson, who graciously granted me permission to quote from their father's materials; to Selma Luttinger of the Robert A. Freedman Dramatic Agency, for permission to quote from the plays of Elmer Rice; and to Berlinda Parra of the Diocese of Tucson, for permission to quote from the plays of Sophie Treadwell.

At Cambridge University Press, I owe a huge "thank you" to series editor Don Wilmeth for guiding the manuscript through the review and revision processes, to the anonymous readers for their insights and suggestions, to Vicki Cooper, Becky Jones, and Liz Davey for overseeing the book's production, to Audrey Cotterell for carefully editing the typescript, and to Mike Leach for preparing the index.

And, finally, an expression of gratitude is due my family, whose encouragement and support throughout the many years of this book's composition allowed me to integrate it into my life. To my parents, Evelyn and Oreon Walker, to Sarah, Liz and Louis Moore, to Carolyn Rieger and Bill Maxwell, Sr., and to Stephanie, Jeff, Anna and Lizzie Binder – many, many thanks. But thanks most of all to my husband, Bill Maxwell, who not only served as the book's primary editor, but played Clark Gable to my Zita Johann, giving me the "spiritual harmony" necessary to write it. To him, our dog Elvis, and our son Bix (who is due even as I write these words), this book is lovingly dedicated.

PART I

Introduction

Aт тне тuгn оf тне тwеnтіетн сеnтuгу, аmегісаn сulтuге was electrified by a revolution in communications technology, with the type-writer, wireless telegraph, telephone, phonograph, cinematographe, and radio appearing within a thirty-five-year span. The typewriter was in production by 1874; the telegraph became wireless in 1896; the telephone generated its own network, reaching from the East Coast to Denver by 1884, becoming fully transcontinental in 1915; the phonograph created a demand for sound recordings which were in mass production by 1893; the cinematographe introduced a new type of entertainment – silent film – in 1895; and the radio made its first broadcast in 1906. As many scholars have noted, the wide-scale implementation of these new communications technologies changed the way Americans experienced distance and time.[1] What has been less discussed, however, is the way these new technologies altered the experience of communication itself. When a pattern of electrical impulses could be sent across the continent and decoded in a matter of seconds, when the grain of the voice could be heard apart from the immediate physical presence of the speaker, when meaningful gestures were presented by bodies removed in both space and time, the messages transmitted through these new technologies must have seemed strange because so unexpectedly distant from the moment of their communicative intent. The act of communication – once experienced as a relatively integrated process – must have felt as if it were suddenly rent apart, splintered into the newly separable elements of bodies, voices, and words.

Floating free in the debris of modernity's shattering blow, these isolated elements posed the problem of where exactly meaning lay: did it reside in or as a function of words alone, or did it include performative features such as gesticulation, intonation, and dynamics? This book argues that such questions and the debates they spawned serve as the founding context of

I

American theatrical modernism. For it was in the theatre – that art form most dependent upon bodies, voices, and words – that fears concerning these new communication technologies were given their most acute cultural expression. Analyzing plays by Eugene O'Neill, Elmer Rice, John Howard Lawson, and Sophie Treadwell, this book locates the origins of American theatrical modernism in expressionism, a dramatic form that has been long misunderstood. Recontextualizing American expressionism within the history of modernity, I show that it is not simply a minor derivation of the better-known German movement, but a complicated artistic response to the forces of modernization. For, giving shape to these experimental plays was the vague but intensely felt anxiety that new communication technologies would displace the human artist from the act of making meaning, mechanically reproducing bodies (e.g., in film), voices (e.g., in phonograph recordings), and words (e.g., the typewriter). Frequently featuring bodies "seen but not heard," "voices heard but not seen," and telegraphically terse dialogue, these plays figure such fears not only thematically in their dystopic vision of modern life, but formally in their expressionistic style.

Readers familiar with recent scholarship on modern technology will recognize an echo of Friedrich Kittler's *Gramophone, Film, Typewriter* (1986; trans. 1999) in this book's subtitle. Indeed, Kittler's work, in bringing the discourse theory of Michel Foucault to bear on media studies, has influenced my understanding of these communication technologies and their impact on modern consciousness. But, as the difference in our titles suggests, we begin our respective studies from separate points of departure. Where he is primarily focused on the technologies themselves, examining the way they shape our understanding of ourselves as conscious subjects, I am more interested in the human body and the crisis it suffered in the moment these new technologies first appeared. For, while they made the body newly visible through the metaphors they offered, these technologies also threatened to displace, replace, or even erase the human body whenever the vehicle of technology was made to substitute for the tenor of the body. Wishing to recuperate a sense of the profound ambivalence – the fears as well as desires – that many turn-of-the-century Americans felt toward these new communication technologies, I propose in this book a way of understanding the cultural expressions that accompanied their emergence.

Walter Benjamin's famous essay "The Work of Art in the Age of Mechanical Reproduction" remains one of the best analyses of this modern ambivalence toward technology. Written in 1935, it stands as an artifact of that ambivalence as well. In speaking of the mechanical reproduction of objects that were once created by hand, Benjamin laments the loss of the original object's "aura," its unique situatedness in space and time. What gives that object its aura, Benjamin surmises, is the artist's relationship to the materials out of which it is made; mechanical reproduction strips the object of that relationship, fetishizing it into instant commodity form. While postmodern theorists are not incorrect to accuse Benjamin of "nostalgia," they often err in reducing his complex ruminations to a naive longing for the past. For, while he does, in fact, lament the loss of an unalienated past, he also recognizes the anti-elitist potential of these technologies in providing more democratic access to powerful works of art. That he saw that potential so quickly put to fascistic ends with the Nazi propagation of film led him to end his essay on a less than optimistic note. But that he saw both potentials existing within such technologies of artistic reproduction has been frequently overlooked.

One of the reasons Benjamin's essay has been misread, I believe, has to do with an anti-Benjaminian tendency to view history through the lens of dominant ideas. That "the culture industry," as his Frankfurt School colleagues deemed it, so quickly assumed hegemonic power in the western world, for example, has led many critics to emphasize the cautionary aspects of Benjamin's essay, as if it were an unambiguous indictment of mass-produced art. But this is to presume a sort of "whig" history of ideas, where the emergence of dominant ideas only is worthy of being traced. A contention of this book, however, is that cultures also develop out of a dialectic engagement with *failed* ideas – those ideas that are disproved, disparaged, and dismissed from the dominant culture but whose negation gives shape to subsequent patterns of thought. In them lie important and largely untapped secrets of cultural history that can shed new light on misunderstood cultural forms such as American dramatic expressionism. Failed ideas are, to be sure, much more difficult to excavate. Their traces are often found only in their negation; "progress," in other words, is a narrative made from successive waves of failed ideas that have been cast off. Turning our attention to those failed ideas, however, can tell us much about how such progress was made. As I show in the first half of this book, they can provide us with a fuller sense of the cultural context out of which American expressionism emerged and may in fact challenge the long-held belief that it was merely a minor derivation of the better-known German movement.

That narrative – first floated by journalists reporting on "the new stage-craft" arriving from Europe in the 1920s – was cemented in 1972 by

Mardi Valgemae's *Accelerated Grimace*, the first full-length critical study of American expressionist drama. Citing the term's first use by French painter Julien-Auguste Hervé in 1901 and its subsequent adoption by German literary critic Kasimir Edschmid in 1917, Valgemae asserts that "expressionism, like most new developments in early twentieth-century art, music, and literature, originated in Europe" (2). He cites the American premieres of Robert Wiene's film *The Cabinet of Dr. Caligari* in 1921, Georg Kaiser's play *From Morn to Midnight* in 1922, and Walter Hasenclever's play *The Son* in 1925 as important and necessary influences on the expressionist plays written by American dramatists, based upon formal homologies such as the stylized presentation of a subjective inner world, compressed syntax, exaggerated caricatures, and episodic action (8–10; 2–3). While it is true that American and German expressionist dramas share many of these traits, it is not necessarily true that German expressionism was the only or even primary influence upon the development of the American form. Yes, German expressionism predates the development of American expressionism, but the German plays were not produced on the American stage until many of the American plays had been written and, in some instances, already produced. Yes, American playwrights had access to copies of the German plays, but they consistently denied having read or been influenced by them. O'Neill, for example, claimed that *The Emperor Jones* and *The Hairy Ape* were written "long before I had ever heard of Expressionism" (quoted in B. H. Clark 83), while Rice insisted that *The Adding Machine* was "a spontaneous thing. I had no experience with German expressionism at that time" (quoted in Elwood 3). Although Lawson and Treadwell made no such public disclaimers about the influences on their plays, Rice offered them his own defense, asserting that "there is no foundation for the belief that the Americans – Lawson, O'Neill, Treadwell, whatever others there were – were imitating German forms" (quoted in Elwood 6). Valgemae, like many critics, dismisses such denials on the grounds that they were likely motivated by the playwright's conscious or unconscious desire to protect his or her artistic vanity. But this seems rather unfair since O'Neill did not fail to credit Ibsen, Strindberg, and Hauptmann as important influences on his work, and Rice allowed that, however unaware he was of any debt he owed to *The Cabinet of Dr. Caligari*, it might indeed have been an "unconscious" influence. There may have been other reasons why these playwrights did not want to admit of German influence, including the anti-German sentiment that persisted in the wake of World War I,[2] but vanity is not a very convincing reason to reject their denials.

What if we were to take these playwrights at their word? What if they were not directly influenced by German expressionism in the writing of their plays? What if there were other – perhaps more influential – sources closer to home? This book contends that there were, demonstrating one such source in speech educator S. S. Curry's theory of "expression." Curry, drawing upon the work of French vocal instructor François Delsarte, challenged conventional elocutionary instruction by insisting that communication was not a function of the voice alone but a whole bodily process that depended upon the perfect coordination of all three "languages" of the body – verbal, vocal, and pantomimic. Tapping into cultural anxieties about the new communications technologies that made these languages visible in their newly isolated form, Curry's theory inspired the "expressive culture movement," a broad-based program of personal and social reform advocating the performing arts as a means of overcoming the alienating conditions of modernity. An example of what Jackson Lears refers to as "anti-modernism," it held that these new technologies alienated human beings from their natural condition, throwing the body's rhythms out of alignment with the spiritual forces of the universe. Indeed, silent film rendered moving lips separate from the words they spoke – words that appeared on intertitles jarringly distant from their imaged source; phonograph recordings reoriented the experience of listening by erasing the spectacle of singers or musicians practicing their craft; even the typewriter altered the act of correspondence – its regular and standardized forms stamped out the idiosyncracies of handwriting that were believed to reveal the writer's "personality." It was thus to repair such losses, to restore a sense of human integrity to the act of communication, that students of the expressive culture movement were taught to re-coordinate their verbal, vocal, and pantomimic languages. By participating in drama, music and dance, students could recalibrate their body's natural rhythms to a state of harmony with the spiritual universe and thus counter the alienating conditions of modern life.

As popularized through the expressive culture movement and implemented in high school and college literary instruction, Curry's theory of expression was well known to all who came of age between the 1890s and 1910s, including the expressionist playwrights discussed in this book. In it, American dramatists had a ready means of representing modern alienation when they sat down to write their expressionist plays in the 1920s. Indeed, Curry's three languages appear to be the source of these plays' distinct formal style; counterpointed, rather than coordinated, they represent the spiritual malaise experienced by each play's central character as he or she comes to terms with the imposition of industrial rhythms on his or her life. That these playwrights did not dispute the term "expressionist" to describe their plays (however much they refused German attribution) suggests a tacit acknowledgment of Curry's theory and/or the expressive culture movement more generally as a source. Audiences schooled in expression and familiar with its popularization may have been confused by these plays' cynical appropriation and ironization of Curry's theory, but they would have known immediately how it was being used and what it was meant to represent.

That we can no longer see the link between Curry's theory and these expressionist plays has to do with the way the expressive culture movement has been erased from cultural memory. Based upon a moral-philosophical understanding of human character and a Romantic belief in mystical sources of inspiration, it was dismissed as a failed idea. So, too, was Curry's theory of expression – despite its legacy in New Critical formalism and methods of oral interpretation. Associated with finishing schools for young ladies and the lost art of elocution, expression was at once feminized within the cultural imaginary and deemed unworthy of serious scholarly attention such that it was little more than a footnote by the time Valgemae began his study. No wonder he did not consider it a possible source – even when he inadvertently stumbled across its path. As Valgemae notes in regard to the epigraph with which his book begins, the term "expressionist" actually first appears in the United States in 1878, in a novel by Charles DeKay. Although Valgemae doesn't pursue its significance, that novel is in fact an early parody of expressive culture enthusiasts.

In identifying the expressive culture movement as an important source of American expressionism, this book not only offers an alternative account of these plays' origin, but does so by fully contextualizing them within the history of cultural modernity. For, only by situating them within this history, can we see how these plays functioned as an aesthetic response to the very real fears and anxieties attending historical modernity. Modernism, in other words, is not simply an aesthetic movement marked by stylistic innovation (as explained by traditional formalist criticism), but must also be understood as a cultural response to the changed conditions of modernity. Appearing within an aesthetic register, it functions as a culture's attempt to represent itself to itself. This is not to say that the artist is an impersonal node through which a culture inscribes its meanings. Rather, as I discuss below, artists often respond in highly personal ways to the cultural and historical changes which find expression in their art. What I wish to emphasize here is that those changes are not merely incidental; they are, in fact, important sources of meaning. That is why it is important to understand dramatic modernism in relation to the historical changes associated with modernity. Where dramatic modernism differs from other forms of cultural modernism, of course, is in the specificity of its medium. Unlike painting, sculpture, literature or music, it utilized the formal languages of the theatre by which to articulate its modernist concerns. But the theatre was not just one site of articulation among many. Given the emergence of new communications technologies, it was a site of anxiety as well. After all, these technologies threatened not only the act of communication (as expressive culture's followers believed), but the very art of the theatre itself insofar as they fractured its formal languages into independent modes of signification. But, even as they functioned as a source of modernist anxiety, these technologies also provided playwrights with a heuristic for thinking about the way meaning is created by bodies, voices, and words. Borrowing Curry's verbal, vocal, and pantomimic languages, these playwrights gave aesthetic shape to their modernist concerns, creating the innovative formal style of American dramatic expressionism. This book thus expands the critical focus on expressionism, zooming out from an exclusively aesthetic consideration of its formal features to a larger cultural examination of the way those features developed in response to modernity.

One reason why the traditional critical narrative of German influence has been uncontested for so long has to do with the fact that German sources were indeed influential in the production and reception of American expressionist plays. As has been well established, many of the scene designers involved in the production of these plays studied the new stagecraft in Europe. Robert Edmond Jones, for example, worked under Max Reinhardt in Germany before designing the sets for O'Neill's and Treadwell's expressionist plays. And even those who didn't study abroad would have been familiar with new trends in the visual arts coming out of Europe – thanks to books by Sheldon Cheney, Oliver Sayler and Kenneth Macgowan, touring productions of Diaghilev's Ballet Russe (1911) and Max Reinhardt's *Sumurun* (1912), and, of course, the 1913 Armory Show. Such images would have been known not only to scene designers but to audiences generally, for whom artistic modernism would have provided a ready reference for understanding the visual style of American expressionist plays. The mistake critics have made is in assuming that the influences that shaped these plays' production and reception necessarily influenced their composition as well.

This, however, is to assume that playwrights wrote their expressionist plays with specific staging effects in mind when, in fact, nearly all of the playwrights discussed in this book were surprised and delighted to see the ways in which their ideas were realized on stage by the creative teams designing their plays' first productions. Indeed, many of the expressionist features singled out for comment by critics were devised by someone other than the playwright (e.g., Jig Cook's plaster dome in *The Emperor Jones*, Blanche Hays's use of masks in *The Hairy Ape*; Lee Simonson's giant calculator in *The Adding Machine*; Mordecai Gorelik's cartoonish backdrop in *Processional*, and Robert Edmond Jones's use of colored lights at the conclusion of *Machinal*). What this reveals is that, even within a theatre collective like the Provincetown Players, the composition and production processes were relatively independent.

This points to a crucial development in the productive relations of the American theatre. Where playwrights in the nineteenth century typically wrote their plays to fit the measurements of a specific company or a commissioning star, playwrights in the early twentieth century were beginning to write autonomous works of dramatic literature. The first part of this book elaborates the conditions that made this possible, demonstrating how technology helped convert what had been an actor's theatre throughout the nineteenth century into a playwright's theatre in the twentieth. Chapter 1 traces the ascent and decline of the actor's interpretive authority, seeing it figured in the "point," an acting technique whereby actors used their bodies to realize their interpretations of a playwright's text. With the rise of new technologies, however, that authority began to disappear, as actors' bodies increasingly became inscribed as signs within a scenic or filmic text that was authorized by someone else, usually the playwright. Chapter 2 discusses how, in the very moment that the artistic mantle of the theatre was passed from actor to playwright, the performative languages of the theatre came under attack. Once gesticulation and vocality could be recorded and reproduced, skills such as acting and elocution were deemed intellectually suspect, necessitating the redefinition of disciplines such as oratory within the new research academy. Tracing this process of redefinition and the debates that propelled it, this chapter shows how a text/performance split became institutionalized, stranding playwrights on the virgule between literary and theatrical values. Their double bind was, in part, resolved by changes in copyright law – the subject of chapter 3. It demonstrates the historically difficult position playwrights occupied in relation to the law. For, while copyright protected them from unlawful publication, it did nothing to protect them against unauthorized "copies" of their plays on stage. Detailing the legislative and judicial battles fought to protect performance rights, this chapter shows how those rights were finally secured with the invention of new recording technologies that rendered a performance "original" from which copies could be made. With texts and performances thus deemed distinct legal entities, the dramatic text could finally be separated from the theatrical apparatus and thus considered its own autonomous art form.

Peter Bürger has described autonomy as a defining condition of artistic modernism. Tracing historical changes within the function, production, and consumption of art, he shows how art became increasingly separated from its social context. Where sacred art served a communal function, for example, modern art reflects the self-understanding of the historical bourgeoisie. Where sacred art was anonymously and communally produced, modern art is produced by individual artists. Where sacred art was meant to be experienced by a collective social whole, modern art is individually consumed. Although this historical evolution was marked by periods of uneven development, it has resulted in the reification of modern art into its own autonomous object (48). As applied to modern drama, Bürger's model suggests a similar – if delayed – process of development. For, though the theatre has long been a collective art form, in the modern period it has undergone a similar process of autonomization. As the first part of this book demonstrates, the playwright's eclipse of the actor was accompanied by a radical devaluation of the performative languages of the theatre and a legal separation of the dramatic text from any performance of it, causing playwrights to assume a new relationship to their art. No longer tied to the producing apparatus of the theatre, playwrights were independent producers of an art form that was increasingly devoted to the portrayal of bourgeois life and consumed by audience members who, plunged into silent darkness, were encouraged to experience it individually rather than as part of a collective social whole. What this means is that the reification of American drama into its own autonomous art form marked the beginnings of American dramatic modernism.

This book demonstrates that expressionism was an important early phase of this development. For, in ironizing Curry's three languages, the expressionists not only represented the technologically induced alienation of their central characters but also found a way to establish their own legitimacy within a regime of literary value that considered drama a "bastard art." This is Susan Harris Smith's apt description of drama's uncertain position within the early twentieth-century American cultural field; born of the theatre, its literary paternity was always suspect. Although, as Smith notes, the roots of such an attitude can be traced to the anti-theatrical prejudice of centuries past, she argues that this "anti-dramatic bias" became acute at the turn of the twentieth century when anxieties over drama's relationship to the category of the literary became particularly rife (5–6). While Smith thoroughly documents the existence of this bias and its legacy in twentieth-century American literary criticism, she nonetheless leaves its origins obscure. Those origins, this book reveals, lie in the anti-performative foundation laid at the base of literary high modernism by figures such as George Santayana and T. S. Eliot. Disputing Curry's claim that all three languages were necessary to the act of communication, they maintained that meaning was a function of verbal signification alone.

With the performative languages of the theatre thus devalued, playwrights faced a serious problem: how to create plays of literary value without forsaking the theatrical medium. Martin Puchner has recently argued that, at the turn of the twentieth century, modern drama gave birth to "a theater at odds with the value of theatricality" (7). He suggests that writers such as Stéphane Mallarmé, James Joyce, and Gertrude Stein got around this problem by writing plays that were simply meant to be read, while playwrights such as W. B. Yeats, Bertolt Brecht, and Samuel Beckett forged a different solution, devising new means of controlling the meanings generated by the stage apparatus. But long before what Puchner calls the "diegetic" theatre of Brecht and Beckett – and in the very moment that Joyce was writing his "closet drama" – there was another group of playwrights who had worked out yet a third possible solution. They were the expressionists who, by disarticulating the performative languages of the theatre from the authority of their texts, were able to secure their otherwise questionable literary status while writing plays that remained theatrically viable.

The second part of this book details the work of four such expressionists, demonstrating how their ambivalence toward the new culture of technology led them to develop their expressionistic style. For, while it helped create the conditions of their artistic autonomy, it also threatened to render them obsolete. Ironically appropriating the three languages that technology made visible in their newly isolated form, these playwrights found a way to give expression to their own personal fears and professional anxieties. Chapter 4 examines Eugene O'Neill's *The Emperor Jones* (1920) and *The Hairy Ape* (1921; 1922), reading both plays as formal allegories of O'Neill's oedipal and professional concerns. Chapter 5 analyzes Elmer Rice's *The Adding Machine* (1922; 1923) and *The Subway* (1923; 1929) against the background of his unhappy experience as a screenwriter in Hollywood. Chapter 6 looks at John Howard Lawson's *Processional* (1924; 1925) as a cynical self-assessment of the role of the bourgeois artist, while chapter 7 treats Sophie Treadwell's *Machinal* (1928) in relation to her career in journalism, a notoriously – and often unrelentingly – masculinist domain.[3]

As I demonstrate in my readings of these six plays, the central character frequently serves as a figure for its playwright's own besieged sense of self, confronting the challenges of making art in an age of technological reproduction. Each play, then, may be seen to function as a "fantasm," or what Fredric Jameson refers to as a fantasy master narrative, in which the author resolves issues of real conflict through imaginative means. Those issues vary, of course, from playwright to playwright, but common to all is a haunting sense of uncertainty about his or her status within the changing cultural field. That is why these plays often read as naturalist allegories where the anti-hero's survival is tested by his or her ability to adapt to a technological environment.

If critics have been unable to recognize autobiographical elements in these plays, it is because such elements do not appear as *narrative* details (as is typical), but exist in the play's thematic and formal design. Themes such as "not belonging," "slavery," "containment," and "reproduction" not only appear in the stories of Brutus Jones, Yank, Mr. Zero, Sophie Smith, Dynamite Jim Flimmins, and Helen Jones, but resonate in each play's use of bodies, voices, and words. Invoking, even as they mock, Curry's theory of expression, these plays encode their playwrights' fears into the poses their characters strike and the voices that they sound. In this way, each play registers not just the playwright's thoughts but, according to Delsarte's originary schema upon which Curry's theory was based, his or her feelings and will, utilizing all three of Curry's languages to become what I will refer to as an "affective autobiography," a play in which the playwright encodes otherwise unrepresentable (and perhaps inadmissable) thoughts and feelings in its formal design.

Together, these plays reveal the struggle playwrights faced as artists in an age of technological change, and of how that struggle gave birth to American dramatic modernism. For, in identifying expressionism as an important early phase of American dramatic modernism, this book maintains that it – no less than any other form of artistic modernism – must be understood in relation to the vast cultural changes wrought by modernity and modernization. Its story lies not only in the dominant ideas that continue to shape our own moment, but in the failed ideas that were cast off as part of their dialectical negation; it lies not only in strips of celluloid, rubber discs, and ribbons of ink, but in all the ways that artists sought to resist these technologies through the reassertion of bodies, voices, and words.

I

Bodies: actors and artistic agency on the nineteenth-century stage

In 1826 – just six years after his stage debut – american-born actor Edwin Forrest favorably impressed visiting British star Edmund Kean with his performance of Iago to Kean's Othello. Where most actors up to that time played Iago as "a sullen and sombre villain, as full of gloom as of hate, and with such sinister manners and malignant bearing as made his diabolical spirit and purposes perfectly obvious," Forrest played him "as a gay and dashing fellow on the outside, hiding his malice and treachery under the signs of a careless honesty and jovial good humor," according to Forrest's biographer William Alger. Forrest's Iago, recounts Alger,

> while working insidiously on the suspicions of Othello, says to him, for example –
>
>> Look to your wife; observe her well with Cassio;
>> Wear your eye thus, not jealous, – nor secure
>
> All these words, except the last two, Forrest uttered in a frank and easy fashion; but suddenly, as if the intensity of his underknowledge of evil had automatically broken through the good-natured part he was playing on the surface and betrayed his secret in spite of his will, he spoke the words nor secure in a husky tone, sliding down from a high pitch and ending in a whispered horror. (Alger 145)

Kean, Alger notes, loved Forrest's rendering of the part, and said everyone thereafter must play it the same.

Using his voice to illustrate Iago's cunning duplicity, Forrest created what in theatrical parlance is known as a "point," a vocal or pantomimic technique designed to elucidate the meaning of the dramatic text. Presenting Iago as a "gay and dashing fellow," Forrest first spoke "in a frank and easy fashion." But, succumbing to the "malice and treachery" in his heart, Forrest's Iago belies his seeming good will with his "husky" voice. In this way, Forrest's change of voice not only helped illustrate Iago's character, but momentarily seduced the audience into being as deceived by Iago as was the unfortunate Moor before jolting them out of their absorption in the narrative and into a recognition of the dramatic irony at work. Such effects were the goal of every actor who sought to create innovative "points." Their reward was the immediate applause of an appreciative audience who obliged them to step out of character in order to accept their thanks.

This was the convention of "points" on the nineteenth-century stage. A signature technique of the Romantic style of acting, it was characterized by the actor's use of his or her body to realize a latent meaning in the dramatic text. In this chapter, I trace the history of the "point" from its critical origins in the eighteenth-century English elocutionary reform movement to its zenith on the nineteenth-century American stage to its eventual disappearance at the turn of the twentieth century, once realism and film had rendered it obsolete. As I show, its emergence, apotheosis, and decline on the legitimate stage can be mapped against the introduction of various communication technologies, from the printing press to the stage machinery of scenic realism to film. Existing in a dialectical relationship to these technologies, the "point" marked the extent to which actors commanded interpretive agency over the texts they performed. Indeed, the "point" itself became a figure for individual agency – both for actors throughout the nineteenth century and – as we'll see – for playwrights in the early twentieth. Ironically inscribing the actor's body into their expressionist plays, these playwrights recuperated the "point" to represent their characters' frustrated agency in a world increasingly dominated by machines.

The "point" in theory and practice

In its theatrical usage, the critical terminology of "points" appears to derive from the late eighteenth-century elocutionary movement in England which aimed to reform the practice of public speaking from both the pulpit and the stage. Citing abuses ranging from monotone to sing-song to rant, critics charged that the delivery of words often ran counter to their sense, and that the accompanying gestures were either stilted or inadequate to the passion being expressed.[1] Such misuse of voice and gesture was typical of the neoclassical style of declamation then practiced on the English stage, where every syllable of dramatic poetry tended to receive pronounced emphasis in order to suggest the gravity or heightened sentiment of the poetic verse.

Hoping to correct this problem by advocating a more "natural" style of delivery, Thomas Sheridan wrote *The Art of Reading* (1775) in which he urged the accent only of those syllables that received emphasis in ordinary conversation. The father of Richard Brinsley Sheridan, Thomas Sheridan acted in and managed theatres in Dublin and London before turning his attention to elocutionary reform (Robb 32). His colleague John Walker also came to elocution from acting, having played second lead to David Garrick early in his career (Robb 34). Like Sheridan, he felt that dramatic poetry should be pronounced as meaning dictated, but expanded his focus from the pronunciation of individual syllables and words to a consideration of the relationship between sound and sense more generally. In his *Elements of Elocution* (1781), he examines how pauses, inflections, accents, and dynamics function to group words into meaningful units for the ear to hear. James Burgh, the son and brother of Scottish clergymen, was also interested in elocutionary reform. Although his own studies for a career in the ministry were interrupted by ill health, Burgh continued to be interested in moral issues, writing a treatise on the education of children and several important books on political reform. His elocutionary manual *The Art of Speaking* (1761) was aimed at improving the methods and manners of public speaking in the hope of promoting civic dialogue. Concentrating on the physiognomic signification of passion or feeling, it advocated "natural" expressions and gestures over those conventionally prescribed by neoclassical decorum. Although Burgh had no theatrical experience as did Sheridan and Walker, he drew many of his examples from the stage, claiming to hold actors in higher esteem than he did most members of the clergy – at least when it came to public speaking (Burgh 35).

As all three critics observed, the problem with effective public speaking was that the declamatory tradition had calcified into a performance style whose conventions were no longer capable of conveying the vibrancy of religious verse or dramatic poetry. But there was also the larger cultural problem having to do with what T. S. Eliot would later identify as a "dissociation of sensibility."[2] For with the introduction of the printing press, the rise of print culture and the increase in public literacy came the problem of how to render the full sense of a text from out of its written form. As we'll see in the next chapter, Eliot would attempt to address this problem by revitalizing poetic language, insisting that it appeal to the emotional as well as rational faculties through the use of an "objective correlative." But Sheridan, in his own moment, attributed the problem to a scholastic overemphasis upon "the dead languages" which taught students to attend only to the meaning of words without regard to their sound (3). It was one thing, he thought, to derive a vocabulary from Greek and Latin grammars with which to analyze the structure of the native English tongue, but it was quite another to assume therefore that meaning was only a function of reason. As Sheridan explains, words are the language of ideas, tones are the language of emotions (150), and

> there is an essential difference between the two, which merits our utmost attention. The language of ideas is wholly arbitrary; that is, words, which are the signs of our ideas, have no natural connexion with them, but depend purely upon convention, in the different societies of men, where they are employed; which is sufficiently proved, by the diversity of languages spoken by the different nations of the world. But it is not so with regard to the language of emotions. Nature herself has taken care to frame that for the use of man; having annexed to every act, and feeling of the mind, its peculiar tone, which spontaneously breaks forth, and excites in the minds of others, tuned invariably by the hand of Nature in unison to those notes, analogous emotions.[3] (150–1)

Sounds, in other words, have an extra-significatory function, expressing the emotions in accord with the thought that is formulated into words.

Walker agreed, criticizing grammarians who presume that "some passion or emotion is contained in the words," where the mere recitation of them conveys the emotion to be expressed (Walker 1, 318–19). Analyzing the relationship between inflection and the structural components of speech, Walker concluded that inflection was often key to meaning. As he illustrates, the sentence "How mysterious are the ways of Providence!" begins with the interrogatory form, but ends with exclamatory punctuation. Thus, the manner in which it is delivered will affect its overall meaning. If given the rising inflection of a question, for example, it may suggest doubt rather than wonder (Walker 1, 319). What's significant about Walker's insight here is that he has stumbled onto the polysemic nature of texts: they allow for multiple interpretations. But where Jacques Derrida sees this to be true of communication generally, Walker specifies it to the written text. Without the author present to speak his or her words with their appropriate inflection and emphasis, readers are left to deduce his/her meaning on their own. With this fact in mind, the elocutionists set out to *regulate* the polysemy of texts – either by delimiting the structural conditions governing meaning (Walker, in an effort much like that of J. L. Austin), or by insisting that printers expand their print vocabulary to include marks of vocal effects (Burgh 3; Sheridan 167). Far from accomplishing their goal, however, what the elocutionists discovered was, in fact, much more important: a text's meaning did not simply inhere within it, but was produced through the act of interpretation.

Printed texts, in other words, were literally multivocal. They could be interpreted in any number of ways, depending upon such variables as the speaker's choice of emphasis and inflection. Or, for that matter, the use of a pause. For, when the elocutionists speak of "points," they appear to mean the "stops" or pauses indicated by marks of punctuation, such as the period, comma, semi-colon, colon, etc. The problem for actors and others who read aloud lay in how to translate such points into speech, especially since printers often differed from one another and were erratic in their own practice, using "points" to indicate grammatical relationships as often as to mark a pause for breath (Sheridan 167).[4] It was for this reason that Sheridan recommended children be taught "to read without points," copying passages without punctuation and learning to insert pauses in accord with the text's meaning (173). Burgh, by contrast, thought children "ought to be taught the use of the *stops*, and accustomed, from the beginning, to pay the *same* regard to them as to the *words*." (8). But, of course, this required a systematic approach to rendering them correctly. Attempting to outline a general rule for translating such marks as pauses, Burgh acknowledges that it "is too exact for *practice*, viz. that a comma is to hold the length of a syllable, a semicolon of two, a colon of three, and a period of four," adding that, "In some cases, there is *no stop* to be made at a comma, as they are often put merely to render the *sense clear*." But, he goes on to observe, "It often likewise happens, that the strain of the matter shews a propriety, or beauty, in holding the pause *beyond* the *proper length* of the stop; particularly when any thing remarkably *striking* has been uttered; by which means the hearers have time to ruminate upon it, before the matter, which follows, can put it out of their thoughts" (8).

This was a remarkable insight! For what Burgh identifies here is the fact that a pause can affect the way we hear the words immediately preceding it. Silence, in other words, is meaningful, too. It can be a rhetorically effective technique for highlighting the import of what has just been said, serving as an aid to comprehension. Thus, while "points" initially referred to pauses, with the length of pause suggested by the type of punctuation used, they eventually came to refer to moments when a pause heightened the meaning or emotional impact of a spoken passage.

In identifying the function of silence to group words into meaningful units, the elocutionists gave a name – the "point" – to a technique that would become an important part of the Romantic style of acting. The fact that "points" or pauses could be variously placed within a dramatic passage meant that it could be rendered in different ways, each offering its own shade of meaning. To illustrate, Sheridan cites several lines of dramatic verse from a play in which the speaking character is challenging another character to a duel. Noting where the actor inserted his pause and the meanings it deployed, he offers an alternative interpretation. The dash indicates where the actor paused:

> West of the town – a mile among the rocks
> Two hours ere noon to-morrow I expect thee
> Thy single arm to mine.

As Sheridan points out, the actor's pause seems to suggest that the character is walking a mile among rocks which are west of the town. But, as James Quin once quipped, had this been right, the character would have broken his shins for all his walking on the rocks! Offering another interpretation, Sheridan suggests the pause should fall after "mile." This would suggest that "a mile" modifies "West of the town" (highlighting the poetic syntax of the line), and "the rocks" is the place where they'll meet: "West of the town a mile, among the rocks" (171).

Although Sheridan's discussion of this passage is meant to correct the actor's mistake, what he does, in effect, is introduce a type of critical discourse in which different styles of vocal renderings are evaluated as interpretive choices. This would suggest evidence for Shearer West's contention that the critical terminology that arose at the end of the eighteenth century to describe various styles of acting developed not in response to a range of different styles so much as out of a culture of connoisseurship in which critics' analyses of actors' performances created the differences that actors then performed. "Such analyses spoke as much of the erudition of the [critic] as the particular manner of the actor," she argues. "An exact and detailed knowledge of the play, down to the nuances of individual lines, was applied rigorously to the performance of actors and became the stamp of critical discernment" (19).[5] Indeed, Sheridan's critique is illuminatingly read against the background of this culture of connoisseurship. What's more, it is a connoisseurship directed at elevating public taste. Clearly, he sees his criticism as having a corrective function. Advising actors to copy their lines without punctuation (since printers often err), Sheridan suggests that they study the meaning of the verse to determine where to insert their pauses: "In this way, the sense alone must guide them, in the right use of pauses" (172).

While he seems to presume that there is only one "right use," Sheridan effectively opens up the possibility that there are *many* possible interpretations. That is, given the multivocality of a printed text, the act of reading aloud involves the exercise of interpretive authority. In the use of "points" or pauses, in the use of force or emphasis, in the use of inflection, the actor imbues the poet's words with extra-verbal meaning through the particular style of his or her vocal rendering. These performative nuances signal a historical shift in the way actors approached their craft and in the way audiences and critics attended to it. Where, in the declamatory tradition, actors subscribed to established conventions to render the poet's words with decorum, in the Romantic tradition, they interpolated vocal and gestural effects in order to render their own interpretations of the poet's words. Accordingly, audiences began to redirect their attention from the poet's text to the actor's interpretation of it.[6] This was the moment of the actor's ascent. And David Garrick, more than any other actor, was responsible for establishing the actor's interpretive authority.[7]

Indeed, Garrick was the quintessential model of effective delivery, one who provided the elocutionists with many of their prescriptive lessons.[8] John Rice, for example, noted approvingly in *An Introduction to the Art of Reading with Energy and Propriety* (1765) that Garrick inserted an unexpected pause in Act v, scene iii of *Richard III* (the battlefield scene), endowing his line with a significance that deepened one's sense of Richard's character. Instead of rendering the line as dictated by the printer's punctuation – "Draw Archers; draw your Arrows to the Head," Garrick paused after the second "draw," giving each of the first three words a strong emphasis with an implicit trochaic inflection, followed by the iambic trimeter of the command: "Dráw Árchĕrs, dráw – yŏur Árrŏws tó thĕ Héad" (Rice cited in P. Edwards 123–4, n.20). Here, the iambic stress pattern of the command not only mimics the action of raising a bow, but, following the trochaic pattern hailing the archers to action, reveals something about the desperate ambition of this character who aspires to victory even in the hopeless face of conquest. This example shows how Garrick used his voice to create a powerful new way of understanding both the line and the character he portrayed. Through such applications, the "point" expanded from the limited sense of marking a pause to the creation of a meaningful gestalt around individual units of words, often serving to bring the actor's character to life.

Garrick created such effects through the use of more than just his voice. Incorporating facial expression, gesticulation, and comportment into his characterizations, Garrick exploited the pause to expand upon the psychological dimension of his character. His contemporary Thomas Davies, for example, commented on the chilling effect he and Mrs. Pritchard created in *Macbeth* when, after having murdered Duncan, the two characters reflect upon what they have done: "His distraction of mind and agonizing horrors were finely contrasted by her seeming apathy, tranquility and confidence . . . Their looks and action supplied the place of words. You heard what they spoke, but you learned more from the agitation of mind displayed in their action and deportment" (quoted in West 64). Here Davies seems to suggest that the two actors' use of looks and gestures served to communicate their characters' respective states of mind, creating an effect more horrifying than the words they spoke. What is more, he suggests that Garrick's and Mrs. Pritchard's simultaneous point-making laid the groundwork for what would become known as ensemble acting.

Davies was not the only one to remark upon the chilling accuracy of Garrick's passions. In fact, as many scholars have noted, his performances appear to have served as a model for both Burgh and Aaron Hill when they compiled their presumably objective catalogues of the physiognomy of the passions (Wood 33; P. Edwards 49). Burgh's descriptions of "wonder" and "fear," for example, evoke both Georg Lichtenberg's first-hand account and Benjamin Wilson's painting of Garrick as Hamlet upon seeing his father's ghost:

> *Wonder*, or amazement, (without any other *interesting* passion, as *love, esteem*, &c.) *opens* the *eyes*, and makes them appear very *prominent*; sometimes *raises* them to the *skies*; but oftener, and more expressively, fixes them on the *object*, if the cause of the passion be a *present* and *visible* object, with the look, all except the wildness, of *fear*. (See Fear.) If the *hands* hold any thing, at the time, when the object of wonder appears, they immediately let it *drop*, unconscious; and the whole *body fixes* in the *contracted, stooping* posture of *amazement*; the *mouth open*; the *hands held* up *open*, nearly in the attitude of *fear*. (See *Fear*.) The *first* access of this passion *stops* all *utterance*. But it makes amends afterwards by a copious *flow* of *words* and *exclamations*. (21–2)

"*Fear*," meanwhile, "*lifts* up the open *hands*, the fingers together, to the height of the breast, so that the palms face the dreadful object, as shields opposed against it. One *foot* is drawn *back* behind the other, so that the *body* seems *shrinking* from the danger, and putting itself in a posture for *flight*." (17).[9] As Paul Edwards wryly observes, such analogies suggest that Burgh may have been in the audience, directly transcribing Garrick's style (49).

Joseph Roach has suggested that the significance of Garrick's style lies in its departure from a declamatory tradition in which prescriptive forms of gesture were meant to regulate the passions or humours that the actor worked up to a more "natural" style based upon a new physiological understanding of the body as a mechanism that gave expression to the passions of the soul. Noting a homology between the stage mechanism that materialized the ghost of Hamlet's father and Garrick's "mechanistic" response, Roach observes:

> The very structure of Garrick's stage business derived from the action and reaction of two mechanisms: first, the ghost rose up from the trap, sprung by counterweights; then, responding like the hydraulic automata of St. Germain at the approach of an intruder, Hamlet's body turned and extended its limbs in an automatically determined reaction to stimulus. Onstage action begot equal and opposite reactions, and mechanical responses followed mechanical stimuli as invisible forces pushed bodies into action. (*The Player's Passion* 87)

If, indeed, a shift in physiological models of the body accounts for the emergence of Garrick's style, it bore within it disconcerting implications for the way that passion had been indexed to class. Those skilled in decorum, after all, assumed a certain class prerogative regarding the appropriate display of passion. Those given to gesticulate freely were simply regarded as uncultured. Implicit to the shift that Roach describes, however, is the idea that passion occurred naturally and spontaneously in everybody alike, with each body responding like a well-oiled machine whose parts were cast from the same universal tool and die shop. What this meant is that the passions – as well as the body's mechanical display of them – could be read as signs within a universal language.

Burgh suggests as much when he notes that "What we mean does not so much depend upon the *words* we speak, as on our *manner* of speaking them; and accordingly, in life, the greatest attention is paid to *this*, as *expressive* of what our *words* often give *no indication* of. Thus *nature fixes* the outward *expression* of every intention or sentiment of the mind" (12–13). Indeed, he goes on to note, "the *variety* of expression by *looks* and *gestures*, is so great, that, as is well known, a whole play can be represented *without* a *word spoken*" (14). What Burgh refers to, of course, is pantomime, the most popular form of theatrical entertainment in the eighteenth century. And pantomime, as Gillen Wood demonstrates, was an important source of Garrick's technique. Having closely observed the pantomimic techniques of John Rich, the harlequin who played in interludes at Covent Garden, Garrick incorporated many of the elements of dumb show into his acting for the legitimate theatre (Wood 32).[10]

On the legitimate stage, silence became a form of signification in and of itself – not only as a meaningful pause between words and phrases but as a moment for highlighting the physicalized meanings of the actor's body. This is why it was so important to keep in character when not speaking – the actions one rendered silently were meaningful nonetheless. At a time when actors were inclined to break character and acknowledge members of the audience, Garrick revolutionized the actor's art by rendering silence not as an absence of signification but as its own type of signification where the body became the text to be read (Wood 35). In this way, the "point" became not only a pause used to highlight a passage within the actor's speech, but a moment when any type of extra-verbal signification – whether vocal or pantomimic – was used to augment the text's meaning.

Many critics, however, began to fear that Garrick's use of pantomime diminished the importance of the dramatic verse. Among them were such literary lights as Samuel Taylor Coleridge, Percy Bysshe Shelley, and Charles Lamb, who disapproved of Garrick's emphasis upon spectacle during his stewardship of Drury Lane – especially since it was one of only two theatres licensed to present spoken verse. "One goes to the theater to see," Lamb complained, "scarcely any longer to hear" (quoted in Wood 44). Such critics clearly disapproved of the way that Garrick's innovations shifted the site of theatrical meaning: where, in the declamatory tradition, it was presumed to reside in the language of the poet's text, in the Romantic tradition it was relocated to the actor's body. Other critics simply disapproved of the effusive displays of passion, considering them unseemly and undignified. Burgh seems to acknowledge such concerns when he allows that some of the passions he describes are extreme and not likely to be observed in men of letters, leading Paul Edwards to conclude that his descriptions may have been a sort of "performance ethnography" of the lower and middling classes who populated the streets, coffee houses, and markets surrounding Covent Garden (49). However "extreme," such passions should be practiced nonetheless, Burgh advocates, since largeness of gesture and vocal resonance are important techniques for reaching and moving large audiences. Besides, practice leads to a greater "ease and fluency" in making transitions between one passion and the next (Burgh 27).

If practice were necessary, thought Burgh, it was because the forces of civilization inhibited our natural responsiveness, making it necessary to relearn unregulated (and therefore authentic) forms of expression. Sheridan agreed that civilization had developed erratically and that regularization was needed, but believed that the model of speech and gesture to be imitated was not that of the lower classes but that practiced at court.[11] Thus, despite their agreement that reform was necessary, the two elocutionists had very different political orientations. Where Sheridan was a political liberal who nonetheless sought patronage at court, Burgh was a political radical who was outspoken in his criticism of court life, including the habit of restraining one's passions in the name of sophistication. Adopting a Rousseauvian perspective, Burgh advocated a return to nature in life, at the pulpit, and on the stage.

Such an attitude flew in the face of most of the connoisseurs then forming the critical establishment. To their neoclassical tastes, the large and seemingly unrestrained passions that Burgh advocated were simply vulgar and incapable of producing aesthetic pleasure, admitting of no proportion and little learning. "Such a view, with its emphasis on eloquent speaking and reasoned, metrically precise discourse," Leigh Woods observes of Garrick's early critics, "contains an inherent class bias – translated into esthetic terms – and it was a critical stance which continued on with some vehemence and frequency through roughly the first half of Garrick's career" (19). Although Woods concludes that "what may have bordered on vulgarity to some in 1741 did not still do so in 1776, when Garrick retired from acting" (23), critical debates continued well into the nineteenth century, opposing the physically impassioned style of a Garrick or a Kean to the comparative restraint of a John Philip Kemble or a Sarah Siddons (West 61).

As West has shown, these debates were frequently figured in terms of the former's "feeling" versus the latter's "judgment" (61). And, though the debates were temporarily resolved by Diderot's paradox, for many critics at the turn of the century, "judgment" became the criterion of choice – especially those who wished to restore a sense of neoclassical order to the stage. "At times," West observes, "this emphasis on judgement superseded the concept of feeling altogether, and much writing on Kemble's acting reflects a certain suspicion, if not distaste, of the idea that the actor could lower himself to such a base level as to 'feel' anything. Kemble's quality was seen to rest in his mental and intellectual abilities, distanced or divorced from sloppy emotionalism" (61). Noting that such critics often sought to distinguish Kemble from his managerial rival at Drury Lane – the politically radical Richard Brinsley Sheridan, West further suggests that their rhetoric of neoclassical order was meant to characterize Kemble as a representative of Edmund Burke's reactionary notions of social order (83). The implication here is that the aesthetic differences that critics used to distinguish between, say, a Kemble or a Kean – with their differing attitudes toward habits of speech, gesture, and bodily comportment – were also encoded with important political significance. As a sign of the actor's interpretive authority, the impassioned "point" increasingly came to be associated with bourgeois individualism and liberal dissent.

Nowhere was this more true than in the United States, where such debates assumed an even greater sense of political urgency. As both Kenneth Cmiel and Jay Fliegelman have discussed, oratory was an important part of political life in the early republic, where a vigorous and spirited public debate formed the core of the new social order. The manner in which that public debate was to unfold, however, was the cause of some concern. Noting the "points" indicated on Thomas Jefferson's hand-written copy of the Declaration of Independence, Fliegelman discusses how Jefferson was nonetheless ambivalent about relying on a theatrical style of oratory to deliver a sentiment that was naturally felt. "For many, but especially for Jefferson, who declared that 'the whole art of government consists in the art of being honest,' the triple injunctions to please yet persuade, to control oneself but stimulate passions in others, to reveal oneself and yet efface oneself, combined to create an exhausting challenge" (Fliegelman 115). What Jefferson found so disconcerting was, in effect, an inconsistency he perceived between form and content.

This problem was mitigated considerably, however, by what Cmiel refers to as the democratization of the English language. As he points out, a general leveling occurred in which Americans at once refused elaborate ornamentation in favor of plain speech, while adopting the titles of "lady" and "gentleman" to refer to citizens of all ranks. Efforts to further erase linguistic marks of distinction included orthographic and grammatical reforms, where correctness was based upon a standard of rationality as opposed to refinement. In this way, Americans developed what Cmiel refers to as a "middling rhetoric," a style that "married the high and low" (58), and was marked by a "willingness to indicate sympathy with one's listeners, not authority over them" (McConachie, "American Theatre in Context" 134). Unique to the American experiment, it was often remarked upon by foreign visitors such as Alexis de Tocqueville who were surprised by the odd combination of speech, manner, and style. "Especially intriguing were the strange farragoes within one person at a given moment," Cmiel observes. "Language contradicted manner, dress belied deportment, one word jarred with the

next. People appeared 'half-formed'" (58). Citing Patrick Henry as a particularly compelling example of such a speaker, Cmiel notes that even the
wary Jefferson found himself moved by the uncommon beauty of Henry's
speech. "What made Henry's eloquence difficult to describe," Cmiel argues,
"was that he did not channel his talent into any recognizable cultural 'slot.'
Classical cadences, passions verging on the evangelical, pronunciation that
smacked of the rustic, and dress and deportment that were genteel – it all
added up to a thoroughly sui generis public performance" (52).

Sui generis, indeed. Language, in America, was the stuff of self-
invention. No longer a fixed marker of social relations that one was obliged
by station to observe, it was a freely traded currency with which one could
purchase an identity of one's own. And the cultivation of vocal and gestural effects was all that one needed to develop a unique personal style.
Thus, it should be no surprise that elocutionary manuals designed to assist
speakers in appealing to the thoughts and sentiments of their fellow citizens were popular in the early republic. Burgh's *The Art of Speaking* was
the first treatise on speaking published in America (Hay 31) and received
nine American printings after its first publication in 1775, while Sheridan's
Lectures on Elocution, and *Rhetorical Grammar* were among the first textbooks used in American colleges and universities (Robb, *Oral Interpretation*
28–9). In this way did the "point" – with all the political significance it had
accrued – become an important part of American self-fashioning. If, within
the theatre, it had helped shift the site of artistic authority from the poet's
pen to the actor's body, within early American culture, it helped shift the
site of governmental authority from royal dicta issued by the throne to
the conscientious deliberations of individual men. As a sign of one's own
interpretive authority, it came to symbolize the power of self-invention.

Within the American theatre this symbolism became especially important, not only to actors who sought to achieve their own success, but to
audiences who saw in them a reflection of their own hopes and dreams. As
C. W. E. Bigsby and Don Wilmeth observe, "the actor was to become the
paradigm of success, an examplar of that ability to transform oneself that
was a cultural and social imperative. He bestrode the stage as the American was to bestride the continent, reinventing himself in a gesture that had
the sanction of national myth" (15). The first American actor to achieve
such success was Edwin Forrest, the same Edwin Forrest whose innovative
"point" in *Othello* won him the respect of Edmund Kean. Known for his
swaggering portrayals of what Bruce McConachie has so aptly identified
as the "Jacksonian hero," a charismatic leader combining a populist appeal

with an affirmation of traditional Republican values, Forrest distinguished himself by the vigorous intensity of his "points." Although partially derived from his study of Edmund Kean, Forrest's physically expressive style was deemed by many to be *distinctly* American. Moreover, Forrest was often taken to represent America itself. As one newspaper reported, "Everything about him was seen to be distinctively American; his voice was like the 'falls of the Niagara' and his thighs were 'carved out of the American forest'" (*New York Mirror* [7 May 1826]; quoted in Buckley 39). A politician of the stage who knew how to please audiences by offering up his "points" for their consideration, Forrest developed a style that appealed to his fans' desire for a democratic hero. Indeed, they even nominated him as a Democratic candidate for Congress in 1838 (McConachie, *Melodramatic* 92). A firm believer in cultural independence, Forrest sponsored playwriting contests to help nurture native-born American talent, and proudly embodied the noble savage of John Augustus Stone's *Metamora*. Bringing such heroes to life on stage, Forrest was quite literally a "self-made man," rising quickly through the stock ranks to increase his earnings from $28 a week to $200 a night within his first seven years on the stage.[12] Thus did Forrest both instantiate and further propagate a narrative of American exceptionalism.

That he was able to do so was at least partially due to the ready availability of a technique that allowed for and highlighted the processes of self-invention.[13] In this sense, the "point" may be seen to be a precursor of theatrical modernism – not only because it signaled a self-conscious break with the declamatory tradition, but because it gave aesthetic expression to the new social order of an emergent bourgeoisie, making the theatre, in Roach's words, a "most propitious forum for a revolutionary society" ("Emergence" 339).

The "point" of attack

The culture of connoisseurship that developed in Britain at the end of the eighteenth century gave rise to the critic's profession. But, given its preference for the criterion of judgment over feeling, the aesthetics of neoclassicism over Romanticism, and the politics of social conservatism over republican radicalism, it was slower to take root in the United States. Indeed, the need for professional criticism was not immediately felt, since audiences in the United States enjoyed their prerogative to assess actors' performances by booing, hissing, or applauding as they felt the performance merited. The role and function of the professional critic did not emerge until the early nineteenth century.[14] And even then, as Tice Miller has discussed, the theatrical review was an uncertain proposition, appearing sporadically and assigned to either random reporters or the newspaper's hired "puff" (vii). Such vagaries and corruption meant that the critic's opinion was often viewed with suspicion. Yet the need for reliable, perspicacious, and enlightening criticism increasingly began to be felt. As one proponent remarked, "The office of a reviewer is[,] in a republic of letters, as beneficial and necessary, though odious and unpleasant, as that of an executioner in a civil state" (quoted in Miller viii). In the young republic, the responsibility of self-rule was understood to apply to all aspects of American culture, including the regulation and, indeed, censorship of artistic expression when necessary. But it was not simply a matter of imposing moral order; it was also a matter of establishing the theatre's cultural legitimacy, especially in a moment when colonial proscriptions against theatrical entertainments were giving way to declarations of cultural independence and the right to free expression.

The question facing early American theatre reviewers was where to look for the values by which to make a critical judgment. Should they adopt the neoclassical standards valued by critics in England? Or should they create new standards in keeping with a nation of self-rule? "In the main classically schooled, the critics, though asserting the need for a vital national theatre in the theatrical magazines, also, ironically enough, urged adherence to traditional subject matters, language, and style," reports Gary Richardson (254). Although Americanist voices such as Edgar Allan Poe's and Walt Whitman's began to be heard at mid-century, most early reviewers tended to look to English critics for their models and to inscribe neoclassical tastes. As Miller writes, "part-time critics drew their critical principles from Europe, from the essays of neo-classical scholars as well as from such English romantics as Samuel Johnson, William Hazlitt, Charles Lamb and Samuel Coleridge . . . For a model, they turned to the English periodical essay as developed in the eighteenth century by Sir Richard Steele and Joseph Addison" (2–3). He describes theatre reviewers William Coleman and William Leggett of the *New York Evening Post*, for example, as "Neoclassical in taste and highly moralistic," seeing them as part of a gentlemen's tradition (4). "In the absence of professional critics," Miller explains,

> the task of maintaining control of [the theatre] fell to the professional men – journalists, men of letters, lawyers, doctors, and businessmen. They served as the voice of the "enlightened public" in an attempt to weigh each play, each actor, by a "permanent standard of taste." While they seldom agreed on a definition of this phrase, they were concerned with art which presented an idealized view of life and upheld conventional morality.[15]

In a sense, this understanding of the critic's role was simply an extension of the prerogative which many upper-class spectators asserted from their boxes within the theatre itself. For, as McConachie has argued with regard to the paternalistic theatre of the early nineteenth century, elite spectators appointed themselves "makers of manners" and used their position high above the pit to "maintain[] the legitimacy of their domination" (*Melodramatic* 15).

The difference was that newspaper critics often pronounced their judgments anonymously, signing their reviews with only initials or a pseudonym (Miller 3). Of course, such critics and the legitimacy of their judgments did not go uncontested. When an anonymous critic, writing under the pseudonym of "Thespis," assailed a local stock actor's interpretation of Macbeth in an 1823 production in Louisville, the actor, T. C. R. Pemberton, took out a letter to the editor of the local paper in which he challenged Thespis's authority.[16] Contending that "some of the 'points' which you may have deemed imperfections are really correct, and that the 'long pauses' were the best means, nay, absolutely necessary, for the elicitation of the passions and feelings with which the mind was agitated," Pemberton goes on to explain what a "point" is, assuming his critic ignorant of the technique. He elucidates that, "tho' the voice was silent, there was a speaking in the eyes and muscles of the face," and admonishes his critic for mistaking silence for an absence of communication.[17] "These 'pauses' of speech," he explains, "are amply supplied by gesture and feature; a *silent acting*, either preparatory or consequent – expressing what *words* never will – never can express. In fact, sir, it is the surest way by which an actor's *power of abstraction* and *art of embodying* character can be *proved*."[18]

Offering a defense of his "points," Pemberton accuses Thespis of having violated the implicit contractual relationship between actor and audience. Not only has he denied Pemberton a chance to respond to his criticism by submitting it anonymously and in print, but, in proclaiming a position of critical authority for himself, he has usurped the dialogue that usually obtains between actor and audience. Furthermore, he has made his judgment without disclosing the grounds upon which it was based. "You have denounced 'points' and 'pauses' in my Macbeth. Your denunciation is before the world," Pemberton half-mockingly complains. "Sir, you have gibbetted them in chains, but have left no evidence to me or the world that they deserve hanging. You ought to have given them judgment, before you took upon yourself the office of executioner." In other words, Pemberton seems to suggest, Thespis not only presumes expertise where he has none, but disrupts the symbiotic relationship between actor and audience by making himself accountable to no one. This was exactly the type of critical presumption and, indeed, arrogance to which many actors and audience members in the United States took great exception.

Not all critics, however, understood their responsibility in such paternalistic terms. Some saw the reviewer's column as a position from which to give voice to, and at times lead, public opinion. Such critics usually appealed to readers to cast their votes at the ballot-box office, withholding support from managers who offended public taste and rewarding those who were responsive to it. For example, an early critic for the *New York Mirror* called upon his readers to refuse to patronize those theatres whose managers did not check reprobate actors from interpolating vulgarities into their dialogue. "We appeal to the good sense of the public," he writes,

> and earnestly ask them if these practices should be permitted? and whether it is not their duty to put a stop to this unwarrantable conduct? We would recommend them to express their feelings on these occasions, and no longer suffer "the indignant blush of scorn to burn upon the cheeks" of those ladies whom they may hereafter accompany to the theatre. Were they to hiss the offender from the boards, and to withdraw their patronage from the manager (for he is also to blame) who suffers these proceedings, they would find it a radical cure for the evil of which we complain. (3.36 [1 April 1826]: 287)

In urging their readers to uphold conventional standards of morality, such critics were certainly no different than the "gentlemen" critics who proclaimed themselves guardians of culture; in terms of appeal, however, the difference was great, and it was a difference that was not lost upon the public.

In advocating the practice of hissing, however, this critic was not necessarily observing conventional propriety, even in the US. In Britain, where professional criticism had largely replaced this sort of audience participation in the legitimate theatres, such behavior was considered boorish and unacceptable. So thought Macready, especially upon being targeted by a hiss during an 1846 performance of *Hamlet* in Edinburgh. Having just instructed the players to set the trap wherein he'll catch the conscience of the king, Macready's Hamlet danced with handkerchief held high upon the line, "They are coming to the play," stopping abruptly to correct his open display of enthusiasm with, "I must be idle" (Rees 230). Imposing his body into the text in order to demonstrate the conceit of idleness, Macready thus sought to illustrate an important theme of the play. But the handkerchief was not simply used to "point" on "idle," it was also a reference to a famous "point" made by the great Garrick who, according to Leigh Woods, had "made rather obtrusive use of a white handkerchief as Hamlet, expressing his triumph after the playing of 'The Mousetrap'" (13). Whether recognized for its clever intertextuality or not, Macready's "point" was not appreciated by Edwin Forrest, then on his second tour of the continent. Apparently, he felt that Macready's physicalization of the concept of idleness overemphasized a relatively unimportant line in the play, while the dance characterized Hamlet as a silly and frivolous man. Assuming the prerogative of judgment accorded to members of the audience, Forrest hissed Macready's "point," sparking a rivalry between the two actors that would later ignite the Astor Place Riots of 1849.[19]

As far as Forrest was concerned, such expressions of audience opinion were simply part of the process of negotiation involved in the actor–audience relationship. And, in the US, this was typically the case. It was not uncommon for audiences to request actors to repeat unusually skillful or uniquely imaginative interpretations of their lines. It was also not unusual for them to chide actors for poor interpretations or even to subject them to noise levels which prohibited them from performing at all. Boos, hisses, catcalls, whistles, stamping, shouting and clapping were typical modes of audience response. So, too, was the occasional projectile aimed at an offending performer, such as a piece of fruit, garbage, coins, marbles, or, as was the case in at least one recorded instance, "the half of the raw carcase [*sic*] of a sheep" (Macready II, 420).

Although this type of audience involvement was not unique to the American theatre, it was frequently characterized as a distinctly American practice by critics and defenders alike. Upon witnessing a performance before a rowdy audience in Cincinnati, for example, Francis Trollope, in a well-known and oft-quoted remark, criticized the audience's behavior as a "patriotic fit" where "every man seemed to think his reputation as a citizen depended on the noise he made" (quoted in Hewitt 119). Utilizing much the same rhetorical strategy, supporters of the practice claimed that audience responsiveness was simply a cultural form of participatory democracy. Since the US has no office of the revels, censorship, or laws prohibiting "indecent exhibition," one apologist argued, it becomes the public's responsibility to perform such restraining functions (Rees 247). "It is the *American people* who support the theatre," the *Boston Weekly Magazine* editorialized in 1824, "and this being the case, the people have an undoubted right to see and applaud who they please, and we trust this right will never be relinquished. No, never!" (quoted in Levine 179).

If audiences felt they had a right to participate in the creation of the theatrical event, it was in part because a structural component of the performance – the "point" – invited their response. By shifting out of character and submitting themselves to the judgment of their audiences, actors who engaged in "points" actively solicited audience applause (whether it was forthcoming or not). Perhaps for this reason, many critics began to disdain the convention and the terminology of "points." The *Mirror*'s critic, for one, claimed to dislike the "point" system of evaluation, remarking as early as 1826 that it was "a term and system to which we are very averse."[20] Although he gives no particular reasons why he dislikes it, there is the suggestion that "points" tend to encourage actors to strive after showy effects, often with little regard for the dramatic text. For, once it had become an accepted technique within the theatrical repertoire, the "point" allowed even actors of limited talent and imagination to extort applause from their audiences in what became known as a "clap-trap." At its worst, such an abuse could degenerate into a form of hammy acting in which the actor drew less attention to the nuances of the text than to him/herself.

The potential for abuse, however, was not limited to actors. Audiences, too, could take advantage of the convention by failing to wait for an invitation to respond. David Grimsted reports that audiences were known to bully orchestra musicians into playing popular favorites such as "Tod-re-I" or "Jefferson's March" instead of the classical program of works originally scheduled to be performed (65). In such instances, the actor–audience relationship was less a negotiation than a fiat by which the audience dictated the terms of the performance. It was for this reason, as historian Peter Buckley has noted, that many critics in the US had been condemning the practice of audience participation since at least 1800 (51). Not only did it limit the actor's authority over his or her own performance but it was perceived as a threat to public safety. What was felt to be a justified demand by one member of the audience might seem outrageous to another, possibly leading to fisticuffs or, worse, rioting.

It was against such a background that the Astor Place Riots took place. What began as a professional rivalry between Forrest and Macready resulted in a full-scale melee between riotous fans and a jittery militia outside the Astor Place Opera House in New York City on 10 May 1849. As many scholars have noted, the riots represented far more than a battle between fans for the preeminence of a beloved actor's professional reputation. Assuming the rhetoric of intense nationalism as well as class struggle, the riots ultimately came to represent a number of deep-seeded social conflicts. Buckley, following David Grimsted, argues that the clash between Forrest's and Macready's fans represented heightening class tensions in New York. He points out that the Astor Place Opera House was literally at the crux of this conflict, situated at the intersection of Broadway – the promenade of the city's fashionable elite – and the Bowery – the urban boardwalk of the working-class "b'hoys" and their "g'hals" (31). McConachie and Eric Lott suggest that the two actors came to stand in for competing models of democracy produced by the slavery debates (McConachie, *Melodramatic* 146; Lott 105). They note that, in the wake of the Farren riot, Macready's Englishness may very well have signified a pro-abolitionist stance to the predominantly white working-class fans who hailed Forrest as their hero. Citing the "apocalyptic melodramas" then popular on the Bowery stage, McConachie further suggests that these plays may have provided the b'hoys with a ready-made scenario for imagining Macready as the villain responsible for all their woes (146).

While the riots undoubtedly revealed class tensions between the social and professional elite who supported Macready's right to perform and the working-class fans of Forrest who sought to challenge the imposition of bourgeois cultural values; and, while Macready's Englishness may have been taken as a multivalent sign of aristocratic privilege and foreign meddling in American affairs to the democratic supporters of the native-born Forrest, these signs of class and nation were not simply grafted onto the two actors after the fact. Rather, I want to argue, such connotations derived from the very ways in which these actors performed on stage. For, however broadly the riots signified within the culture at large, their theatrical source was not simply incidental. As we have seen, the "point" was overlaid with a political significance that was understood differently by British traditionalists and American liberals. Thus, Macready's and Forrest's styles of acting may very well have been what the riots were *about*.

To be sure, twenty-two people were not killed over a difference in aesthetic taste. But language – and its use – was a highly charged political issue at the time. As Cmiel has documented, a debate over language use, similarly overlaid with Anglophilic and nationalist meanings, occurred two years prior to the Astor Place Riots. That debate, known as the "war of the dictionaries," concerned two rival abridgements of Webster's American Dictionary, one edited by a Cambridge, Massachusetts schoolteacher named Joseph Worcester – which jettisoned much of Webster's innovative orthography – and one edited by a Yale professor of rhetoric, Chauncey Goodrich, who was also Noah Webster's son-in-law. Printed in 1846–7, the two dictionaries vied for sales – and loyalties – all across the country, with Worcester's version tagged "Anglophilic" for its traditionalist stance and Goodrich's deemed "nationalistic" for its association with the Webster name. As Cmiel points out, the difference between the two versions was less pronounced than the ensuing battle would suggest (especially since Goodrich initially had overseen and largely approved of Worcester's revision), but it loomed large in the national consciousness, with various regions of the country adhering to one version as opposed to the other. Worcester was deemed authoritative by the literati of Boston and New York and was accepted as such in the South, while Webster was championed throughout the Midwest, especially by Yale alumni, partisans of Goodrich, who were founding many small colleges there (Cmiel 84–8). Language use – from spelling to pronunciation to vocabulary – came to connote a political stance. Thus, if Macready were seen as a representative of Englishness, aristocracy, or foreign-meddling, it may have been because his relationship to the English language reflected such traditional values. And, if Forrest were seen as a representative of Americanness, democracy, and self-rule, it may have been because his relationship to the English language was marked by a more fluid process of self-invention. Their differing attitudes toward language were reflected moreover in the different material forms of their respective acting styles.

Although both were schooled in the Romantic tradition and adept at the "point" technique, the difference between their styles was notable (and was writ large in the eyes of their fans). Where Macready understood acting as part of a long tradition which honored the contributions of those who had come before him, Forrest understood it as a process of individual self-expression. Where Macready understood "points" as a means of elucidating key passages within the playwright's text, Forrest understood them as a means of authorizing one's own interpretation. Where Macready harnessed an intense but tempered power,[21] Forrest unleashed a thunderous energy that was the trademark of his physically expressive style.[22] Where Macready often disdained his audiences, feeling that few were capable of appreciating the subtle "points" he devised from careful study of the text, Forrest played to his fans with pointed displays of physical bravado meant to bring his characters to life. Simply put, the differences between the two actors concerned the extents to which each engaged his physical powers of interpretation and appealed to audience desires. As we'll see, the physicality of an actor's performance would become the defining issue in debates about acting in the third quarter of the nineteenth century. But, at mid-century, the issue of audience participation could no longer be ignored. As the Astor Place Riots demonstrated, it had become simply untenable to allow audiences the amount of control formerly granted to them.

As Grimsted has shown, sometime around the middle of the century, what was once *the* American theatre became splintered and hierarchized into several different types of theatrical venue. Where, early in the century, a typical evening's entertainment might consist of a full-length play, a farce, and a musical interlude, by the middle of the century, separate venues had appeared to showcase a single type of entertainment, whether opera, drama, comic burlesques, model artist shows, or blackface minstrelsy. Within a few short years many of these venues would specialize further, distinguishing between "legitimate" and melodramatic drama, and add concert saloons and variety shows to the ever-expanding list of entertainments.[23] Arguing that this process of specialization was the result of mid-century class tensions, Grimsted suggests that, after the Astor Place Riots, several theatrical venues were needed to meet the needs and tastes of an ever-diversifying society (75). Buckley concurs: "No longer was there a shared or a sharing culture, but rather a host of different cultural forms catering to specialized audiences" (645). Lawrence Levine likewise argues that, with the bourgeoisification of American culture, various types of expressive culture became distinguished according to a "high/low" cultural divide.[24]

Although this specialization of venues did not, in and of itself, put an end to the practice of audience participation, it did tend to contain audience behavior to theatres that catered to like-minded (and often class-specific) audiences. In venues that featured "low" forms of cultural expression, audiences maintained their right to active participation and the "point" continued to be practiced much as it was in the early part of the century. Indeed, the bawdy puns and physical humor of comic burlesques, blackface minstrelsy, and concert saloons provided actors with plenty of opportunities to stand on "points." But, with the rise of what McConachie refers to as "business-class theatre," audiences began to defer respectfully to the judgment of professional critics, admiring actors' performances in a silence punctuated only by moments of appreciative applause. Without an actively participating audience, actors in the legitimate theatre were forced to reconfigure their relationship to their craft. On its stage, actors' "points" began to change.

"Pointing" the way to realism

With the rise of scenic realism, audiences increasingly fell under the spell of spectacular new visual effects wrought by innovations in stage machinery and lighting technology. Such technological effects materially altered the actor–audience relationship. First, as has been well established, the introduction of gas – and later electricity – allowed for variations in lighting that plunged audiences into silent darkness while illuminating actors on stage. This not only disrupted the active social exchange between actors and their audiences, but did so by completely separating the realms of social and fictive reality. Second, the space of the stage thus became a fictional landscape that induced actors to remain in character rather than assume their own identities to accept applause. Third, actors began to create their characterizations out of new relationships to props and other actors on the stage; where before they were understood to be interpreters of their roles, within the framework of the fictional illusion, they were beginning to be perceived as the characters they played. Fourth, this shift in the actor's relationship to character meant that acting became less a bodily than an imaginative skill, creating a distinction between so-called physical actors and intellectual ones.

Within a theatre marked by such changes, the "point" began to be regarded as old-fashioned, hyper-theatrical, and overly physical. Yet, without it, this new regime of realistic acting could not have been. After all, the "point" introduced the use of voice and gesture to enlarge upon the significance of the dramatic text. Where it differed from realism was simply in its frank acknowledgment of its own theatricality. But as stage machinery and lighting technology created the illusion of a seamless fiction, the "point" began to be sustained throughout entire scenes and, eventually, the course of the play so as to become almost unrecognizable. Accordingly, it began to disappear from the critical vocabulary.

For example, L. Clarke Davis, a reviewer for the *Atlantic Monthly*, observed of Joseph Jefferson's 1867 performance of *Rip Van Winkle* that, "[His] impersonation is full of what are technically known as *points*; but the genius of Mr. Jefferson divests them of all 'staginess,' and they are only such points as the requirements of his art, its passion, humor, or dignity, suggest" (quoted in Hewitt 200). Although Davis invokes the term "point" to describe Jefferson's performance, he recognizes its inability to fully capture the "passion, humor, [and] dignity" of Jefferson's characterization of Rip. Its insufficiency seems to lie in its connotation of "staginess" – something that Davis says is refreshingly absent from Jefferson's acting.

While it may seem strange for a comic actor's performance to be praised for its lack of staginess – in effect, for its incipient realism – Jefferson was widely acclaimed for his ability to enlarge simple comic caricatures into fully realized human beings without compromising their comic potential. His Rip, like his Asa Trenchard in Tom Taylor's *Our American Cousin* and his Salem Scudder in Dion Boucicault's *The Octoroon*, was a simple back-woodsman whose humble honesty and rustic good nature allow him to triumph over his follies and foibles, making him the quintessential American stage-type. But, as Jefferson notes in his autobiography, Rip's extra-comic humanity derived from an unusual source:

> I was so bent upon acting the part that I started for the city, and in less than a week, by industriously ransacking the theatrical wardrobe establishment for old leather and mildewed cloth, and by personally superintending the making of the wigs, each article of my costume was completed; and all this too before I had written a line of the play or studied a word of the part.

Although he admits that this method of characterization goes against both experience and advice, he allows, "I can only account for my getting the dress ready before I studied the part to the vain desire I had of witnessing myself in the glass, decked out and equipped as the hero of the Catskills" (171). What this story reveals is the way that actors were beginning to imagine their characterizations through a relationship to commodities and commodity culture with the imposition of the fourth wall. Where they once created their characters out of the social relationship between actor and audience, by the third quarter of the century, actors were beginning to create them out of a relationship to things.[25]

Further evidence of this new trend appears in the advice British actor Henry Irving gave to the students of Harvard University in an 1885 lecture. Referring to his performance as Henry Bertram to Charlotte Cushman's Meg Merrilies in the stage adaptation of Sir Walter Scott's novel *Guy Mannering*, Irving recounts that

> It was my duty to give Meg Merrilies a piece of money, and I did it after the traditional fashion by handing her a large purse full of coin of the realm, in the shape of a [bag of] broken crockery, which was generally used in financial transactions on the stage, because . . . the clatter of the broken crockery suggested fabulous wealth. But after the play Miss Cushman, in the course of some kindly advice, said to me: "Instead of giving me that purse[,] don't you think it would have been much more

natural if you had taken a number of coins from your pocket, and given me the smallest? That is the way one gives alms to a beggar, and it would have added to the realism of the scene."

"I have never forgotten that lesson," Irving concludes, "for simple as it was, it contained many elements of dramatic truth" (62–3). Here, as with Jefferson's costume, character is produced out of the actor's relationship to a thing, a property whose significance is no longer conventional (where meaning is static and seen to reside in it) but conditional (where meaning is produced out of the momentary conjunction of various social forces).

Such was the beginning of realism on the American stage. And no actor was more exalted for heralding the new order than Edwin Booth. Entering quietly and remaining in character throughout, Booth never invited applause. Critics commented wonderingly on his refusal to take "star turns." For example, at his 1870 performance of *Hamlet*, his entrance sparked the comment that, "It was many moments before he could make his voice heard . . . he stood, with pale face and glowing eyes, clad in the mourning garb of the Danish prince, inclining his head slightly with stately grace, but not for an instant separating himself from the part he had assumed" (quoted in C. H. Shattuck 69).

No longer shifting in and out of character, Booth assumed a new relationship to his "points," prompting J. Palgrave Simpson to note in his 1880 *Theatre* review that,

> Instead of being the slave of "tradition," I found him constantly neglecting old traditional points . . . for effects which commended themselves better to his true matured intelligence. [An] instance may be given in his delivery of the words, "I'll rant as well as thou," which were not howled and ranted, as is commonly the case, but uttered with a profound contempt for the *ranting* of *Laertes*. . . . Edwin Booth was eminently natural, and to be looked on as an admirable exponent of the more approved "new school". (quoted in Matthews and Hutton 72–3)

Explicitly rejecting the critical language of "points," Simpson recurs to the more general term "effects" to describe Booth's style, illustrating the perceived difference between the two techniques by noting Booth's treatment of Hamlet's line "I'll rant as well as thou." Had Booth stood on "old traditional points," had he ranted the line (as other actors had), he would have used his voice to realize the word "rant." By *not* ranting, Booth still used his voice to create an effective interpretation, but, because he used it in such a way as to communicate Hamlet's utter *distaste* for ranting, he was better able to realize Hamlet's overall character.

Booth's acting suggests a new relationship to character, one which is based upon the text as a whole rather than upon a careful excavation of individual words and meanings (and is not unlike that described by Gay Gibson Cima as having developed in response to the writing of modern drama). Sustaining his "points" throughout a line, a scene, or the entire length of the play, Booth was seen to transform the actor's relationship to the text. But he does not appear to have been the first to do so. As early as 1845, Forrest was reported to have sustained his "points" admirably in a London production of *King Lear*.[26] And, in 1857, Matilda Heron had entered in character without pausing for star recognition, spoken in conversational tones, occasionally turned her back to the audience, and often engaged in "commonplace business" about the stage (Wilson 123). What struck critics as new about Booth's performance style may not have been the mere suspension of his "points," but their contextualization within a new ethic of performance – one that applied to actor and audience alike. For the key distinction between Heron's and Forrest's physically impassioned performances, on the one hand, and Booth's nuanced characterizations, on the other, seems to be one of class-based habits of bodily comportment. Where Heron and Forrest were often accused of indulging in exhibitions of emotional excess, Booth was usually praised as a veritable model of bourgeois restraint.

Charles Shattuck notes that, as an example of the bourgeois values that his performances conveyed, Booth cut lines that might have offended the sensibilities of his audience. For example, in the scene where Hamlet meets the Ghost in the cellarage, he excised the lines where Hamlet taunts the Ghost since "audiences disliked to hear the good son addressing his father's spirit disrespectfully." He also cut any lines containing sexual innuendo or "filth," which Shattuck explains by quoting a note Booth wrote to another actor in which he remarked that "Hamlet is not merely a Prince, but a most delicate and exquisitely refined creature – an absolute gentleman." Nowhere was this more in evidence than in the scenes where Hamlet has fun at Polonius's expense. Instead of issuing his insults at him directly, Booth crossed downstage, delivering his lines in an aside to the audience so as not to portray Hamlet as an insensitive churl who would intentionally hurt the old man's feelings (Shattuck xvii–xx). Such asides suggest that this is a realism hardly capable of holding a mirror up to nature. But in the late nineteenth century, it was a realism that reflected the values and manners that bourgeois audiences recognized as their own.

Indeed, as historian John Kasson has observed with regard to the development of nineteenth-century manners, "self-control" and "restraint" were verifiable markers of one's having achieved the highest stage of social evolution. For example, he quotes Ward McAllister, "the arbiter of New York's fashionable elite in the nineteenth century," as having said, "The highest cultivation in social manners enables a person to conceal from the world his real feelings" (148). No wonder the vast proliferation of etiquette manuals in the second half of the century was greedily consumed by members of the middling classes who wished to emulate (and be mistaken for) their social betters. No wonder, too, that Booth's Hamlet caused Simpson to gush with praise. Booth simply presented as "natural" the behavior and manners that his mostly bourgeois audiences recognized and valued as their own.[27]

Compared to Booth's restraint, then, the traditional "points" of an aging actor like Edwin Forrest could only be registered by bourgeois audiences as excessively physical and overwrought. So they were, as George William Curtis, the editor of *Harper's*, reported in 1863 in an oft-quoted anecdote: Unable to choose between two theatrical performances – one by Edwin Forrest, the other by Edwin Booth – Curtis and a friend decided to go to both. Staying only long enough to get a feel for Forrest's "muscular school; the brawny art; the biceps aesthetics; the tragic calves; the bovine drama; rant, roar, and rigmarole," Curtis reports that his friend had had enough. Proceeding to the theatre where Booth was performing, the play-goers were struck by the difference: where Forrest's audience was passionately absorbed, crying "good hearty tears," Booth's audience is described as "refined," "cultivated," "intellectual," clearly appreciating Booth's "articulately" rendered Iago (quoted in Levine 57–9). As Levine observes of the story, the splitting of American entertainment into high culture and low was manifested not only in terms of content and venue, but as a "stylistic bifurcation" as well (68).

This "stylistic bifurcation" was usually discussed in terms of intellectuality versus physicality, with Booth and Forrest as the respective models of each. And, though Forrest's style was vigorously defended as requiring thought as well as physical skill, the dominant critical narrative at the time held that his was a lesser form of art.[28] Even the supposedly objective and scholarly account of Forrest's career – Montrose Moses's *The Fabulous Forrest* – bears this bias into the twentieth century. For example, Moses quotes approvingly William Winter's 1908 retrospective of Forrest's career in which Winter claims that "No actor of the nineteenth century has been the theme of such acrimonious controversy as Edwin Forrest occasioned; the reason being that absolute harmony can never exist between the antagonistic systems of muscle and mind. Forrest was an uncommonly massive and puissant animal, and all of his impersonations were more physical than intellectual" (Moses 333–4). Back in 1820 when Forrest made his stage debut, this opposition between "physical" and "intellectual" would have been unthinkable – acting was understood to require skills in both abilities, neither of which excluded the other. What had happened to create "antagonistic systems of muscle and mind" by century's end?

One reason may have had to do with the way that new types of work were redefining class distinctions, implicitly calling into question the status of the actor's work. As historian Stuart Blumin has shown with regard to the formation of the middle class, the creation of new positions in sales and management and the realignment of artisanry with industrialized labor in the latter half of the nineteenth century led to a sharper distinction between non-manual and manual labor – a distinction more commonly understood as a distinction between "headwork" and "handwork" (316). Thus, actors who defined their work in terms of its physicality – such as actors who continued to stand on traditional "points" – made themselves vulnerable to the charge that theirs was "handwork," or manual labor, while actors who defined their work in terms of its intellectuality could identify it as "headwork" or, as was becoming more common, a "profession."

Theatre historian Benjamin McArthur has detailed the rise of the actor's profession, noting that, with the specialization of venue at mid-century, came a change in the way the business of theatre was conducted: "Verbal agreeements gave way to written contracts. The various theatrical trades became more insistent on their rights, and in the twenty years after 1880 actors, producers, stagehands, musical directors, and agents each formed associations" (89). These often grew out of protective societies such as The General Theatrical Fund (1829), The Actor's Order of Friendship (1849), and The Actors' Fund of America (1882), each of which was established to assist actors in financial need. But with the specialization of labor and the elaboration of financial alliances among theatre managers and booking agents, actors quickly found themselves in need of greater protection. After first reassuring its prospective constituency that it was not a trade union, the first professional actors' society – The Actors' Society of America (1894) – was formed (McArthur 105). Not only did it help effect new laws protecting actors against unscrupulous managers and agents, but it established a legal standard for professional credentialization (McArthur 110). As McArthur observes,

The ASA's attempt to polish a public image and confidently assume a professional stature fits the pattern often followed by striving occupations. At its founding it issued two resolutions expounding actors' social and professional virtues. They declared acting to be a "fine art," rebutting a common inference that it was inferior to the established arts of music, literature, painting, and sculpture. The resolutions also asserted that the "practice of acting is an entirely honorable profession," one "worthy of the support of the best social influence." Responding to lingering prejudices toward amusements, the ASA also resolved that all public amusements that "entertain and do not demoralize are legitimate." In short, the ASA began its work by defending players' honor against the still-frequent charges of disrepute. Recognizing the increasing importance of entertainment in American life, it entreated the public for a corresponding respect toward its providers. (105–6)

So effective was the ASA in helping actors achieve professional stature that it managed to win the sympathies of even their harshest critics. As McArthur relates, members of the clergy and the social elite – once the most powerful voices against the actor's profession – began to recognize its legitimacy, with clergymen hailing the theatre as an instrument of moral reform and society mavens hosting actors as guests in their homes (123–42).

This push toward professional stature, however, involved making a distinction between those who acted on the legitimate stage and those who did not, those who observed bourgeois codes of behavior and those who did not. Such distinctions appear in many of the acting manuals that began to proliferate at the end of the century, as the call for credentialization included a call for professional instruction. As early as 1869, for example, feminist Olive Logan invoked the language of professionalism to distinguish between female burlesque performers who merely exhibited themselves and those actors whose "years of toil and study" gave them the "right" to appear on the legitimate stage (130–2).[29] Similarly, Percy Fitzgerald remarked in his 1892 acting manual, "Indeed, we might say that there are *actors*, and that there are *performers*. This distinguishes the cultured from the uncultured 'acting of commerce'" (1). Writing under the pseudonym Alfred Ayres, Thomas Osmun Embley concurred, lamenting in his 1894 treatise that, "There are so few players that practice their vocation as an ART, and so many that practice it only as a TRADE!" (Ayres 48).

By the end of the nineteenth century, the traditional "point" style of acting had become associated with the lower classes not simply because it was they who comprised the bulk of the audience in those theatres where it continued to be practiced (*pace* Grimsted), but because the explicit physicality of the style marked it – and its actors – as lower class. On the boards of the legitimate stage, the "point" was being practiced in a very different way. Marked by a suspension and redirection of the actor's energy, it had become thoroughly transformed – so much so that it demanded an alternative critical vocabulary. But, for all the rhetoric of professionalism, this new style of acting was no less physical than the traditional "point"; it simply utilized a different manner of physicality – one marked by changing attitudes toward the body and its movements through social space.

The Delsarte technique

Of course, the body's movement through aesthetic space was changing, too, thanks in large part to the stage technology introduced in the last quarter of the nineteenth century. With cage lifts and rotating platforms facilitating changes in scenery, the fictional illusion could be sustained for longer periods of time. In addition to these devices were newer inventions such as the elevator stage (which allowed for fully decorated sets to be assembled on three different floors of the theatre and then raised or lowered into place), the sliding stage (which operated on the same principle but horizontally rather than vertically), the floating stage (which allowed for greater range of movement, including curvilinear patterns), the illumiscope (which mimicked the changing quality of sunlight by season or time of day), the colourator (which accomplished the same effect but with colored tints), the luxauleator (which created a veritable curtain of light), the nebulator (which mimicked the shadows cast by clouds), and the proscenium-adjustor (which changed the size and shape of the proscenium opening) – all invented by one man, Steele MacKaye (Vardac 141–3). As Nicholas Vardac notes, MacKaye's mechanisms were designed to heighten the effect of the stage spectacle, preparing audiences for the arrival of film (144). "Carried to its proper conclusion, such a system would have resulted, as would his over-all productional approach, in the complete elimination of dialogue," Vardac concludes. "Drama then would have become a series of visual symbols, pictures envisioned by the scenic artist and created by the stage mechanic and by the body of the actor" (144). Indeed, thanks to MacKaye, the body of the actor *was* practically reduced to a mere visual symbol – not only because of the way it was recontextualized by these stage mechanisms, but because of an influential acting method that he introduced.

Specifically, I refer to the Delsarte method, a system of actor training created by French vocal instructor François Delsarte, with whom
MacKaye began training in 1869. Upon quickly mastering Delsarte's
method, MacKaye returned to the United States in 1871 with the hope
of raising enough money from a lecture tour to help Delsarte flee from
the chaos of the Franco-Prussian War. Unfortunately, Delsarte died before
MacKaye could come to his aid, but MacKaye's lectures generated such a
tremendous interest in the Delsarte method that it became the most popular
program of actor training in the US from the 1870s until 1900, inspiring a
host of other methods that traveled in its path (Shaver 202; Kirby 55).[30]

Just what was the Delsarte method? A catalogue of gestures and expressions to which Delsarte had ascribed specific meanings, it instructed actors
in using their bodies to create various character types for the stage. As illustrated by figures 1–3, for example, Delsarte analyzed various expressions of
the eye, hand, and leg to determine the emotive significance of each. The
hooded brow over a wide-open eye, for instance, communicates "firmness"
or resolve, the open hand with fingers fully extended "exaltation," and the
wide-spread legs "intoxication." In this way, the actor wishing to represent
any one of these emotional states could refer to Delsarte's schema, reproduce the appropriate gesture, and thus communicate an aspect of his or her
character's inner state.

With a specific meaning assigned to each expression, stance, and gesture,
the Delsarte method was like the neoclassical system of rhetorical gesture in
its codification of bodily movement. Unlike neoclassical decorum, however,
it held that its significations were discovered in nature rather than produced
by convention, having been based upon Delsarte's own empirical observations. In this way, it may be seen as an extension of Burgh's efforts a century
before. Surreptitiously noting the behavior of people in the streets, parks,
and cafés of Paris, Delsarte would record the various expressions, stances,
and gestures he witnessed, even traveling to the scene of a mine disaster and
visiting an insane asylum to observe expressions in the extreme (B. Lewis
115). From such observations, Delsarte then divided the body into expressive
zones, systematizing the various possible combinations of movement and
ascribing a meaning to each. Thus, actors, wishing to represent with scientific accuracy the various emotional states of their characters, could appeal
to the "natural" laws of expression recorded by Delsarte.

The technique involved more than simply reproducing a prescribed set
of gestures, however. It also required the actor to coordinate expressions and
gestures according to various character templates outlined in a complicated

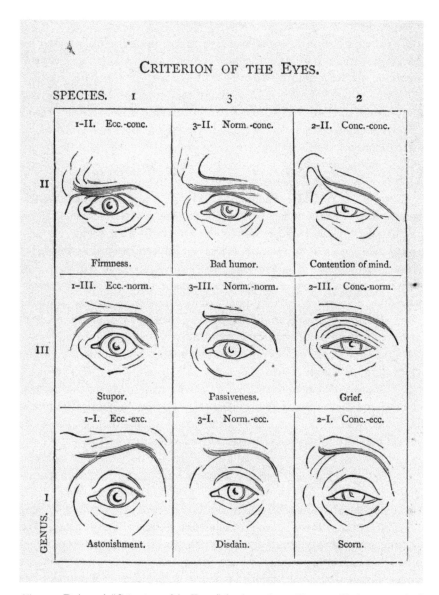

Figure 1. Delsarte's "Criterion of the Eyes." As these charts illustrate, Delsarte ascribed a specific meaning to each expression and gesture based upon his analysis of its governing faculty and movement in relation to the rest of the body.

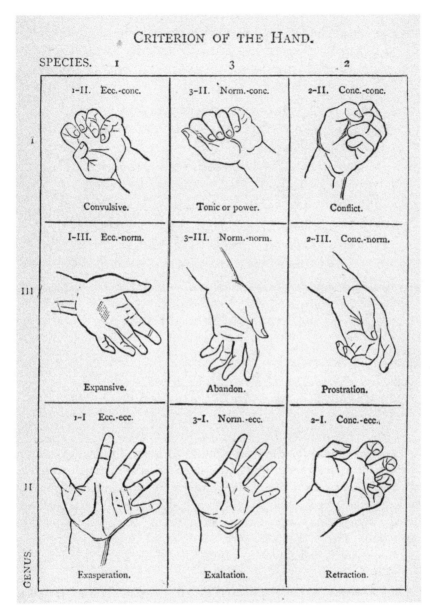

Figure 2. Delsarte's "Criterion of the Hand."

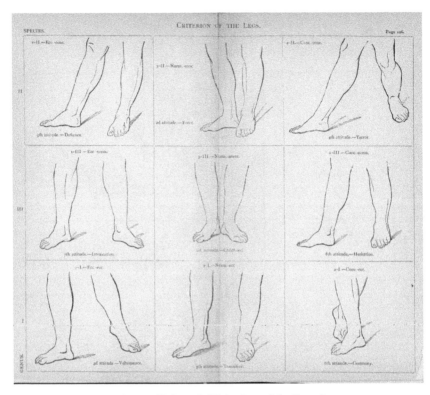

Figure 3. Delsarte's "Criterion of the Legs."

quasi-philosophical system. According to Delsarte, the human body is divided into three zones – the limbs, the head, and the torso – each of which is governed by one of three faculties – life, mind, and soul. In assigning these three faculties to the three bodily zones, Delsarte borrowed heavily from Johann Caspar Lavater, an eighteenth-century moral philosopher whose theory of physiognomy localized the three principal human faculties – vitality, morality, and intelligence – within specific regions of the body.[31]

But Delsarte did more than simply appropriate Lavater's moral-philosophical schema. From it, he elaborated a theory of bodily movement which indicated the dominant faculty within a person's soul: movement about a center (normal) is moral and expresses soul; movement away from a center (eccentric) is vital and expresses life; and movement toward a center (concentric) is mental and expresses mind.[32] Each of the three zones was

capable of all three types of movement, allowing for nine possible combinations (e.g., concentric–normal–normal, normal–eccentric–normal, etc.).
Thus, the three faculties operating within the three bodily zones produce a range of nine basic gestures which are themselves variable by the
nine types of movement for a total of eighty-one expressive possibilities
(Kirby 65).[33]

For its American proponents, what was important about the Delsarte
method was that it was a *method* which could claim for itself the rigor of
a science. Genevieve Stebbins, author of one of the most popular Delsarte
manuals published in the US, spoke for many when she affirmed the scientific credentials of Delsarte's empirical method: "What Comte has done for
exact science, Buckle and Mill for history, Spencer for culture, and Ruskin
for painting," she asserts, "Delsarte has tried to do for action, for expression"
(5). The conditional quality of her rhetoric notwithstanding, Stebbins, along
with MacKaye, saw Delsarte's "course of applied aesthetics" as a means of
bringing the rigor of science to the study of acting, further helping it to be
recognized as a legitimate profession.[34]

Indeed, Delsarte appears to have had a great interest in the scientific
experiments of his day, especially those of Sir Charles Bell and G.-B.
Duchenne de Boulogne.[35] But, as science emerged as the dominant discourse of knowledge in the late nineteenth century, it was often conflated
with what we would now refer to as pseudo-science, especially when the
latter invoked the rhetoric of the former to advance speculative theories as
conclusive facts. Delsarte happened to have subscribed to many pseudo-
scientific theories, ultimately ensuring the obsolescence of his work. And
though the false premises underlying the pseudo-sciences are easy to see
from our historical perspective, in their own moment, their truth claims
often appeared as common sense. Physiognomy, as we've seen, attempted to
provide physical evidence for the widely accepted moral-philosophical pre-
cept that human behavior was governed by three reigning faculties: reason,
sentiment, and will. Similarly, phrenology sought to identify various personality traits by analyzing the shape and regions of the head.[36] Its analysis
of the forehead survives to this day in the common parlance of "highbrow"
and "lowbrow" to describe relative degrees of intelligence (albeit often manifested as "taste"). Mesmerism, too, along with its sister art hypnosis, seemed
to explain the motives of human behavior by introducing the notion of a
"subconscious" mind. It gave further impetus to the study of expression
by suggesting that subconscious motives often reveal themselves in bodily
attitudes that belie professed thoughts and beliefs.

The vogue for such seemingly scientific explanations of human behavior was further enhanced by Darwin's theory of natural selection and its application to the expression of emotions. But, given Darwin's emphasis upon instincts, the moral-philosophical model of human behavior that had dominated much of nineteenth-century thought began to be modified, as reason, sentiment, and will no longer seemed sufficient categories of analysis. "These terms faded as psychology became an academic discipline at the end of the nineteenth century," cultural historian Fred Matthews reports, "but the vision of the self [outlined in moral philosophy] . . . remained powerful in popular thought and in the psychology taught in schools" (Matthews 146). Indeed, this vision of the self continued to dominate discussions of acting where it not only shaped the practice of bourgeois realism but influenced a popular understanding of character. In the theatre as in the culture at large, moral philosophy combined with pre-Freudian psychology to create a pseudo-scientific hybrid I refer to here as "moral psychology."[37]

These moral-psychological principles could be applied to an empirical reading of one's bodily expression. Delsarte postulated, for example, that when we are drawn by sentiment toward another person our torsos incline toward the object of our affection, as in most gestures of greeting (e.g., a handshake, a kiss, a hug). This would indicate a movement from the moral center outward, where various degrees of vitality would be evinced, depending upon the amount of affection one felt for the person greeted. But experience often proved contrary to theory. As Delsarte discovered, there were sometimes instances of behavior which seemed to contradict the otherwise rational explanation of Lavater's physiognomy. For example, Delsarte caught himself by surprise one day when his beloved cousin unexpectedly came to visit him in his garden. Instead of inclining toward him, as theory held, Delsarte found that he threw his arms back in surprise, tilting his torso away from his cousin, the object of his affection. What inspired him to assume such a posture? Reflecting upon this seeming anathema, Delsarte speculated that the arms were thrown toward heaven "as if expressing thanks for an unexpected joy." This necessitated that the head be lowered onto the torso with chin touching chest in order to provide the body with balance as the back arched backward, while allowing him to keep the object of his affection in full view (Delsarte 397). Here, as elsewhere in Delsarte's studies, the data needed to be reconciled with the physiognomic system of meaning and that system of meaning needed to be modified in light of new data.

Even so, the core assumptions of Delsarte's method remained faithful to Lavater's theory. From it, Delsarte derived his important principle of the "ninefold accord," the rule that each of the three zones is capable of giving expression not just to its own governing faculty but to each of the other two as well.[38] What was important about the principle of the ninefold accord was that it allowed Delsarte to account for differences among individuals. After all, if the governing faculties, zones, and types of movement were the same for all human beings, how could we account for the uniqueness of each and every individual? As Angélique Arnaud, a French disciple, cautions, Delsarte's schema, however useful as a model for analysis, is not something to which an individual's personality can be reduced:

> [T]his division into three modalities or into three states is far from giving the number of the manifestations of being. Nature is not reduced to this indigence. From the fusion of these three states, in varying and incessant combination, and from the predominance of one of the primitive modalities, whether accidental or permanent, countless individualities are formed, each with its personal constitution, its shades of difference of education, habits, age, character, etc. (quoted in Delsarte 173)

Indeed, allowing that some types of movement are acquired through inheritance, some through habit, and others as a result of accident, Delsarte held that, though individual movements could be understood to have universal significance, the particular combination of them as exhibited in a single person's body revealed the uniqueness of his or her "personality" (Giraudet quoted in Shawn 109).

Historian Warren Susman has observed that the concept of "personality" – suggesting energy, charisma, and charm – came to replace the Victorian notion of "character" – with its connotations of moral constancy – in the early twentieth century (217). Like George Lukács, he sees the new model of the self suggested by this linguistic turn as an overdetermined response to the economic shift from a producer to a consumer culture.[39] Doubtless, pressure on the idea of individuality intensified in a culture of mass-produced goods, where the production of such goods threatened the cult of individual difference so important to bourgeois ideology. Ironically, the consumption of such goods became the means by which one cultivated one's own unique sense of self since it allowed for the assertion of individual preferences and desires. But this dialectical tension between mass-produced types and individual differences already exists in Delsarte's notion of "personality," given the infinite variability of combinations that can be made from among the elements identified among its types. Susman is right, however, to insist upon the peculiar Americanness of this idea. For, though it appears to originate in Delsarte's writings, the notion of personality was given special prominence by his American followers. Anna Morgan's instructional manual *An Hour with Delsarte* (1890), for example, goes so far as to list it as a "law" among Delsarte's nine laws of expression:

> The Law of Personality is that which marks a man's individuality and distinguishes him from other men. Personality is the result of heredity and culture. We work upon the material received at birth from our ancestors, striving to efface or emphasize its peculiarities accordingly as they are advantageous or detrimental to us; the result at manhood, colored by experience, is personality. It is that by which we recognize a friend by his walk, a mother by the inflections of her voice as she speaks to her child, the words of a favorite author by the style of the composition. (Morgan 55)[40]

While Morgan's rhetoric is perfectly in keeping with Delsarte's own theory of personality as that which makes every individual unique, no such "law" appears in Delsarte's own fragmentary writings, suggesting that this particular formulation is of American origin.

However useful the schematic shift that Susman describes, personality did not so much replace character as simply transform it. For, within Delsarte's theory of personality, substantial residue from the Victorian notion of character persists. As we've seen, Delsarte drew heavily from eighteenth-century moral philosophy. Its presumption of a soul or moral essence within each individual was also at the core of the Delsarte method, with its "Law of Correspondences," the rule that one's outward action necessarily revealed his or her inner essence. As its name suggests, this law was based upon Emanuel Swedenborg's mystical belief in "correspondences," parallel realities existing between this life and the next, spirit and matter, soul and form. Likewise, Delsarte held that there was a mystical yet identifiable correspondence between one's inner moral character and the expression, gesture, and comportment that were its outward signs. His system of "semeiotics" (*sic*) was simply the science of reading such signs.

Using Swedenborgianism to mystify the assumptions used to structure his empirical findings, Delsarte effectively naturalized late nineteenth-century conventions of bourgeois morality. As this passage from a transcript of one of MacKaye's lectures demonstrates, for example, habits of expression, gesture, and comportment signified in not just moral but class-specific terms:

> You take different types of character. You take a type of character that is self-poised, self-controlled, and under the influence of a similar motion there will be very little expansion in its gesticulation; whereas if it is a frivolous character, if it is one of those little pots that get soon hot, it will under the influence of the same motion gesticulate much. So you will find common and vulgar people under the influence of pleasure make a great deal of gesticulation, while self-controlled and noble types of humanity make very little expansion, but that little expansion means more in their case than the violent expansion of gesticulation in the other. The farmer and the boor are always full of gesticulation. He says, "I am glad," "How are you?," "Pshaw I didn't care." He makes a great deal of gesticulation and protestation, whereas the other type will say, "I am very glad to see you," under the influence of the same amount of emotion, and the expansion may be very slight. (Mackaye 82)

Although we cannot benefit from seeing the expression and gestures that accompanied MacKaye's lecture, his language stunningly reveals that moral psychology bore within it a distinct class bias.[41] While gestural excess is "common and vulgar," the self-restraint practiced by the bourgeoisie is indicative of "noble types of humanity."[42] With thinking such as this, it's no wonder that Forrest fared poorly when compared to Booth!

Although the Delsarte method was designed to help actors express various moral-psychological states of being, its focus on the body – the arms, legs, head, eye, etc. – continued to leave actors vulnerable to the charge that theirs was a manual rather than intellectual type of work. This was due in large part to the particular emphasis MacKaye placed on the physical or "gymnastic" element of Delsarte's method. Although MacKaye variously attested to the authenticity of, yet claimed credit for, the physical training method he referred to as "harmonic gymnastics" (also known as "aesthetic gymnastics"), his wife attributed it to her husband after his death, explaining that, while "Delsarte did indeed teach a series of gestures which were very beautiful and expressive in character, [they were] exceedingly intricate and difficult of imitation." MacKaye, having mastered them in three short months (much to the delight of his teacher), realized that he could assist others in learning these "mento-muscular movements" by devising a series of exercises that would condition the body to perform Delsarte's gestures with greater ease. "[T]he principles at that time discovered,"

Mrs. MacKaye concludes, "are the foundation stones of that system now known as Harmonic Gymnastics" (188).

Taught by enthusiasts less knowledgeable than MacKaye, however, harmonic gymnastics were often put in the service of something other than learning the intricacies of the Delsarte method. Associated with the exercise regimens that became part of women's health reform at the end of the nineteenth century, MacKaye's harmonic gymnastics were sometimes practiced as part of the "physical culture movement" popularized by Dio Lewis. Henrietta Hovey, for example, combined Delsartean principles with her own vision of personal reform which advocated corset-less dressing for women and the many benefits of the yawn (Ruyter 43). The result was often an amalgam of ideas assembled under the name of Delsartism which bore only a family resemblance to the method itself. When Delsarte's daughter, Madame Giraldy, came to the United States to observe the success of the Delsarte method, she was amazed by the proliferation of practices and products that went by her father's name. Upon visiting a class on Delsartean movement for young ladies, she was surprised to be handed a pair of dumbbells, remarking that, however healthful the program of exercise, it bore no relation to her father's method (see Delsarte 561–2). Advertisements for "Delsarte" corsets and even prostheses appeared in the back pages of several leading magazines.

Even without these misappropriations of its name, the Delsarte method began to come under attack for overemphasizing the physical instrument of the actor's body. Among those critical of the Delsarte method was Alfred Ayres, who complained, with a sneer apparently directed at MacKaye,

> I am one of those that believe in attacking the actor's art from the intellectual, not from the gymnastic side; one of those that believe in giving one's best energies to the cultivating of the brain rather than of the brawn: one of those that believe if the mind goes right the action is pretty sure not to be far wrong. The brain, not the muscles, is the seat of emotion, and emotion is well-nigh everything to the actor. (39)

The Delsarte method might have been the single greatest influence on legitimate actor training at the turn of the century but its emphasis upon the body again posed the problem of whether or not acting required intellectual skill.

Thus, even actors on the legitimate stage were faced with what feminist historian Faye Dudden refers to as the "body problem." As she discusses, the general shift from an aural to a visual orientation in the nineteenth-century theatre meant that actors' bodies were subject to an objectifying gaze. This posed a particularly vexing problem for female actors, she argues, since they were already suspected of moral laxity for exhibiting themselves in public (3–6; 183). But the body problem was not unique to female actors. Nor was it simply a matter of spectacularizing the actor's body. Rather, the problem was one of spectacularizing the actor's body in such a way as to strip it virtually of any agency whatsoever. And this had less to do with the general shift from an aural to a visual orientation than with the ways in which the actor's body was framed. Under the traditional system of "points," the theatrical fiction was exposed, allowing actors to shift in and out of character in order to reveal it as their own invention. Under realism, however, the theatricality of the fiction was increasingly obscured, as the actor's identity was folded into the character's until the house lights came back up. Where the former method was premised upon an intersubjective relationship between actor and audience, the latter depended upon a model of object relations to situate the actor within the viewer's scopic field. The body problem, then, was not simply a spectacularization of the actor's body so much as the spectacularization of a body that, in being situated as a sign to be read rather than a person with whom to interact, was effectively denied its own agency.[43]

This was precisely the problem: reduced to the function of a sign, the actor was no longer a maker but a bearer of meaning. Where, early in the century, the actor was the primary interpreter of the dramatic text, by the end, he or she was simply one of many signs within the text of the *mise-en-scène*. Such a shift was, of course, facilitated by the rise of scenic realism and the emergence of the producer-director, or *régisseur* (Hewitt 219). Nonetheless, the Delsarte method further foreclosed the actor's interpretive agency by prescribing a semeiotic notation of moral-psychological character types. Although, in principle, its theory of personality allowed for an infinite number of manifestations, providing the actor with a potentially infinite range of interpretations, in practice, it limited the actor's interpretive choices to those expressions, gestures, and movements described by Delsarte. The fact that such expressions and the supposedly natural laws that governed them were reported to have been observed in real life meant that actors wishing to represent their characters in a realistic manner were obliged to reproduce them just as they had been recorded by Delsarte. In this way, the actor's interpretive agency was diminished.

From spectatorium to cinematographe: the actor's body on film

Steele MacKaye's inventions were not simply incidental devices meant to magnify various aspects of stage realism. Together, they were supposed to combine in the magnificent totality of his proposed "spectatorium." Comprising twenty-five stages arranged around the periphery of an immense theatre, the spectatorium was imagined as a life-sized kinetoscope with the audience seated inside. On its stages, audiences would witness monumental scenes detailing the story of Columbus's discovery of the New World, performed by actors who were basically "reduced . . . to pantomimists" (Vardac 149). Alas, the financial panic of 1893 put an end to the project before it could be completed, but MacKaye managed to realize his plans in a modified and scaled-down version known as the "scenitorium" (Vardac 149–50). Although MacKaye died before he could see his inventions reach their apotheosis in the new medium of film, they were instrumental to its success, as Vardac persuasively argues. Not least among his contributions was the introduction of the Delsarte method. In many ways, it was the perfect vehicle for film. Indeed, early silent film may be seen as a veritable time capsule of Delsartean technique. For, without sound, film had to rely on the silent gesticulations of its actors to communicate the stories that it told.

In her pioneering study of silent film acting, Roberta Pearson has identified an important shift between 1908 and 1913, when what she refers to as a "histrionic" method is replaced by a "verisimilar" code of acting. Comparing films such as *A Drunkard's Reformation* (1909) and *Brutality* (1912), Pearson demonstrates how the same basic reform melodrama story is rendered in radically different ways. Where actors in the earlier film appear to rely on theatrical conventions, using overly large gestures which are often repeated to underscore their significance, actors in the later film use more restrained gestures to create a more realistic, psychologically nuanced effect. Although Pearson identifies Delsartism with the histrionic code, suggesting that its complicated system may have been misunderstood by inexperienced actors and thus rendered in an overly stylized way, the Delsarte method was probably the cornerstone of what she refers to as the verisimilar code.[44] After all, Delsarte's innovation was to record and systematize actual patterns of gesture and expression as he had observed them in real life. The more likely source for the histrionic code was the "point." After all, the first actors to appear in film were often from the melodramatic theatre where the "point" tradition continued to flourish at the turn of the twentieth century. On its stage, gestures were not considered overlarge; they were simply the conventional means of emphasizing or illustrating passages in the dramatic text. Early film actors trained on the melodramatic stage would not have been inclined to regard their style of acting as excessive or overmuch. But they would have been faced with an unexpected challenge in the practice of their craft – the new and limiting condition of silence. Without the spoken language of the dramatic text to make their "points" intelligible, actors may have felt the need to enlarge or repeat their gestures – much like the tourist who, when trying to communicate with an uncomprehending native-speaker, repeats him or herself in a much louder voice. The solution is ridiculous, of course; it does nothing to advance the disabled act of communication. But, if we laugh at such compensatory actions, it is because we can recognize the difference between verbal signification, and the vocal and gestural effects which function to supplement it. In this early moment of silent film, however, such distinctions were not yet fully understood. Film, in fact, helped to make them so.

The Delsarte method was perfectly suited to this new medium. Promising to be its own systematic, free-standing "language," one without need for the spoken word, the Delsarte method offered itself as a substitute for verbal communication, shifting spectating habits further away from an attention to poetic language and narrative toward a concern with the psychology of individual characters (and/or the "personality" of the actors creating them). As Pearson notes, "the mixture of conventional gestures, glances, and by-play" became the hallmark of the verisimilar code, revealing the psychological causality behind a character's actions (62). Such an emphasis on psychological portraiture was facilitated by the development of film techniques that were dialectically advanced by the Delsarte method. The close-up, for example, rendered subtle facial expressions visible, allowing in turn for the development of editing techniques such as the point-of-view shot. What made such techniques possible, argues film historian Mikhail Yampolsky, was Delsarte's anatomization of the body into discrete zones of signification (51–2). Knowing that a convulsive hand signified agitation and thwarted desire, for example, the filmmaker could focus on that alone, cropping the rest of the actor's body out of the frame.

Thus, if theatre threatened to reduce the actor to the function of a sign, then film actually followed through on the threat. As film theorist Barry King has discussed, the very process of making a film limits the actor's interpretive agency by containing his or her movements in the still image of the frame (33). The film's meaning is located not so much in the actor acting as in its assemblage of still images, the ordering and temporality of which, as Lev Kuleshov proved, affects the narrative chain of associations produced in the viewer's mind. Kuleshov's famous experiment, as Yampolsky demonstrates, was indebted to Delsarte's insights (51).[45] Thus, it would appear that much of modern film technique grew out of theatrical techniques that had been absorbed by the cinematic apparatus. Indeed, even before advances in editing transformed the director into an *auteur*, the camera was already beginning to inscribe the actor into the director's text.

D. W. Griffith's 1912 Biograph film *The Old Actor* serves as an interesting case in point. As "the old actor," played by W. Christie Miller, passionately declaims a passage from Shakespeare, the camera moves in for a close-up. What was new was not the close-up per se, as Charles Musser points out, but that it was trained on an actor other than the studio's star, Mary Pickford. Since Miller himself was an old actor, Musser speculates, the close-up appears meant to intensify the audience's awareness of his relationship to the character he plays: "Role and reality converge" (Musser 61). If early film audiences knew how to read Griffith's visual pun, it was because they were already familiar with a similar technique on the nineteenth-century stage. For however new it was in film, what Musser describes here is a "point." But where the *actor* used to shift between social and fictive identities, here the *camera* effects this oscillation by suggesting an overlay of Miller's character and Miller himself. Zooming in to intensify this effect, the camera performs both the significatory work of the actor and the interpretive work of the audience. In this way, the camera could create "points" without need for the actor's histrionics. Sergei Eisenstein drew upon his theatre work with Vsevelod Meyerhold to refer to such moments of visual intensity as "attractions," developing his theory of montage as a way of using film to link attractions together in a rhythmically effective manner.[46] Thus, in addition to appropriating the Delsarte method, the camera appears to have absorbed the "point" as well.

From a technique used to highlight the actor's interpretive skills, the "point" (and, indeed, the actor's body generally) was pressed into the service of a technology used to advance the director's vision. On the screen as on the stage, actors were increasingly (and, at times, unwittingly) obliged to cede their interpretive authority to the director. Although, as we've seen, film was not responsible for delimiting the actor's artistic agency, its emergence in the moment when such developments were unfolding allowed it to become a totem of fear for many actors overwhelmed by the changes sweeping through their profession. For, in addition to the aesthetic changes occurring on stage, the rise of the theatrical syndicate further foreclosed what little artistic agency actors had left. Film simply provided an identifiable source for many actors' fears.[47] Locked in celluloid, they were able to assume only a mute significance as they signaled through the frames.

Where, early in the nineteenth century, actors stood on "points" to render words made flesh, by the turn of the twentieth, flesh was made word as actors' bodies became signs within Delsarte's system of gestural semeiotics. Both on stage and in film, the actor's body ceased to be a site of his or her interpretive agency, but rather became a mere sign whose meaning was inscribed by someone else. In this way, it came to function as an element of a new theatrical and filmic language that was soon to become the medium for a new dramatic art. For, insofar as it was no longer a site of self-authorization, the actor's body became a symbol of modernist alienation that a new generation of playwrights would inscribe in their expressionist texts. Much like the featureless figure in Edvard Munch's painting *The Scream*, unable to make its voice heard or even emerge into the picture plane with an individuated persona, the actor's body came to emblematize the modern malaise of frustrated agency. If in film the actor was mute, in the theatre, at least, the actor still had a voice; but, as we'll see in chapter 2, even that became a point (so to speak) of increasing anxiety.

Voices: oratory, expression, and the text/performance split

In THE BACK PAGES OF AN 1897 EDITION OF *WERNER'S MAGAZINE* is an advertisement, pitched to the voice teachers and elocutionists who were the magazine's chief subscribers, for a device called a "graphophone" that combines the recording features of a dictaphone with the play-back features of a phonograph. The ad, shown in figure 4, depicts a panoply of artists floating on the waves of sound funneling from the machine's horn, and promises to assist teachers of "music, elocution . . . language, or . . . anything where accuracy of tone, inflection or pronunciation is important." Touting that "exercises may be recorded on cylinders by the instructor," and that "such a cylinder becomes at once a patient, tireless teacher, ever ready to repeat," the ad goes on to claim that this instrument is "more valuable than any text-book, because it speaks to the ear with the living voice." What's more, it adds, a permanent record of students' voices can be made. Clearly, the appeal here is to help ambitious vocal coaches extend their pedagogical reach beyond the sound of their own voice, proving Friedrich Kittler's observation that, by transforming bodily traces into material artifacts, these new communications technologies promised a kind of immortality. But they also helped to induce an element of anxiety by implying that, like John Henry and the locomotive, technology ultimately would be unmatched. The ad, for example, concludes with the testimonial that "Progressive teachers who have adopted the Graphophone for an assistant have greatly multiplied their power and effectiveness as instructors," adding somewhat ominously that "The Graphophone cylinders go on teaching while the teacher rests." That teachers tired might have been a point upon which to close the sale, but it also must have been a disquieting thought to anyone who feared being replaced by these machines.

As this ad suggests, the new communications technologies appearing at the turn of the century were the source of some ambivalence, if not

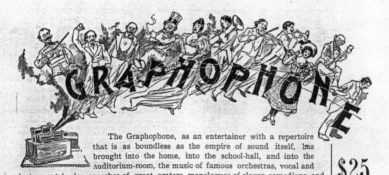
Figure 4. An ad from an 1897 edition of *Werner's Magazine.*

outright anxiety, over the possible threat they posed to the human beings whose voice and gesture they mechanically reproduced. Indeed, regardless of whether they actually replaced human voice teachers or not, such machines entered the symbolic imaginary as figures for them, given the imitative and repetitive methods of traditional elocutionary instruction. Once voice and gesture could be mechanically reproduced, the traditional methods by which speaking and acting had been taught began to be regarded with suspicion, especially in a moment when the new research academy was insisting upon a higher standard of intellectual rigor and redefining each of its core disciplines as a science.

So it was that oratory – the central pillar of a university education throughout much of the nineteenth century – was deemed a structural obstacle in the field of scientific inquiry on which the new research academy was built. In this chapter, I revisit the institutional history that led to oratory's reconfiguration as an intellectual discipline, showing how the merely imitative practice of elocution was transformed into a fully theorized method for interpreting written texts through the use of voice and gesture. Known as "expression," it revolutionized literary instruction and gave birth to a popular turn-of-the-century movement advocating performance as a means of de-alienation. It also spawned influential critical debates concerning the autonomy of the poetic text, the poet's agency in its composition, and the extent to which performance was necessary to the realization of its meaning. Never fully resolved, these debates reached a temporary solution in the text/performance split. As I show, it not only defined the category of the literary in explicitly anti-performative terms, but, in doing so, changed the shape of the cultural field in which playwrights could practice their newfound autonomy.

Oratory as a discipline

Throughout the early nineteenth century, oratory was the central part of an American university education, being considered essential training for the leaders of a new nation responsible for debating issues and addressing their constituencies (Applebee 4). But, by the third quarter of the century, with the expansion and reorganization of the classical curriculum into separate disciplines, oratory either saw its constituent elements assigned to other departments such as English, newly formed out of rhetoric and belles lettres, or was made to justify itself as its own autonomous department (D. Smith 448–51).[1] At Boston University, oratory was made into its own school, the first in the US, founded in 1872. Under the direction of its dean, Professor Lewis B. Monroe, Boston's school of oratory became a leading center of influence on the study and practice of vocal expression.

Monroe's chief contribution was to shift oratory away from a concern with vocal technique per se to a focus on the expression of ideas. To do so, he drew upon the theories of François Delsarte to expand the category of speech to include all forms of communication issuing from the body. As we've seen in chapter 1, Delsarte's "method" purported to be drawn from empirical observation even as it was premised upon the speculative theories of eighteenth-century moral philosophy. As we have also seen, its practice in the United States was primarily focused on the physical training of the actor's body, turning it into the physiognomic signifier of a character's moral-psychological essence. But, while Delsarte is mostly remembered for his method of actor training, his early research was primarily devoted to voice and speech. Indeed, Delsarte himself was once a vocalist who turned to teaching only after his own prospects for an operatic career were ruined by the early misuse of his voice.

As with his gestural schema, Delsarte's vocal schema was tripartite in structure, in which the vocal apparatus was analyzed into three parts, each of which correlated to a principle within his moral-philosophical system, yet abiding by the "ninefold accord."[2] And, as with his gestural schema, Delsarte often found himself having to modify his theory in accord with his empirical findings, especially when they challenged the accepted wisdom of conventional voice theory. For example, Delsarte noticed that mothers cooing to their children often spoke in a high-pitched register with a low degree of acuity, or force. This was at odds with the traditional understanding among voice teachers that force should increase with the ascension of scale. Nonetheless, Delsarte had to acknowledge that "it would be very bad taste to bellow the words at [the child] on the pretext that, according to singing teachers, the intensity of the sound is augmented in direct ratio to its acuteness" (Delsarte 415). At a loss for how to explain this phenomenon, Delsarte hit upon the solution when he distinguished between the *sentiment* expressed by mothers and the *passion* expressed by singers on stage or "uncultured persons" in everyday life (Delsarte 420):[3] Thus did Delsarte deduce the "laws" of vocal force in relation to scale. By distinguishing between the different emotional states that were expressed (not to mention the different classes of person expressing them), he was able to reconcile his empirical findings with his theoretical principles and thus justify his system.

As this example reveals, Delsarte's musical training provided him with a way of analyzing the features of everyday speech, from inflection and intonation to rhythm and phrasing, and of assessing their effect upon auditors. According to his disciple Angélique Arnaud, Delsarte revolutionized vocal music performance in France through his interpretation of "appoggiatura," the technique of using one's voice to emphasize or sustain a note. Although most vocalists throughout the nineteenth century interpreted "appoggiatura" to indicate an emphasis, Delsarte understood the term to derive from the same root as the French verb "appuyer," to press or sustain. Thus, instead of emphasizing a randomly picked note in the phrase – often, one that was high or showy to demonstrate vocal range – singers who trained with Delsarte were taught to sustain the most dissonant or unresolved note (e.g., the subdominant fourth) in the musical phrase (Delsarte 190). This had the effect of prolonging the phrase and of heightening audience anticipation of its resolution in the tonic base.[4] Delsarte thus redefined the reigning paradigm of vocal instruction, shifting its emphasis away from a concern with vocal technique per se to an interest in how such techniques could be used to engage the audience's understanding and emotional experience of the musical piece.

Delsarte brought such insights to bear upon speaker training as well. Realizing that the effect of a sustained emphasis in a musical phrase might be comparable to that of a sustained emphasis in a spoken phrase, he postulated rhetorical effects that could enhance an audience's engagement with spoken language. Intonation, for example, indicated which words were to receive emphasis – whether by vocal force or, as Delsarte was fond of pointing out, by a softness which elicited the audience's desire to hear more (both literally and figuratively). So, too, could emphasis be deflected to a seemingly insignificant word in order to enhance the meaning and effect of other words adjacent to it. To illustrate, Delsarte once asked a lecture audience which word they would emphasize in the following lines of poetry:

> The wave draws near, it breaks, and vomits up before our eyes,
> Amid the surging foam, a monster huge of size.

One respondent proposed "monster" since it evoked an object of terror that should be rendered in a terrifying way. Another suggested "huge" since the vocal emphasis would appropriately enlarge the sound of the word itself. A third proposed "vomits" to underscore "the ugliness of that which it expresses." But Delsarte demurred in favor of an alternative point of stress. According to Arnaud,

> It was on the word *and* that he concentrated all the force of his accent; but giving it, by gesture, voice and facial expression, all the significance lacking to that particle, colorless in itself, as he pronounced the word, the fixity of his gaze, his trembling hands, his body shrinking back into itself, while his feet seemed riveted to the earth, all presaged something terrible and frightful. He saw what he was about to relate, he made you see it; the conjunction, aided by the actor's pantomime, opened infinite perspectives to the imagination. (Delsarte 204)

Thus, as with music, emphasis could be used in speech to sustain a phrase in order to increase the audience's desire to hear it to conclusion.

In this example, Delsarte breaks with John Walker's rule that a conjunction should be grouped with the phrase it precedes,[5] but, like Walker and other eighteenth-century English elocutionary reformers, he understood meaning to exist as much in the *way* words were spoken as in the semantic content of the words themselves. Meaning also existed in silences, in emphases, in vocal and gestural cues. It was not simply a function of the word's (arbitrary) relationship to the idea it named, *pace* Saussure, who would soon deliver his lectures on the signifier's relationship to the signified at the University of Geneva.[6] Meaning, for Delsarte, was the product of all these elements combined. But where the elocutionary reformers tended to prescribe proper language use, Delsarte was more interested in describing and analyzing actual language use, shifting the study of speech away from the mastery of conventional techniques toward an understanding of the meanings and effects that such techniques created.

With Delsarte as his model, Boston University's Monroe likewise shifted speech training away from the acquisition and mastery of vocal technique toward a cultivation of the voice for creating meaningful effects within an auditor's mind. Prior to Monroe, American speech training had been based on an amalgam of prescriptive lessons taken from the elocutionary reformers, a physiological understanding of the vocal apparatus contributed by Dr. James Rush, and a universal system of pronunciation developed by deaf-educator Alexander Melville Bell (father of Alexander Graham Bell). Collectively known as the Rush–Murdoch system, this compendium of methods provided a total system for analyzing the vocal properties of pitch, force, abruptness, quality, and time, and formed the backbone of speech training throughout the second half of the nineteenth century (Robb, *Oral* 103). With its emphasis on the vocal apparatus and its range of possible sounds, the Rush–Murdoch system served as a sort of vocational training for public speakers such as lawyers, statesmen, ministers, and of course actors. This was all very well and good, but, as Monroe came to realize, its exclusive focus on training the speaker's voice neglected an important part of the art of speaking, specifically the relay of meaning. The Delsarte method, however, did not; it offered a systematic way of understanding the relationship between various vocal techniques and the emotional effects they created in the auditor.

This, for Monroe, was what was most exciting about Delsarte's work. By attending not simply to the act of speaking but to the transfer of meaning from speaker to auditor, Delsarte put the communion back into communication – with all of that word's spiritual significance. For Delsarte, speaker and auditor alike are transformed by a process in which a spiritual truth is made flesh in the speaker's physiognomic signification, and is made spirit once again in the mind of the auditor. Upon first learning of Delsarte's method, Monroe is reported to have remarked that it was "Swedenborg geometrized" (Renshaw 302). Indeed, the link Delsarte draws between the three zones of the body and the spiritual forces of life, mind, and soul suggests that he did adhere to Swedenborg's theory of correspondence between the spiritual and material worlds (despite, or perhaps in addition to, his Catholicism).[7] In any case, a profound sense of mysticism lies at the heart of Delsarte's "course of applied aesthetics," with its three principles of ontology, semeiotics, and aesthetics.

By "ontology," Delsarte appears to mean a divine principle of being very much like the Hegelian notion of mind or spirit which both produces and seeks to recognize itself within the material realm. As particular instances of this principle of being, we, too, seek to recognize its manifestations in nature and human activity. To do so, we practice "semeiotics," which Delsarte defines as "the science of organic signs," the ability to recognize this principle of being as it appears in the material form of nature, such as the passions moving through the human body. When such passions are objectified in art, we draw upon "aesthetics" in order to comprehend the relationship between form and feeling. "The object of art," Delsarte deduced, "therefore, is to reproduce, by the action of a superior principle (ontology), the organic signs explained by semeiotics, and whose fitness is estimated by aesthetics" (Delsarte 460). Delsarte delineates his "laws" thus:

1. If, from a certain organic form, I infer a certain sentiment, that is Semeiotics.
2. If, from a certain sentiment, I deduce a certain organic form, that is Aesthetics.
3. If, after studying the arrangement of an organic form whose inherent fitness I am supposed to know, I take possession of that arrangement under the title of methods, invariably to reproduce that form by substituting my individual will for its inherent cause, that is Art. (Delsarte 461)

Art, in other words, is the activity wherein ontology, semeiotics, and aesthetics all come together. Although the universal spirit moves through us all, it finds special expression in the artist whose soul is at peace, whose mind is open, and whose body is lent as instrument to the creation of a work of art (Delsarte 460–3).

To Monroe and other American followers, Delsarte's model of aesthetic communication must have struck a familiar chord – not only because it resonated with a popular strain of Romantic thought but because that resonance had already been sounded by the American Transcendentalists. Indeed, a familiarity with the Transcendentalist writings of Ralph Waldo Emerson must have prepared many Americans to hear and respond to Delsarte's message.[8] There was certainly an affinity between the two thinkers. Both posited a universal spirit that manifested itself in nature and in art. Where Emerson spoke of the "oversoul," Delsarte invoked the "spirit of God" when formulating his principle of ontology. Furthermore, both subscribed to the ancient idea that nature was a book whose lessons we must learn to read. Where Emerson held that "It is not words only that are emblematic; it is things which are emblematic" (49), Delsarte posited "semeiotics" as the ability to read natural signs, whether in bodily gesture and comportment, in vocal expression, or in nature generally. Finally, both held that art was the translation and expression of such lessons whereby the universal spirit was revealed through the instrument of the artist. Where Emerson spoke of art as "nature passed through the alembic of man" (47), Delsarte developed his principle of "aesthetics" as the objectification and/or comprehension of the divine relationship between form and feeling.

Thus, an infusion of American Transcendentalist thought entered into a peculiarly American understanding of the Delsarte method, especially as adapted by Monroe for the teaching of speech.[9] Although he died in 1879, only seven years after having assumed his position as dean, Monroe had a tremendous impact on speaker training, despite never having set his ideas in print. In his obituary, the *Boston Herald* eulogized him as a "leading influence" in the growing field of elocution, which boasted close to 5,000 students in the Boston area alone (Renshaw 302). His legacy proved long-lasting both in terms of his contribution to the study of speech and in the influence he exerted upon his students. Among his most celebrated students was S. S. Curry, who not only recorded Monroe's theories in print in several influential and widely adopted textbooks, but expanded upon them to such a degree that he rechristened the field of study "expression" in order to distinguish it from "elocution," its discredited forebear (Robb, "Elocutionary" 196).[10] Other prominent pupils included Anna Baright, who, shortly after marrying Curry, merged her school with his to found the School of Expression (later Curry College); Charles Wesley Emerson, who established the Emerson College of Oratory (later Emerson College); Franklin Sargent, who, along with MacKaye, founded the Lyceum Theatre School which became, under his directorship, the American Academy of Dramatic Arts; and Leland Powers, who, with his wife Carol Hoyt (a former student of Emerson), instituted the School of the Spoken Word (Renshaw 304–6; Hodge 561; Blanchard 626). As teachers, these students of Monroe proved no less of an institutional influence upon their students than Monroe had been on them, prompting many of their pupils to go on to found schools of their own. For example, two of Emerson's students – Mary Blood and Ida Riley – founded the Columbia School of Oratory in Chicago in 1890, renamed the Columbia School of Expression in 1904 (Renshaw 305).[11]

S. S. Curry and the theory of expression

S. S. Curry was Monroe's heir apparent, assuming his duties as Boston University's Snow Professor of Oratory immediately following Monroe's death. Like his mentor, Curry was critical of the way oratory was typically taught at the end of the nineteenth century, accusing many of its practitioners of being stilted and mannered – even those such as Robert Fulton and Thomas Trueblood who attempted to merge Rush's attention to mechanics (quality, force, abruptness, pitch, time) with Delsarte's triune focus on mental, vital and emotive faculties (Robb 162–3; 194–5). Curry felt that such efforts all too often ended in the creation of a single vocal standard to which the student's voice was rigidly calibrated. Believing with Alexander Melville Bell that "What is wanted is not a Rule for this or that species of sentence, but a power over the voice generally," Curry sought to create a more flexible method of study that would serve as a corrective to the "mechanical" delivery that tended to result from the strict observance of rules (Robb, *Oral* 156–7). Indeed, the term "mechanical" was Curry's favorite pejorative for the prescriptive protocols then in use. Speaking specifically of the Rush–Murdoch method, for example, he claimed that "The greatest evil . . . of the whole system, is that it introduces mere rules, founded upon a mechanical mode of procedure. The whole action of the mind is focused upon the modes of execution by the voice, and not upon the successive ideas" (*Province* 317). In such approaches, "Nothing is left to difference of personality or the unconscious or spontaneous impulse of the soul. All must not only be conscious and deliberative, but must be given by every person in the same way" (*Province* 324).

Although recent speech historians frequently use the term "mechanical" to describe earlier methods of voice training that calcified into rote practice or a rigid set of rules, this application does not actually appear in the historical record until Curry, as Paul Edwards has pointed out (19). Prior to the industrial revolution, after all, "mechanical" tended to refer not to machines but to an artisan who worked with his hands (e.g., Bottom, Snout, Flute or any of the other so-called "mechanicals" from *A Midsummer Night's Dream*). By the end of the nineteenth century, however, the term had taken on a very specific connotation having to do not only with things of the "machine age," but with the way such things threatened to efface individuality. We see traces of this in Curry's quote above, as when he complains that, in mechanical methods such as Rush's, "all . . . must be given by every person in the same way." Clearly, the metaphorical value of his favorite epithet lay in its ability to evoke a set of associations not unlike those we saw at work in the Graphophone ad.

Curry's solution was to reassert the importance of the individual in the act of speaking. But, of course, such an emphasis upon the *self* in self-expression allowed for the possibility of grandstanding or charismatic display. Indeed, one of the common complaints against public speakers and actors at the turn of the twentieth century was that they succumbed to a rather indulgent tendency to showcase their own personalities. As we've seen in chapter 1, "personality" was an overdetermined term at the turn of the twentieth century, with actors invoking it vigorously and often to secure a diminishing sense of artistic agency in their work. So was it freighted with extra significance in the debates leading up to the text/performance split, with expression itself often taken to mean the cultivation and public display of one's signature "personality." Between 1891 and 1907, when he wrote his influential textbooks, Curry was careful to insist upon a proper balance between the *matter* expressed and the *manner* in which it received expression. He seems to speak to this problem of balance when he describes the proper movement expression should take:

> As the leaf manifests the life at the root of the tree; as the bobolink's song is the outflow of a full heart; so all expression obeys the same law; it comes FROM WITHIN OUTWARD, from the centre to the surface, from a hidden source to outward manifestation. However deep the life, it reveals itself by natural signs.
>
> Expression in man is governed by the same law. Every action of face or hand, every modulation of voice, is simply an outward effect of an inward condition. Any motion that is otherwise is not expression. (*Foundations* 10)

The willful imposition of the speaker's personality onto that which is to be expressed, in other words, breaks the bond of unity otherwise created between the universal life force and the speaker, and halts its reach to the audience. According to Delsarte enthusiast Marion Lowell, however, one could err in the other direction by not expressing one's personality enough. Believing that personality is what establishes the speaker's relation to the object of his/her expression, Lowell suggests that it typically functions as an index of domination or deference: "When a gesture is made without any indication of the person of the object or subject precedent to its motion, the gesticulation becomes impersonal in its nature" (Lowell 100). Thus, in order to facilitate the perfect balance between the cosmic spirit and the speaker's own personality, Curry developed a method of study designed to help the speaker communicate the subjective impressions that a text evoked within his or her mind (Robb, "Elocutionary" 196). In this way, he further established oratory as an intellectual discipline, shifting its emphasis once again from the training of voice and gesture onto the training of the speaker's mind.

Curry's "think-the-thought" method was essentially a program of textual explication which anticipated that of the New Critics by emphasizing attention to such features as figurative language, meter, and the significance of line length.[12] Beginning with a work of literature, Curry's speaker was asked to conceptualize the meaning of the work as a whole. Then, concentrating upon the various figures and images that produced that conception, the speaker communicated it to the audience through the expressive means of his or her entire body. These expressive means included the three primary "languages" of the body: verbal (the conventionalized symbols of language), vocal (e.g., tone-color, rhythm, and inflection, which register emotion), and pantomimic (gesture and bodily comportment). Only through the effective and unified use of these three languages, Curry held, could the individual achieve authentic self-expression.

In identifying three languages of expression and insisting upon their coordination, Curry essentially follows Delsarte's method. His modifications are so extensive, however, that they effectively constitute a new system. Where Delsarte is mystical, for example, Curry is mostly secular. Where Curry delineates verbal, vocal, and pantomimic languages, Delsarte distinguishes among "vocal" (i.e., tone) "dynamic" (i.e., gesture), and "buccal" (i.e., articulation) modes of expression (Stebbins 36). More than a simple difference in vocabulary, these separate nomenclatures reflect a different understanding of how such languages convey meaning. Where Delsarte keeps his focus on the body of the speaker as a site of enunciation, Curry sees the speaker as one element in the communicative process. By using the word "verbal" – as opposed to Delsarte's "buccal," for example – Curry seems to open up the category of language to take in the shared signs and thus social nature of communication.

Nonetheless, Curry followed Delsarte in believing that expression was basically a process through which an inner idea was outwardly manifested in and through the speaker's body. The gradual process by which an idea was pressed outward, or "ex-pressed," was called the process of "evolutions" or "successions." Genevieve Stebbins explains, for example, that an emotion first reveals itself in facial expression, then bodily gesture, then in language, where it is given articulate form. "Expression of face precedes gesture, and gesture precedes speech . . . It takes many words to say what a single look reveals . . . The gesture shows the emotional condition from which the words flow, and justifies them" (Stebbins 170; see also Lowell 25). Delsarte himself held that "Gesture is . . . always anterior to speech, which is but a reflected and subordinate expression" (Delsarte 234). Some of Delsarte's followers interpreted this to mean that vocality and gesture were more important than, because prior to, speech. For example, the Abbé de Delaumosne proclaimed that, though speech is a gift from God (ranking humans highest on the evolutionary scale), it is the last mode of communication acquired in human development and therefore last in the chain of successions to be expressed and thus make itself known (Delaumosne in Delsarte 127).

For his part, Curry did allow that "verbal expression . . . is the most complete and adequate means of revealing ideas" (*Province* 52). But, he maintained, it is not adequate unto itself; vocal and pantomimic languages complete the expression by introducing nuances which can augment or even reverse the presumed meaning of a verbal utterance (*Province* 54). "The writer arranges his ideas and endeavors to embody thought in words," Curry explains,

> while the speaker not only endeavors to embody his ideas in words, but to reveal all the phases of experience arising from these ideas or associated with them through a co-ordination of all the living languages of his personality. Not only must he have 'words that burn,' but tones and inflections, motions and actions, which breathe and live with the deepest life of his soul. (*Province* 39)

As he explains, "The true orator knows that every language natural to man is intended to perform a certain function in his great work of speaking, and that unless all these languages are brought into co-ordination, unless the testimony of each is made to bear out the same purpose, he knows that one will contradict another, and his expression thus weakened" (*Province* 58). This was important because only if his or her ideas were well expressed could the speaker arouse the sympathetic identification of his or her auditors so as to make the conceptualization that had manifested itself to him or her manifest itself to them. "The soul of all true expression is sympathy," Curry explains. "The imagination conceives the scenes and situations, reproduces them in a natural order, and thus awakens sympathy, and creates an emotional response" (*Imagination* 199–200). In this way, the circuit of communication was complete: from its impetus in the spiritual forces of the universe to its revelation within the speaker's mind to its perfect expression in the three languages of the speaker's body to its sympathetic reception by the auditor, insight became idea became fully embodied and experiential knowledge.

The expressive culture movement

Whether because it served as a bridge between religious and secular world-views, or because it tapped into a distinctly American preoccupation with the self, or because it easily lent itself to the burgeoning Reform Movement, "expression" quickly became the "expressive culture movement" in the first two decades of the twentieth century. Essentially a program of de-alienation, it promised to help individuals overcome the alienating conditions of modernity by applying Curry's theory of expression to everyday life. Encompassing poetry and drama, music and dance,[13] the expressive culture movement purported that, through these forms of artistic self-expression, one could restore one's body to the natural rhythms of the universe. For, with the mechanization of work, transportation, and even leisure activities, the human body had been altered by the imposition of industrial rhythms, its own natural rhythms having been thrown out of alignment. The only way to restore the body to a state of spiritual harmony, proponents believed, was to help it unlearn the awkward habits it had acquired in adapting to its changed environment. "There seemed to be a general assumption, which was probably correct," one student later recalled, "that everyone's body was constricted and because of that fact exercises in relaxation were given from the start" (M. Oclo Miller quoted in Robb, *Oral* 168). Those exercises in relaxation were typically known as "decomposing exercises," a physical regimen designed to relax the body's musculature from bad habits of breathing, speaking, gesture, and movement which, if left unchecked, inhibited authentic self-expression. These were followed by a set of "recomposing exercises" which allowed for the body to be properly retrained.[14] Once its movements and rhythms had been recalibrated to a natural – as opposed to industrial – standard, the body was ready to give expression to a work of art. This, however, was not an end in and of itself. The performing arts simply offered a means by which to experience one's body as an agent of meaning-making once again. For, by reciting a poem or a dramatic monologue, playing a musical instrument or dancing, one could remember what it was to feel, to be in a body, to live life in relation to a larger spiritual design.

It was, in a way, a means of healing the alienation caused by the mind/body split that developed in the wake of capitalism's historical emergence. As dance theorist Randy Martin observes, this split has intensified in the modern period, given capitalism's ever-expanding logic of rationalization (70). Arguing that the power to resist this logic lies in the kinetic body, Martin's analysis bears a striking resemblance to that made by many turn-of-the-century thinkers. Like him, they identified the problem as a profound sense of alienation from the experience of one's own body. As cultural historian Tom Lutz has discussed, this problem was often given the medical diagnosis of "neurasthenia" by late nineteenth- and early twentieth-century doctors. Under the care of physicians such as S. Weir Mitchell, female neurasthenics were prescribed a mandatory "rest cure," while vigorous outdoor activity was recommended for male patients suffering from the nervous disorder. Those associated with the expressive culture movement, however, diagnosed the problem of alienation as a *cultural*, rather than medical problem, believing that the problem lay less in the individual than in the alienating conditions in which the individual lived.[15]

In its concern with the felt distance between mind and body, the individual and nature, modernity and a less-alienated past, the expressive culture movement recalls Emerson's essay "Nature," in which he laments the fact that humankind has become so habituated to the natural rhythms of the universe that they cease to be felt as such. Where once we stood in awe of nature, reveling in the experience of being alive, now we take it for granted, mining its resources for our keep. Calling for a renewed relationship to the natural forces of the universe, Emerson heralds that "A life in harmony with Nature, the love of truth and of virtue, will purge the eyes to understand her text. By degrees we may come to know the primitive sense of the permanent objects of nature, so that the world shall be to us an open book, and every form significant of its hidden life and final cause" (54–5). Proponents of the expressive culture movement took inspiration from Emerson, promising to restore their followers to a "life in harmony with Nature."

Whatever was causing the current state of *dis*harmony, however, was rarely named beyond a vague reference to the processes of modernization. But, given expression's emphasis upon reintegrating the three languages of the body, it would seem to have been at least exacerbated by the new communications technologies appearing at the turn of the century. After all, these technologies effectively fractured the sense of bodily integrity involved in the act of communication. When mute bodies gestured on the screen, and disembodied voices poured forth from phonograph horns, telephones and radios, signification must have seemed strange, floating free from its bodily source.[16] What's more, its inscription on celluloid, wax cylinders and rubber discs meant not only that it could exist as a material artifact separate from the individual who produced it, but that it was endlessly reproducible, thus calling into question the heretofore assumed primacy of the individual in the act of self-expression.

Whether these new technologies were causative or merely incidental, the expressive culture movement appears to have provided a forum for Americans to come to terms with the vaguely perceived anxieties they wrought. It certainly tapped a nerve in the American cultural psyche, generating a large and enthusiastic following throughout the first two decades of the twentieth century. Indeed, the movement was so popular, its influence so pervasive, its precepts so widely accepted that it could be referenced with barely a mention of its name (which perhaps explains the scholarly neglect it has received from American cultural historians). Nonetheless, as speech historian Fred C. Blanchard observes, its ubiquity "is amply illustrated by the numerous schools and private teachers of expression, by the great popularity of platform reading, by the inevitable 'reader' in Chautauqua and other lyceum circuits, by journals devoted to the subject, by associations and conferences of elocutionists and 'expressionists'" (Blanchard 624).

Among those most responsible for the success of the expressive culture movement was Solomon Henry Clark, who, as director the Chautauqua Summer School of Expression from 1894 until his death in 1928, reached not only the thousands of students who came to Lake Chautauqua for a dose of cultural uplift but the thousands more who followed his curriculum while participating in similar "Chautauquas" around the country or attending its traveling roadshow.[17] Shortly after assuming his duties at the Chautauqua Summer Institute, Clark was invited by fellow Chautauqua assemblyman William Raney Harper to join the faculty of the University of Chicago as Head of the Department of Public Speaking. There he continued to spread the gospel of expression, reaching a new generation of students in the Midwest. Poet Vachel Lindsay, for example, heard him give a series of extension lectures in Springfield, Illinois during the winter of 1896–7, while still a student in high school, and again at the Art Institute of Chicago, where he studied from 1901 to 1904. According to Davis Edwards, it was Clark who introduced him to the concept of "tone-color,"[18] an important compositional technique that Lindsay used in poems such as "The Congo" (1914), made famous through Lindsay's own charismatic performance of it (D. Edwards 183). Indeed, the manner in which his poems were vocalized was so important to their overall significance that Lindsay included marginal instructions on how they should be performed.[19] The following excerpt from "The Congo" – part III, "The Hope of Their Religion" – illustrates:

A good old negro in the slums of the town	*Heavy bass.*
Preached at a sister for her velvet gown.	*With a literal*
Howled at a brother for his low-down ways,	*imitation of*
His prowling, guzzling, sneak-thief days.	*camp-meeting*
Beat on the Bible till he wore it out	*racket, and*
Starting the jubilee revival shout.	*trance.*
And some had visions, as they stood on	
chairs,	
And sang of Jacob, and the golden stairs,	
And they all repented, a thousand strong	
From their stupor and savagery and sin and	
wrong	

And slammed with their hymn books till
    they shook the room
With "glory, glory, glory,"
And "Boom, boom, Boom."
THEN I SAW THE CONGO, CREEPING THROUGH   *Exactly as in*
    THE BLACK   *the first section.*
CUTTING THROUGH THE JUNGLE WITH A   *Begin with*
    GOLDEN TRACK.   *terror and*
                                        power, end with joy.

Like Eugene O'Neill's *The Emperor Jones*, which it heavily influenced (see chapter 4), "The Congo" imagines the atavistic pull of the primitive on otherwise civilized Black Americans. From a camp-meeting revival where the preacher chastises his flock for their luxury, vanity, lechery, intemperance, and thievery to the jungle's surprising reassertion of its mysterious power, this section, Lindsay tells us, is to be intoned with a voice that mimics the preacher's "heavy bass," imitates a "camp-meeting racket," segues into a "trance," and then, shifting into a "deliberate [and] solemn" cadence, concludes "with terror and power," that is transformed into a final note of "joy."

Clearly, the poem's verbal significance is meant to be realized through the speaker's voice. The struggle it depicts between the organized religion of Christianity and primitive pantheistic beliefs is also *enacted* by the speaker's voice, demonstrating the complex interaction between the body and soul of both the poem's performer and its African-American characters. Lindsay explicitly staged this struggle in terms of the poem's rhythms, interweaving the cadences of the traditional church hymn "Hark Ten Thousand Harps and Voices" and something approaching a Gregorian chant that he said came to him unconsciously (D. Edwards 191). Thus, "The Congo," as Cary Nelson has observed of modern poetry generally, absorbs the sacramental functions of religion into its very form in order to situate religion itself as a site of political struggle (Nelson 131).

Lindsay's use of competing rhythms to stage the struggle for his African-American characters' souls came from a lesson he had learned from expressive culture's Clark. By "tone color," Clark meant an "inherent quality of vowels and consonants" that has the ability to change a line's rhythm, even when it conforms to a regular metrical pattern (D. Edwards 187–8). The sibilant "s," the long smooth "o," the gutteral "g" – all have the ability to shape our sense of the ideas named by the words they're in, and in so doing have the ability to affect the overall mood of the poem. Tone color, in other words, is an aural quality that can evoke a specific mood or emotion in a listener's mind, whether on the level of word or phrase. To cite but one example from "The Congo," Lindsay tells us that the preacher "preached," illustrating his moral righteousness with a clean "e" sound that ends in a short, sharp and definitive "ch'd." In the next line, however, Lindsay tells us that he "howled," suggesting an ambiguous moral slippage both by way of its diphthonged "ow" and its echo in the sinner's "prowling." Even in these two words, Lindsay uses tone color to foreshadow the preacher's spiritual de-evolution along with his lapsed congregants.

For poets influenced by expressive culture such as Lindsay, sound was important. But it wasn't important simply because it was pleasing to hear a poem recited out loud (or, for that matter, in the mind's ear); it was important because it shaped the way we hear it *mean*. Thus, terms such as "tone color" are drawn from music not simply for their metaphorical value but for their ability to describe a dimension of experience that exceeds the printed sign. As we've seen, a major source for this musical vocabulary was Delsarte, whose work Monroe and Curry integrated into expression which itself blossomed into the expressive culture movement.[20] Meaning, in other words, lay as much in the aural form of a work of art as in its conceptual content. With such lessons among its teachings, the expressive culture movement influenced not just the performance of literature but also its composition.

The text/performance split

As with any popular movement, however, expressive culture had its critics. Indeed, many came from within the movement itself as even supporters noted that "expression" had come to mean many different things to many different people. Others came from outside. Prominent among them was Harvard philosopher George Santayana, whose influential *Interpretations of Poetry and Religion* (1900) appears to have been written in response to the expressive culture movement. As Santayana himself explained to his assistant Daniel Cory, the issues which prompted him to write it "were very much 'in the air' at the turn of the century" (quoted in Porte xxv).[21] No doubt they were; wafting across the Charles River from their headquarters at Boston University, the principles of the expressive culture movement formed an important cultural and critical context to Santayana's thought.

In his essay, "The Elements and Function of Poetry," for example, Santayana identifies expression by name, complaining that, by diffusing the act of meaning onto the cosmos, the speaker, and his or her audience, it effectively erases the poet's agency. "Expression," he contends,

> is a misleading term which suggests that something previously known is rendered or imitated; whereas the expression is itself an original fact, the values of which are then [mistakenly] referred to the thing expressed, much as the honours of a Chinese mandarin are attributed retroactively to his parents. So the charm which a poet, by his art of combining images and shades of emotion, casts over a scene or an action, is attached to the principal actor in it, who gets the benefit of the setting furnished him by a well-stocked mind. (158)

Expression, in other words, not only misattributes to the poem the poet's skill, but effectively denies poetic agency by suggesting that the poet is simply a conduit of some larger universal truth which he or she merely inscribes upon the page.

Moreover, he continues, expression is vulnerable to the pathetic fallacy, that tendency of projecting emotion onto an inanimate object (not to mention the as-yet-unnamed affective fallacy, whereby one projects an emotion onto a work of art rather than responding to the emotion expressed by the work itself). While Santayana agrees that emotions are the stuff out of which poetry is made, he goes on to insist that poetry does not present us with an unmediated experience of them; rather, it presents us with emotions that have been transformed first within the poet's imagination. Through the poetic process, the poet turns his or her emotion inward and works upon it until it can be rendered in terms that are ideal, terms that induce in us the simultaneous shock of recognition and truth of revelation. The key to the poet's success, Santayana avers, lies in his or her ability to find the "correlative object" by which that emotion may be expressed.[22]

As many scholars have observed, Santayana's notion of a "correlative object" is the probable source of T. S. Eliot's "objective correlative."[23] Eliot was, after all, a student of Santayana at Harvard in the first decade of the twentieth century. Thus, insofar as the expressive culture movement was "very much 'in the air'" for Santayana, it was most likely "in the air" for Eliot, too. Indeed, Eliot's formulation of the objective correlative can also be read as a reaction to Curry's theory of expression, in particular his emphasis upon the speaker and the performative features of language as the source of poetic meaning.

Eliot's famous critical phrase first appears, of course, in "Hamlet and His Problems" (1919), where he criticizes Shakespeare's play for its inability to objectify in language the correlating emotion which propels its central character to speak. Eliot explains that the play "is full of some stuff that the writer could not drag to light, contemplate, or manipulate into art. And when we search for this feeling, we find it, as in the sonnets, very difficult to localize" (267). This "stuff," he suggests, is comprised ultimately of Hamlet's inexpressible feelings for his mother, feelings which are "in excess of the facts as they appear . . . Hamlet is up against the difficulty that his disgust is occasioned by his mother, but that his mother is not an adequate equivalent for it; his disgust envelops and exceeds her. It is thus a feeling which he cannot understand; he cannot objectify it, and it therefore remains to poison life and obstruct action" (268). Eliot adds that, just as Hamlet is unable to express adequately his feelings, so, too, is Shakespeare unable to express adequately the artistic aims of his play. He has created, in Eliot's estimation, a flawed work of art. Sounding much like his mentor, Eliot explains, "The only way of expressing emotion in the form of art is by finding an 'objective correlative'; in other words, a set of objects, a situation, a chain of events which shall be the formula of that particular emotion; such that when the external facts, which must terminate in sensory experience, are given, the emotion is immediately evoked" (268). Note that, for Eliot, it is not a matter of an actor's interpretation of Hamlet's emotional expressivity that is the problem; rather, it is the author's construction of his character in words.

The suggestion that the play's language cannot fully account for the meanings generated by its action did not originate with Eliot but derives from book XVII of Friedrich Nietzsche's *The Birth of Tragedy*, first translated into English in 1910. Here Nietzsche cites Shakespeare's play as an example of what he refers to as "socratism" – an overemphasis on reason at the expense of feeling. According to Nietzsche, this tendency began with Euripides and has marked tragedy's decline ever since, removing it from its origins in Dionysiac revelry when music, sung by the chorus, transported audience members out of an awareness of their individual identities into a participation in the collective whole. Expressing only the *principium individuationis*, post-Euripidean tragedy fails, says Nietzsche, since language alone is insufficient to realize the artist's tragic vision. In order to restore the dialectical tension between Apollonian and Dionysiac forces, language must be reunited with music – as in Wagner's operas – so that the audience can experience the dialectic of individuation and transcendence once again.[24] Specifically invoking Shakespeare's play, Nietzsche claims that Hamlet "talks more superficially than he acts" such that the meaning generated by the play's action is unable to "find its adequate objectification in the spoken word."

Clearly, Nietzsche provides the source of Eliot's critique of the play, as F. N. Lees first suggested. Nonetheless, there is a curious difference between Nietzsche's and Eliot's understandings of where the play's "problem" lies; for Nietzsche, it lies in tragic drama's movement away from music; for Eliot, it lies in the playwright's inability to find the exact verbal expression "which shall be the formula of [a] particular emotion." The difference appears to be in their understanding of where the drama's meaning lies. For Nietzsche, it cannot be reduced to language, whereas, for Eliot, it must be.

Although we cannot know for certain whether Eliot was motivated to formulate his notion of the "objective correlative" by Curry's theory of expression, his desire to locate meaning in verbal signification alone functions as an implicit challenge to Curry's insistence that all three languages are necessary to effective communication.[25] It would seem that Eliot took issue with the distinction Curry makes between the writer, who merely "arranges his ideas and endeavors to embody thought in words," and the speaker, whose "co-ordination of all the living languages of his personality" required superior skill; between a work of literature, which "is a representation of thought and truth in verbal language," and expression, which is "the presentation of truth by personality" (*Province* 41–2).

For Eliot, this emphasis on "personality" was exactly what was wrong. Observing in "Tradition and the Individual Talent" (1919) that "when we praise a poet . . . we pretend to find what is individual, what is the peculiar essence of the man," Eliot suggests instead that we situate the poet in relation to literary history, measuring the extent to which "the dead poets, his ancestors, assert their immortality most vigorously" in his/her work (*Selected Essays* 14). In urging a reconsideration of tradition as it shapes and is shaped by the poet's contribution to his or her craft, Eliot seems to be tacitly challenging not only the Romantic obsession with "genius" – as scholars have observed – but, more specifically, the precipitate of that idea as it filtered into the expressive culture movement's notion of personality. Indeed, Eliot's concern with personality here is near obsessive. He says: "The progress of an artist is a continual self-sacrifice, a continual extinction of personality" (*Selected Essays* 17), and "Poetry is not a turning loose of emotion, but an escape from emotion; it is not the expression of personality, but an escape from personality" (21). Struggling to make himself clear, he all but names expression as the target of his critique: "The point of view which I am struggling to attack," he opines, "is perhaps related to the metaphysical theory of the substantial unity of the soul: for my meaning is, that the poet has, not a 'personality' to express, but a particular medium, which is only a medium and not a personality, in which impressions and experiences combine in peculiar and unexpected ways" (19–20). Again sounding much like Santayana, Eliot identifies the poet's function as that of a catalyst, forging alchemical bonds between thoughts and feelings, words and images. In this way, the poet's mind becomes a crucible in which the elements of the poem are combined and its form crystallized. No longer a charismatic religion, poetry in Eliot's laboratory would become a truly modern science, free from the contaminating presence of an oral interpreter.

In "The Possibility of a Poetic Drama" (1920), Eliot elaborates this point, noting that it is the fact of performance and the need for actors to perform it that is the greatest difficulty in creating poetic drama:

> [W]e must take into account the instability of any art – the drama, music, dancing – which depends upon representation by performers. The intervention of performers introduces a complication of economic conditions which is in itself likely to be injurious. A struggle, more or less unconscious, between the creator and the interpreter is almost inevitable. The interest of a performer is almost certain to be centred in himself: a very slight acquaintance with actors and musicians will testify. The performer is interested not in form but in opportunities for virtuosity or in the communication of his "personality" . . . (*Selected Essays* 69)

But, for all of his apparent hostility toward performance in these early essays, Eliot began to modify his position in the 1920s, just as he was beginning to explore the dramatic form for himself.[26] Writing in 1923, upon the death of popular music hall performer Marie Lloyd, for example, he expresses admiration for Lloyd's ability to give near-perfect expression to the lives of her working-class audience. As he notes, her every gesture resonated with their values, as if it were a sort of gestural equivalent of the objective correlative (*Selected Essays* 419). Such a willingness to reconsider the artistic merits of performance appears again in "Four Elizabethan Dramatists" (1924) where Eliot challenges William Archer's claim that modern drama represents the pinnacle of the genre's evolution. He argues that, if – as Archer maintains – there is a problem with Elizabethan drama, it is not that its conventions are not sufficiently logical or realistic; the problem is that it doesn't have *enough* conventions to regulate its expression.[27] And what is true of Elizabethan drama is no less true of modern drama: both lack conventions that would provide them with a self-consistent form (*Selected*

Essays III–12). In the absence of such conventions, Eliot concludes, a dramatic work makes itself vulnerable to the performer who supplements its gaps with his or her personality. Four years later, Eliot went on to elaborate the type of conventions necessary for drama to achieve such a self-consistent form: in *A Dialogue on Dramatic Poetry* (1928), his mouthpiece "E." proclaims, "the perfect and ideal drama is to be found in the ceremony of the Mass" (*Selected Essays* 47). It, above all other modes of performance, realizes Eliot's ideal: it locates meaning in the Word; it uses ritual and the incantatory power of language to evoke a particular emotion (much like the objective correlative); it demands that one's personality be subordinated to tradition; and – most important – its conventions adequately regulate the performers' and participants' self-expression. Thus did Eliot arrive at a protocol for composing drama as a *verbal* art form – one that he would attempt to realize in *Murder in the Cathedral, The Family Reunion*, and other full-length plays written in the later part of his career.

Of course, Eliot was not alone in his objections to Curry's insistence that a work of literature was not fully realized until its meanings were deployed through all three "living languages of man." As we have seen, Santayana was just as adamant about curbing the habit among expressive culture enthusiasts of attributing the poet's creativity to the spiritual forces of the universe, effectively denying the poet's authority and diffusing the poem's meaning. What's more, Ezra Pound and the Imagists appear to have been similarly critical of "the cosmic poet, who seems to us to shirk the real difficulties of his art."[28] If I emphasize Eliot's importance here, it is because he provides us with a fairly neat documentation of a shift in cultural attitudes toward performance in relation to language and meaning. Coining his famous phrase "objective correlative" in order to locate meaning in language alone, Eliot proceeds to rail against the vanity of performers and, indeed, the fact of performance in realizing a piece of dramatic literature. Although he pauses briefly to consider the expressive potential of popular forms of entertainment, Eliot concludes that there never can be a poetic (i.e., literary) drama unless and until its expression is regulated by proper conventions such as those that govern the Mass. Seeking to rescue the dramatic genre from performative excess, Eliot ultimately ends up confining it – and the category of the literary more generally – to verbal signification alone.

That Eliot's later plays were critically acclaimed for their literary qualities speaks as much to the way that category came to be defined by Eliot's early critical writings as to their ability to conform to that definition. For, however ambivalent Eliot may have felt about performance, his early critical writings – with their unmistakeable antipathy toward performance – helped define literary high modernism in anti-performative terms. Canonized within the Anglo-American university through the work of I. A. Richards and F. R. Leavis, and New Critics Cleanth Brooks, Robert Penn Warren, and Robert Heilman, this influential model of literary high modernism bore within it a bias against explicitly performative modes of communication that, as Susan Harris Smith has argued, made much of drama a "bastard art."

The New Criticism of the 1940s, however, was simply the practical extension of the text/performance split that already had been effected within the American university system in the middle of the 1910s. This was when departments of English were rent in half, between those who advocated expression and those who found it too subjective for the new research academy. Where the first group believed in a generalist approach toward education, championing expression's emphasis upon reading comprehension and aesthetic appreciation, the other preferred a more specialist approach, advocating the scientific analysis of literary texts through historical source study and the application of German philological methods (Applebee 36). The split between these two perspectives developed into a professional fissure, with the research-oriented scholars affiliating with the Modern Language Association (MLA) and the generalists breaking off to form the National Council of Teachers of English (NCTE) in 1911 (Rarig and Greaves 497).

But even within the ranks of the NCTE, factions developed – this time between those who felt the study of literature was best served by silent reading and those who insisted upon the importance of oral expression, or what was increasingly being referred to as "oral English." Here again, the debate was pitched in terms of intellectual seriousness versus the cultivation of the student's whole being. Although prominent figures such as Cornell University's Hiram Corson argued that oral English was important "as a means to a disciplined knowledge of the text" (Applebee 61), others such as the University of Chicago's Solomon Henry Clark tempered their earlier enthusiasm, contending that it took up too much valuable classroom time, silent reading having proved itself wholly sufficient as a means of comprehension. "Beautiful as is the adequate vocal interpretation of literature," Clark allows, in his *Interpretation of the Printed Page* (1915), "it is of infinitesimally less worth in a system of education than the ability to interpret silently" (14).

Clearly, the move toward intellectual rigor and scientific objectivity bore within it an anxiety over performance-oriented modes of knowledge. But, in its desire to separate performance out from the study of literary texts, the new research academy found itself unable to contain it, let alone keep it safely outside the curriculum. A well-known case in point is that of Harvard English Professor George Pierce Baker, who developed a workshop component for his influential "English 47" playwriting course. Arguing for the instructive value of allowing students to test the stage-worthiness of their ideas, Baker sought to garner academic credit for the workshop throughout the nineteen-teens. The Harvard administration, however, denied his request on the grounds that, however useful the workshop may be, it was not intellectually demanding enough to merit credit toward a degree.

Finally, on 28 November 1914, the Public Speaking Section of the NCTE broke from its parent organization to form the National Association of Academic Teachers of Public Speaking (NAATPS), later to become the National Association of Teachers of Speech (NATS).[29] With a professional organization to give them national visibility, advocates of oral expression managed to get their courses of instruction recognized as part of a legitimate course of academic study by forming their own departments of theatre and speech. One by one, universities around the country began to invite performance back into the academy with the promise of credentialization. Pacific University in Oregon, for example, offered its first course in play production in 1911–12 (Hamar 587), and in 1914 courses in play production were officially on the books at the University of Wisconsin, the University of Nebraska, Drake University, and the University of Oregon. That same year saw the first autonomous department of drama founded at the Carnegie Institute of Technology. After 1914, other colleges and universities followed suit, with Yale University offering the deanship of its new School of Drama to the long-suffering George Pierce Baker in 1925 (Beckerman 350–2).[30] Even so, anxieties over the intellectual merits of performance had not abated; they were simply lessened by the fact that theatre, too, had recast itself as a "science" (complete with practicum and lab).

That the text/performance split was institutionalized in the very moment when literary high modernism was being born is no simple coincidence. By distinguishing between performative and verbal modes of signification, it made textuality an object of analysis in its own right, defining the category of the literary in a way that enabled the production of literary high modernism. Astradur Eysteinsson has suggested just such a link between the institutionalization of literary study and the development of literary high modernism, noting a dialectical relationship between the formalism of the New Critics and modernist experimentation (75–83). The missing term in his dialectical triangle, however, is the antithesis of performance. For, within the category of the literary that grew out of the text/performance split is an explicitly anti-performative bias. As we'll see in part II, this would pose a particularly vexed problem for modern dramatists with literary aspirations. Caught between an anti-performative bias and the performative medium of their craft, they were placed in a nearly impossible double-bind.

Having assumed the actor's artistic mantle within the theatre, playwrights nonetheless found themselves constrained by changes within the cultural field. If they continued to write theatrically viable plays for the stage, they risked losing their newfound status as literary authors. Yet if they wished to secure their literary credentials, they would have to refuse the performative languages of the stage. As we'll see in chapter 3, this paradox was partially resolved by changes within the juridico-legal field. After the federal copyright revisions of 1909, playwrights were able to assume a new relationship to their craft. For, with the emergence of new recording technologies that rendered a performance "original" from which copies could be made, the law had to recognize a distinction between playscript and performance. What this meant was that playwrights were no longer tied to the producing apparatus of the theatre, but were free to write their own autonomous plays.

3

Words: copyright and the creation of
the performance "text"

In 1903, THE UNITED STATES SUPREME COURT RULED ON THE
case of *Bleistein v. Donaldson Lithographing Co.*, in which the defendant
had unlawfully copied three chromolithographed circus posters designed
by the plaintiff. The question before the court was whether or not these
posters, designed as advertisements, were eligible for copyright protection.
The Sixth Circuit Court had decided they were not, ruling that the law,
based upon its Constitutional charter, was intended to protect only the
"useful arts." The three posters, having been created solely for commercial
purposes, did not fall under this category of protection. Not only were they
not "works connected with the fine arts," they were deemed "immoral,"
depicting as they did "a ballet, a number of persons performing on bicycles,
and groups of men and women whitened to represent statues." As Sixth
Circuit Judge Walter Evans wrote, "The court cannot bring its mind to
yield to the conclusion that such tawdry pictures as these were ever meant
to be given the enormous protection of not only the exclusive right to print
them, but the additional protection of a penalty of a dollar each for reprints
from them" (*Bleistein v. Donaldson* 2).

Although the Supreme Court agreed that, "Picture-posters or show
bills . . . are not designed for close inspection or long-continued study,
like an oil painting, a steel or wood engraving, or an etching," that, rather,
they are "intended to catch the eye of the passer on the street, or any one
who merely glances at them, and to challenge his attention, – if possible to
compel him to look again, so that he will observe what is the subject of the
poster and have this forced upon his mind, and will be attracted by it," it
overturned the lower court's decision, arguing that such posters are eligible for copyright protection since they "require artistic ability, and above all
things creativeness or originality of a high order, but peculiar." Such posters,
it held, *do* belong to the category of art; indeed, do belong to the *useful* arts,

however "peculiar" their use might be. Their status as art lies not in their content, which, tasteful or not, was drawn from life, but in the manner in which that content was rendered by the artist.[1] While any one is free to copy the original as it appears in life, Justice Oliver Wendell Holmes reasoned, "[t]hey are not free to copy the copy. The copy is the personal reaction of an individual upon nature. Personality always contains something unique. It expresses its singularity even in handwriting, and a very modest grade of art has in it something irreducible, which is one man's alone. That something he may copyright" (*Bleistein v. Donaldson* 8).[2]

What is significant about the *Bleistein* decision is not that the court recognized the copyrightability of mechanically reproduced art, nor that it extended protection to such art when used for commercial purposes, but that it located its status *as* art in the expressed personality of the artist. Clearly Justice Holmes was drawing on the rhetoric of the expressive culture movement where "personality" meant that which was wholly unique and unreproducible within the individual. As we've seen in chapters 1 and 2, this concept emerged as a dialectical response to technologies of mass communication, which, by mechanically reproducing bodies, voices, and words, appeared to threaten the integrity of the individual. "Personality" thus became a way of identifying what such technologies could not reproduce. That the law found it necessary to call upon such rhetoric in order to recognize the rights of the individual whose art was being mechanically reproduced is interesting, but it was not the first time that the law had encountered such a problem. Indeed, copyright itself was founded upon the need to protect the individual from technologies of mechanical reproduction with the invention and widescale implementation of the printing press. As such technologies proliferated, copyright protection was expanded and adapted to include new types of protection.

The revolution in communications technology at the turn of the twentieth century was simply one such moment, albeit one that required a thorough revision of existing copyright statutes. That the new "texts" produced by recording technologies such as film and phonography were, in fact, *performances* meant that that the law finally had to address a problem that had long confronted dramatists whose plays were often "re-produced" without their consent. In this chapter, I focus on the neglected history of dramatic copyright, demonstrating how drama's precarious position between the realm of literature and the realm of theatrical production made it conform imperfectly to the initial provisions of copyright law. As the law was modified to accommodate the special needs of drama, drama was likewise modified to accommodate the special needs of the law such that, by the early twentieth century, the conditions were in place for the emergence of modern drama. As I show, that emergence was premised upon these new recording technologies. Not only did they allow for a performance to be analogized to a print original capable of generating copies (on cylinders, discs, and celluloid) that deserved protection under the law, but, in turning performance into its own distinct copyrightable identity, they allowed for the dramatic text to assume an autonomous identity all its own. As we'll see in part II, that new autonomous identity meant that playwrights were able to develop their plays free from the production concerns of the theatrical apparatus. Distinguishing themselves apart from and, in some cases, against the theatre, playwrights began to introduce new dramatic forms such as "expressionism."

The historical background of dramatic copyright

Historians of Anglo-American copyright typically begin their story in 1710 when the British Parliament enacted the Statute of Anne, the first law to recognize authors' rights to control the printing of their works. Prior to this act, a monopoly over published materials was held by the Stationers' Company, a printers' guild, given a royal patent in 1557 (formalized by the Star Chamber decree in 1586) in exchange for censoring materials deemed immoral or seditious. After the patent expired in 1695, the Statute of Anne was enacted in order to protect the economic interests of those involved in the making of books – printers, of course, but also the authors whose books they printed. Entitled, "An Act for the Encouragement of Learning by vesting the Copies of printed Books in the authors or Purchasors of such Copies during the Times therein mentioned," the Statute of Anne was designed to guarantee authors and printers adequate compensation for their labors in order to stimulate the production of books for the public good. Thus seeking to balance private and public interests, it recast the total monopoly held by the Stationers' Company into a limited monopoly of fourteen years (with the possibility of renewal), after which the work entered into the public domain. Effecting what Jane Gaines refers to as a "double movement of circulation and restriction" (9), the Statute of Anne laid the groundwork for modern copyright law.

Like all British territories, the American colonies were subject to the Statute of Anne upon its enactment in 1710, and used it as a model for their own copyright provisions when drafting the Articles of Confederation in

1783 (Abrams 1173). Accordingly, American courts looked to British courts whenever important cases concerning copyright produced new interpretations of the law. Thus, we see the US Supreme Court ruling in *Wheaton v. Peters* (1834) follow closely the British court's deliberations in *Millar v. Taylor* (1769) and *Donaldson v. Beckett* (1774). All three were seminal cases in the history of copyright and concerned the extent to which an author maintained a common-law right in his or her work beyond the statutory limitations of the law. In *Millar*, the court affirmed the author's right to select the printer to whom to entrust the printing of his or her work, thus affirming a common-law right. In *Donaldson* and *Wheaton*, however, that right was seen to terminate in the statutory provisions of the law. Thus, copyright was found to be the right of the author, but only insofar as it pertained to the printing of his or her manuscript. Once printed, the work was subject to the limited terms of the monopoly granted by the law; the author retained no further rights. Copyright was quite literally the right to copy, in both senses of the term – the right to control the "copy" or manuscript, and the right to reproduce it (Rose 12). What is important about this, as Mark Rose points out, is that, in this early moment of copyright jurisprudence, the author's rights were understood to pertain only to the manuscript – the physical artifact of ink and paper – not to what we might refer to more broadly as the "text." Simply put, the notion of intellectual property did not yet exist.[3]

Tracing the emergence of this idea, Rose follows Martha Woodmansee in linking it to the Romantic conception of the author that developed toward the end of the eighteenth century. As she demonstrates, the construction of the author as an original creative genius appeared in response to a changing literary market where the patronage system of honoraria was being absorbed by capitalist relations of exchange. As long as writers were financially supported by patrons, there was no explicit equivalence between the cultural value of their work and the honoraria they received, thus writers were disinclined to understand the flat fee they received from printers in exchange for copyright as a measure of their work's worth. But as the publishing industry became more and more profitable, meeting the growing demands of an increasingly literate public, writers began to rely on the market for their keep, expecting a greater share of the profits from their work. The problem, of course, was that these new productive relations suggested an equivalence between a work's cultural and market values. Thus, in order to distinguish between the two systems of value, there arose a concomitant distinction between different types of writers: in the words of Lord Camden, who deliberated on the *Donaldson* case, it was a difference between "those favoured Mortals, those sublime Spirits, who share that Ray of Divinity which we call 'Genius'" and those "Scribblers for bread, who teize the Press with their wretched Productions" (quoted in Rose 104).

The "author" thus emerged as an original creative genius whose openness to divine inspiration distinguished him or her from the wordsmith who merely applied time-honored rules of composition to the subject of his or her work (Woodmansee 427). In such an author's mind, the creative process unfolds like a seed germinating into full flower. At least this was the metaphor used by Edward Young in his *Conjectures on Original Composition* (1759) – a seminal document of Romantic theory which, more than any other, propagated the conception of the author as original genius. Woodmansee demonstrates that it was in this organic metaphor that the seed of intellectual property itself took root since the work could be seen to consist not only of the idea (which may have been revealed through divine inspiration) but also the form in which that idea was expressed by the author. As elaborated by Johann Gottlieb Fichte, this distinction between the idea and its form gave a material dimension to the author's unique contribution, allowing it to assume the status of a property eligible for protection under the law. Only when the author was recognized as contributing something original, and only when that contribution was recognized as a property under the law, could the author be deemed the "owner" of that property and thus emerge in its current legal configuration.

It is against this general background of copyright's development that we should understand the special case of dramatic copyright's evolution. For, insofar as it was a literary genre, drama fell under the same laws that protected against the infringement of an author's copyright. But, of course, drama is not simply a literary genre; and insofar as it is not, it fell outside the law's protection, posing special problems which took another century or two to address.

Those special problems were primarily two. The first concerned the fact that drama is an aesthetic form that originated out of a premodern social formation. As such, it tends to reflect residual communal values in both its collaborative mode of production and its formal design, posing an immediate problem to a law that recognized a single discrete author. Even as late as the Elizabethan period, when playwrights were already beginning to be recognized as authors in this sense, the play typically belonged to the acting company, not the playwright who, as Joseph Lowenstein observes, was usually referred to collectively in the prologue as "*our* poet" (102). And, for most acting companies in this early moment of print's domain, printing was little more than a subsidiary interest. If a company decided to register a play with the Stationers' Company at all, Lowenstein reports, it might have been to profit from the publication of a play whose popularity was beginning to wane, or to prevent the publication of unauthorized editions of a popular play, regardless of whether the company ultimately intended to publish it or not (105). Thus conceived as a collaborative art form, drama did not lend itself easily to the historical conjunction of "printing technology, market-place economics, and the classical liberal culture of possessive individualism" that Rose sees as formative influences on copyright law (142). Furthermore, drama's aesthetic form retained elements of its collaborative design. Its conventional five-act structure and stock character types, for example, may have enabled companies to quickly mount and efficiently rotate productions, but such schematic elements militated against the drama's "originality," at least in the sense conceived by the Romantics. Such a bias delayed the law's recognition of drama's status as intellectual property and persisted well into the twentieth century when, in 1931, US Supreme Court Justice Learned Hand ruled against the plaintiff in a copyright infringement case on the grounds that the situation and character types found both in her play and in the defendant's film were so common as to reflect no authorial originality.[4] Making a Fichtean distinction between ideas and their expression, Hand appears to fault the plaintiff for her lack of artistry: "It follows that the less developed the characters, the less they can be copyrighted; that is the penalty an author must bear for marking them too indistinctly" (Hand quoted in Kaplan 50). Although apparently unaware of the extent to which his reasoning was the product of its own historical moment, Hand clearly assumes that good drama – copyrightable drama – must conform to the standards of psychological realism, an aesthetic movement that, as George Lukács points out, is specific to the historical period of modernity as a "drama of individualism" (Lukács 430). Considering that, up to the late nineteenth century, dramatic character was written so broadly as to allow it to be individuated by the actor in performance, the implication of Hand's ruling seems to be that drama (or, at least, premodern, non-psychological realist drama) is inherently uncopyrightable.[5]

The second problem had to do with the fact that drama is not a freestanding work of literature, but also functions as a template for theatrical productions. As such, it was only half-protected by the early law since copyright was, from its inception, a provision designed to regulate publication – not any other use to which a text could be put. Insofar as drama was considered literature, it was protected by the same law that regulated other types of printed material. But insofar as it was a script to be acted by players on a stage, it was something else, and that something else was not regulated by copyright law. This is not to say that performances were not regulated. In England in 1574, the Office of the Revels was charged with responsibilities not unlike those assigned to the Stationers' Company.[6] But, since the Office of the Revels was concerned primarily with censoring materials deemed offensive to the crown, it made no provisions against the "copying" of a performance against a playwright's consent. Such an idea was inconceivable. First, without a concept of intellectual property, there could be no legal distinction between the author's manuscript and the ideas it contained, let alone an interpretation of those ideas in performance. Until this concept entered the law, a performance could not be recognized as a separate entity deserving protection. Second, the fact that any one performance necessarily differed from another meant that – until the invention of the phonograph in 1877 and the cinematographe in 1895 – performances themselves could not be copied. Only then, only when technologies of mechanical reproduction made it possible for performance to be analogized to print, could an individual performance be recognized as an original work of art that deserved protection against unauthorized copies. Only then did the performance – and its central architect, the producer-director – come into its own. Paradoxically, it was only then that the play and playwright did, too.

The playwright's rights (or lack thereof)

Throughout the nineteenth century, the American theatre was primarily an actors' theatre, attracting audiences with the magnitude of its star power rather than the promise of a well-written play. The quality of verse was not unimportant, to be sure, but most audiences attended less to the craftsmanship of a play made familiar through repeated repertory offerings than to its interpretation by the various actors who essayed its central roles. Even when a new play was introduced, it was often to showcase the talents of its commissioning star. As we've seen in chapter 1, Edwin Forrest was one such star – the first American to commission original plays – holding his first play contest in 1828–9, when John Augustus Stone's *Metamora, or the Last of the Wampanoags* won the prize purse of $500 plus half the proceeds of the third night's performance (Quinn 270–1). The play not only helped secure Forrest's professional success but strengthened his star image as the consummate American hero by casting Forrest in the title role of the noble

savage whose defiant death testifies to his exceptional courage and love
of his people. Little of the glory generated by the play's success, however,
extended to its author, Stone. For, while Forrest reaped the enormous profits
yielded by his numerous productions of the play, Stone was left only with
his first-prize earnings. Though Stone challenged Forrest for a larger share
of the play's proceeds, Forrest refused him on the grounds that he had been
sufficiently remunerated for his work, leaving Stone so despondent that he
killed himself in 1834 (Quinn 271). Unfortunately, Stone's relationship to
Forrest as playwright to star was all too typical; Robert Montgomery Bird,
whose plays *The Gladiator, Oralloossa,* and *The Broker of Bogota* served as
further star vehicles for Forrest, found himself also having to dispute the
star's claim that he had been properly paid for his work (Quinn 244).[7] When
Forrest refused to grant him permission to publish his plays out of fear that
another actor would have access to them, Bird was forced to abandon his
playwriting career for novel writing instead (Quinn 246–7). It was a less
drastic measure than that taken by Stone, to be sure, but it likewise signaled the impossibility of making a living on the writing of plays. As Gary
Richardson observes, "playwriting as a profession arguably did not exist in
early-nineteenth-century America" (251).

The chief problem playwrights faced had to do with the inadequacy
of existing copyright law. The first general revision of the law was made
in 1831, extending the term to twenty-eight years with the possibility of
a fourteen-year renewal and adding musical compositions to the list of
protected works (Patterson 201). This provided some hope for playwrights
such as Stone and Bird in that musical compositions, like plays, were written
to be performed. But, because copyright developed out of a context of
publishing rights, the new law was seen to apply only to the *printing* of
written scores, leaving other uses – such as their performance – unaddressed.
This was a problem that Stone or Bird would have run into had they pled
their cases in court. Copyright per se did not apply. Besides, by having
accepted Forrest's commission for their plays, they probably would have
been found to have transferred their rights in the dramatic properties to him.
If Forrest did not wish to publish, that was now his prerogative. As Arthur
Hobson Quinn explains, "The American dramatist was unprotected by the
copyright laws, and the play having once been purchased by a producer he
usually ceased to have any rights that the public or the producer respected"
(245).

Indeed, in selling their properties outright, playwrights were understood
to have given up any further claims on them. Such was the price of their

independence. For, when the playwright was an integral part of a theatre company, he (or, less often, she) was entitled to participate in the system of benefits whereby various members of the troupe took turns designating the proceeds from an evening's performance to themselves (with those serving dual functions – e.g., as playwright or manager – taking the profits from a second night's performance as well). As Richardson notes, such semi-professional "men and women rarely had the economic freedom to live solely by their pens and, as often as not, saw their work as an extension of their other theatrical activities" (297). With the rise of an independent literary marketplace in the eighteenth century, however, it was possible for the playwright to separate from the theatrical establishment and write as a freelance, selling his or her work to the manager with the highest bid.

This change in productive relations redefined the playwright's relation-ship to the theatre, thus raising new problems concerning production and copyrights. Without being a member of a theatre company whose wel-fare was his or her own, the playwright could no longer depend on the system of benefits for compensation but had to rely entirely upon the fair market value that his or her play could command. From the old system of patronage (whether aristocratic sponsor or the public) to what Bruce McConachie – following Raymond Williams – refers to as a "post-artisanal" phase, the playwright became an independent agent, selling his or her work to the "distributive intermediary" of the publisher or the "productive inter-mediary" of the manager (McConachie, "Historicizing" 173). In selling these rights to a publisher, the playwright assumed the same protection extended to other authors under the copyright act of 1831. But there were no such protections extended to the playwright whose property was reproduced in repeated stage productions. It commanded a one-time sale price, regard-less of the number of times the purchaser wished to produce it on stage. And, to make matters even worse, the availability of standard repertory fare (e.g., Shakespeare), cheap translations and/or adaptations, and pirated manuscripts meant that managers' bids were never very high to begin with, making the playwright's profession a poor one throughout most of the nineteenth century. "Bluntly put," Richardson summarizes, "there was little economic incentive to enter upon a career as [a writer, and even less of one for becoming] a playwright" (253).

The reason for this disparity in the playwright's fortunes had to do with the uneven development of the literary and theatrical markets in the late eighteenth and early nineteenth centuries. In the literary marketplace, play-wrights, like other writers, became "market professionals," assuming a direct

relationship to the market as a whole. In the theatrical marketplace, however, playwrights remained in a post-artisanal phase throughout much of
the nineteenth century. Where, on the one hand, the playwright's play was
literature, a freestanding work of art whose proper domain was print, on
the other, it was a template, an important but not yet fully realized part
of a theatrical work of art. Printing technology, in creating a distinction
between an original and a copy, had necessitated the enactment of copyright laws to protect the author's (including the playwright's) rights over the
printing of his or her manuscript. But, in the theatre, residual assumptions
regarding the manuscript remained well into the nineteenth century. Here,
as in the copyright provisions predating the Statute of Anne, the manuscript
was considered a material artifact – mere ink and paper – which could be
purchased outright from its author, with no further rights obtaining, for a
single sum. The play-as-template, then, was understood to be a material
form no different than a cookie cutter purchased from a tinsmith in that it
was capable of generating as many iterations as the baker or manager wished
to make. From the baker or the manager's point of view, this was only fair;
the tinsmith and the playwright were duly paid for their work – regardless
of whether the cookie or the production satisfied public taste. In terms of
manufacturing costs, the risk was all theirs. But, from the playwright's perspective, a play's success had at least as much to do with the form he or
she created as with the ingredients the manager poured in, especially since
those ingredients remained fairly consistent from one stock production to
the next.

The fact that one play was a success and another a failure suggested that
the value of the play lay less in the material artifact of the manuscript than in
the ideas it contained. That the play's value lay in its ideas was certainly seen
in the fact that the manager was often not the only one to capitalize upon
his or her purchase. Piracy, rampant throughout the nineteenth century,
implicitly called into question the play's status as a single material entity.
And piracy took many forms, some of which were only beginning to become
visible. First, there was the pirating of plays published in foreign countries.
Without an international copyright agreement, foreign plays became fair
game for American publishers as well as theatre managers who risked little
on a proven success that cost them nothing. Second, there was the pirating
of unpublished – and thus unprotected – manuscripts (both foreign and
domestic). In such cases, the courts generally recognized the common-law
rights of their authors, but only to control printing – not performance.
In fact, an unauthorized performance was almost unthinkable before the

mid-nineteenth century. As an interpretation of a printed manuscript, a performance was generally considered fair use. So, too, was the adaptation of a non-dramatic work for the stage.[8] By mid-century, however, this was all beginning to change as the courts increasingly recognized the concept of "work."

From the beginning, interpretations of the copyright statute understood the protected property to be quite literally the physical manuscript – a specific composition of letters, spaces, and punctuation – not the ideas contained therein. But, as we've seen, once the Romantic notion of the author as original genius was introduced in the late eighteenth century, a distinction arose between the physical form of the manuscript and its content, and between its ideas and their expression. It was not until 1835, however, when a British court heard *D'Almaine v. Boosey*, that such a distinction entered into jurisprudence, introducing the concept of "work." The case concerned a musical composition in which the defendant reset the tempo of several airs from Auber's opera *Lestocq* (to which the plaintiff had rights) for the purpose of dancing quadrilles and waltzes. In previous cases, as legal historian Benjamin Kaplan discusses, the courts had ruled that certain elements of separate compositions were necessarily the same (e.g., the contours described by maps, the dates of historical calendars, etc.), especially given the imitative nature of learning. Where they previously had held that what was needed to distinguish between a new work and an unauthorized copy was evidence of original labor, here the courts ruled that this was not enough. Clearly, effort was involved in resetting the tempo of the tunes. But, "Substantially," Lord Chief-Justice Baron Abinger wrote, "the piracy is where the appropriated music, though adapted to a different purpose from that of the original, may still be recognized by the ear. The adding variations makes no difference in the principle" (quoted in Kaplan 21).

What was important about this case was the way it shifted the standard of infringement away from identicality toward likeness in overall conception or design. Thus, the "work" was abstracted from the physical text to become the proper subject of copyright protection. This was an important bellwether for the recognition of performance as something more than fair use; for, insofar as a play was understood to be a "work," a performance of it was a veritable copy in which the playwright should have legal rights. Prior to *D'Almaine*, courts regarded non-identical versions (e.g., translations, abridgements) as new properties. According to this logic, the addition of actors, costumes, properties, and scenery were sufficient to deem a theatrical performance distinct from a play. Indeed, as theatre historian

John Russell Stephens reports, this is exactly what the British courts found in *Murray v. Elliston* (1821) when Lord Byron's tragedy *Marino Faliero* was "altered and abridged" for Robert Elliston's production at Drury Lane (89). The decision in *D'Almaine*, then, would prove to be a promising first step toward the protection of the abstract and immaterial property at the heart of both play and performance.

The problem was that, in the US, the concept of "work" took much longer to be incorporated into the framework of the courts' deliberations. In the famous case of *Stowe v. Thomas* (1853), the presiding judge, Justice Grier, ruled that a German translation of Harriet Beecher Stowe's novel *Uncle Tom's Cabin* was sufficiently different from her original English manuscript to be considered a separate text. In making his ruling, Grier explained that, by claiming property in the novel's ideas (as opposed to the text), the plaintiff's case rested upon an overly broad interpretation of copyright that threatened to erase the line between a copyright and a patent. Refusing to admit the concept of "work," Justice Grier's opinion "ended with the sweeping statement that by publication of the book all of Mrs. Stowe's 'conceptions and inventions' not excepting her characters were made free to the world and could be 'used and abused' by playwrights among others" (Kaplan 30). Indeed they were, as Stowe's novel was freely adapted by Henry J. Conway and George Aiken in their rival stage productions.[9] By 1879, however, legal consensus had turned against Grier. *Drone on Copyright*, explicitly responding to his ruling in *Stowe*, wrote that

> Literary property, as has been shown, is not in the language alone; but in the matter of which language is merely a means of communication. It is in the substance, and not in the form alone. That which constitutes the essence and value of a literary composition, which represents the results of the author's labor and learning, may be capable of expression in more than one form of language different from that of the original . . . The translation is not in substance a new work. It is a reproduction in a new form of an existing one. (quoted in Jaszi 477)

Once introduced, the concept of work allowed for the eventual recognition of performance as a right invested in the play insofar as it, too, was a "reproduction in a new form" of an existing work. Thus considered as a sort of "copy," performance endowed the dramatic manuscript with a greater potential for financial reward in that it, too, was subject to the playwright's control. The problem was that this understanding of performance was not yet formally recognized by the law. As we've seen, the line between fair use and piracy was often too fine to draw, with managers capitalizing upon others' investments once a play proved to be a hit. By changing a few key details, they could claim that their productions were completely different, leaving the penniless playwright in the lurch. In such circumstances, the best that playwrights could do was maintain private control over their manuscripts while negotiating with as many managers in as many different markets as possible. But, because managers were disinclined to bid on unread manuscripts, few playwrights were in a position to do this.

One who was in such a position was Dion Boucicault, the actor-manager-playwright whose wildly successful plays *The Colleen Bawn*, *The Shaughraun*, and *The Octoroon* (to name just a few) changed the level of the field on which playwrights pitched their plays. Because his plays were so popular, their near guarantee of making money allowed Boucicault to pit manager against manager for the production rights to his plays (Stephens 56–7). In this way, he was able to negotiate terms that were most advantageous to him, including a sliding scale over and above a fixed weekly sum where percentages increased as profits increased (Stephens 54; 65). Known as a profit-sharing system, Boucicault's standard contract single-handedly changed the way plays were negotiated, guaranteeing playwrights adequate compensation while allowing managers to meet overhead costs before either was able to take a share of any profits. So skillful a businessman was he that Boucicault extended his profit-sharing agreements to cover touring productions which ran simultaneously with the original production in New York or London (Stephens 55). Not only did these "combinations" allow him to make even more money on his properties, but they helped ensure against piracy by beating his competition to the punch. Thus, Boucicault helped playwrights begin to make the transition from post-artisanal production to the status of "market professional"; although they did not yet have a *direct* relation to the market as a whole, the possibility of controlling multiple productions of a single play at one time was on the table, laying the groundwork for future developments such as the Minimum Basic Agreement. "In his assertion of the playwright's proprietary rights over his labor," Richardson observes, "Boucicault helped secure the economic futures of American writers" (297).

The emergence of performance rights

However profitable, Boucicault's combination companies were not enough to control the unauthorized production of plays, necessitating the passage of a new American copyright law in 1856. Indeed, Boucicault was instrumental in mustering support for this new law, which extended the copyright protection accorded to published plays to stage productions, giving playwrights the right to grant stage rights (Stephens 104).[10] Under the new law,

> the author or proprietor of any dramatic composition, designed or suited for public representation, shall be deemed and taken to confer upon the said author or proprietor, his heirs or assigns, along with the sole right to print and publish the said composition, the sole right also to act, perform, or represent the same, or to cause it to be acted, performed, or represented, on any stage or public place during the whole period for which the copyright is obtained. ("An Act supplemental to an Act . . ." 139)

At last, the law provided playwrights special protection against unauthorized productions of their plays! Hereafter, they would have the right to control not just the printing of their plays, but the performance of them as well.

With the 1856 law in place, manager Laura Keene felt confident in filing suit against rival managers in Boston and Philadelphia who were presenting Tom Taylor's *Our American Cousin*, to which she had obtained exclusive performance rights in 1858 for the sum of $1,000. But in both *Keene v. Kimball* (1860) and *Keene v. Wheatley* (1861), she was disappointed to find the courts rule against her claims. In *Kimball*, the defense filed a demurrer which the court granted and, upon appeal, sustained. In *Wheatley*, the judge issued a rather loquacious ruling in which his reasoning proved much the same. In short, both courts found that while Keene had cause for grievance, the law upon which her suit was based simply did not apply because it concerned only published plays and Taylor's play had not been published. Under the new law, performance rights were effectively embedded in publishing rights; that is, they were secondary to and contingent upon the primary right to copy. Performance, in other words, was not yet recognized by the law as a separate artistic entity which was, in and of itself, copyrightable.

That, in sum, was the finding. But there were differences between the two cases, including the two courts' reasoning on the question of whether Taylor's play had been "published." Judge Hoar in *Kimball* interpreted the term narrowly to refer to the registration and appearance of a manuscript in print; since Taylor's play had been neither registered nor printed, the 1856 law did not apply. Judge Cadwalader in *Wheatley* interpreted the term more broadly to include any means of disseminating a work's contents to the public, including performance. Nonetheless, because Keene, as Taylor's "assign" in the United States, had authorized a public performance of the play without registering it first, she was found to have forfeited her exclusive rights by "dedicating" the play to the public (i.e., depositing it in the public domain). Judge Cadwalader ruled, "the literary proprietor of an unprinted play cannot, after making or sanctioning its representation before an indiscriminate audience, maintain an objection to any such literary or dramatic republication by others as may be enabled, either directly or secondarily, to make from its having been retained in the memory of any of the audience."

Furthermore, the circumstances giving rise to the two cases were considerably different. In *Kimball*, the manager of the Boston Museum had sent a secretary to Keene's theatre to copy the dialogue and business – a common if unethical practice dating back to the Elizabethan era (Stephens 86). Here, Judge Hoar found that the practice of copying itself was not illegal since the dialogue and business weren't formally copyrighted under the law (Dudden 131). In *Wheatley*, the Philadelphia managers claimed to have acquired a copy of Taylor's play from the widow of an American actor once employed by the Adelphi Theatre in London, to which Taylor had once licensed his play. The legitimacy of the serpentine provenance of the manuscript notwithstanding, there remained the question of how the defendants' production came to match Keene's exactly, especially in the dialogue and business that had been added by Joseph Jefferson, a member of Keene's company, in rehearsal. The defendants testified that they had acquired these emendations from Jefferson himself, an admission that the judge found especially disconcerting. In his ruling, Justice Cadwalader determined that

> If the defendants, in taking advantage of Mr. Jefferson's breach of duty to his employer, had been innocent parties, not aware of his confidential relation to the complainant, the jurisdiction of the court . . . would have been preventive only. As, however, they were privies to and participants in his breach of confidence, if not the procurers of it, they were liable to make her pecuniary compensation.

Thus, he awarded Keene the fund put in escrow by the defendants at the start of the trial as indemnity against her injunction to cease their continued performances.

Judge Cadwalader's displeasure over Jefferson's breach of confidence motivated his finding of damages against the Philadelphia managers who sought to profit from Keene's success. But it also reveals something about the difficulties in applying the notion of "property" to a theatrical production. Noting that Jefferson's interpolations were material to the success of the play (especially since an earlier version was found wanting), Cadwalader muses on the nature of "gags" and their relationship to the dramatic text:

> A "gag," in dramatic language, is a word, a sentence, or a passage of two or more sentences, not in a drama as composed by the author, but interpolated, and uttered on the stage by a player. Gags, in general, are violations of dramatic propriety. But theatrical regulations which prohibit them are not always enforced with strictness, and are sometimes much relaxed as to comedians in public favor. Sometimes gags are sanctioned by the manager's approval at the rehearsal of a play. They are, occasionally, in comedies of the lighter kind, licensed more or less, if not encouraged, by dramatic authors, who attend rehearsals of their own plays. (*Keene v. Wheatley* 13)

With a wild imagining of "theatrical regulations" that "prohibit" actorly deviations from the playwright's text (whether strictly or carelessly enforced), Cadwalader presumes that the playwright's text has the function of authorizing all subsequent productions. While this assumption is certainly in keeping with the 1856 law that embedded performance rights in publishing rights, it contradicts actual theatre practice where a text typically undergoes numerous revisions, often incorporating suggestions made by actors in performance. What Cadwalader's stunning pronouncement shows is a certain incongruity between the notion of a proprietary text as outlined in the law and the actual manuscript composed through the residual practices of theatrical collaboration. Furthermore, he presumes that such gags may be "sanctioned" by managers and, upon occasion, "licensed more or less, if not encouraged, by dramatic authors, who attend rehearsals of their own plays." The assumption here is that, no matter how extensive the actor's innovation, the authorizing presence behind it is the playwright (or, in his or her absence, the manager to whom the author has conferred performance rights). While Cadwalader goes on to acknowledge that Jefferson's gag is important to the success of Taylor's play, he cannot allow it to assume the status of a property itself except insofar as it becomes part of the author's dramatic text. "If unwritten gags could be a subject of proprietary right, as they never can be," he reasons, "they would[,] as between the dramatic author and the player uttering them, be the player's" (13–14). But since gags are intangible, they "never can be" property unless rendered in a tangible form, such as an author's stage direction. Once so rendered, however, they become part of the author's – not the actor's – legal property. Thus we see, here again, how the collaborative nature of theatre, while leaving its residual mark on the dramatic text, is unable to be accommodated by legal principles premised upon an authorizing text. Rather, the law must assume a single authorizing presence behind the text, even retrofitting one in those cases where the text is preceded by its own performance.

This assumption about the relationship between text and performance reappeared in the case of *Daly v. Palmer* (1868), where the authorizing primacy of the dramatic text was invoked to determine the proprietary rights of stage action. Specifically, the case concerned the right to use a scenario in which a character, lying incapacitated on a railroad track, is rescued by another character who breaks free from his or her confinement just as a train steams into view. Expressing widespread fears about the forces of modernization that threaten to crush anything in their path, the scenario first appeared in a short story entitled "Captain Tom's Fright," published in *The Galaxy* on 15 March 1867.[11] Augustin Daly, recognizing the potential for a thrilling stage spectacle, scripted the scene into his 1867 play *Under the Gaslight*, much to the delight of his audiences. Perhaps wishing to capitalize upon Daly's success, Boucicault included a version of the scene in his 1868 play *After Dark*, to which the defendant held American copyright. Daly then filed suit, seeking to prevent A. M. Palmer from publicly representing or publishing Boucicault's play on the grounds that it infringed his copyright. Evidence in the record suggests that Boucicault, long familiar with court cases involving dramatic copyright, anticipated Daly's move and hoped to avoid culpability by varying key elements in the scene. Where Daly's scene featured a woman rescuing a man tied to the track, for example, Boucicault's called for a man to rescue another man; where Daly's was set above ground, Boucicault's was set in an underground railroad; where Daly's rescuer broke down the door to the railroad station in which she was locked, Boucicault's rescuer broke through the wall of an adjacent cellar. If Boucicault devised his scene with the hope that a standard of non-identicality would be observed, he must have been sorely disappointed. The court found for the plaintiff, invoking the concept of "work" to rule that "the two scenes are identical in substance, as written dramatic compositions, in the particulars in which the plaintiff alleges that what he has invented, and set in order, in the scene, has been appropriated by Boucicault" (*Daly v. Palmer* 20). Here, as in *Keene v. Wheatley*, the decision rested on the fact that what made the stage action distinctive and unique was recorded in the dramatic text, the only property protected under the law. But Boucicault must have anticipated this, too. By scripting his scene as a pantomime, he appears to have calculated that the court would find the dramatic text to consist only of dialogue and thus dismiss Daly's claim on the grounds that copyright did not apply to stage action. In determining that the action was authorized by the dramatic text, however, the court ruled that the law did, in fact, apply. Justice Blatchford's ruling is worth quoting at length:

> A composition, in the sense in which that word is used in the act of 1856, is a written or literary work invented and set in order. A dramatic composition is such a work in which the narrative is not related, but is represented by dialogue and action . . . To act, in the sense of the statute, is to represent as real, by countenance, voice, or gesture, that which is not real. A character in a play who goes through with a series of events on the stage without speaking, if such be his part in the play, is none the less an actor in it than one who, in addition to motions and gestures, uses his voice . . . A written work, consisting wholly of directions, set in order for conveying the ideas of the author on a stage or public place, by means of characters who represent the narrative wholly by action, is as much a dramatic composition designed or suited for public representation, as if language or dialogue were used in it to convey some of the ideas . . . Indeed, on an analysis of the two scenes in the two plays, it is manifest that the most interesting and attractive dramatic effect in each is produced by what is done by movement and gesture, entirely irrespective of any thing that is spoken. The important dramatic effect, in both plays, is produced by the movements and gestures which are prescribed, and set in order, so as to be read, and which are contained within parentheses. (*Daly v. Palmer* 6–7)

"Writing in the *American Law Review*, defendant's counsel Mr. T. W. Clarke lamented that this 'is the first decision which has established a property in incident'" (Kaplan 32). Although, technically, the incident was seen to be a feature of the propertied text, Clarke was not far wrong. Within fifteen years, the courts would establish property in the incident of a scene set before a photographer's camera. The engines of modernization were at full throttle.

The case in question was *Sarony v. Burrow-Giles Lithographic Company* (1883) and a subsequent appeal in which the Supreme Court upheld the eligibility of a photograph for copyright protection. Its decision rested upon an analogy between a photographic composition and a written composition in which an original idea could be inscribed once and copied several times over; the specific technology of inscription was unimportant. With still photography quickly developing into continuous motion photography at the end of the century, the *Sarony* decision would help establish copyright protection for performances captured on film. The metaphor of inscription, however, would ensure that performance continued to be viewed as a secondary right of publication.

Even so, a new way of thinking was beginning to emerge. Although in its 1870 general revision of copyright statutes Congress retained much of the language of the 1856 law, its discussion of public performances or representations of dramatic compositions "for which a copyright has been claimed" appears in a new context. Read narratively, the statute concerning dramatic compositions (section 101) follows the statute concerning "any map, chart, musical composition, print, tint, engraving, or photograph, or chromo, or of the description of any painting, drawing, statue, printing, or model or design intended to be perfected and executed as a work of the fine arts" (section 100; "An Act to revise, consolidate, and amend . . ." 681). Here the intent appears to be to elaborate the concept of "writing" in order to establish the copyright eligibility of non-verbal works such as the photograph at issue in *Sarony*. It makes clear that such art forms are protected under copyright law as long as evidence of an original (e.g., a print) is duly registered with the copyright office. What is worth noting, however, is its provision for *descriptions* of "any painting, drawing, statue, printing, or model or design *intended to be perfected and executed as a work of the fine arts*." That is, it recognizes a mere description of an original idea as sufficient for the registration of copyright, but it also recognizes that the realization of that idea is itself a work of art. Thus, read narratively, the general revision suggests that section 101, concerning dramatic compositions, may be understood to follow from the logic of section 100 whereby a performance could be viewed as the realization of an idea registered in the form of a copyrighted play but which is itself a separate work of art. What is embedded as a secondary right in the statute concerning dramatic compositions – the right to performance – thus emerges as an incipient primary right according to the logic following from section 100. Although the legal separation of publishing and performance rights would not be fully recognized until the next general revision in 1909, a conceptual distinction between text and performance was beginning to be made.

The machinery of space and time

Meanwhile, in Britain, the problem of how to protect the performance rights of plays under the copyright law of 1842 was being given a notably different solution. Upon the advice of a Royal Commission established in 1875, it was decided that, just as performance rights were extended to dramatic manuscripts registered for copyright, so, too, should publishing rights extend from the public performance of a play. In other words, both publishing and performance rights were embedded in one another, but, unlike in the US, there was no necessary primacy attached to publication. An unpublished play performed in Britain would, upon the occasion of its first performance, automatically receive the protection of copyright in a practice that became known as "stage-righting" (Stephens 100).[12]

The only problem was that, given the different protections afforded playwrights by the two countries, a playwright might find that the protections secured in one country were not recognized in the other. This, in effect, is what happened to Tom Taylor and *Our American Cousin*. Because he had granted Keene permission to perform it in the US before it had been published or performed in England, he was found to have forfeited his rights to copyright protection in the UK. And, because Taylor was a British citizen, he was ineligible to register his play for copyright protection in the US. This was part of the problem that Keene ran into in both of her suits. Without publishing rights under American law, Taylor had no performance rights to assign her legally. As this case makes clear, the incompatibility of copyright laws between nations led to numerous entanglements, necessitating an international agreement by the end of the nineteenth century. But, because those entanglements were often profitable to various home industries, a definitive agreement took several years to work out.[13]

Meeting in Berne, Switzerland in 1885, delegates from fourteen countries hammered out an agreement to honor the rights of foreign writers. The only hold-out was the United States. Although it sent a delegate to observe the proceedings of the Berne Convention, the US decided not to sign the 1886 international agreement until its own ongoing deliberations on the issue were completed (United States Congress House Report No. [51-1] 2401). Domestically, arguments on behalf of both sides of the issue had been put before Congress since 1837. On the one hand were the publishers, who argued that an international agreement would make it difficult for their fledgling industry to compete against the more established British press. Besides, by printing cheaper editions of British novels, they pled, they were making reading materials available to a larger and geographically diverse portion of the American public, thus helping the cause of literacy. On the other hand were American authors, who argued that the availability of inexpensive British books made it difficult for them to earn a living on the sale of books for which the publisher had to pay a fee for copyright.

However noble the cause of universal literacy, they pointed out, it was being advanced on the backs of native-born authors at the cost of a flourishing national literature (United States Congress House Report No. [50-1] 1875).

By 1888, however, even the printers' unions were willing to support an international agreement. What had changed was that, in the intervening years, the publishing industry had grown to such an extent that it had generated competition within its own ranks between producers of high-quality books who employed union printers and producers of cheap books who employed non-union women and shared each other's plates. In the face of such competition, Siva Vaidhyanathan sardonically notes, "The printers' unions realized that while the lack of an international copyright was protecting the jobs of more American printers, the workers who filled those jobs were the wrong kind – women instead of men. By the late 1880s, the unions flipped sides and joined the major publishers and authors in support of some measure of international copyright" (55). With this shift in political pressure, the US Congress was finally able to pass a bill securing the rights of foreign authors whose home countries reciprocally recognized and protected the rights of American authors. The 1891 amendment was immediately signed into law. In urging its passage, the House Judiciary Committee touted the cultural and financial benefits of the international agreement, reporting that it would "unquestionably raise the standard of literary taste" at home, and that it would allow American authors to "obtain a wider market – that of the whole world" (United States Congress House Report No. [50-1] 1875).

Indeed, as British literary and cultural historian N. N. Feltes has argued, the relaxation of national boundaries effected by the international copyright agreements not only opened up the world market to individual authors but introduced a new operational logic into the book trade. Identifying two coordinates at work – the spatial domain in which a play or book received protection and the temporal limitations placed upon that protection – Feltes argues that, with the passage of an international copyright agreement, "The spatial and temporal dimensions of copyright and their interaction were thus recast": instead of subordinating time to spatial domain, where a national polity's interests were in making sure that native works of enduring value were made widely available, space was subordinated to time, where international capitalist investment encouraged the rapid turnover of new titles in as many markets as possible (540). Thus, the impetus to forge an international copyright agreement, Feltes provocatively argues, "arose less out of a desire for juridical consistency than from the material contradictions of time and

place for which 'modernism' was the resolution elsewhere on the ideological level" (535). International copyright, that is, streamlined the market's
operations by smoothing the incongruities along the national borders of
the publishing industry. Those incongruities, he suggests, were largely the
result of a changing experience of space and time.

   In identifying international copyright with "modernism," Feltes makes
a powerful insight into the way that the law was having to adjust to a new
cultural moment marked by a changing experience of time. For, in subordinating spatial limitations to temporal ones, the law only magnified a
problem that had been lurking in the application of print copyright to temporal art forms from the very beginning. As we saw in the case of *D'Almaine
v. Boosey*, the problem of applying copyright to a musical composition was
temporarily resolved by the concept of "work." In determining that the
quadrilles and waltzes, though non-identical to the original operatic air on
paper, "may still be recognized by the ear," the court effectively located the
protected property not in the printed composition but in the performance
of it. This remedy, however, was not recognized as specific to the temporal
arts but was broadly applied to printed works, transforming the protected
property from the print itself to the substance of the matter communicated
by that print. Thus, the concept of "work" is fundamentally premised upon a
model of performance, even if obscured by its analogy to the act of reading.
In making this application general, however, the law left the specific needs
of the temporal arts unaddressed for another seventy-five years. Although
those needs were revisited in 1868 in the case of *Daly v. Palmer*, the court
pointed to the authorizing primacy of the text as the grounds upon which
the "work" was protected, again failing to recognize the specific needs of
the temporal arts in applying copyright protection.

   Those special needs, however, were beginning to be vaguely acknowl-
edged at the turn of the twentieth century. In 1894, for example, the
House introduced a bill to extend copyright protection to "operatic" (later
"musical") compositions, remarking that "The existing law relative to copyrights has been found to be inadequate to properly protect authors and
producers of American plays and operas in the enjoyment of their rights of
property in these duly copyrighted productions" (United States Congress
House Report No. [53-2] 1191). What is interesting, though, is that a report
accompanying the bill focuses its attention not on the ephemeral nature
of these art forms, but on the ephemeral – or, rather, transitory – nature
of their infringers. Noting that offenders of print copyright are usually "of
fixed habitat," the chairman of the House Committee on Patents observes
that the offenders of this kind of piracy

are almost uniformly men without attachable means, and defy all the ordinary processes by which they might be mulcted in damages. The representation of these pirated productions is generally given for a night or two only at a given place, and the offenders flit from section to section and from State to State, and bid defiance to the processes of the courts seeking to restrain their unlawful acts.

The report thus recommends that the penalty for this kind of piracy be increased from a fine to imprisonment. Although this penalty would later be retrofitted to accord with the standard copyright infringement of a fine, it suggests that this particular type of piracy was felt to be categorically different from that of print manuscripts; unauthorized performances were somehow closer in kind to authorized performances than an unauthorized copy was to its print original (see United States Congress House Report No. [59-2] 7083, 15).

Interesting for the way it half-acknowledges the difficulties in applying a model of copyright derived from printing to the protection of temporal arts forms such as theatre, this report reveals a growing awareness of the fact that performances were not quite "copies." From the 1856 law in which performance rights were seen to be embedded in and secondary to printing rights to the 1870 general revision where there is a dawning recognition that, in certain forms of art, the realization of a copyrighted design is not a copy but itself an original, the dramatic composition and its performance were beginning to be recognized as their own separate entities, each of which deserved its own protection. What made that recognition finally possible was the invention of technological means by which the performance could become an original, capable of generating its own copies. These means, of course, were the new recording technologies developed at the end of the nineteenth century, inscribing sound and image on cylinders, discs, and celluloid – tangible forms with verifiable spatial dimensions from which multiple copies could be made.

No mere consequence of the space–time inversion Feltes so astutely analyzes, these technologies and the cultural transformations they effected were part of the impetus behind the shift he describes. For, when representatives from the fourteen countries met in Berne to discuss an international copyright agreement, they did so at the behest of the Swiss government, which was anxious to protect one of its major industries, the manufacture of mechanical music boxes.[14] Such mechanical devices, however, raised knotty questions as to what exactly was being reproduced (the music or the performer) and who had a right to claim property.[15] This may have been a major reason for the United States' decision to delay signing the international accord; as the home country of many of these new recording technologies, it may have wished to work through all the legal implications of these provisions carefully before committing itself to an agreement that could potentially hinder the development of industries based upon new and promising patent designs. Its prudence was well rewarded as the situation remained unsettled for several years. France, for example, interpreted the Berne Convention to allow only mechanical appliances that reproduced music but not music and words, while Germany distinguished between those that had limited repertoires (e.g., the music box and barrel organ) and those that had exchangeable parts (e.g., "the talking machine" or the "automatic piano"), and Italy provided blanket protection to composers whose works were used in any automatic musical record appliance (United States Congress House Report No. [59-2] 7083, part 2, 4–5; United States Senate Report No. [59-2] 6187, part 2). Noting the widespread disparity in interpretations of the Berne accord as well as the fact that a case involving the use of perforated music rolls for player pianos was pending before the US Supreme Court, Congress decided to delay further deliberations on the 1906 proposed general revision of copyright until 1909.

That case was *The White–Smith Music Publishing Company v. The Apollo Company* (1908), in which the Supreme Court upheld a lower court's decision that "perforated records or sheets adapted to mechanically reproduce the music upon the pianoforte, pianola, and other musical instruments" were not copies of musical compositions on the grounds that, unlike printed sheets of music, they could not be "deciphered and learned" (1–2). In other words, they clearly served a different function – one that pertained to mechanical inventions, not to individuals wishing to perform the copyrighted piece. Thus, on the question, strictly considered, as to whether the defendant's perforated rolls were an infringement of the composer's copyright to his songs "Little Cotton Dolly" and "Kentucky Babe Schottishe," the Court said "no." But, recognizing that composers' rights were potentially at risk by such inventions, the Court urged Congress to create new legislation that would offer protection to composers for the use of their music on such music rolls. In writing for the majority, Justice Day insisted that

> A musical composition . . . is not susceptible of being copied until it has been put in a form which others can see and read. The [existing] statute has not provided for the protection of the intellectual conception apart from the thing produced, however meritorious such conception may be, but has provided for the making and filing of a tangible thing, against the publication and duplication of which it is the purpose of the statute to protect the composer. (10–11)

Thus, by insisting on the "tangible thing," he strictly limited the law's protection to the manuscript on which the composition had been musically
notated. Justice Holmes, although concurring with Day's general ruling,
issued a separate statement in which he urged a broad, not strict, interpretation of "writing" such that the composition was not limited to the
tangible thing registered for copyright but the ideas and conceptions registered therein. What is significant about this distinction between tangible
and abstract properties is that it reveals the difficulty, in this moment, of
locating the concept of "property" that was to be protected. By urging a
broad interpretation, Holmes opened the door for a performance – a temporal, and thus ephemeral thing – to be considered property under the
law.[16]

When the 1909 law was finally drafted, it attempted to recognize judicial precedent in view of the new methods of mechanical reproduction, and
to balance the rights to private property against the benefits to the public. Thus, with regard to the concerns made evident in the *White–Smith*
case, the law gave composers the right to prohibit their music from being
mechanically reproduced, or, if they didn't wish to prohibit such reproductions, the right to receive royalties on the use of their compositions, all
the while ensuring the public's right to access and enjoy music by placing
restrictions on the formation of trade monopolies among music publishers.
"It is not the intention of the committee to extend the right of copyright to
the mechanical reproductions themselves, but only to give the composer or
copyright proprietor the control, in accordance with the provisions of the
bill, of the manufacture and use of such devices" (United States Congress
House Report No. [60-2] 2222). Extending the term of renewal from fourteen to twenty-eight years after the intial twenty-eight-year period had
ended, the new law laid out a thoroughly modern conception of copyright,
one in keeping with the spirit of the Statute of Anne while allowing for the
growth of new industries based upon the mechanical reproduction of sound
and image.

Throughout deliberations on the *White–Smith* case, concerns about how to
protect the rights of composers while allowing for the growth of the nascent
audio and visual recording industries made one thing clear: performance,
once seen as a secondary feature of a written composition, had to be recognized as a fully separate entity from any written composition on which
it was based. Although implicit in the 1870 general revision, performance
finally emerged as its own legal entity in 1909. What made this possible, of

course, was the invention of mechanical means of recording performances, for, by them, the metaphor of inscription could be realized fully. For the first time in history, there could be such a thing as a performance "original" from which "copies" could be made. This meant not only that performance was recognized as its own separate legal entity apart from the dramatic text, but that the dramatic text was likewise separable from the theatrical apparatus. The conditions for a modern dramatic literature were finally in place.

PART II

Introduction

Throughout the nineteenth century, the lack of an international copyright agreement as well as the difficulties of ensuring both publication and production rights within a single country had had a chilling effect upon dramatic writing. There was virtually no tradition of dramatic literature in English during that time. Even today, much of what was written or produced then has been lost or exists only in fragments. By the 1890s, however, the situation had improved greatly as adequate legal protection created better conditions for writing, better conditions allowed for a greater volume of production, and a greater volume meant more noteworthy plays for the dramatic publishing industry to print, advertise, and sell.[1] Besides the stalwart Samuel French Company, early twentieth-century play publishers included Walter H. Baker Company, Dramatic Publishing Company, Penn Company, Dick and Fitzgerald Company, and the Eldridge Company – all of which had a ready audience in the members of newly formed cultural clubs such as the American Drama Society (1909), the MacDowell Club (1910), and the Drama League (1911) (Kozelka 606).

Founded in Chicago by the city's Woman's Club, the Drama League began as a screening committee to identify which local commercial theatre offerings were worth patronizing (and, indirectly, which were not). From its reviews published in the club's newsletter, to a backlist of recommended titles fit for reading or producing amateur theatricals, the committee's influence grew, inspiring woman's clubs around the country to adopt its regulative function in their own local communities. Eventually blossoming into a national organization, it boasted 114 chapters and over 100,000 members by 1915 (S. Smith 84). Its mission expanded accordingly, seeking not only to elevate and educate the public taste but, in doing so, to influence the type of theatre that was produced. One of the ways it sought to do so was by exerting consumer pressure on the commercial theatre, awarding patronage to plays that were morally uplifting and withholding it from those that were not. Another strategy was to encourage the founding of alternative, non-commercial theatres, such as Chicago's own Little Theatre, which produced plays of serious literary and artistic merit. Thus was born the little theatre movement, introducing a demand for artistic and morally uplifting plays that American-born dramatists could help to supply. Such plays, noted in the League's list of approved titles, were typically produced and acted by amateurs (often club members) who welcomed the opportunity to practice their lessons in expressive culture, coordinating their bodies and voices with the playwright's words. "By 1917," Susan Harris Smith notes, "there were more than fifty Little Theatres firmly established across the country, some specializing in American work and all committed to intimate productions, a high standard of acting, and 'good' drama. As part of both the educational and Little Theatre movements," she justly concludes, "the Drama League's influence should not be underestimated" (85).

In this moment when economic, legal, and cultural forces were aligning in such a way as to give American plawrights what they never had before – the opportunity to make a living writing plays – they were faced nonetheless with an irresolvable contradiction. For, as we've seen, the category of the literary had been redefined in explicitly anti-performative terms: in order to attain literary status for their plays, playwrights would have to subscribe to an anti-performative bias. Yet, in order to create theatrically viable plays, they would have to include performative modes of expression. The question that faced them was how to break free from this seemingly inescapable double-bind.

One answer to this question lay in the very conditions of their new freedom. For, having been legally separated from the producing apparatus of the theatre, they could begin to regard their plays as autonomous works of art. And, though it took a while for playwrights to realize the full extent of this new relationship, they eventually began to explore the artistic freedoms that it offered. As Eugene O'Neill wrote in a 1925 playbill for the Provincetown Players: "The present theatre of the future is in the actor. Until he goes on we others – I speak as a playwright – can't, except by the inadequate written word. My motto just now is 'write 'em and leave 'em!'" (quoted in Gelb, *O'Neill* 588). Giving up on the state of acting when this program note appeared, O'Neill self-consciously makes a distinction between his plays – he announces his speaking position as that of a playwright – and the ways in which those plays are enacted. Claiming that his motto is simply to "write 'em and leave 'em," he nonetheless acknowledges the limitations of his craft when he refers to the "inadequate written word." Eventually, this most literary of American dramatists would more than accommodate himself to the written word, but the ambivalence evident in his statement suggests that he – like many playwrights in the mid-1920s – was not yet ready to forsake fully the theatre's performative modes of expression.

Throughout the first half of this book, I have demonstrated how performative modes of expression were being resignified at the turn of the twentieth century by various technological and cultural forces. Film simultaneously showcased the meaningfulness of gesture while limiting the actor's interpretive agency. Recording devices such as the phonograph and "graphophone" revealed the power of the voice while paradoxically replacing its physical source. But, even as the power of the written word was threatened by these technologies, the law reasserted its authority by defining performance as a text. That early twentieth-century American culture was marked by intense debates over the significatory power of bodies, voices, and words we have already seen. How those debates gave shape to American dramatic modernism is the subject of this book's second half. Identifying expressionism as an important early phase of American dramatic modernism, I demonstrate how it provided playwrights with a formal vocabulary by which to express their ambivalence toward the theatre and its performative modes of signification without fully disengaging from the theatre altogether. For, though playwrights longed to secure their literary credentials, they were often hesitant to forsake the theatrical medium for which they wrote. To understand how expressionism allowed them to effect the transition from theatrical playwright to literary dramatist, we must analyze the conceptual – if not chronological – evolution of the form. In what follows, I briefly analyze two expressionist plays from the 1920s, demonstrating how each instantiates an important phase in expressionism's emergence. The first phase involves an ironization of Curry's theory of expression as a gentle rejection of the theatre itself. The second is characterized by a more intensely ironic stance. Here the theatre's performative languages are reappropriated as a formal vocabulary with which to explore the playwright's ambivalence toward his or her art. As we'll see, these plays are often deeply personal, revealing their playwright's fears that technology will render them obsolete.

Rachel Crothers's *Expressing Willie* (1924), a perennial favorite of little theatre groups all over the country, provides an illustration of the first phase.[2] A parody of the expressive culture movement, it pokes fun at the vogue for authenticity among a social set used to exchanging flattery for favors. The play opens on the "overdone" parlor of the "ridiculously magnificent" house of Willie Smith, a hardworking Midwestern-boy-made-good who is now the magnate of a toothpaste fortune, as he awaits the arrival of his fashionable house guests – social climbers Dolly and George Cadwalader, the artist Taliaferro, and the gold-digging Frances Sylvester. Before they arrive, however, we are introduced to Minnie Whitcomb, a music teacher and Willie's former hometown sweetheart whom his no-nonsense straight-talking mother has invited without his consent. Although Minnie serves as an unwelcome reminder of Willie's humble origins, embarrassing him with her awkwardness and rustic simplicity in front of his sophisticated urban friends, she is a true original, a classic modern primitive uncorrupted by civilization if temporarily intimidated by its mystique. Her rival for Willie's affection is Frances, the cigarette-smoking fashion plate whose pretense of soulful honesty masks her true ambitions of becoming a permanent fixture in Willie's overly sumptuous home. In contrast to Minnie's authenticity, she merely flatters Willie into thinking that she alone is able to truly perceive the inner greatness of his soul, speaking of their private encounter as a "magic moment" sparked by a "current of sympathy" (Crothers 52).

As the play's title suggests, the characters are all swept up in the vogue for expression, for "absolute freedom" (12), the power to reveal "the God within us" (31). Taliaferro, an artist whom Willie has commissioned to paint his portrait, is its chief spokesman, urging Minnie to "*free* that thing that is pounding in you," advising her that, "Until you let your soul speak through your music you will never have lived" (31). In fact, it is he who frees Minnie from her fear and inhibitions, allowing her to overcome her initial timidity and reveal her true self in a piano performance that leaves her audience "exhilarated and honestly thrilled" (40).

With characters such as Frances and the aptly named Cads, Crothers deftly parodies the expressive culture movement and the charlatans who practiced in its name.[3] What's more, she targets parvenus like Willie whose class anxieties make them vulnerable to such transparent ploys. Nonethe-less, there is also a sense that Minnie's transformation from timid piano teacher to soulful musician would not have occurred had it not been for the catalyst of Taliaferro, the artist, whose ministrations of expressive culture's balm have freed her from her stifling inhibitions. The play's critique, then, is ambivalent; while expression may be a fad whose excesses are worth ridicul-ing, it also seems to be a means of genuine self-realization. This ambivalence is crystallized in the play's centerpiece – a song that not only made the play a huge success (running for 281 consecutive performances on Broadway) but was a hit in its own right (Lindroth 56).

EXPRESS YO'SE'F MY CHILE

When I was a chile, my mammy say
"Hush yo' mouf – go 'long an' play
Don' you fuss nor fret nor cry –
You can be good ef you des try.
*Sup*press yo'se'f my chile. – *Sup*press yo'se'f."

But now dey say to a li'l chile
"Laf and holler, sing an' cry.
What you don' wan do don' eben try.
When you feel lik yellin' – yell like hell –
*Ex*press yo'se'f an' do it well:
*Ex*press yo'se'f my chile. – *Ex*press yo'se'f."

When I wus young an' growin' tall
Dey say "You a chile – you don't know all.
You gotta wait an' listen an' grow.
You too young an' in'cent to know.
*Sup*press yo'se'f my chile. – *Sup*press yo'se'f."

Now dey say to a gal right out –
"Speak up plain what you t'inkin' bout.
What you feelin' let fo'kes know.
Don' hide nothin' an' say 'taint so.
*Ex*press yo'se'f my chile. – *Ex*press yo'se'f."

"Let all yo' emotions rise to de top.
Ef you got convolutions don't let 'em stop."
Dat's what dey say to a gal now-days.
Express yo'se'f is de latest craze.
*Ex*press yo'se'f my chile. – *Ex*press yo'se'f.

(Crothers 42–3)

As seen in the lyrics of her song, Crothers's barbs are directed not only at expressive culture but also at the fad for psychoanalysis, suggesting like Susan Glaspell and Jig Cook that a little suppression just might be a good thing. At one point, Willie's plain-spoken mother remarks, "If we were were all running around without any *suppressions*, we might as well have tails again" (72). Yet the parody does not lie in the content of the lyrics so much as in their form. For, in both spelling and diction, this is a black-face minstrel song. And, while its marriage of form and content are strange enough, the song's very appearance in the middle of a comedy of manners is even stranger still. Strange, that is, until we consider the various ways that blackface was used in 1920s drama. As we'll see in chapters 4 and 6,

Eugene O'Neill and John Howard Lawson use the conventions of blackface minstrelsy, appropriating them ironically and metonymically to represent class concerns. Crothers, too, appears to use the blackface idiom to represent something other than what it would seem to be. In her play, where it appears only in the narrative voice of the song, blackface seems to represent a feigned primitiveness, a pretense of authenticity, a mask used to hide the face of civilized cynicism, much like the behavior of the bounder characters in her play. By indirectly invoking blackface, Crothers seems to be suggesting that the performance of authenticity, in being performed, is thus rendered inauthentic. Thus, she would seem to mock the expressive culture movement's claims to reveal one's soulful, pure, and absolutely unmitigated feelings.

But the play, like blackface minstrelsy itself as Eric Lott has demonstrated, is ambivalent: for, even as it mocks the expressive culture movement, it demonstrates an unavowed love for authentic expression. While it asks us to find the antics of the urban sophisticates appalling, it also asks us to applaud Minnie's transformation from dowdy spinster to exalted artist. At the end of the play, when Willie comes to recognize Minnie's inner beauty and Frances's self-interest, we expect this romantic comedy to resolve in a traditional way. In fact, Willie does ask Minnie to marry him, offering to take care of her, but Minnie demurs – not only because she recognizes that Frances, with her high style and savoir-faire, is what Willie with his new life really wants, but because *she* wants something else. When Willie asks her what it is, she replies, "To express myself." Although he protests that she can express herself and marry him too, Minnie insists, "I must be free" (78). This is certainly in keeping with Crothers's feminist concerns; Minnie recognizes the trade-off implicit in Willie's offer and explicit in his question: "Wouldn't you rather be happy as a woman than a successful musician?" (76), and she chooses to be free. In expressing herself, she has become free because she has come to recognize and accept responsibility for her own creative potential. Her triumph is the play's own. As Sharon Friedman observes of another Crothers heroine, "art becomes a way of expressing her female identity" (79).

But there is yet more to this play than its apparent mixed response to the expressive culture movement. It also seems to be saying something about art, artifice, patronage, and commerce. Minnie, after all, is an artist whose musical self-expression is her gift to the world. Taliaferro, too, of course, is an artist, but, unlike Minnie, who insists upon her own freedom, he is obliged to flatter and cajole wealthy patrons into supporting him in his work.

Willie, the toothpaste magnate, represents capital whose seductive power lures all of them to the comforts of his palatial home. But it is only Frances, artificer of urban manners, high style, and haute couture fashion – and thus representative of the decorative arts – who is comfortably at home with him there. This is what Minnie recognizes upon meeting Frances and seeing how Willie's life has changed. Thus, insofar as we are asked to identify with Minnie and experience her epiphany as our own, the play seems to suggest that expression is, indeed, the true source of art, but only if untainted by the demands of commerce.

We see this same theme treated in George S. Kaufman and Marc Connelly's 1924 comedy, *Beggar on Horseback*, the second of my two examples. In it, Neil McRae, a struggling composer, is torn between marrying Gladys Cady, the daughter of a wealthy business tycoon whose money would buy him the time he needs to complete his symphony, and Cynthia Mason, his equally destitute neighbor, a fashion designer whose own artistic orientation to life allows her to recognize his true genius. Upon the advice of his pragmatic best friend Albert, a doctor who is concerned about his health and welfare, Neil impetuously decides to ask Gladys to marry him. But, sick and tired from overexerting himself with meaningless "hack work" to pay his bills, he immediately falls into a deep sleep racked by nightmarish visions of what married life to Gladys would be. Presented in a series of surrealistic episodes whose comic absurdity reaches Ionescan proportions, Neil's dream reveals that the Faustian contract sealing the marriage between art and commerce would lead to his soul's damnation. The demands of courting capital's favor never end, leaving him little time to compose his music. Thus, in a feverish attempt to escape the suffocating banality and material excess of the life he's chosen, Neil murders Gladys and her family, only to have them reappear in the courtroom as he is being sentenced to a life of hard labor in the Cady Consolidated Art Factory. Here Neil takes his place among novelist/pulp-fiction-purveyors, painter/advertising-illustrators, and poet/jingle-masters, churning out popular ditties such as "mammies, sweeties, and fruit songs" in addition to the jazz rags that the philistine Mrs. Cady loves so much (220). The only way out of this hellish existence, Neil learns, is death. Thus, with the promise that Cynthia will accompany him to the other side, Neil submits to the executioner, only to wake up to the opportunity of making the right choice this time around.

The message here, as in Crothers's play, is clear: when the fine arts capitulate to the demands of commerce they are necessarily degraded into industrial or mass forms of art. But, while money is the primary source of anxiety for these artist-figures who must fend for themselves, it is not money per se that threatens to corrupt their art. Rather, it is the combination of money and philistinism (represented here by the Midwestern Cady family) which cannot distinguish between high and low art. Throughout the play, strains of "The Frog's Party," a jazz tune, are heard from across the street. Where Neil marvels at how "people [could] actually enjoy that" (41), Mrs. Cady cannot help but sing to it, Gladys cannot help but dance to it, and Mr. Cady cannot help but admire its financial prospects, remarking, "Great song! A man I played golf with yesterday tells me that for the first six months of the fiscal year that song'll make a hundred thousand dollars. Write something like that," he advises Neil, "and you're fixed. That's music" (64). Ever the source of contempt, the new-moneyed philistines threaten the cultural order not only by equating economic and aesthetic value, but by using the power of their money to impose their uneducated tastes upon the public at large. At least this is what Kaufman and Connelly suggest in their dream sequence. In Neil's waking life, Mr. Cady is merely a boorish businessman with no particular interest in music or the arts. When he offers Neil a job, it is with the understanding that he could "write a little music now and then in [his] spare time" (63). In Neil's dream, however, Cady is the owner of an "Art Factory," a prison house where artists toil ceaselessly to fulfill the base demands of an insatiable public who gawk at the inmates uncomprehendingly like visitors at a zoo. No hard-hitting Frankfurt School critique of the culture industry, Kaufman and Connelly's play nonetheless draws a link between industrial forms of art and the manufacturing of public taste.

It is this subtle yet persistent emphasis on industrial forms of mass communication that holds the key to the play. For, throughout this comedy, Kaufman and Connelly make reference to various forms of technology that have altered the experience of communication if not also the production of art: the dictaphone, the typewriter, the radio, the telephone. Further reference is made to newspapers, posters, movies, and theatre itself as mass forms of communication. The penetration of these technologies and communications into everyday life is represented as at once normal and exceedingly alien, appearing both in Neil's waking reality and in his phantasmatic imaginings of a world gone awry. Such double coding suggests a profound ambivalence toward mass communication, especially with regard to Kaufman and Connelly's own medium, the theatre. In the sequence where Neil is being tried, for example, the courtroom is made up to look like a theatre, with posters of Judge Cady on display and groups of fawning fans deliberating over which of his past performances was the best. Jurors are ushered to their seats by a ticket taker, who has to clear up some confusion resulting from a juror who has mistakenly taken another's seat – a bit of physical comedy no doubt made humorous by the audience's recognition of its real life counterpart. When Judge Cady appears, he is grand in his judicial robe and wig, but "throws away all dignity . . . by lifting the skirts of his gown and skipping into view." Like a character out of a Monty Python sketch, "Cady curtsies toward the jury box in response to unanimous applause, and blows a kiss. He goes up to his chair and holds the picture of a satisfied actor as he waits for another burst of applause to subside" (182). Groan-worthy vaudeville-esque puns are "pointed" when the prosecuting attorney "objects" to the defendant's looks (194), and when Neil seeks a "higher court:"

> CADY: About how high a [court] would you want?
> NEIL: I'd want the highest I could get.
> CADY: All right. (*Judge Cady slowly goes up in the air, as his stand grows two or three feet higher.*) Is this high enough for you?
> NEIL: I guess so. Is this the superior court?
> CADY: Oh yes. Much superior. And more up-to-date. We send out all our verdicts by radio. (198–9)

What is this self-ironizing meta-theatricality all about? Given the call for a serious, more literary drama, and given the pejorative connotations attached to the theatre and performance more generally, such self-ironizing moves appear to represent an attempt by the playwrights to work both in and against their theatrical medium. Using performative modes of communication to establish the play's viability within the theatre, Kaufman and Connelly nonetheless ironize them in order to cast the theatre as despised low other to their high cultural ambitions. When vocal and pantomimic languages are used, for example, they are often stylized in such a way as to make the actors appear as if they are parts of a theatrical machine. In the opening dream sequence, we see ushers and bandsmen who all look alike, reciting their lines in a "rhythmic chant" (99). Subsequent scenes feature butlers, waiters, and dancing teachers whose numbers expand exponentially and "of course" are dressed "exactly alike" (105; 108; 146; 159). Catch phrases are repeated over and over, while banal conversations are simultaneously overlaid in an endless reproduction of nonsense (117). In his vision of their married life together, we hear Neil respond "automatically" (110) and "mechanically" (139) to anything Gladys says. Cady barks random business orders into a "telephone attached to his chest" (107), and is accompanied by four businessmen who are, of course, all dressed alike (122). They "walk in stiffly, in a line, repeating the phrases 'Overhead,' 'Turnover,' 'Annual Report,'" and "fall into mechanical positions" (135–6).

While all of these examples illustrate how Kaufman and Connelly use sound and movement to depict a world transformed by industrial rhythms, the most extraordinary example appears at the beginning of the Art Factory sequence when, with lights dimmed, we hear a "burst of noise. Pianos are playing discordantly; there is the sound of machinery in the distance, a voice is singing a jazz tune, and other voices are heard in loud declamation" (211). Such cacophony is the hallmark of "expressionism" and, indeed, *Beggar on Horseback* has been described as an "expressionistic" play.[4] But it is not, as critics have long maintained of American expressionism more generally, a derivation from the German movement. Rather, it is a response to the particular set of demands American playwrights faced in this moment of dramatic modernism's birth. As we've seen in chapters 1 and 2, film had captured the actor's body, phonography the singer's voice, suggesting that the art of the theatre lay in its ability either to integrate bodies, voices, and words (*pace* Curry and expressive culture enthusiasts), or to distinguish between the theatrical machinery and the literature performed on its stage (*pace* Eliot and the New Critics). What the so-called expressionists did was effect an ingenious solution to this dilemma by borrowing Curry's three languages but *counterpointing* rather than coordinating them to express the spiritual disharmony of their artist-figure alter-egos. In this way, they could explore their own ambivalent feelings toward their craft without having to forsake it fully. They could call upon performative modes of communication to ensure the viability of their plays, while disavowing those same modes through irony to secure their literary status.

As we'll see in chapters 4, 5, 6, and 7, Eugene O'Neill, Elmer Rice, John Howard Lawson, and Sophie Treadwell all follow this same pattern. In their expressionist plays, we find:

(1) a central character (often an anti-hero) who functions as a figure for the artist,
(2) an agon between the central artist figure and the forces of commerce and industry,
(3) the theme of technology as a source of spiritual malaise, and
(4) a formal disarticulation of the play's verbal, vocal, and pantomimic languages.

But, unlike Crothers, who limits her expressionistic technique to a black-face minstrel song and Kaufman and Connelly, who limit theirs to a dream sequence (albeit a long one), these playwrights develop their expressionistic technique throughout the full length of their plays. By doing so, they prove that it is possible to write for the theatre while conforming to a high modernist conception of literary value. This was an important early stage in the development of American dramatic modernism. For what it signaled was the playwright's tentative break from the producing mechanism of the stage. After these expressionist experimentations, playwrights could finally divest themselves from the theatre to become self-conscious literary authors writing autonomous modern plays.

4

The *"unconscious autobiography"*
of Eugene O'Neill

JAMIE O'NEILL, EUGENE'S DISSOLUTE OLDER BROTHER, OFTEN
played minor roles in *The Count of Monte Cristo* alongside his father, actor
James O'Neill, whose performance in the title role earned him a considerable
fortune and made him a star. While James was the consummate professional,
who early in his career caught the favorable attention of Joseph Jefferson
and Edwin Booth, Jamie was anything but. Scornful of his father's success
and contemptuous of his bravado – both on-stage and off – Jamie frequently
used his stage appearances as opportunities to embarrass his father. On one
occasion Jamie took to striking poses upon the apron of the stage while
dressed in leggings tight enough to reveal his most intimate proportions.
But it was neither the posturing nor the leggings that embarrassed the elder
O'Neill. Accustomed to such tricks himself, James condoned the leggings
since they were likely to please the ladies in the audience. What mortified
him was the fact that Jamie made explicit eye-contact not with the "ladies"
but with the prostitutes whom he already knew well (Gelb 107).[1]

If Jamie's antics were meant to be outrageous, it was not because they
included a public recognition of prostitutes, but because they made explicit
the unspoken relationship between theatrical and social codes of propriety.
For Jamie knew (as perhaps his father did not) that, by the early twentieth
century, his father's melodramatic style of acting had become associated
with theatres catering to lower-middle- and working-class audiences. By
standing on gratuitous and exaggerated "points" and recognizing prostitutes
in the audience, Jamie simply sought to make explicit his father's professional
disrepute.

Jamie was not the only one to recognize that James's "point" technique had
become marked as belonging to a lower order of theatrical fare. Eugene, too,
was embarrassed by his father's brand of histrionics. "My early experience
with the theatre through my father really made me revolt against it," he

once recalled. "As a boy I saw so much of the old, ranting, artificial romantic stuff that I always had a sort of contempt for the theatre" (quoted in Gelb 64). Perhaps contributing to Jamie and Eugene's embarrassment was their father's inability to see what they so clearly could.

Although James's acting career provided the family with a sizeable income, it did little to elevate the family's prestige. Even the thoroughly bourgeois background of Ella Quinlan O'Neill, Jamie and Eugene's mother, was not enough to counter James's reputation as an actor – and of working-class origin, no less. As one of their neighbors in the tony town of New London, Connecticut, curtly remarked, "We considered the O'Neills Shanty Irish, and we associated the Irish with the servant class" (quoted in Sheaffer 49). Such snubs no doubt rankled Jamie, Eugene and, indeed, their mother's feelings, but instead of hiding behind an alcohol- or morphine-induced haze, Eugene turned his resentment into first a rejection and later a revision of his father's theatrical legacy.

By now, it is well established that much of O'Neill's work derives from and deals with the family romance – from Doris V. Falk's pioneering psychological study of his plays, to landmark biographies by Arthur and Barbara Gelb and Louis Sheaffer which read O'Neill's work as that "of an eternal son, a man constantly examining and dramatizing his ambivalent feelings toward his mother and father" (Sheaffer 49), to Stephen Black's more recent attempt to apply a clinical diagnosis to O'Neill's life and work. My intent here is not to reassert the claim that O'Neill's career as a playwright was motivated by an oedipal desire to transform the American theatre from which his father derived his fame. Rather, it is to examine how this oedipal conflict bore within it class tensions, and how the theatre functioned as both the source of this multiply coded conflict and the site of its resolution.

In my examination of *The Emperor Jones* (1920) and *The Hairy Ape* (1921; 1922), I show how these two early experimental plays – so seemingly unrelated to O'Neill's autobiographical corpus – in fact encode these psychodynamics in their expressionistic style. The key to finding and understanding them is not to presume a close parallel between the narrative events depicted in the plays and O'Neill's own life (as *Long Day's Journey Into Night* invites us to do); it is to trace a parallel between the structures of feeling recorded in these plays and in the surviving details of his life. To do so, I propose reading each of these two plays as a "fantasm" in which, as Fredric Jameson points out, issues of real conflict are imaginatively resolved (180). The work of literature, that is, functions as a sort of wish fulfillment wherein the author creates an imaginative solution to a problem that cannot be solved in real life. As we'll see, these plays propose imaginative solutions to O'Neill's oedipal conflict as well as his own professional and class anxieties not only in their narrative unfolding but in their formal design.

If scholars have had difficulty detecting the psychobiographical elements encoded in these plays, it is because they have persisted in viewing the plays through the analytical lens of New Criticism, with its exclusive focus on verbal signification. Such elements become clearer, however, if we also examine O'Neill's use of vocality and gesture, the performative languages that Delsarte and S. S. Curry identified as the special province of emotion and will. Thus resituating these plays within the context of the expressive culture movement and the debates that followed in its wake, I challenge the long-held belief that O'Neill's expressionistic technique was derived solely from the German movement.[2] As I show, it is expressive culture that is the primary source for these plays' psychological portraiture; it is expressive culture that is the primary source for their experimental form. In drawing upon its performance conventions, O'Neill not only arrives at an aesthetic resolution to his issues of real psychological conflict, but paradoxically writes himself into the position of "literary" dramatist to herald the arrival of modernism on the American stage.

The Emperor James

The story of an African-American man who escaped his oppressors in the US to assume imperial command of a small West Indian island, *The Emperor Jones* shows us his fall from power, descent into madness, and death at the hands of the subjects he once ruled. From the moment the play begins, we learn that the natives are restless and Brutus Jones, as Emperor, is about to be overthrown. This exposition is accomplished in fairly short order in the dialogue between Smithers, the English trader who has profited from his collusion with Jones to exploit the natives, and an aging native woman whom Smithers stops as she prepares to flee into the hills. When Jones appears, looking majestic in his "light blue uniform coat, sprayed with brass buttons, heavy gold chevrons on his shoulders, gold braid on the collar, cuffs, etc.," we see a "tall, powerfully-built, full-blooded negro of middle age" who appears "not altogether ridiculous" in his grandeur (O'Neill 1, 1033). Although he may look his part, Jones is revealed to be a grandstander, an impostor, who has hoodwinked an entire island nation into thinking he is a deity through luck and his ability to manipulate the natives' superstitions. Believing him to be a demi-god who can be killed only with a silver bullet, the natives have retreated to the hills in order to prepare themselves to bring Jones down. This conflict, established in the first scene and resolved in the last, is sustained throughout the middle scenes which trace Jones's flight into the jungle and his consequent psychological and spiritual disintegration. Confronted in turn by the "little formless fears," the ghost of his gambling partner Jeff, visions of a chain gang, a slave auction, a slave ship, and a Congo witch-doctor who summons forth a primitive crocodile god, Jones undergoes a process of de-evolution which ends in his ultimate extinction.

According to O'Neill's own accounts, the character of Brutus Jones was inspired by Vilbrun Guillaume Sam, the President of Haiti who, in 1918, was murdered by an angry mob intent upon his overthrow. Like Jones in the play, Sam is supposed to have boasted of his invincibility, saying that, if anyone wanted to kill him, he would shoot himself first with the only thing befitting his rank and honor – a silver bullet (Gelb 438). But as O'Neill's biographers point out, Brutus Jones also bears traces of sources closer to O'Neill, such as Adam Scott, a New London bartender, and Joe Smith, a Greenwich Village drinking buddy – both of whom may have provided some of Jones's distinctive dialogue (Gelb 439; Sheaffer 29).[3] Like nearly all of O'Neill's plays, *The Emperor Jones* was based at least in part upon his own experiences. Unlike much of the O'Neill canon, however, *The Emperor Jones* does not appear to deal with the psychodynamics of O'Neill's family life.[4] But, given that O'Neill finished the script only two and half weeks after James O'Neill's death, we might want to consider that the narrative structure O'Neill found for such details of African-American history and culture lay in the story of his father's life.[5]

For months before his death on 10 August 1920, James O'Neill lingered bedridden, lapsing in and out of consciousness with occasional periods of lucidity. During such periods, he liked to show his visitors the telegram he had received announcing Eugene's Pulitzer Prize for *Beyond the Horizon*. Remarking, "Well, lad, I tried to drag you in by the back door of the theatre and now you're on the stage," James wanted Eugene to know he was proud of his success. But for all of his pride in his son's achievements, he could not help harboring some bitterness over his own failures. Having sacrificed a once-promising career for financial and popular success, an anguished James confided to Eugene that *Monte Cristo* had been his ruin. "How keenly he felt this in his last years," O'Neill later told a friend, "I think I am the only one who knows, the only one he confided in" (quoted in Gelb 430).[6] Although Eugene must have been saddened by this revelation, he must have been a little heartened by it as well. For if he felt some oedipal guilt over having supplanted his father's theatrical legacy with his own playwriting success, Eugene must have been relieved by his father's confession that he had caused his own demise. "My father died broken, unhappy, intensely bitter, feeling that life was 'a damned hard billet to chew,'" O'Neill remarked. "This after seventy-six years of what the mob undoubtedly regard as a highly successful career! It furnishes food for thought, what? . . . his words . . . are written indelibly – seared on my brain" (quoted in Gelb 431).[7]

As a player of melodrama, James O'Neill had become so associated with the flamboyant and emotionally expressive title role in *The Count of Monte Cristo* that he found it difficult to cross back over into the legitimate drama he had performed earlier in his career. Although he sometimes lamented having limited himself to the performance of a single role, he had not suffered financially and, in being identified with a single character, he was certainly in good company – Joseph Jefferson was primarily known for his poignantly comic Rip Van Winkle, while in the public mind William Gillette practically *was* Sherlock Holmes. As with these actors and their trademark roles, audiences loved James as Edmond Dantes; they simply refused to conceive of him in other dramatic roles. But whether James realized it or not, his lack of success in other, especially newer, roles toward the end of his career had as much to do with his particular performance style as with recalcitrant fans.

Trained in the "point" technique, James O'Neill was in the habit of assuming poses and postures to vividly illustrate images or metaphors in the dramatic text. Early in his career, for instance, James won praise from the eminent Edwin Booth for an innovative "point" he made while playing Othello to Booth's Iago. After Booth suggested that he not wear his sword in Act III, scene iii, since it was unnecessary and tended to get in the way, James decided to put the sword to dramatic use. Pulling it halfway from its hilt, James addressed it (not Iago, as was usual practice) with the line "Nay, stay, thou shouldst be honest," and let it clang back into its sleeve, thus using the action of resheathing the sword to illustrate Othello's change of heart (Gelb 29).

As we have seen, the "point" – once an accepted part of the Romantic style of acting that dominated the nineteenth-century stage – came to be associated with lower orders of theatrical fare by the turn of the twentieth century. Although it continued to be practiced on the boards of the melodramatic and vaudeville stage, its emphasis on the actor's body was not in keeping with the new regime of moral-psychological realism then being practiced on the legitimate stage. But, as we have also seen, that new regime bore within it a distinct class bias. The Delsarte method both moralized and naturalized class-based habits of behavior. Thus, not only were actors who stood on "points" associated with the lower-middle- and working-class audiences for whom they performed; according to the logic of moral-psychological realism, their highly expressive style of self-presentation marked *them* as lower class.

Occurring over the course of several decades, this classifying of acting styles was subtle and often imperceptible to many actors who, like James, had once been adept at performing a range of dramatic roles in a variety of theatrical venues. When O'Neill's *The Count of Monte Cristo* opened on 17 February 1883, it was at Booth's, the most respectable of theatres, to the most respectable of audiences (Hewitt 244). Within twenty-five years, however, its respectability had gone the way of the grand old theatre in which it premiered. Sometime between his first and 6,000th performance of *The Count of Monte Cristo*, James O'Neill became irrevocably linked to a style of acting that was marked and that marked him as "lower class." Although Eugene could see how the theatre had changed, he believed his father to have been blissfully unaware.

Perhaps that is why James's agonizing deathbed confession struck him as especially tragic. After a long and financially successful career, James's recognition of his professional disrepute must have made him a tragic figure in Eugene's mind, one whose fate was made inevitable by his own blindness and whose moment of anagnorisis, as always, came too late. Stunned by his father's self-recognition, O'Neill sought to come to terms with both his grief and his guilt for having formerly regarded his father with contempt.[8] Perhaps he also noted the irony of his own blindness: it wasn't that James did not know the truth; it was simply that the truth was too painful to acknowledge. Such truths, as O'Neill suggests in later plays such as *The Iceman Cometh* (1939; 1946) and *Long Day's Journey Into Night* (1939–41; 1956) where his father's revelation appears in James Tyrone's climactic speech, can only be sustained in brief moments of clarity before becoming enshrouded again in a pipe dream or metaphysical fog. Clearly, this revelation was important to O'Neill, not only in understanding his father's life but in comprehending the larger problem of self-alienation and spiritual disharmony that afflicted modern humanity.

In the example of his father – a once-powerful man who experienced a great fall – O'Neill found a modern tragic figure upon whom to model his psychological conception of Brutus Jones.[9] For, like James, Jones is a "tall, powerfully-built" man whose strength and physical presence stand in stark opposition to his psychological frailty.[10] Like James, Jones is a consummate showman, a con artist, whose once-loyal supporters turn against him. If for Jones betrayal comes at the hands of superstitious West Indian islanders who once worshiped him as Emperor, for James it comes at the hands of fans and critics who once proclaimed him a beloved star.[11] Forced to take a final account of his life, Jones – like James – experiences a fleeting moment of recognition before succumbing to his inevitable death.

Of course, unlike James's life retrospective, Jones's is not limited to his personal consciousness, but extends to his "racial consciousness" as well, reviewing historical episodes in the slave trade which document the subjugation of Africans in the New World. This apparent emphasis upon Jones's racial identity has led scholars to assume that Brutus Jones is based strictly upon historical and contemporary Black figures and to overlook the parallels between his character and James O'Neill. But as an Irishman, James O'Neill would have been subject to a type of racial discourse similar to that used to describe African-Americans during the nineteenth and early twentieth centuries, as recent cultural historians have well demonstrated.[12] Examining English attitudes toward the Irish, John Szwed, for instance, has noted that, although the Irish were long thought to be culturally distinct from the English, by the nineteenth century they were considered to be racially distinct as well (20). Described as having "Africanoid" features, the Irish were believed to have descended directly from African peoples. Such suppositions were given scientific credibility when, in 1885, John Beddoe, President of the Anthropological Institute of England, created an "index of Nigresence" which distinguished the peoples of Ireland, Wales, Scotland, and Cornwall from England according to varying degrees of physiological difference (Szwed 21).

In the US, attitudes were not much different. Even the American census bureau observed a similar racial logic in the mid-nineteenth century. According to David Roediger, it "collected statistics on . . . 'native' and 'foreign' populations, but kept the Irish distinct from even the latter group" (133). And, such official distinctions were translated both from and into cultural attitudes, with the Irish immigrant frequently caricatured in the pages of American periodicals as an ape and depicted on stage as a simpleton, clown, or servant. According to Szwed, such stage characterizations of the Irish prefigured the blackface grotesque: "before the Negro was mimicked on the stage, the Irishman had served the same purpose; in fact, [with the rise of blackface minstrelsy] Negro speech was simply grafted on to

Irish tunes" (Szwed 27). Joyce Flynn extends Szwed's insight to suggest
that the Americanization of white ethnic immigrant groups such as the
Irish often took place on the American stage through negative portrayals
of them in blackface (426). "*Low-browed* and *savage, grovelling* and *bestial,
lazy* and *wild, simian* and *sensual* [were all] adjectives used by many native-
born Americans to describe the Catholic Irish 'race' in the years before the
Civil War" (Roediger 133), when James O'Neill was just a boy. Although
Irish-Americans were able to assimilate into white America with somewhat
greater ease than were African-Americans in the years following the Civil
War, the notion that they were racially inferior to the other "civilized white
races" lingered well into the twentieth century. As late as 1924, Joel Pfister
reports, "Congress heard 'scientific' testimony that Irish immigration should
be restricted because the Irish were the most 'degenerate' and 'defective' of
all immigrant groups" (124), suggesting that this kind of racial prejudice was
not unknown to Eugene.

Drawing upon this cultural history, Shannon Steen has recently argued
that Jones's blackness functions as a cipher for O'Neill's own feelings of
social marginalization. Suggesting that Jones's mildly eroticized black body
is a fantasmatic object of identification that is both "almost the same but not
quite" (347), she theorizes that it provided O'Neill a "pleasurable distance"
(349) from which to experience his melancholy loss of social acceptance.
While I think she is right to read Jones's blackness as figure for social
marginalization and to theorize it as a means by which O'Neill was able
to explore feelings of abjection, I believe those feelings are not so much
O'Neill's own as his father's (or at least are deflected onto his father within
his imagination). After all, O'Neill cast his father as a Black man in other
plays. In *All God's Chillun Got Wings* (1923; 1924), for example, O'Neill
represents his father as the African-American Jim, dramatizing his parents'
mixed-class marriage as an interracial relationship (Flynn, 428; Gelb, 534–5).
In *The Iceman Cometh*, we hear echoes of his father again in the Black Joe
Mott, whose heightened self-conception is at odds with the racist opinions
others have of him. It should be no surprise, then, that in Brutus Jones
James O'Neill is figured as a Black man. Using race to explore the issue of
class, O'Neill can probe the problem at the heart of his father's professional
disrepute without having to confront it directly.

Of course, this is to presume that race and class are distinct epistemo-
logical categories when in fact they have often been tightly intertwined.
The institution of slavery, with its neat justfication that Black bodies were
"naturally" better able to perform hard labor, made sure of that (as did the

labor conditions and social attitudes that the immigrant Irish faced). Even into the twentieth century, when O'Neill was writing these plays, race was deeply imbricated in the experience of class as was class in the experience of race. Thus, as with many naturalist writers, O'Neill's conception of class and class identity is not surprisingly racialized, subscribing more to a Darwinian vision of biological and environmental determinism than to the ideology of bourgeois liberalism with its emphasis on class mobility.

O'Neill's racialization of what is essentially an experience of class, then, explains why *The Emperor Jones* does not satisfactorily address the problems arising from the history of American race relations that it would seem to invoke. After all, as Eleanor Flexner has pointed out, the events from Jones's racial past are not presented within their social contexts, but appear as episodes within his racial consciousness to suggest a biological determinism that is fundamentally racist (144). Most critics agree. Travis Bogard, for example, condemns the play, arguing that, unlike Joseph Conrad, "O'Neill makes no generalization . . . that there is a savagery in the hearts of all men. Instead it is the Negro who is essentially uncivilized, wearing contemporary sophistication as a loosely fitting mask over an incorrigibly savage countenance" (139). Other critics are more circumspect, pointing to evidence of what John Cooley refers to as O'Neill's "racial ambivalence" (76). Gabriele Poole, for example, argues that the play dramatizes a conflict between Black and white discourses, with "neither discourse . . . clearly privileged" (21). Still others find that the play transcends the specificity of race altogether. Reading *The Emperor Jones* as a morality play, Norman Kagan places Jones at the end of a long line of characters destroyed by conscience, including Oedipus Rex and Lady Macbeth (162), while Frederic Carpenter concludes that the play's "fundamental themes are those of human life itself – the eternal conflict of good and evil, of sunlight and moonlight, of civilization and savagery, of the clearing and 'the Great Forest . . . Its hero is a perfect mixture of the dual opposites of man's nature'" (89–90).

Without apologizing for the racist assumptions upon which both the play and the character of Brutus Jones appear to be based, many critics – even those who excoriate it – have tended to defend the play on the grounds that Brutus Jones "was the first important role written for a Negro actor that was more than a walk-on part, a comic turn, a vaudeville sketch" (Bogard 139). But this is not entirely true. Gary Richardson reports that "the first play by an American to elevate a black man to heroic stature" was William Henry Brown's *The Drama of King Shotaway*, written in 1823 (289). And, in

1915, Ridgely Torrence had also written serious roles for African-American actors in his *Three Plays for the Negro Theatre*.[13] This is not to say that *The Emperor Jones* is not an important – even historically significant – play. But its significance lies not so much in the fact that its central character is Black, as in the fact that, throughout the course of the play, he is shown to undergo a process of psychological change.

Intrigued by his father's capacity both to know yet not be able to functionally acknowledge something important about himself, O'Neill set out to explore the complexity of the human psyche. Thus, within the framework of the external conflict between Jones and the insurrectionary islanders, O'Neill presents an internal conflict within Jones's mind, pitting him against the fears that threaten to subvert his sanity. In this way, Jones is both the agent and the site of the dramatic action. As critics generally agree, the play thus metaphorizes Jones's flight into the jungle as a journey into the psychological recesses of his mind. Where they differ is in the psychological model that O'Neill is supposed to have used; while almost all critics cite the play's debt to Carl Jung's notion of the "collective unconscious" (which O'Neill himself acknowledged), some insist that it bears Freudian elements as well. But, while both Jung and Freud may have influenced the narrative rendering of Jones's psychological descent, neither accounts for the play's experimental form, opening up the possibility of another – pre-Freudian – source for Jones's psychological portrait.

That source, I propose, is S. S. Curry's theory of expression and its popular dissemination through the expressive culture movement. As we've seen in chapter 2, the moral-psychological model of the self that it popularized was derived from Delsarte. Relating the psychological faculties of reason, sentiment, and will to their supposed physical manifestations in the head, torso, and limbs, the "expressionists" believed that individual neuroses or maladjustments were the result of modernization where the rhythms of industry and mechanization had thrown the body's natural rhythms out of alignment. Such alienation was not merely a problem of physical well-being but affected one's spiritual health as well, causing one to feel out of harmony with the universal life force. Thus, to restore that harmony, the individual must recondition his or her body through a program of physical exercise and realign the three languages of expression. Those three languages, of course, are verbal, vocal, and pantomimic, the perfect coordination of which would result in the individual's return to a state of spiritual harmony.

Considering that the play represents Jones's spiritual *dis*harmony, we should not be surprised to find that O'Neill places these three languages in counterpoint.[14] Indeed, the play's haunting effect derives not simply from the fact of Jones's psychological deterioration, but in the way it is represented in the play's form. Consider, for example, O'Neill's famous use of the drumbeat. Although he claimed that the idea to represent a pounding heartbeat came from a bout with malaria he contracted while prospecting for gold in Honduras (Bogard 135), O'Neill was no doubt also aware of the drum's expressive use in Vachel Lindsay's poem, "The Congo." There, as in *Jones*, the drum represents what is imagined to be the mysterious and irresistible power of the jungle to lure Black Americans back from civilization to more primitive ways. There, as in *Jones*, it functions to seduce the (presumably white) audience who hears it as well. But where the poem's third-person narrator mitigates this performative effect of seduction, the play intensifies it with a heart-pounding rhythm that places the audience directly inside Jones's head. They, like Jones, experience the dislocation of being both inside and outside his reality.[15]

Consider, too, the play's use of pantomime. While O'Neill calls for pantomimic scenes in earlier plays such as *Thirst* (1913; 1916), they appear here in marked proliferation, as Timo Tiusanen has observed (102). Almost all of Jones's visions appear in pantomime – the convicts working on the chain gang, the auctioneer soliticiting bids from the belles and dandies at the slave auction, the captives rowing themselves to enforced servitude, the witch-doctor beckoning Jones to his sacrifice. Although Jones speaks to these visions, they never speak back; the only sounds we hear are the "low mocking laughter" (1, 1046) of the little formless fears, "the queer, clicking sound" (1, 1047) of Jeff's dice, the "low, melancholy murmur" and "long, tremulous wail" (1, 1055) of the captives on the ship, and the witch-doctor's "weird monotonous croon, without articulate word divisions" (1, 1058). The effect is otherworldly, disconcerting. Even in those scenes where sound and image would seem to match – such as scene 3, where Jeff throws the dice – there is a sense that they do not (the sound is described as "queer"), as if the spatial and temporal planes of a parallel universe were joined together in syncopated time.

Edward Murray has remarked upon the cinematic nature of these scenes, noting that O'Neill's stage directions effectively metaphorize the camera's eye – focusing in on Jones as if in a close-up, zooming out to describe the setting, and using fade-ins and fade-outs to introduce and conclude individual scenes (18). In fact, Murray comments, the play is so visually oriented that "much of the dialogue could be omitted without real loss" if it were made into a silent film (18).[16] Dong-Ho Sohn agrees, extending

Figure 5. Scene 5 from Eugene O'Neill's *The Emperor Jones*. Belles and dandies bid on Charles Gilpin's Brutus Jones in a silent pantomime that evokes a scene from early silent film.

Murray's insight to argue that the play almost subordinates Jones's dialogue to his actions (1089). Thus, it would seem that, with these pantomimic images, O'Neill inscribes his father's "point" technique into the play. Indeed, given that their significance exceeds, or at times even contradicts, the verbal constructions appended to them, these pantomimic images appear to tell a story all their own, leading C. W. E. Bigsby to observe that "The collapse of language creates rather than destroys meaning." He goes on to explain that "At the level of language lies are possible; at the level of instinctual behavior, of gesture, and of unconscious impulse, there is an available truth" (56). By separating gestures and words, then, O'Neill is able to present two stories at once – one that reveals how Jones feels and one that recounts his self-willed thoughts. In this way, O'Neill is able to represent what was, for much of his father's life, simply unrepresentable. What I mean, of course, is the sad truth of his father's professional demise and the lie he told himself to deny it. Thus, scenes 2 through 7 may be read as James's final accounting – the proverbial life's retrospective – played back, as Sohn has described it, like a movie in reverse time.[17]

Thinking about these pantomimic scenes through the lens of silent film opens up a new range of meanings in the play having to do with the significance and cultural status of the film medium in the moment that the play was written.[18] As we've seen in chapter 1, early cinema, by locating artistic control primarily in the director, effectively foreclosed the artistic agency that actors enjoyed on the nineteenth-century stage. Of course, this was not simply a function of film; as we've also seen, the rise of the producer-director on the legitimate stage yielded much the same effect. Nonetheless, the mechanism of the cinema allowed it to be associated with the threat posed by modernization more generally. This may explain why, insofar as he consciously draws upon cinematic effects, O'Neill repeatedly refers to his stage figures as "automatons" and describes their movements as "mechanical." Jeff throws his dice "with the regular, rigid, mechanical movements of an automaton" (1, 1047). Similarly, the convicts' movements "are those of automatons – rigid, slow, and mechanical," prompting Jones to pick up a shovel and mime "weary, mechanical gestures of digging up dirt and throwing it to the roadside" (1, 1050). The belles and dandies at the slave auction are "stiff, rigid, unreal, marionettish" (1, 1053). Speaking of Jones's compulsion to join in these "mechanical" movements, Robert Conklin has observed that "These performances threaten to place him in a prearranged part, to deny him any sense of performative freedom" (104).

Only the Africans' movements appear to be natural, suggesting that O'Neill sees them as part of a premodern, unalienated past. Jones's movement toward this premodern past suggests a redemptive ending; the closer to nature he gets, the less alienated he becomes.[19] But, of course, in reuniting him with the spiritual forces of the universe (represented by the pantheistic crocodile god), this process of de-alienation leads to his death. Thus, it would seem, spiritual harmony can only be had in the absolute obliteration of self. Perhaps this is a pessimistic vision, as O'Neill's critics have often complained, but the persistence of this Greek tragic vision, this "higher optimism" in O'Neill's writings suggests that he did not think it was (Tornqvist 13–14). As Egil Tornqvist observes: "Belonging and peace are invariably the attributes of death in O'Neill's plays; life is characterized by the opposite qualities: loneliness and struggle" (18). In *Long Day's Journey Into Night*, for example, Edmund reveals that the most beautiful moments of his life have been those when he completely lost himself in the vastness of existence. Such moments, however, are fleeting at best: "For a second you see – and seeing the secret, are the secret. For a second there is meaning! Then the hand lets the veil fall and you are alone, lost in the fog again, and you stumble on toward nowhere, for no good reason" (O'Neill III, 812). James Tyrone experiences such a moment, but it, too, is fleeting. Upon confessing his professional shame to his son, he quickly reverts to his old boastful habits. So does Brutus Jones. Upon recognizing the imminence of his death (represented by the call to sacrifice), he clings to life by firing his last silver bullet into the gaping maw of the crocodile god. It is an excruciating moment for the audience. For, in having spent his last bullet to save his life, Jones, we recognize, has condemned himself to die at the hands of Lem and his men. But there is an ironic twist. As we discover in the play's final scene, Jones has died just as he wanted; the islanders, believing that "He got um strong charm" (I, 1061), have killed him with a silver bullet. If we feel remorse and pity for Jones's hubristic fall, we also feel relief at the realization that his struggle is finally over. The tom-toms cease and we know that at last he is at peace with the spiritual universe.

If, as I've suggested, Jones figures James O'Neill, we may assume that such feelings were also felt by O'Neill as he scripted the play's conclusion. For, though he was apparently struck by the tragic dimensions of his father's life and career, imagining him as a tragic figure brought down by his own blindness, he must also have felt some relief at the thought that his father's struggle was now at an end. Fittingly, O'Neill's hero is killed with the very prop he had devised to maintain the theatrical illusion of his power, and it has been forged from melted money. While such a detail provides evidence for Michael Hinden's thesis that the play – like much of the O'Neill canon – is an indictment of the American drive for happiness through the acquisition of material possessions (4), it also suggests, within the play's fantasy narrative, that his father's artistic career was shot dead in its tracks by his own financial success.

Like all such fantasy narratives, however, this one does not satisfactorily address all the issues it brings into play.[20] A year and a half later, O'Neill returned to take up many of its central themes in *The Hairy Ape*. He also returned to its expressionistic style. As O'Neill once remarked in explaining that play's experimental form, "*The Hairy Ape* is a direct descendant of *Jones*, written long before I had ever heard of Expressionism" (quoted in B. H. Clark 83). As I shall show, it is indeed a "descendant"; for, while it revisits the oedipal and professional/class dynamics dramatized in *Jones*, its story is not his father's but his own.

The literary ape

Drawing on the expressionistic technique developed in *Jones*, O'Neill returns to the theme of self-alienation in *The Hairy Ape*. The story of Yank, a ship's stoker, who finds himself unable to reconcile his understanding of the world with his experience of it, the play is ostensibly about his inability to achieve class consciousness. It begins with Yank celebrating the virtues of speed and strength – virtues which place him at the top of a social-Darwinian world order in which the strongest not only survive but rule. "Who d'yuh tink's runnin' dis game," he shouts to the unseen engineer blowing the whistle for him to work, "me or you?" (O'Neill II, 136). This world order is turned upside down, however, when Yank is confronted by Mildred Douglas, the steel heiress, who is horrified by his brutal appearance, likening him to a "filthy beast" just before she faints. Yank initially wants to respond to the insult with physical violence but is waylaid by his shipmate Long, who wishes to tutor him in the subject of class struggle in order to raise his class consciousness. Frustrated by Yank's inability to understand Mildred's insult in anything but personal terms, Long eventually gives up, leaving Yank in a state of utter confusion. After a stint in jail, Yank becomes convinced that his belief in might makes right is shared by members of the International Workers of the World and seeks to join their brotherhood. They, however, are wary of his terroristic rhetoric and, thinking he is a Pinkerton spy, cast him back out on the street alone. Finally, in an attempt to see the beast that Mildred saw in him, Yank goes to the zoo, where he encounters a caged gorilla. But, just as he is groping toward an understanding of his situation, explaining to the gorilla, "She wasn't wise dat I was in a cage, too – worser'n yours – sure – a damn sight – 'cause you got some chanct to bust loose – but me – (*He grows confused*)" (II, 161), Yank surrenders to the fatal embrace of the ape and to the ideology that only the strongest are meant to survive.

Largely based upon O'Neill's experience as a seaman aboard the *S.S. New York* in 1911, *The Hairy Ape* has traditionally been read as O'Neill's attempt to come to terms with the suicide of his drinking buddy Driscoll who, like Yank, was a fireman. By O'Neill's own admission, the play was a "search for an explanation of why Driscoll, proud of his animal superiority and in complete harmony with his limited conception of the universe, should kill himself" (quoted in Gelb 488). O'Neill first attempted to search for an explanation for Driscoll's suicide in a short story he wrote four years earlier in 1917. Never quite happy with the story's resolution, however, O'Neill later had the manuscript destroyed (Sheaffer 389).[21] Doris Falk insists that, since the story for the play was first outlined in 1917, it should be read within the context of that period of O'Neill's life (10), but I want to argue just the opposite. Considering that O'Neill once referred to the play as an "unconscious autobiography" (Sheaffer 76; Gelb 488), and that it, like *Jones*, was written quickly – over a period of only ten days[22] – we may conclude that something happened in the fall of 1921, to crystallize in O'Neill's mind the final shape of his play.

What happened that fall was that O'Neill became a victim of his own success. Having won a Pulitzer Prize for *Beyond the Horizon* the year before and moved *The Emperor Jones* to Broadway earlier in the year, O'Neill found himself in hot demand, with two plays in production at two different theatres, opening little more than a week apart. Because of the hectic schedule, O'Neill was unable to see the New London production of *The Straw* (1918; 1921) before it closed, but he was not surprised by the mixed reviews it received. He fully expected audiences to be as yet unprepared for a play about a tuberculosis patient who finds hope in an unrequited love affair. Although *Anna Christie* (1920; 1921) also dealt with a subject that most middle-class audiences would find unsavory, its naturalistic treatment of a woman's fallen virtue and her father's futile attempt to save her from such a fate was, for the most part, well received; it would go on to earn him a second Pulitzer Prize. Given these recent and soon-to-be triumphs, O'Neill had every reason to take pride in his accomplishments and further pursue his professional ambitions. According to Stella Hanau and Helen Deutsch, those ambitions were, from the beginning, what marked him apart from Provincetown Players founder Jig Cook.[23] But, while he was no doubt pleased with his successes, O'Neill was also probably wary about identifying too closely with the theatrical medium that had ruined his father's life. As he well knew, the proverbial bitch-goddess of the theatre could be capricious in her lusts, embracing a lover one day and casting him aside the next.

Perhaps these were the thoughts running through his mind in December 1921, as he began work on his new play. The problem he had queried with regard to Driscoll's suicide in 1917 was one he was currently dealing with himself – the problem of identifying so closely with one's work that one risked becoming blind to the actual conditions of one's life. Turning to the play, we see that this is, indeed, the problem addressed by its primary conflict. In scene one, Yank proudly identifies with his work, bragging,

I'm de ting in coal dat makes it boin; I'm steam and oil for de engines; I'm de ting in noise dat makes yuh hear it; I'm smoke and express trains and steamers and factory whistles; I'm de ting in gold dat makes it money! And I'm what makes iron into steel! Steel, dat stands for the whole ting! And I'm steel – steel – steel! I'm de muscles in steel, de punch behind it! (II, 128–9)

Yet, by scene seven, after ruefully discovering the folly of his identification, he despairs, "Steel was me, and I owned de woild. Now I ain't steel, and de woild owns me" (II, 159). Thus, the play reveals the perils of false consciousness, tracking Yank's fall from identification to disidentification and eventually death.

What motivates Yank's initial display of "frenzied self-glorification" (II, 129) and unqualified identification with the ship of modernity in scene one are the nostalgic reminiscences of Paddy, "an old wizened Irishman" who longs for the decks of the sailing ships of yore. Remembering "clippers wid tall masts touching the sky," "warm sun on clean decks," and "wind over the miles of shiny green ocean like strong drink to your lungs," Paddy despairs of their life in the stokehole, asking

Is it one wid this you'd be, Yank – black smoke from the funnels smudging the sea, smudging the decks – the divil a sight of sun or a breath of clean air – choking our lungs wid coal dust – breaking our backs and hearts in the hell of the stokehole – feeding the bloody furnace – feeding our lives along wid the coal, I'm thinking – caged in by steel from a sight of the sky like bloody apes in the Zoo! (II, 126–7)

Paddy's rhetorical question is prescient in more ways than one. Besides foreshadowing Yank's disgrace in the eyes of Mildred and his demise at the hands of the gorilla, Paddy's question situates Yank within the forces of history, asking him to see the consequences that his identification holds for him when advancing age will compromise *his* strength, too.

Yank, however, refuses to identify with Paddy, to see in him a future version of himself. In his ears, Paddy's lament is pure *ressentiment*, the plaintive cry of the weak. To him, Paddy simply doesn't belong:

He's old and don't belong no more. But me, I'm young! . . . He can't breathe and swallow coal dust, but I kin, see? Dat's fresh air for me! Dat's food for me! I'm new, get me? Hell in de stokehole? Sure! It takes a man to work in hell. Hell, sure, dat's my fav'rite climate. I eat it up! I git fat on it! It's me makes it hot! It's me makes it roar! It's me makes it move! . . . It – dat's me! – de new dat's moiderin' de old! (II, 128)

As this last line suggests, the relationship between Yank and Paddy isn't simply marked by a generational difference; the conflict between them is clearly oedipal, too. Yank not only disparages the life that Paddy yearns for, but revels in having rendered it obsolete. Thus, if O'Neill were reveling in his own theatrical success, if he were celebrating the death of his father's theatre, he also might have feared that, in identifying too closely with the theatre himself, he, too, would someday be rendered obsolete.[24]

But, of course, this isn't the only – or even most important – fear to which the play gives fantasmatic expression. Paddy is not the only one to try to convince Yank that his worldview is wrong. With just one look, one phrase, and one faint, Mildred Douglas succeeds where Paddy fails. But Yank is confused by the lesson she offers, requiring extra tutelage from his shipmate Long. A radical socialist agitator, Long tries to raise Yank's class consciousness by pointing out that real power is configured not in terms of strength or raw brute force but in terms of capital, ownership, and class. Revealing that Mildred is the daughter of "a bleedin' millionaire, a bloody Capitalist," the man who "owns this bloody boat," Long proselytizes that he and Yank are nothing more than "'is slaves" and "'er slaves, too!" (II, 139). Yank scoffs at Long's explanation, deriding it twice as "Salvation Army–Socialist bull" (II, 125, 140). "Say! What's dem slobs in de foist cabin got to do wit us? We're better men dan dey are, ain't we? Sure! One of us guys could clean up de whole mob wit one mit . . . Dem boids don't amount to nothin'" (II, 125). In rejecting Long's Marxist analysis of the economic relations of power, Yank reveals himself to be a particular kind of lumpenproletarian, one who not only is ineducable on the subject of class conflict but persists in maintaining a specifically masculinist view that might makes right. Though he tries to think critically about his situation, emblematically striking the pose of Rodin's *The Thinker* throughout the play, Yank always gives up thinking in favor of force. And that force is always directed at Mildred – a "skoit," a "skinny tart," a "white-faced bum" – who, if not a representative of her class, is representative of Woman, the presumed source of all Yank's problems.

As James A. Robinson reads him, Yank is strongly identified with the culture of the "masculine primitive," a term he borrows from historian Anthony Rotundo. According to Rotundo, the ideology of the masculine primitive developed at the end of the nineteenth century in reaction to the emergence of the New Woman, defining "man as 'the master animal who could draw on primitive impulse when reason would not work,' evaluating men 'according to their physical strength and energy,' seeing life as a 'competitive jungle struggle'" (Rotundo, quoted in Robinson 97–8). Robinson suggests that, in Yank, O'Neill represents his own youthful identification with this ethos. The young O'Neill, he argues, found the ethos of the masculine primitive appealing since it allowed him to indulge in a youthful rebellion against his parents' middle-class values (97). By shipping out to sea, drinking to excess, whoring with prostitutes, living in flophouses, and associating with anarchists, O'Neill could happily defy his parents' bourgeois expectations. But, by the time he wrote *The Hairy Ape*, Robinson argues, he had begun to rethink his investment in this identity. "O'Neill's rebellion against a middle-class style of existence would end with this play," Robinson concludes. "For – not coincidentally – the playwright's theatrical successes had given him the independent income to maintain a bourgeois lifestyle himself" (107).

Robinson's explication of the late nineteenth-century ideology of the "masculine primitive" is illuminating in many respects. Not only does it provide us with the cultural-historical background necessary to understand Yank's code of self-identification, it points further to O'Neill's own crisis of identification with this ethos. But where Robinson sees O'Neill's disidentification as the necessary result of his playwriting success and thus enhanced class status (which made it unnecessary for him to rebel any more), I see it as a considerably more complicated process. For, as inscribed in the play, Yank's identification and subsequent disidentification is tragic. It would seem that O'Neill mourns the loss of this masculinist self even as he is acutely aware of its limitations.

To understand O'Neill's apparently conflicted feelings toward the masculine primitive, we should consider his professed identification with it in his early sea plays. After all, they not only feature this ethos as it defined the lives of Yank's predecessors aboard the *S.S. Glencairn*,[25] but reveal something about O'Neill's own youthful infatuation with this relentlessly masculine code – and perhaps his difficult initiation into it. Although little is known about O'Neill's actual seafaring experiences, critics have reasonably surmised that they provided the basis for many of the stories dramatized in the Glencairn cycle. W. David Sievers has gone even further to suggest that the character of Smitty is a figure for O'Neill himself (99). Indeed, Smitty's relationship to the other sailors would seem to describe the comfortably middle-class O'Neill's own sense of difference from the hard-living seamen he likely encountered. In *The Moon of the Caribbees* (1916–17; 1918), for example, Smitty sits apart from the rest of the men, philosophizing about the nature of human suffering while they mindlessly drink and whore. In

In the Zone (1916–17; 1917), this temperamental difference begins to mark him as an outsider deserving of suspicion. Thinking him a German spy, Smitty's shipmates break into his belongings, only to find that the tin box he has been hiding contains love letters from a woman who has since spurned him. In Edwin Engel's perceptive reading, Smitty is a "man of feeling,"

> a pensive figure with an acute consciousness, lonely and life-weary. O'Neill, shortly after he had first created the character, professed to regard the type with disdain, pointing out that "his gestures of self-pity," "his thin whine of weakness," "his sentimental posing" are "much more out of harmony with truth, much less in tune with beauty, than the honest vulgarity of his mates." He felt, in short, that the latter were in accord with external nature, that the former was an anomaly. Yet he later set about either to banish or to transform the mates and to elevate the man of feeling, making him the perennial hero upon whom he was to bestow his attention, understanding and sympathy. (10–11)

As Engel points out, O'Neill was ambivalent toward the man of feeling, disdaining him in his youth, only to become more sympathetic toward him later in his career. For, though he claimed to find him overly sentimental, insincere, or perhaps even effeminate in the 1919 letter to Barrett Clark that Engel cites, these early plays suggest that O'Neill in fact identified with him. *The Moon of the Caribbees*, for example, shows us a man who, like his playwright-creator, attempts to trace larger patterns of meaning out of the petty lives of men. *In The Zone* gives us a man under suspicion simply for having an interior emotional life. However much O'Neill may have been attracted to the ethos of the masculine primitive described by Robinson, the ambivalence in these early plays suggests that he is the man of feeling himself – a sensitive boy with a touch of the poet about him trying to be a man among men. Like Smitty, he may have found that his tendency to think and feel deeply marked him apart from the other men. Like Yank, he may have found that he simply didn't "belong."

Despite his claim to despise the "sentimental posing" of the man of feeling and genuinely admire the "honest vulgarity" of his mates, O'Neill began to shift his perspective when he wrote *The Hairy Ape*. What had changed was the existential milieu which defined him. Surrounded by writers who shared his desire to express intense feelings in their art rather than seamen who shared his desire for masculine camaraderie, O'Neill gave freer rein to the sentimentality he had previously mocked in himself, and began to rethink his commitment to the masculine ethos of his past. To be sure, he did not completely forsake his investment in a masculine prerogative; an element of Strindbergian misogyny persists. But he did give up his idealization of the masculine primitive as somehow less alienated and more in harmony with nature than his own philosophical restlessness; Driscoll's suicide may have pressed him to do that.

With this shift in context, however, O'Neill was no less vulnerable to a fear of not belonging. Did he, for example, truly "belong" to the intellectual circle of college-educated writers and artists with whom he mixed, or was he, like Yank, capable only of striking the thinker's pose? Pfister reports that O'Neill was apprehensive about literally assuming such a posture when, in 1919, he was asked to pose for a promotional photograph with pen in hand in front of the sea. O'Neill refused, lest he be thought *only* to pose. Explaining why, O'Neill snapped, "An author whose work is sincere and honest should see to it that he remains likewise . . . His best place is – out of sight in the wings" (quoted in Pfister 8–9). By the late 1920s and 1930s, however, he apparently began to feel more at ease with such images, recommending a photo to Barrett Clark for his 1926 biography and sitting for such chroniclers of the modern as Edward Steichen and Carl Van Vechten (Pfister 9). Examining several of these photographs, Pfister argues that they helped establish his reputation as a writer of deep psychological truths. Picturing O'Neill in a pin-striped suit at his desk with furrowed brow and pen in hand, one photograph not only attests to the playwright's "depth," but also casts him in the ready-made image of professional writer by evoking a well-known photograph of August Strindberg, a serious *literary* dramatist (1–4). O'Neill may have consented to such photographs only a decade after his initial refusal because, having been awarded three Pulitzer Prizes, a gold medal, and an honorary degree, he felt such an image had some basis in reality.

But in 1921, as O'Neill wrote *The Hairy Ape*, he was only just beginning to receive such recognition. Though he had every reason to be confident that more theatrical successes would be forthcoming, he likely harbored some doubts about his place in the literary world. As we saw in chapter 2, it was in this moment that the category of the literary was being redefined specifically to exclude performative modes of communication. O'Neill was no doubt well aware of these debates. As a student in George Pierce Baker's English 47 playwriting class at Harvard in 1914–15, he would have been at their epicenter, absorbing the shock waves in the very marrow of his bones. Thus, even if O'Neill felt confident about writing plays, his choice of medium left him vulnerable to suspicions that his was a lesser form of art. After all, we should remember that, just ten years after its legal separation from the theatrical apparatus, the drama had yet to emerge as a fully recognized literary art form. For playwrights such as Susan Glaspell or Edna St. Vincent Millay who were also developing literary reputations in fiction and poetry, the drama's "subliterary" status (as Susan Harris Smith puts it) may not have caused much concern. But, for those such as O'Neill whose literary reputations depended solely upon their dramatic writings, the genre's uncertain literary status was a source of great anxiety. Again, he may have felt that he didn't "belong."

What I have been suggesting is that the set of professional concerns that O'Neill confronted in early December 1921 were akin to those he had experienced as an ordinary seaman aboard the *S.S. Ikala* and *S.S. New York* ten years earlier. That is, he may have felt an affinity between the two experiences which prompted him to revisit the story of Driscoll's suicide and propose a new resolution. As we'll see, that resolution, born of his unconscious, does more to address O'Neill's own professional concerns than to explain the circumstances surrounding Driscoll's fate. But here, as in *Jones*, it is cast in universalizing terms.

Reading the play as "unconscious autobiography" can explain why it, like *Jones*, doesn't satisfactorily resolve the social issues it would seem to address. As many critics have noted, O'Neill's treatment of the theme of alienation is not truly concerned with the economic exploitation of labor. Rather, it is abstracted and de-politicized into philosophical – or, more properly, spiritual – terms. This understanding of Yank's problem as primarily spiritual was first advanced by O'Neill himself in an interview printed in the New York *Herald Tribune* in November 1924. Here, O'Neill claimed that Yank "was a symbol of man who has lost his old harmony with nature, the harmony which he used to have as an animal and has not yet acquired in a spiritual way" (quoted in B. H. Clark 84). O'Neill's somewhat unexpected emphasis on spirituality in this play seemingly concerned with class conflict has perplexed scholars who have tried to understand it through the lens of Christianity, or more specifically Catholicism. But, if we remember that a loss of "harmony with nature" was how expressive culture enthusiasts explained the alienation that resulted from the conditions of modernity, then we might have better luck unlocking the play's meanings.

In speaking of "the harmony [Yank] used to have as an animal and has not yet acquired in a spiritual way," O'Neill clearly evokes the expressive culture movement's understanding of alienation. But, rather than regard nature pantheistically, as the physical manifestation of the spiritual universe,

O'Neill seems to view it in Darwinian terms, as the primordial sludge from which humankind has emerged into its current state of existence. Yank's alienation from nature, then, is simply the condition of humanity more generally. Though he tries, he cannot reason himself into a higher state of being (à la the Nietzschean *Übermensch*), nor even ascend to a higher plane of spiritual awareness. O'Neill illustrates these strivings throughout the course of the play. From a presumably unalienated state in which he is in harmony with his own "honest vulgarity," Yank falls from grace with the knowledge Mildred brings that there is a higher state of being to which he doesn't "belong." Ironically, both her exclamation (filthy beast) and Paddy's interpretation of it (hairy ape) would seem to reconcile Yank to a state of nature, but he remains alienated from nature throughout the rest of the play. Nor is he able to effect a reconciliation with heaven. As Ann Hughes and D. G. Kehl have pointed out, the parishioners whom Yank encounters on Fifth Avenue seek to erect obstacles between man and God.[26] Literally unable to challenge or stop them, Yank is deemed a nuisance and thrown in jail. "Thus, not being able to find [harmony] on earth nor in heaven," O'Neill tells us, Yank finds himself "in the middle, trying to make peace, taking the 'woist punches from bot' of 'em' . . . Yank can't go forward, and so he tries to go back. This is what his shaking hands with the gorilla meant. But he can't go back to 'belonging' either. The gorilla kills him" (quoted in B. H. Clark 84). Too highly evolved to be content with his position in nature, Yank is not highly evolved enough to find spiritual peace. Yet with his death comes an end to his unappeasable strife. "And, perhaps," O'Neill suggests, "the Hairy Ape at last belongs" (II, 163).

Clearly, Yank's alienation takes a spiritual form. His life has been so restructured by the rhythms of industry that he can no longer integrate himself back into society, let alone nature. Such a reading accords with O'Neill's account of the play in a letter to Kenneth Macgowan shortly after he had completed the manuscript. As he relates, "I have tried to dig deep in it, to probe in the shadows of the soul of man bewildered by the disharmony of his primitive pride and individualism at war with the mechanistic development of society" (quoted in Bryer 32). Indeed, the mechanistic development of society figures not only in the play's content but also in its form.

Pulling apart the layers of verbal, vocal, and pantomimic signification in his play, O'Neill calls for his actors to speak their lines in voices that mock the words they speak and to strike poses whose meanings they cannot possibly realize. For example, Yank's buddies make fun of him when he tries to think, shouting, "Think!" in a "brazen, metallic" bark, "as if their

Figure 6. Scene 5 from Eugene O'Neill's *The Hairy Ape*. Yank encounters "a procession of gaudy marionettes" on Fifth Avenue, while his shipmate Long looks on.

throats were phonograph horns" (II, 139), thus undermining the referential function of the word by calling for it to be given an ironic vocal inflection. This mocking continues when one of Yank's buddies facetiously suggests that Yank's problem is having fallen in love – "Love!" It continues again when Long suggests Yank take his case before the law – "Law!" – that they have the power to change governments – "Governments!" – and that they're equal before God – "God!" (II, 139–40). By having these words repeated by voices which are "brazen," and have a "metallic quality," O'Neill severs the presumed connection between verbal and vocal expression in order to dramatize his character's inability to grasp what these words mean.

Several critics have commented on O'Neill's use of language to suggest the mechanization of the stokers' lives. Bogard surmises that "The chorus effect was intended to suggest that the men were no more than machines" (246), while Tornqvist comments on "the spirit of the steel made verbal" (189). Speaking to the difficulty of translating *The Hairy Ape* into other languages, Ann Massa has remarked upon the "Unexpected consonants and the repetitively-emphasised, twisted vowel sounds [that] make for [Yank's] idiosyncratic speech." She sees the vocal quality of his speech as a further metaphor for the bonds from which he struggles to break free, arguing that "Yank can only break the bounds of his vocabulary and his style in the same violent and ultimately frustrated way that he bends the bars of his cell. Neither speech nor experience yield to him in real terms. He can't break the mould of the apparently flexible yet imprisoning medium that is language and that is life" ("Intention" 43).[27] And, in a rhetorical reading of the play, Tiusanen argues that "O'Neill uses the chorus and the sound effects in order to bring closer to us the feeling of alienation experienced by his inarticulate hero." Where, early in the play, Yank identifies with steel and the men bang their fists against their steel bunks in solidarity with him, here they cast him out from their ranks with a mocking "voice of metal" (Tiusanen 120).

Although apparently unaware of Curry's theory of expression, all of these critics perceptively point out O'Neill's innovative use of sound to illustrate Yank's frustration, alienation, and spiritual disharmony. Such insights, taken together, demonstrate the effectiveness of O'Neill's expressionist strategy – with or without an understanding of the context from which it emerged. Yet, without an understanding of this context, critics have tended to neglect or misunderstand his equally effective use of pantomime. Bogard, for example, finds O'Neill's use of *The Thinker*'s pose to be both inappropriate and immaterial to the play's thematic design.[28] "Under any circumstances," he argues, "deletion of the pose would not materially damage the scenes. What is important is that Yank should think, not that he should quote Rodin" (246–7). But, of course, insofar as we are supposed to understand Yank as a product of modernity afflicted by self-alienation, it *is* important that he affect a pose that he simply cannot realize. As we have seen, Yank is stunted in his ability to think. Thus, modeled in soot if not in bronze, Yank's pose is meant to inscribe him ironically as a material and sensuous being, an element of nature unable to ascend to a higher plane. This pose recurs in scenes six, seven, and eight – each time registering the futility of the pose to realize what it is meant to represent. And if his audience holds out hope that Yank will in fact become the thinker that he "apes," O'Neill not only dashes their hopes but mocks them when, in the final scene, not Yank but the gorilla assumes *The Thinker*'s pose.

Mildred Douglas assumes poses, too. When we first meet her she is on deck with her aunt, a society matron whose only virtue (and dramatic function) is to reveal that Mildred's interest in sociology is merely a pretension. Although the two of them are described as "incongruous, arti-ficial figures, inert and disharmonious," the aunt seems unperturbed by her own imperfect facade, preferring to scold her niece: "[F]or a fresh pose I have no doubt you would drag the name of Douglas in the gutter!" And, as Mildred embarks upon her adventure in class tourism, her aunt calls after her, "Poser! . . . I said poser!" (II, 134). Like Yank, it would seem, Mildred is unable to act upon her aspirations; she can only affect a futile pose. But while such actions have no real impact upon their lives, they are not mean-ingless, especially if understood in relation to the play's formal design. For, with these poses, O'Neill is in effect redeploying his father's "point" tech-nique, but in a way that underscores his characters' frustrated agency. That is, while Yank's and Mildred's poses effect nothing in terms of the play's narrative action, they are not merely empty signifiers (as Bogard supposes). In terms of the play's form, their very meaninglessness becomes mean-ing*ful* insofar as they become ways of figuring these characters' inability to act – despite their desire to do so. Like James and other turn-of-the-century actors stuck in the "point" technique, they are trapped within a structure of signification they ultimately cannot control.

In representing both Yank and Mildred as afflicted by modernity's malaise, O'Neill not only defuses the class conflict that initially motivates the play's crisis, but universalizes it as a struggle between the facticity of the human body and the desire to transcend that body's boundedness. Though critics have been confused by this unexpected turn to abstraction, it, too, can be explained by the influence of expressive culture with its roots in American Transcendentalism, itself largely based on Hegelian thought. For what O'Neill is essentially dramatizing here is the classic Hegelian conflict between spirit and flesh, subject and object, idea and materiality. Though Hegel sees the struggle of this dialectic as a necessary course toward the attainment of absolute knowledge, O'Neill is considerably less sanguine. For him, all that we can know is the affliction of the struggle itself. Both Yank and Mildred suffer from this affliction simply because they are human.

Though class enemies, Yank and Mildred are existential equals, as O'Neill illustrates when he has Yank ask with regard to Mildred, "Ain't she de same as me?" (II, 142). To emphasize this point, he has both characters identify themselves with steel. "Steel, dat's me!," Yank says, accosting the Fifth Avenue socialites, "Youse guys live on it and tink yuh're somep'n. But I'm *in* it, see!" (II, 148). Mildred, too, identifies herself with steel. As the heiress of a steel fortune built by her father and grandfather, she recognizes that steel has made her what she is: "I'm a waste product in the Bessemer process . . .

Or rather, I inherit the acquired trait of the by-product, wealth, but none of the energy, none of the strength of the steel that made it" (II, 132). If this identification with steel allows Mildred to explain her physical and moral corrosion, it initially galvanizes Yank's sense of self: "Sure I'm part of de engines! Why de hell not! Dey move, don't dey? Dey'r speed, ain't dey? Dey smash trou, don't dey? Twenty-five knots a hour! Dat's goin' some! Dat's new stuff! Dat belongs!" (II, 128). While O'Neill uses the metaphor of steel to establish Mildred and Yank as fundamental equals based upon the facticity of their being, he also uses it to suggest the difference between their self-conceptions: Mildred likens herself to slag while Yank is "what makes iron into steel" (II, 129).

Despite these self-conceptions, it is the neurasthenic Mildred who is finally able to break Yank's steely self-conception, where Long and Paddy each has failed. For, when Yank's understanding of the world is finally challenged, it is not through reasoned debate but through an insult that is only vaguely understood, an insult that strikes Yank like a visceral punch. Although he tries to understand what has happened to him, all he knows is what he feels. As he tells the gorilla in the final scene, "It beats it when you try to tink it or talk it – it's way down – deep – behind – you 'n' me we feel it" (II, 162). Thus, here, as in *Jones*, we see O'Neill dramatize thought and feeling as separate – and often incompatible – registers of meaning. Yank's problem is that he cannot reconcile thought with feeling, nor spirit with material existence. Unable to process his thought at all, he is hopelessly trapped within his body.

This was why it was so important that the role of Yank be properly cast. O'Neill wanted an actor whom the audience would register first and fore-most as a physical presence. Well before the play was even written, O'Neill asked his friend Charles Kennedy if he thought a relatively unknown actor named Louis Wolheim would be willing to play "Yank" (Gelb 478). Explain-ing his choice of Wolheim in a letter to George Jean Nathan, O'Neill wrote, "He is the only actor I know who can look it, who has by nature the right manner. Whether he can act it or not, I doubt; but I also doubt if any actor can act it. It is a tremendous part" (quoted in Bogard and Bryer 161). What was important to O'Neill was not that Wolheim could "act it," that is, meld seamlessly into his role, so much as that he could "look it," which is to say corporeally instantiate the part.

Described as a man with "a hulking build and a face like a battering ram," Wolheim was "plug-ugly," as Sheaffer unqualifiedly asserts (69, 80). His brutal appearance derived from his experience as a boxer and Cornell

Figure 7. Louis Wolheim as Yank in Eugene O'Neill's *The Hairy Ape*. "He is the only actor I know who can look it, who has by nature the right manner," O'Neill wrote of his casting choice. "Whether he can act it or not, I doubt; but I also doubt if any actor can act it. It is a tremendous part." Years later, O'Neill would cite Wolheim as one of only three actors who perfectly rendered his character on stage.

football player, which Wolheim took great delight in recounting. "'That guy,' he used to say, 'smeared my nose from ear to ear'" (Sheaffer 80). O'Neill was thus confident that Wolheim could "look" the part. But there was also every indication that Wolheim could "act it." With three years of experience acting on stage and five years in film (Gelb 491), Wolheim was a "man of superior intelligence" who held degrees from two schools and was a linguist who spoke at least four languages (Sheaffer 80). Nonetheless, for O'Neill he was first and foremost a physical presence who could make the character of Yank palpably real.

Wolheim's raw physical presence was important to O'Neill because it allowed him to create Yank as a material being unable to come to terms with the ideas that order his world. He wanted Yank's materiality, constituted through Wolheim's body, to stand in sharp relief against the play's narrative structure of ideas. In this way, the play encodes a Hegelian dialectic in both its narrative and form which resolves, as the play does, with Yank's death. For, after Yank has submitted to the gorilla's fatal embrace, O'Neill's stage directions tell us that Yank "slips in a heap on the floor and dies. The monkeys set up a chattering, whimpering wail. And, perhaps the Hairy Ape at last belongs" (11, 163). Only in death, it would seem, can Yank's alienation be overcome; only by casting off his body, can his spirit reunite with the oversoul.

But if, as I have been arguing, Yank is a figure for O'Neill in this fantasmatic imagining of his own professional anxieties, why would this be a satisfying conclusion? Why would he have Yank die? Such a conclusion would seem defeatist. Yet, it is not. O'Neill's stage directions make clear that Yank has achieved a conditional transcendence. But what are we to make of it? What is the "body" that O'Neill desires to cast off? And what is the "oversoul" with which his spirit wishes to unite? Remembering that O'Neill was confronted with the anti-performative bias of literary modernism, I would like to suggest that it is the body of the theatre O'Neill seeks to cast off in order to unite with the rarefied circle of literary authors. After all, O'Neill has ironized bodily modes of expression (e.g., vocality and pantomime) throughout the play, while locating much of the play's primary meanings in his authorial text (e.g., his novelistic stage directions).[29] Thus, the play invites us to read it symptomatically, as O'Neill's attempt to resolve aesthetically the double-bind that he and other playwrights faced with regard to the text/performance split. Figuring the theatre as the body, and literature as mind or spirit, the play suggests that drama can only achieve literary status by casting off its associations with the theatre. This is why

O'Neill disarticulates the play's formal languages, juxtaposing verbal, vocal, and pantomimic modes of signification against each other to make each visible as such. By doing so, O'Neill not only represents Yank's spiritual disharmony (in much the same way as he did for Brutus Jones), but also resolves his own professional conundrum by inscribing an anti-performative bias.

O'Neill's contemporary, Virgil Geddes, remarked upon the playwright's "apparent distrust of the theatre as a medium" (8), feeling that he was, indeed,

> a man at war with art. Expression with him is something he does not love to do; it is too much like a confession, an embarrassment of the heart wrung from him against his will. As long as he must out with it, he endeavors to make it heard in loud and roaring effects, but one seldom feels he cares overmuch for the profession. (7)

The profession that Geddes speaks of in these 1934 observations was not, of course, the same profession that O'Neill had started out in. Indeed, O'Neill had helped considerably to transform it into what it was. In the moment of that transformation, when O'Neill wrote *The Hairy Ape*, the profession Geddes speaks of did not exist as such. In that moment, O'Neill was no doubt vulnerable to concerns about "belonging" to the literary world – a world in which authors possessed greater cultural capital than did mere "hacks" for the stage. Thus, we should not be surprised to find his concerns expressed in both the form and content of this play. On the narrative level, Yank can be read as a figure for O'Neill, who, in casting off the body of the theatre, is able to ascend to a higher (read "literary") plane. On the formal level, the play ironizes the languages of the theatre in order to attest to the intellectual seriousness of its playwright-author. Such a reading is not as far-fetched as it may seem; shortly after having written these two expressionist plays, O'Neill refused any further involvement in the staging of his work. As he remarked to Provincetown director Nina Moise, "When I finish writing a play, I'm through with it" (quoted in Tornqvist 23).

O'Neill's expressionistic technique has been long misunderstood by critics who have assumed that he simply borrowed his technique from German Expressionism and adapted it to his own dramatic ends. To be sure, the success of these two plays was due in large part to the European staging methods used to produce them. As reviews of *The Emperor Jones* attest, the enthusiasm which greeted the play's opening was as much for the atmosphere created by George Cram Cook's plaster dome (modeled upon the German *Kuppelhorizont*) and the interpretation of the title role by Charles Gilpin as for the play itself; similarly, reviews for *The Hairy Ape* hailed the stark contrast between Louis Wolheim's powerful performance and the cramped, claustrophobic stage settings designed by Cleon Throckmorton and Robert Edmond Jones, who had studied in Europe. But while European staging techniques may have been used to foreground the formal experimentation in O'Neill's plays, we should not assume that O'Neill's formal experimentation necessarily developed in response to these new techniques – especially since O'Neill repeatedly disavowed any German influence.

One reason critics may have been confused is O'Neill's own use of the term "expressionism" to describe the style of these two plays. Responding in frustration to critics who judged *The Hairy Ape* according to a standard of realism, for example, O'Neill complained: "People think I am [trying to] giv[e] an exact picture of reality. They don't understand that the whole play is expressionistic. Yank is really yourself, and myself. He is every human being" (quoted in Gelb 499). In other words, "expressionism" for O'Neill is a means of universalizing human experience. Unfortunately, this use of the term "expressionistic" caused him problems as well. For, as practiced and imported by German theatre artists, Expressionism tended to reduce character to an abstraction, a cipher, a mere symbol – exactly the opposite of his aims for this play. Possibly thinking of German Expressionism, some critics saw Yank as a pure symbol of the exploited worker, leading them to regard the play as a call for radical reform, for which O'Neill was either heralded or scolded, much to his amusement if not also his chagrin (Sheaffer 88). With regard to the German movement, O'Neill later said, "I personally do not believe that an idea can be readily put over to an audience except through characters . . . When [an audience] sees A Man and A Woman – just abstractions, it loses the human contact by which it identifies itself with the protagonist of the play" (quoted in Gelb 499).

The problem lies in two different uses of the term "expressionism." On the one hand, it appears to describe applications of Curry's theory of expression (whether faithful or not). On the other, it refers to the specific practice of German playwrights such as Frank Wedekind, Georg Kaiser, and Ernst Toller. Thus, the mistake that critics have made from O'Neill's day to our own is in associating the term exclusively with the German movement. What has been overlooked is the important cultural and critical context of the expressive culture movement and the artistic practices that it spawned. As I hope to have demonstrated here, it was the expressive culture movement – not German Expressionism – that provided O'Neill with a formal vocabulary for creating his early psychological portraits of humanity in conflict with the spiritual universe. It was the expressive culture movement that provided him with the ability to tell two stories at once – one on the level of content, one on the level of form. Where the former allowed him to express feelings of guilt and fear, the latter allowed him to fulfill his wish to put such feelings to rest. Understanding these two plays as affective autobiographies, then, allows us to place them back into the corpus of O'Neill's mostly autobiographical drama.

Confused and annoyed by critics' attempts to pigeon-hole the stylistic experimentation in his work, O'Neill once complained, "To be called a sordid Realist one day, a grim, pessimistic Naturalist the next, a lying Moral Romanticist the next, an immoral violent Expressionist the next, etc., etc. is quite perplexing" (quoted in Bogard and Bryer 195). Thus forced to retreat from giving his stylistic choices names at all, O'Neill remarked with exasperation, "Whether *The Hairy Ape* . . . is to be classified as an Expressionistic play or not is of little consequence . . . Its manner is inseparable from its matter" (quoted in Gelb 499).[30]

5

Elmer Rice and the cinematic imagination

IN A LETTER DATED 21 AUGUST 1922, POSTMARKED EAST HAMPTON, Elmer Rice writes his boyhood friend and legal counsel Frank Harris to say that he has just emerged from an experience that has left him "limp." "It was grand though!" he declares. "The best time I've had in years and years." The experience to which he refers was the intense composition of his expressionist work *The Adding Machine* (1922; 1923), a play he wrote in only seventeen days. "It's very different from anything I've ever done," he notes. "It's new – a radical departure in technique and subject matter (for me, at any rate)." Although he goes on to admit that he doesn't know whether the play is any good, he enthuses that it was "the most spontaneous, the most deeply-felt thing I've ever done."

> For the moment, then, I'm out of the bog in which I've been floundering. The sense of frustration which has been choking me for four years has abated. I actually feel a consciousness of liberation, a relief from a state of psychic congestion which I cannot help believing strongly akin to that physical congestion which the physiologists tell us finds relief in a sexual orgasm. This may strike you as far-fetched, but it comes nearer to conveying my present condition than anything else that occurs to me. (letter 8/21/22)[1]

Comparing the psychological experience of writing the play to sexual release, Rice provides his literary biographers with important information about the composition of this critically misunderstood play. For, where scholars have long insisted that the play was modeled on German expressionism, Rice's correspondence provides evidence for his long-held claim that it was "a spontaneous thing. I had no experience with German expressionism at that time" (Elwood 3). Revealing the state of creative possession in which *The*

Adding Machine was composed, Rice's letter invites us to read the play in much the same way we did O'Neill's expressionist works – as a fantasm, encoding both a psychological problem and its resolution in imaginative form.

Rice himself suggests that the play functioned as a fantasm in his 1963 autobiography, *Minority Report*. There, he ingenuously tells us that the play allowed him psychologically to unburden himself of the mixed feelings he had for his father,[2] a bookkeeper whose epileptic condition kept him from holding a steady job or inspiring much affection in his son:

> Not the least puzzling part of the cathartic effect that the writing of the play had on me was the purging of my lingering antagonism toward my father. I had never really hated him, but I had always resented his failure to measure up to my standards of fatherhood. Now my animosity was washed away and replaced, not by love certainly, but by a kind of pity. I cannot explain the connection between this abatement and the writing of *The Adding Machine*. It was not as though I had vented my ill-will by portraying my father in an unfavorable light. For, though he had many of Mr. Zero's prejudices and malevolences, he was proud, self-assertive and anything but a conformist. My release is part of the mystery that enshrouds the whole creation of the play. (*Minority Report* 191)

Thus, it would seem that, like O'Neill's *The Emperor Jones*, Rice's *The Adding Machine* functioned as a wishful resolution to the author's oedipal crisis, its expressionistic form a means of effecting that resolution.

But, as Rice acknowledges, the play is not simply about his feelings for his father. The issues of pride, self-assertion, and non-conformity – or, rather, the lack thereof – are central to his conception of Mr. Zero, suggesting that there is another source for his main character. Indeed, as his letter to Harris attests, the play seems to be as much about himself as about his father (or perhaps himself refracted through the lens of his father) insofar as it released him from the "bog in which [he'd] been floundering." But what exactly was that "bog"? What was causing the "sense of frustration" that had been "choking" him for four years? And, most important, how did the play function to release him from this "state of psychic congestion"? In this chapter, I draw from Rice's personal correspondence to suggest answers to these questions and propose a reading of the play. As I demonstrate, many of these questions can be answered with reference to Rice's experience in Hollywood, working for Samuel Goldwyn and Jesse Lasky between 1919 and 1921. For it was there, working within the Hollywood dream factory, that Rice first felt what it was like to be a "zero," ground down by an industry that threatened to replace him (and the theatrical values he represented) with a machine. And it was there that he learned to disarticulate verbal and vocal languages from a story that was told through pantomimic means.

Life by the numbers

As its title indicates, *The Adding Machine* is about a machine that adds figures. But the machine to which it refers is not the one that replaces the central character, Mr. Zero, in his job – it is Zero himself. Programmed to perform a set task, Zero is able to do little else, rarely deviating from the script society has handed him on how to live his life. Though he takes furtive pleasure in watching a woman across the courtyard undress, he outwardly adheres to conventional moral standards, channeling his voyeuristic desires into watching the films that his shrewish wife demands to see. Like his name, Mr. Zero is a nonentity, a cipher, the empty set, null. A poor working drudge, he lives only to fulfill this routine. Thus when his boss fires him after twenty-five years of faithful service, Zero finds himself unable to cope and, in a moment of unexpected passion, plunges a bill file through his boss's heart. Returning home to a dinner party with "red ink" on his collar, he waits for the police. The "red ink," of course, is blood but its significance is the same – Zero's luck is running at a deficit. The man who simply "ain't got the nerve" to take a mistress (*The Adding Machine* 57), confess his love to his co-worker, Daisy (102), or tell his boss to shut up (55) is summarily sentenced to execution by a jury of his peers. Passing into the afterlife, Zero – along with Shrdlu, a fellow traveler across the river Styx – is disappointed to find that the conventional morality they lived by on earth is not the morality that abides in heaven. Ironically, the very misdeeds for which they were punished are their passports to paradise. Unable to accept this new state of affairs, Zero leaves the Elysian Fields and the happy life he and the recently suicided Daisy could have there in order to return to the familiar comforts of routine: he operates an adding machine in limbo. From there he is called up for active duty by Lt. Charles, the commanding officer of a "repair and service station – a sort of cosmic laundry" for recycled souls (129). Noting that Zero's past lives have traced a pattern of evolutionary descent, Lt. Charles nonetheless manages to convince

Zero to return to a life of even more unimaginative drudgery by con-
juring up an illusory vixen named Hope, whom Zero hastily pursues off
stage.

As this synopsis makes clear, the play, though a comedy, is remarkably cynical. Not only does it suggest that life is literally a hopeless
journey, marked by stupidity, conformity, and fear, but its central character
is completely without redemption. Although, as we've seen in chapter 4,
O'Neill's anti-heroes are similarly unredeemed, they are not without hope.
In death, at least, they are allowed the possibility of finding some kind of
ameliorating solace, one we desperately long for them to find. In *The Adding
Machine*, by contrast, Rice gives us a character who is unable to achieve transcendence – even in death, even when it is freely offered him and ready for
the taking. Refusing to accept the Nietzschean code of individual morality
that governs the Elysian Fields, Zero prefers to conform to a moral standard that is comfortingly familiar and requires only thoughtless obedience.
He is a "poor, spineless, brainless boob" (138) to whom we respond with
derisive laughter. But even the laughter is unsettling. For, if we laugh with
Joe, Lt. Charles's assistant, who finds Zero's gullibility utterly ridiculous,
we find ourselves immediately chastened, as Charles punches Joe in the jaw.
Rubbing his jaw in surrender, Joe leaves to prepare for the next soul's arrival,
while Charles shakes his head and despairs, "Hell, I'll tell the world this is
a lousy job!" As the curtain falls, "He takes a flask from his pocket, uncorks
it and slowly drains it."[3]

Critic Robert Hogan describes Charles's last line as "a bitterly apt fillip
to end on" (31), arguing that "The play is, despite its amusing satire, a grim
and black comedy dissecting the soul of the machine-conditioned man and
finding nothing there" (31). Frank Durham agrees, describing Zero as "a
less cerebral J. Alfred Prufrock" (49), whose tragedy lies in his fearful relationship to a world where technological progress "is accompanied by human
retrogression" (51). Even so, Durham is discomfited by the pessimistic mood
of this play, finding it uncharacteristic of Rice's work. Arguing that Rice
both lived and dramatized the promise of the American Dream, Durham
suggests that, in painting such a dire portrait of modern man in this play,
Rice may have been advocating a "cataclysmic revolution . . . to force an
exchange of positions by the masters and the slaves" (52). Although I appre-
ciate his attempt to reconcile *The Adding Machine* with the rest of Rice's
corpus, I find Durham's interpretation untenable. There is simply no evidence to support his contention that the play was meant to rouse its audience

to protest or revolution. The play is pessimistic, yes, in terms of the story it tells, but the optimism that Durham sees as characteristic of Rice's work is there, too. It is just less evident, being encoded in the play's expressionistic form.

On the level of narrative, however, the play is cynical, indeed. A Nietzschean fable of modern man, it is the tale of a hapless man, a "slave," who is in thrall to a "herd mentality" of conventional morality, and thus incapable of evolving into an *Übermensch* for the future. From the moment the play begins, we see Zero silently subjected to the pressures of work and home. As his wife harangues him about his various inadequacies, he distracts himself with thoughts of nothing, residue of the day's work having co-opted his brain. This impression is masterfully created by the tableau of a man lying in bed, surrounded by numbers projected on the wall, while his wife sits talking at her vanity, undressing as she dresses him down. Indeed, as we'll see, tightly constructed visual images like this form the backbone of the play, often standing alone from or commenting ironically on the characters' dialogue. Yet, as Hogan points out, Mrs. Zero's monologue is not unimportant. Although it would seem to simply verbalize the visual image of the scene, "its effect depends upon the beautiful variations of exasperation that an actress gives to the constant repetition of a single idea. It must be a repetition stressing that each rephrasal is to her not a rephrasal but almost a new discovery of bitterness" (Hogan 33). Besides providing an aural accompaniment to this visual tableau, however, Mrs. Zero's monologue is important for the Nietzschean themes that, in it, Rice lays out. For, if we listen to the substance of Mrs. Zero's complaints, we hear the echo of a *ressentiment* that is particular to the American middle class, born of its uncomfortable capitulation to a punitive morality internalized as "respectability."

Speaking of the films she has seen, wants to see, or probably never will see, Mrs. Zero declares in the play's opening line, "I'm gettin' sick o' them Westerns." Presumably, this genre is a favorite of Zero's. She, on the other hand, prefers comedies or "them sweet little love stories" such as *For Love's Sweet Sake* or *A Mother's Tears* (*The Adding Machine* 2). Anthony Palmieri has pointed out the irony in "Mrs. Zero's purported predilection for movies," given "her own ugly love relationship with her husband" (61). But there is another irony at work as well. Them sweet little love stories are not as "nice an' wholesome" as she insists; for, in recounting the stories that they tell, Mrs. Zero reveals that they often revel in the depiction of their heroine's threatened virtue. Although the heroine is saved and the villain punished at the end, the moral order that these films restore is less their vaunted goal than the rationale that allows them to represent villainy in its most salacious form.

The so-called reform melodramas to which Mrs. Zero refers only began to appear after 1908, when filmmakers were forced to respond to complaints that movies were corrupting society's morals. As film historian Lary May explains, 1908 was the year when New York City mayor George B. McClellan, Jr. ordered all of the city's nickelodeons and movie houses closed (43). Although the owners and operators of these mostly Lower East Side establishments managed to evade this injunction long before it was officially rescinded, they soon found themselves subject to Mayor William Gaynor's Motion Picture Ordinance of 1912. That ordinance, too, was aimed at elevating the moral tone of the city's amusements. But, instead of prohibiting films, it increased licensing fees "in an effort to bring a 'better' class of businessmen into the movies," and enforced safety inspections in order to assure the well-being of middle-class patrons (May 57). In this way, the Motion Picture Ordinance of 1912 implemented an official system of regulation that could be used unofficially to police the content of films shown.

Such unofficial regulation came from the National Board of Review, a volunteer organization of citizens who independently rated films. Determining which films were fit for viewing and which were not, the National Board of Review exerted a tremendous influence on the viewing habits of audiences. Its influence, moreover, extended well beyond the limits of New York, with many communities adopting its recommendations when determining their programming needs (May 57). The Board's seal of approval, then, meant greater profits for those filmmakers whose films conformed to its moral standards. In this way, reformers were able to influence the making as well as showing of films. As Frederic Howe, the Board's president, explained: "If a producer refused to abide by the action of the Board, pressure is brought to bear on him by the rejection of his output by the local agencies throughout the country, which if continued long enough will destroy his concern, his standing, or seriously cripple his business" (quoted in May 57). Given such pressures, films made in the 1910s began to reflect a greater concern for conventional morality, often adopting the formula of the reform melodrama so popular on the stage. Those that did not risked having scenes cut or being censored altogether. For, if a movie house showed a film that did not meet the Board's approval, it could be shut down for any

Figure 8. Scene 3 from Elmer Rice's *The Adding Machine.* As Zero's dinner guests assemble, he still has work on his mind.

one of a number of "safety" violations. The trick, then, for filmmakers was to include sensational scenes that could be contained within a putatively moral framework. Even so, such scenes often ended up getting cut, especially by the time they made it uptown to the second-run movie houses. This would seem to be the subtext of Mrs. Zero's complaint that they never get to see first-run films. Lamenting that she missed the presumably titillating cabaret scene cut from *The Price of Virtue* (*The Adding Machine* 4), Mrs. Zero mollifies herself by claiming to be above all the "rough stuff" they show in films these days. Rice's critique, then, would seem to be directed not only at the hypocrisy of a culture that sells titillation in the guise of salvation, but at that of its citizens who vicariously indulge their basest appetites while pleading their own moral goodness. The Zeroes are Nietzschean slaves, subject to a "herd mentality" that thoughtlessly subscribes to a standard of conventional morality, despite the longings of their own individual wills. Palmieri identifies this as one of Rice's persistent themes – "the destructiveness of Puritanical morality" (84).

The coercive power of this herd mentality is shown in scene three during the dinner party that the Zeroes throw for their friends, the Ones, the Twos, the Threes, the Fours, the Fives, and the Sixes. Although Zero has just broken free from the Judaeo-Christian ethic "Thou Shalt Not Kill" by murdering his boss, he meekly returns home to his wife and the conventional middle-class values which define their and their friends' lives. Rice demonstrates their conformity in comically grotesque fashion, noting that the "men are all shapes and sizes, but their dress is identical with that of Zero in every detail. Each, however, wears a wig of a different color. The women are all dressed alike, too, except that the dress of each is of a different color" (36). If their clothes serve as a badge of their conformity, their conversation testifies to the oath of stultifying likemindedness they have sworn. The women cannot discuss the merits and demerits of lace trim without immediately reconciling contradictory viewpoints into agreement. The men similarly forge a sense of solidarity by defining themselves against a whole host of others, from unruly women who make too many demands at home to foreign agitators who make too many demands at work. Counterpointing the women's and men's conversations in a sort of theme and variation on inanity, Rice unifies them into a final rousing chorus when, in response to Six's strident shout "America is for the Americans is what I say!," they chant: "That's it! Damn foreigners! Damn dagoes! Damn Catholics! Damn sheenies! Damn niggers! Jail 'em! shoot 'em! hang 'em! lynch 'em! burn 'em!" (47). The herd is stomping mad and ready to charge anyone who threatens their pride.

Even Zero. For, as we see in scene four, Zero's dinner guests are also the jurors at his trial. Although Zero admits to killing his boss, he is not strong enough to take responsibility for his action.[4] Rather, he capitulates to convention and dutifully toes the moral line, explaining that he didn't kill his boss on principle, as the representative of an unjust system of labor; he killed him because he "didn't have the nerve" to tell his boss to shut up. Throughout Zero's testimony, the jurors are implacable, "staring stolidly before them" (51). But, when Zero implicitly implicates them in his guilt, affirming that he's "just a regular guy like anybody else. Like you birds, now," the jurors look "indignantly at each other" and shout "GUILTY" in unison (59–60).

One would think that Zero would disidentify with a way of thinking that condemned him to death. The play's doleful comedy, however, lies in its repetition. Zero never learns and never will. And there is nothing in the cosmic universe that will lead him toward salvation. As Palmieri observes,

the eight courses of ham and eggs that the incarcerated Zero has ordered
for his final supper only further reveal that "he lacks the imagination and
the inclination to break the pattern of repetition to which he has become
inured" (66). As Zero sits in his jail cell, lapping up his ham and eggs, "The
Fixer" stands nearby, picking his teeth if not paring his nails, his indifference
nonetheless evident.[5] If for Nietzsche God is dead, for Rice he is absent at
best, sending in The Fixer and Lt. Charles to do his dirty work.

The play's repetition, then, is not only comic but cosmic as well, as Zero
returns to earth, destined to repeat his mistakes. Following the path of
evolutionary descent, Zero is the antithesis of Nietzsche's *Übermensch*. He
is unable to assert his individual will and break the bonds of servitude to
chart a path of progress into the future for humankind. Rather, he will
chart its regress, a downward spiral circling back over the tired old theme of
life's unending struggle. With a knowing wink, Rice does much the same,
scripting Zero's life out of tired old storylines borrowed from recent films.

The Clerk (1914), for example, concerns "the slave of the office who has
no labor union to champion his cause and faces a lifetime of drudgery,"
according to a contemporary issue of *Motion Picture World*. In Lary May's
terms, it is about "a young man constrained by a drab office, a time clock,
and a boring job. Seeking relief, he turns to romance with a young secretary
in the office. Though they fall in love, the hero eventually loses her to
his boss. In despair, he kills his employer and goes to jail" (102–3). Clearly,
Georg Kaiser was not the first to detail the anomie and sordid desperation of
modern clerical work in his play *From Morn to Midnight*. Indeed, it would
seem that much of the plot to the first half of Rice's play was borrowed
not from the 1922 American stage debut of Kaiser's play but from this and
perhaps other films.

A Bedroom Blunder (1916), for example, similarly "opens on a young clerk,
Mr. Murphy, who slaves at his office, rarely finding any excitement in life."
Returning to May for a synopsis, we find that

> Finally he takes his staid wife to Atlantic City, one of the new amuse-
> ment beaches. But when she "was careless enough to let him sit by the
> window," the sorry hero looks out to the strand where beautiful women
> sunbathe. Among the Sennett Bathing Beauties is Mary, whose flouncey
> stride makes her "the chief wigglette of Wigglesville." To make matters
> worse, during the dinner hour when Mrs. Murphy is out, the hotel clerk
> accidentally puts Mary in Mr. Murphy's room. Soon the police are called
> in, along with the house detective, to put a stop to what seems to be a
> bedroom affair. (104)

A farce, "where the police, the hapless couple, and Mary are all made to look ludicrous" (May 104), this film would seem to provide the germ of the story concerning Judy O'Grady, the good-time girl who lives across the courtyard. As we learn in scene one, Mrs. Zero has also been "careless enough to let [her husband] sit by the window," where he has indulged his voyeuristic fantasies by watching Judy undress every night. In an effort to punish them both, Mrs. Zero has Judy arrested for indecent exposure, calling her a "dirty bum" who has no right living "in a house with respectable people" (6). But, where *A Bedroom Blunder* gently ridicules the beleaguered Murphy and his staid wife for their repressive attitudes toward sex, Rice's play contemptuously mocks the equally beleaguered Zero and his staid wife for internalizing their repression as *ressentiment*.

Long before Theodore Adorno and Max Horkheimer came to the United States and were horrified by the proto-fascistic "culture industry," Rice was making his own sort of Frankfurt School critique. What he seems to be saying here is that the stories lifted from these films were never original to begin with.[6] Even when these films were first released, they were already hackneyed and stale. What is worse is that film audiences not only are moved by them but substitute them for their own emotional lives. Poor Daisy has gone her whole life without a kiss, but imagines what it would be like from having seen *The Devil's Alibi*. Only when she gets to heaven does she allow herself to experience the real thing. And it is from film that she gets the idea to kill herself. Although she hates the smell of gas and is afraid to ask for carbolic acid or poison, she fantasizes that suicide is glamorous, having seen Pauline Frederick do it in the movies (15). In borrowing or alluding to plots that are so recognizably unoriginal, then, Rice would seem to be suggesting that his characters' lives are similarly not original; that they think they are is what makes them pitiable and ridiculous.

How strange, then, that a play that is so cynical toward its central character and, indeed, toward life in general should have filled its author with so much joy upon its completion! What could possibly have motivated Rice to write it, let alone take so much pleasure in having done so? The answer, I believe, lies in the play's many references to film. For, when Rice wrote this play, he had just returned to the East Coast after an unhappy two-year stint working in Hollywood. Finally released from his contractual obligations to resume his playwriting career, Rice reflected back on this period in which his initial optimism about the film industry had turned sour, plunging him into a profound funk from which he was able to emerge only upon regaining his artistic freedom. What I want to suggest here is that the play may have functioned as a sort of exorcism, allowing Rice to cast off his feelings of servitude to the Hollywood system. Writing from the distance of East Hampton, a year after leaving California, he was able to look back and simultaneously lament having been a slave to the Hollywood system and revel in having broken free from its constraints. Understood as an affective allegory of his Hollywood sojourn, then, the play figures Rice both as its downtrodden central character and as its triumphant playwright, the *Übermensch* who evolves out of his former slave self.[7]

"Continuity man"

In the summer of 1919, Rice moved to Hollywood, lured by the burgeoning film industry's promise of more consistent and better-paying work. Although he had shrewdly conserved much of the profit from his smash hit *On Trial* (1914), Rice knew that he could not live on its proceeds forever. He needed another success, but was having difficulty finding a producer willing to mount any of the plays he had written. He was also having a creative dry spell, unable to write anything new. Further compounding the problem was the fact that his financial obligations had grown. Having won the hand of Hazel Levy, who had earlier spurned him for his poor financial prospects, Rice found himself with a wife and, quickly thereafter, a child to support. In his autobiography, Rice recalls this period of his life, remembering that he

> had heavy economic responsibilities, and I wanted to be free to experiment and to find my way without being harassed by money worries. I remembered Mr. Micawber's dictum, "Annual income twenty pounds, annual expenditure twenty pounds ought and six, result misery." I had before me, too, the image of my father, sitting night after night, covering sheets of paper with columns of tiny figures, trying to solve the daily problem of making ends meet. (*Minority Report* 133)

He was beginning to feel like he was becoming his father – a man so beaten down by life and work that he was little more than an adding machine. With financial concerns thus heavy on his mind and no prospects of another theatrical success, Rice decided to accept Samuel Goldwyn's offer of a five-year contract and move to Hollywood, feeling that "a complete change of scene and a wholly new activity might pull me out of the bog in which I was floundering" (*Minority Report* 170).

Curiously, Rice's critics have failed to consider the significance of his Hollywood adventure, briefly dismissing it, if they discuss it at all (Hogan 27; Durham 27, 34; Palmieri 54, 56; Vanden Heuvel makes no mention whatsoever). But an examination of his correspondence with Frank Harris during this period reveals that it was an important period in his life – both in terms of his personal development, and also in terms of his career. In Hollywood, Rice not only further developed his talent for plotting action, but learned to do so almost wholly through visual means.

Writing to Harris shortly after his arrival in Hollywood, for example, Rice describes his new duties at the Goldywn Studios in remarkable detail:

> The first job . . . is to work out a story synopsis giving in narrative form the thread of the story. This is read and passed upon by any number of people – usually the director and sometimes the star is called into conference. That means as a rule, a re-hashing of the material. When the story thread is satisfactory, the continuity work begins. What is called a continuity synopsis is worked out. In this the action, motivation, and so on are set forth in great detail and more or less in sequence, but without actually breaking it up into scenes for the camera. Titles, too, are roughly indicated. (Titling, by the way, is one of the most important features of the work.)
>
> After the continuity synopsis has been approved, the continuity is written. This is nothing less than a detailed scene synopsis of exactly what you see upon the screen. In other words, if the continuity man does a good job, his script when it goes to the director indicates every camera angle, every close-up, every title, every bit of business which appears in the finished picture. A picture averages about 250 scenes, so you can readily see that the continuity man has plenty to do. Of course, it's hack-work routine, a good deal of it – but a skillful continuity can camouflage a bad story, whereas a good story can easily be bungled by bad continuity. (Letter 9/10/19)

As he notes, writing for film is quite different from writing for the theatre, being less the domain of an individual artist than the corporate body of the film industry. And, though he acknowledges that "it's hack-work routine, a good deal of it," he is mostly optimistic about his responsibilities as a "continuity man" in the exciting enterprise of film. Part of his enthusiasm comes from the way he is learning to think in new ways about his craft. As he tells Harris, "It's a distinct medium adapted to the portrayal of action, and to nothing else. You can't be subtle, you can't put over ideas (unless they are extremely obvious) and you can't develop character in any real sense." There is also, he tells Harris, great potential for the writing of original screenplays: "The demand for material is simply enormous and eventually they'll exhaust the supply and then they'll have to turn to the men who can give them original material." Brimming with hopeful energy at the artistic possibilities offered by the film medium, Rice concludes his letter by encouraging Harris, his sometime collaborator, to submit any story ideas he might have. Try to "aim at variety of scene and put in all the incident you can," he advises. Think "stirring, quickly-moving action. Tricks, surprise, mystery, all help" (letter 9/10/19).

Unfortunately, Rice's optimism quickly turned sour – not so much because of the work itself, but because of his boss's mercurial manner. Inspired by Goldwyn's vision that film was soon to become a writer's medium, Rice was surprised to find Goldwyn so indifferent toward him when he arrived and so casual about when he reported to work (*Minority Report* 171). Yet, when Rice requested a temporary leave to oversee the troubled production of his play *Find the Woman* in September, Goldwyn refused (letter 9/26/19), leaving Rice at the mercy of Richard Bennett, the producer and star actor of the play, who had assigned himself the task of making revisions to Rice's script.[8] Bennett, it seems, enlarged his part so substantially that he felt it was a new play and so retitled it *For the Defense*, copyrighting it in his own name (Palmieri 10). Understandably, Rice felt betrayed, initially seeking to sue Bennett but settling for the restoration of copyright. But further aggravating his frustration was Goldwyn's refusal to let him leave. Goldwyn later relented, granting him a two-week leave to right the wrong that had been done him and salvage what he could of the play (*Minority Report* 175–7).

Three months later, Rice was still in a funk, sickened not only by Bennett's vanity and greed, but by his indenture to the Hollywood system. Increasingly, he began to resent his work, complaining bitterly about the astronomical salaries of stars and directors when "it's the story that counts" (letter 2/9/20). One director made $1,200 a week, he reports, compared to the disproportionate (but nonetheless respectable) $200 he brought home weekly. For all of Goldwyn's promises to nurture writers and establish the art of screenwriting, Rice found that Hollywood was first and foremost an industry where storylines were written by committee and/or added after the fact.

Indeed, Hollywood was an industry and had been deliberately created as such between 1912 and 1920. This was the period, according to May, when businessmen such as Samuel Goldwyn, who started out as a glove-maker, applied their organizational skills to the art of filmmaking, merging methods of mass production with a system of mass distribution to create the film industry (176). Their strategy proved successful: "Assembly line techniques and specialization encouraged high production, and yielded seventy films a year" (May 187). But such methods necessarily compromised any one contributer's artistic control, since he or she was responsible for only one portion of the process. Thus, as a writer, Rice may very well have felt like the screenwriter depicted in *The Original Movie* (1922), puppeteer Tony Sarg and filmmaker Herbert Dawley's animated spoof of the film industry. Poking fun at the specialized labor processes used to generate films, it traces the progress of a movie script from its author's typewriter to the producer's desk to the cast's adaptations to the director's film to the censor's edits to the editor's cutting room and back to the author who, sitting in the audience, is no longer able to recognize his script in the finished film.

In fact, Rice himself admits to having been enlisted in the cause of altering someone else's scenario – even after it had been produced. By cutting some scenes, reintroducing discarded footage and writing new intertitles, Rice changed a "heavy-handed 'satire' on 'parlor Bolshevism'" into the story of a woman swept up in the belief that human souls could be reborn in the bodies of animals. "It was still a bad picture," Rice concedes, "but was now releasable," earning far more than he made the entire time he was employed at the studio (*Minority Report* 174–5). Despite his obvious pride in the film's success, this account provides only further evidence for Rice's general complaint that, in Hollywood, "Everything went into the old sausage machine and . . . came out looking and tasting alike" (179). In this case, he had got to play sausage grinder; more often than not, he provided the meat.

By December 1919, Rice was thoroughly fed up with the Hollywood system. Even a visit to a local vaudeville house could not chase away his blue devils. In a letter to Harris, he reports that it not only proved disappointing, but made him "more firmly persuaded than ever that the human race is damned" (letter 12/22/19). Such hopelessness is strange in that it begins a letter that should be full of hope, as Rice meditates on the anticipated birth of his second child. Reflecting fondly on the young life of his first child, Rice's initially optimistic ruminations quickly turn black again upon considering how the immense potential within one little life remains largely unrealized in the great mass of humankind.

And even admitting that progress [is] an illusion, that life is an endless cycle, a meaningless riddle – what you will; even admitting that, it seems to me that the task [of rearing a child] is not a contemptible one; for at least, the individual's span of life is real and vivid and filled with potentialities, the era in which he moves can be enriched or debased by the emanations of his personality.

Briefly mocking himself for "his highfalutin method of giving a grandiose flourish to what may be merely a purely animal instinct to perpetuate the race," Rice concludes with despair that he is "beginning to think that mankind is a failure: certainly, a failure as a race of god-like creatures, possessed of immortal souls, and to judge by the physical conditions in which the bulk of men live, a failure as a species of animal, too" (letter 12/22/19). Sounding much like Lt. Charles, Rice reflects upon sending a life "filled with potentialities" into a world full of cowardice, conformity, pettiness, and greed.

Although Harris's response does not survive, it must have expressed anxious concern for his friend, reminding Rice that he had many more reasons for living than despairing of life. For, in his next letter, Rice replies that Harris has simply not understood his meaning; he never said life was not worth living. "What I did say is that it appears to me – at this moment, at least – that human progress is an illusion, the utopian future a mirage. My leaving New York has completed the process of disillusionment which five years of war and the aftermath of war, began and advanced." In speaking of having left New York, Rice notes that he has left the familiar comforts behind to face the stark reality of life without such blinders. Here in California, he explains, "I see things more objectively."

I see a welter of God's images stewing in all the lusts and cruelties of the jungle . . . I no longer see the potential god shining through the thick skin of my fellow-man. Do you? Do you see anything godlike in your naive neighbor in the subway or your learned opponent in the municipal court? I tell you I am sick unto death of the joyless, brainless, humorless optimism which fills the air with its stink. (Letter 1/15/20)

Although his plaints appear to be directed at life in general, his lament about the "the joyless, brainless, humorless optimism which fills the air with its stink" would seem to be directed at Hollywood more specifically, its canned entertainments more specifically yet. Although he says the move from New York to California has made him see things "more objectively," it is also clearly responsible for his new perspective on life. Reconciling himself to this gloomy awakening, Rice suggests that the only thing we can do is live our lives as best we can. "The answer is not suicide or negation," he concludes,

> but rather the determination to make one's life – the one physical certainty! – more useful and more complete; to expend one's energies in bringing happiness to oneself and as many others as possible; to do what one can to make the world more beautiful, less cruel, less stupid, here and now. In a word[,] to spend one's talents upon one's own generation, instead of investing them in a mythical after-life or an equally mythical racial future. (letter 1/15/20)

Perhaps mocking his youthful ambitions of success, Rice resignedly suggests that his children alone rather than his work are capable of providing him with meaningful satisfaction.

Eventually, Rice did crawl out of his slough of despond. His spirits marginally improved with his reassignment from continuity to title editing. "I'm rather glad of the change," he tries to convince himself in a letter of 18 March 1920.

> Continuity writing is fairly interesting, but much of it is purely mechanical. After the story is blocked out, the detail work is rather tiresome. There is not much scope for originality or imaginativeness. And it's work that doesn't lead one anywhere, in particular. Besides, it's more likely than not to be thankless: if the picture is successful, the director gets the credit. If it fails, the continuity writer is blamed. (letter 3/18/20)

Such attempts to will himself into a better mood were not enough, however, to keep him satisfied for very long. A month later he was debating about whether or not to renew his contract, about whether or not to give up financial security for greater freedom to pursue his own work (letter 4/15/20). "There are moments when I long to be free again and the motion picture industry is not always absorbing," he remarks in an understatement devoid of irony. "On the other hand, my surroundings are pleasant, I am well-treated, the work is not irksome – and a salary of $250 per week is not to be [despised]" (letter of 5/27/20). Indeed, as May reports, good salaries, a comfortable work environment, and access to leisure facilities were among the perks offered by the studios to keep organized labor at bay (187).[9] They certainly proved a strong enough inducement to convince Rice that he was happy for a while. Informing Harris that he had received verbal assurance that nothing in his contract prevented him from pursuing his own playwriting work,

Rice decided to renew his contract in May of 1920 (letter of 5/27/20). Upon reviewing the contract, however, Harris reported that he found nothing to support such an assurance. Rice replies that he is disappointed but resigned (letter of 6/20/20).

Two months later, however, Rice was still trying to talk himself out of despair: "I don't regret at all having come out. On the contrary, my movie experience has been very valuable in more than one way and I wouldn't have missed it, for a great deal. But I feel that I've had enough; that henceforth, I'd be wasting my time – and I'm anxious to get back to work" (letter 8/27/20). By getting back to work, Rice meant getting back to the writing of plays. But, while he flirted with the possibility of working as a freelance in order to make his time his own, he could never quite bring himself to leave his job and the reliable income it represented.

Finally, an opportunity presented itself for Rice to buy back his freedom. On a train from San Francisco to Los Angeles, Rice had a chance encounter with Will Rogers, one of Goldwyn's biggest stars for whom he had written scenarios in the past. As Rice recounts in his autobiography, Rogers "complained about the poor quality of his story material and asked me to try to write something suitable for him" (180). He did. Drawing upon the anachronism so humorously treated in Twain's *A Connecticut Yankee in King Arthur's Court*, Rice wrote a story about a cowboy who, frustrated by his inept skills at lovemaking, dreams that he is Romeo to his beloved's Juliet. "It gave Rogers a good opportunity to display his gaucherie amid the trappings of the Renaissance," Rice approvingly assessed (*Minority Report* 180). Entitled *Doubling for Romeo*, the film was a big success at the box office. It was also a success in terms of Rice's career. With Rogers's support for the screenplay, Rice was able to leverage a deal whereby the sale of the scenario was conditioned upon his release from the studio's contract. The studio – in the person of his superior, Thompson Buchanan – agreed, but with an added condition: Rice had to invest half of his proceeds from the sale into a speculative (and ultimately unprofitable) oil company that Buchanan was setting up. Although Buchanan probably thought he had put one over on the inexperienced young writer, Rice felt the extortionate price was well worth paying for his freedom (*Minority Report* 180–1).

Thus, in December 1920, Rice finally and irrevocably made up his mind to leave the studio. In a spirit of renewed self-confidence, Rice wrote to Harris with the news of his decision, justifying his reasons for leaving: production is slow, the economy's bad, people are being laid off, and the hostility toward theatre practitioners, he reports, has never abated (letter 12/14/20). "So I shan't be sorry when my connection with the Goldwyn company ceases," he writes. "No one possessed of an independent spirit or the desire to create should be a job-holder. The great mass of men seems to have a taste for time-serving and petty intrigue. I know no meanness like the meanness attendant upon self-preferment" (letter 12/14/20).

Undoubtedly a reference to Buchanan's strong-armed tactics, Rice's vigorous pronouncements against "self-preferment" reveal the extent of his disgust at Hollywood and the business of filmmaking. But his lament for the "great mass of men" who seem "to have a taste for time-serving and petty intrigue" appears to be aimed at himself. That is, in defining himself against such a category of men, it is almost as if Rice is casting off a version of what he fears he has become – a man who willingly sells his "independent spirit" and "desire to create" for the financial security of being "a job-holder." Perhaps ashamed of having sold his soul for such a meaningless reward, Rice renounces Hollywood with the passion of a newly converted zealot – his anger compensatory for his previous self-deceit.

Having severed his ties with Goldwyn, Rice nonetheless remained in Los Angeles for the next six months, working as a freelance for Jesse Lasky, while trying to finance a move back to the East Coast. Although he was considerably happier in his new job (which Lasky offered to make permanent), Rice was forced to conclude that, "at best, motion-picture work is hack-work (for anyone who can – or thinks he can – do something else) and I don't feel like going back to it, unless I can see in it enough money, *immediately*, to assure my increasing my capital considerably" (letter 4/26/21).

That qualification "unless" reveals the extent to which Rice continued to be dogged by financial concerns. His play *Wake Up, Jonathan*, co-written with Hatcher Hughes, had opened in January 1921 to disappointing reviews (Vanden Heuvel 22). Further playwriting efforts were proving just as hard won. Even after returning to the East Coast, Rice "was finding it difficult to get back to playwriting," Palmieri tells us.

> Plagued by self-dissatisfaction, disheartened about his work, and doubtful about his future as a writer, he was toying with a multitude of ideas, inspired by none. Finally, it seems almost in desperation, he accepted an invitation from Walter Jordan, a theatrical agent, to dramatize Haydon Talbot's unpublished novel, *It is the Law*. The play, bearing the same title, and sharing its fate of being unpublished, ran for only fifteen weeks in New York in 1922. It provided Rice neither financial nor aesthetic satisfaction. (Palmieri 56)

To make matters worse, Jordan absconded with most of the money and, though threatened with prosecution, was unable to pay Rice back (Palmieri 11).[10] Like *For the Defense*, then, this crime drama featured as many misdeeds behind the scenes as were represented before the audience.

If he had thought that, by leaving Hollywood, he could escape the Scylla of unscrupulous business partners and the Charybdis of unrewarding work, he soon discovered that he was wrong. Perhaps for that reason, Rice allowed himself to be lured by Hollywood's siren song again.

This time it came from Mary Pickford and Douglas Fairbanks, founding principals of the new United Artists studio, who invited him to head their scenario department at a beginning salary of $700 per week. Rice was tempted by the prestige and, needless to say, the money, but ultimately lashed his desire to the mast, feeling that he did not want to surrender his artistic autonomy again. "I came away feeling virtuous," he admits, "but doubtful about the soundness of my judgment."

> In fact, I was doubtful about everything, ridden by uncertainty, discontent, and self-dissatisfaction. I felt I was getting nowhere, accomplishing nothing. I wanted knowledge, experience, understanding. I was disheartened about my work, wondering whether I really had a future as a writer. After two years in Hollywood, I found it hard to get back to playwriting. I toyed with one idea after another, but found none that fired me. The trouble was that everything was mentally contrived; what I wanted was something charged with emotion. But there was an emotional barrier that I seemed unable to break through. (*Minority Report* 188)

Thus, he found himself floundering in the bog once more, unable to think clearly or write freely, his emotional reservoir dammed. Until, that is, the waters rose and *The Adding Machine* rushed fully complete into his head.

Motion pictures

The Adding Machine, as we have seen, unfolds as a Nietschean fable. It is, in Rice's words, "the case history of one of the slave souls who are both the raw material and the product of a mechanized society" (*Minority Report* 190). But it is also, as we have seen, a fantasm in which Rice was able to express a tentative identification with and empathetic understanding of his father, based upon his own experience of trying to support a family by working at a soul-destroying job. The play, then, functions as an affective allegory of Rice's life in Hollywood, where Zero is a figure for

Rice himself, refracted through the lens of his father. Like Rice, Zero is a wage slave who limits his ambition to a culturally acceptable standard of success,[11] and unquestioningly defers to the authority of his boss. But if Zero is a figure for Rice-the-Hollywood-flunkie, he is also a figure that Rice-the-playwright definitively (and oedipally) rejects – not only in his cynical treatment of the character, but in the play's experimental form. By telling his story in a way that both uses and critiques the visual images he had learned to script as a "continuity man" in Hollywood, Rice ultimately trumps the industry that once oppressed him. For, having learned to plot stories through purely visual means, having worked within the limitations of the film medium like a poet perfecting his craft, Rice returned to the theatre with the ability to disarticulate and redeploy its verbal and vocal languages in new and complicating ways. This, as we'll see, not only helped reinvigorate the theatrical medium, but allowed him to critique the film industry's uncritical celebration of the image.[12] Thus, to return to Durham's concern that *The Adding Machine* is uncharacteristically pessimistic, we see that, while it recounts the dispiriting story of a man who is little more than a Nietzschean slave, it formally encodes that man's *übermenschean* triumph over his former slave self. Such "optimism" is only discernible, however, in an analysis of the play's use of verbal, vocal, and pantomimic languages.

As discussed earlier, the play begins with a densely packed visual image of a man prostrated by the pressures of work and home. Indeed, visual tableaux often illustrate the relationships between characters throughout the play. At the end of scene two, for instance, Rice depicts the anomie of modern office work in Zero's relationship to his co-worker, Daisy. With the shrill blast of a whistle, work is done, and the dramatic action shifts from speech to pantomime:

> *With great agility they get off their stools, remove their eye shades and sleeve protectors and put them on the desks. Then each produces from behind the desk a hat – Zero a dusty derby, Daisy, a frowsy straw . . . Daisy puts on her hat and turns toward Zero as though she were about to speak to him. But he is busy cleaning his pen and pays no attention to her. She sighs and goes toward the door at the left. (The Adding Machine 24)*

Zero says goodnight, "But she does not hear him and exits. Zero takes up his hat and goes left" (25). As Durham observes, the pantomime makes "clear the desolate separateness of these two, their failure to communicate" (42).

More pantomimic action ensues as the play's most powerful image closes the scene. Just as Zero is about to leave, he encounters his boss, who, rather than promote him or grant him a raise as expected, fires Zero with remarkably callous indifference. The boss continues to speak, spouting platitudes and insipid excuses, but, as Durham notes, his speech "breaks down into jagged stock phrases, disconnected but meaningful in their very emptiness" (43). Meanwhile, Zero's mind begins to whirl: "[T]he sound of the mechanical player of a distant merry-go-round" is softly heard. "The part of the floor upon which the desk and stools are standing begins to revolve very slowly" (29). Gradually, the music increases in volume and the floor rotates more quickly. Although the boss's jaw continues to move, we are unable to hear what he says.

> *The music swells and swells. To it is added every off-stage effect of the theatre: the wind, the waves, the galloping horses, the locomotive whistle, the sleigh bells, the automobile siren, the glass-crash. New Year's Eve, Election Night, Armistice Day, and the Mardi-Gras. The noise is deafening, maddening, unendurable. Suddenly it culminates in a terrific peal of thunder. For an instant there is a flash of red and then everything is plunged into blackness.* (30)

This "brainstorm," as Rice called it, is at once a visual and aural metaphor for Zero's state of mind. Witnessing it, we feel his anger and confusion and are paralyzed by its force. Much to Rice's delight, the Theatre Guild production, directed by Philip Moeller, added even more stage elements to augment this effect.

> At the end [of the scene], when the boss fires Zero, the lights go out and the walls become alive with revolving figures. This is done by two discs operated by clock-work and projected by stereopticons. The effect is quite breath-taking. As the numbers revolve on the luminous walls, the desks and men revolve more and more rapidly and the off-stage noises swell. Then the numbers fade out and there is a huge gout of blood, thrice repeated. Then blackness. It's really quite over-whelming. (letter to Marc Connelly 4/18/23)

This description suggests that the two clockwork mechanisms controlling the rates of rotation operated at different speeds. While the number projections rotated at one speed, the platform rotated at another, intensifying the effect of Zero's being "out of sync" with the forces in his life.

The play's final image also functions as a powerful metaphor for these forces. When scene seven opens, we discover Zero in limbo, hard at work on the very machine that replaced him in his past life. Rice's stage directions indicate that,

> *Before the curtain rises the clicking of an adding machine is heard. The curtain rises upon an office similar in appearance to that in scene two . . . In the middle of the room Zero is seated completely absorbed in the operation of an adding machine. He presses the keys and pulls the lever with mechanical precision. He still wears his full-dress suit but he has added to it sleeve protectors and a green eye shade. A strip of white paper-tape flows steadily from the machine as Zero operates. The room is filled with this tape – streamers, festoons, billows of it everywhere. It covers the floor and furniture, it climbs the walls and chokes the doorways.* (123)

Once again, Zero is dwarfed by forces much larger than he. Once again, he finds satisfaction in generating and being consumed by the debris of modern life. "The billowing strip of paper," Hogan points out, neatly demonstrates Zero's "cosmic unimportance" (36). And – once again – the Theatre Guild production exceeded Rice's hopes of realizing his intent. In a memorable set positively cited by many reviewers, scene designer Lee Simonson created a huge adding machine on which Zero, played by Dudley Digges, jumped, hopping from key to key, pulling the lever with all of his weight. Writing to a friend, Rice enthusiastically described the scene thus: "At the rise of the curtain, Digges in his absurd full-dress suit runs up and down on it like a monkey, gleefully pressing down the keys and pulling the gigantic handle which makes them spring back into place. His pantomime is wonderful and he gets a big laugh" (letter to Marc Connelly 4/18/23).

Such images are powerful and proved memorable to the play's audiences and critics. But equally effective was Rice's use of sound. In scene two, for example, before we see Zero and Daisy's inability to make contact with each other, we *hear* them fail to do so as they recite numbers to each other. "They chant figures unceasingly throughout and the terrible monotony beats at one's brain like the tom tom in *Emperor Jones*," Rice explains, "except that here it relates directly to the action and punctuates the sub-conscious thoughts" (letter to Marc Connelly 4/18/23). Interspersed into this endless chain of numbers are, as Rice indicates, Zero's and Daisy's subconscious thoughts – thoughts of romance, thoughts of lust, thoughts of hurt feelings and grudges past. From this jumble of thoughts we hear how the meaningless exchange required of their work is made to pass as a social exchange of another kind. It is as if they have to create an imaginary social relationship out of the otherwise meaningless words they speak in order to

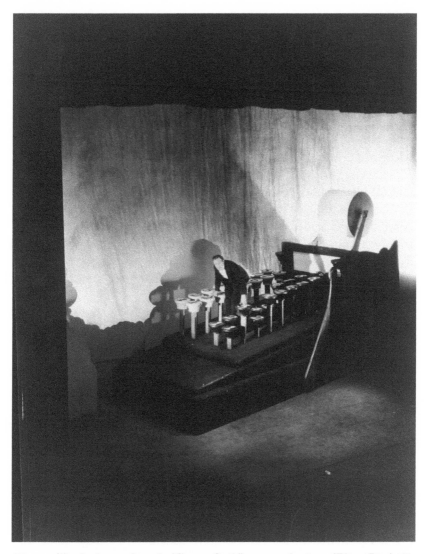

Figure 9. The final scene from the Theatre Guild's 1923 production of Elmer Rice's *The Adding Machine*. Dudley Digges, as Zero, jumps from key to key on Lee Simonson's giant adding machine.

get through their day. Yet, as we discover at the end of the scene and learn from their remembrances in scene six, they are never able to activate that imaginary relationship; they are forever stuck in their own atomized shells. This technique of layering dialogue and spoken thought is one that Rice would use again in *The Subway* (see discussion below).

As we've seen in scene three, Rice similarly orchestrates the voices of the Zeroes' dinner party guests. The stage directions in his original manuscript indicate that the talk between the men and women "grows louder and more staccato until it acquires a sort of rhythmic beat. Strophe and anti-strophe."[13] Although these instructions do not appear in the published version, his original intent nonetheless comes through; Hogan, for example, refers to the scene as a "brilliant modern adaptation of the chorus" (36). But, unlike Nietzsche, who lauded the chorus for its ability to overcome the *principium individuationis*, Rice is sceptical of that same dynamic for its potentially fascistic appeal. He thus resolves the dinner guests' chant into an ironic rendition of *My Country 'Tis of Thee*, "giv[ing] to this mordant scene a climax of great impact" (Hogan 36).

Like O'Neill, then, Rice disarticulates verbal, vocal, and pantomimic modes of signification in order to represent his character's spiritual malaise. But unlike O'Neill, who sought to secure his literary credentials, Rice was less invested in the verbal per se. An unapologetic man of the theatre, he seems to adopt Curry's tenet that no mode of signification is capable of standing on its own.[14] The play offers several examples of how one mode can contradict or at least militate against the tyranny of another. For instance, in scene five, Zero pops his head out of his grave, thinking that he hears Judy O'Grady: "That's funny!," Zero remarks, looking around. "I thought I heard her talkin' and laughin'. But I don't see nobody. Anyhow, what would she be doin' here? I guess I must 'a' been dreamin'. But how could I be dreamin' when I ain't been asleep? (*He looks about again*)" (67). Although we have just seen and heard Judy try to convince her date to desecrate Zero's grave by having sex on it, Zero has had his head in the ground. But, not seeing any visual evidence to corroborate the source of the voice he thought he heard, Zero doubts himself. Thus, even as a ghost, Zero is a loser, unable to invisibly penetrate obstacles and omnisciently perceive with a "sixth sense."

This scene and the next feature several corny vaudeville-esque puns. Emerging from his grave with "hands . . . folded stiffly across his breast," Zero walks "woodenly," grousing, "Gee! I'm stiff!" Referring at once to his uptight personality and his rigor mortis, Zero is himself a "stiff." Later, in scene six, he dismisses Daisy's concern for privacy by pointing to Shrdlu's self-absorption and explaining, "He's dead to the world" (96).

What are these puns doing in this cynical play? Aside from providing a little humor, they illustrate the unreliability of language to say exactly what it means. Puns, after all, condense two meanings into a single word, requiring us to revise what would appear to be the manifest meaning with a more latent one. What is more, there is verbal significance to Shrdlu's name. As Professor Jean Collette observed in a 1953 letter to Rice, "shrdlu" is the sequence of keys on the second line of a linotype machine (comparable to "qwerty," for example, on a computer keyboard today).[15] This suggests that he represents an arbitrary – and therefore meaningless – order. Indeed, the character of Shrdlu seems to exist simply to make us see the meaninglessness of the conventional moral order. Like Zero, he has committed a crime that is so horrible (in his case, matricide) that he expects to and wants to go to hell. His mother, however, was not the "saint" he insists she was, but, as we easily deduce from his story, a controlling, moralizing monster who ultimately reaped the abuse that she sowed. Shrdlu, then, represents an order that is merely orderly; there is no meaning behind it, just as there is no meaning in letters or even combinations of letters, considered only as such. His is a case of abiding by the letter which killeth the spirit of the law.

But language is not the only mode of signification whose autonomy Rice puts into doubt. Sound and image are likewise represented as inadequate on their own. In scene six, for example, Daisy and Zero are surprised by the other's confession of love, having previously relied on a body language that told another story. They reminisce, for example, about coming home from a company picnic when Zero put his arm across the back of Daisy's seat, while pressing his knee against hers. Daisy moved away to see if he really "meant it," but, in doing so, she made Zero think that she was "sore" (101). Zero's inference then made him stop making advances, leading Daisy to think that it was an "accident" all along. Misreading each other's body language, Daisy and Zero missed an opportunity to acknowledge the love they actually felt toward each other. And, as with gesture, sound is unreliable, too, as we see in the play's final scene. Poor gullible Zero stumbles off stage in pursuit of Hope, after Lt. Charles ventriloquizes her voice (140).

Thus, by disarticulating bodies, voices, and words and revealing their individual limitations, Rice would seem to accept Curry's tenet that all three "languages" are necessary to the act of communication. He would seem to believe that the theatre is superior to the impoverished medium of film. In writing this play, then, Rice not only cast off the specter of his former Hollywood self in his mocking account of the hapless Zero, but reaffirmed a new sense of himself, one committed to the art of the theatre, as his masterful deployment of verbal, vocal, and pantomimic languages attests.

The Subway

Five months after completing *The Adding Machine*, Rice began work on another expressionist play (letter to Harris 1/30/23). Entitled *The Subway*, this piece did not meet with nearly the success that the earlier play did. Indeed, it took him six years to find someone willing to produce it.[16] Even today, critics are divided in their estimation of its worth.[17] But, from the very beginning, Rice seemed to have some inklings of doubt that it would ever find an audience, given its tragic as opposed to comic tone (letter to Harris 7/14/23). Nonetheless, he wrote to Harris,

> I must do it. It's full of emotion and much more personal than *The Adding Machine*. It answers my present need for some vivid[,] intense form of expression.
> It's curious that although my mind runs so much to satire and so many of my ideas are satiric, I seem able to lose myself only in the things that are emotional and tragic.
> I suppose the reason is that my satiric, flippant manner is really a mask, an affectation – a defense mechanism to conceal my hyper-sensitiveness. (letter 7/14/23)

Thus, it would seem that, like O'Neill, Rice returned to a second expressionist play in order to penetrate further the personal issues first treated in the earlier play. Unfortunately, the trail of correspondence between Rice and Harris ends with this letter, bringing with it an end to such artifacts of self-revelation. To find out more, we must turn to the play itself – a play that, like *The Adding Machine*, appears to function as an affective autobiography.

In a filing room, deep in the bowels of the Subway Construction Company, Sophie Smith works with "maximum efficiency" (*The Subway* 15). An office boy brings her a basket of letters to file, which she no sooner empties than another is brought in. When the third office boy, George Clark, enters, however, this mundane workplace scenario changes as the rear wall "becomes transparent," revealing a suburban landscape, complete with "a cheap, suburban bungalow covered with clamboring roses"(4). George, it becomes clear, is Sophie's love interest. But when he moves to Detroit to find a better position, Sophie is left despondent, and, moreover, vulnerable to the seductive charms of Eugene Landray, a commercial artist who has come to the Subway Construction Company to illustrate an article for a popular magazine. Charmed by her naivete, youth, and beauty, Eugene asks Sophie out, offering her a respite from both her dull, unimaginative job and her dull, unimaginative family. They go to the movies where, in an aside, Eugene reveals the torments of his lust battling with his conscience. Sophie, too, speaks in asides, laying bare her confusion: while she is flattered by his interest and aroused by his charms, she knows she should conform to the dictates of propriety. Eventually, however, she succumbs. We know this because she lets herself into his studio with her own key and the studio is filled with nude portraits of her. Her happiness here is shattered, however, when she discovers that Eugene is due to leave for a job in Europe. Seduced, betrayed, pregnant, and ruined, Sophie flees from her nightmares to the subway where she submits to its seduction, throwing herself upon its tracks as a train rushes into the station.

If critics comment on *The Subway* at all, they usually discuss its expressionistic use of sound, light, dialogue, and movement.[18] More difficult to pinpoint is its central theme. Depicting the fall of a young girl from innocence to ruination, the play is clearly tragic. Yet Sophie is less a human being than a symbol in this largely allegorical play. The subway of the play's title, like the locomotive before it, is clearly a symbol of modernity; representing technological ingenuity, efficiency, and progress, it also threatens to violate the human values of a premodern past. Scene two, for example, shows Sophie commuting home from work, pressed tightly against the window of the subway car, and pressed tightly against her fellow passengers. When another train roars past, obscuring the car in darkness, the flickering lights come back up to reveal Sophie amidst the leering, menacing passengers who now wear "hideous, grotesque, animal masks: a dog, a pig, a monkey, a wolf, a rat" (31). Sophie shrieks, as the scene ends in blackness.

"This strong theatrical scene makes quite unnecessary any overt statement of the theme of the play," Hogan asserts, though he is vague in identifying what that theme might be, suggesting only that "the symbolic subway drains the humanity from people and reduces them to beasts" (38). Insofar as the subway symbolizes modernity, the play does seem to be a critique of its potentially dehumanizing force. But there is much more going on in this play. Sophie, herself, is a symbol – of beauty, truth, goodness or, as her name literally suggests, wisdom. Her seduction by the outwardly charming Eugene suggests the capitulation of a Romantic conception of art to the superficial charms of commerce. He is, after all, a commercial artist who, in seducing Sophie, prostitutes his muse, dispensing with her when she no longer satisfies him. Her suicide, however, is not the act of despair that it might seem;[19] in throwing herself under the train, Sophie seeks to redeem herself in terms of the narrative Eugene has written in her honor. An "epic of industrialism," Eugene's story is itself an allegory of modernity. He describes it to Sophie as an apocalyptic vision:

> The city . . . steel and concrete . . . industrialism, rearing its towers arrogantly to the skies . . . [. . .] Up and up . . . fists of steel shaking defiance at the skies . . . still higher and higher . . . All mankind joining the mad mechanistic dance . . . bondsmen to the monsters they have created . . . slaves to steel and concrete . . . [. . .] And under the earth . . . miles and miles of burrows . . . hundreds of miles . . . walls of concrete . . . rails of steel . . . winding and winding . . . the subway . . . the entrails of the city . . . Speed . . . Speed . . . Faster and faster . . . a labyrinth . . . an inferno . . . a great roaring and the clatter of steel upon steel . . . A subway train . . . a monster of steel with flaming eyes and gaping jaws . . . Moloch devouring his worshippers . . . Juggernaut crushing his tens of thousands . . . A subway train. (94–5)

After the apocalypse, after the buildings are razed, after "Destruction rained from the skies," mankind is reduced to "a herd of terror-stricken animals . . . seeking refuge . . . fleeing down to their burrows . . . down under the earth . . . down in the subway" (96). A thousand years later, a team of scientists lead an expedition down into the "mountain of concrete and twisted steel," only to discover the charred and blackened remains of Western civilization. In the midst of the rubble, however, they stumble upon a miracle – "the body of a young girl . . . preserved miraculously . . . inexplicably . . . through all those centuries . . . a young girl asleep . . . warm . . . radiant . . . in that chamber of death . . . A vision [. . . of] eternal beauty . . . beauty that survives death . . . that endures forever . . . that cannot be destroyed" (98). Thus, in killing herself, Sophie seeks to make an apotheosis of her ruined self, "a vision of eternal beauty that cannot be destroyed."

That this allegory appears within the allegory of the play suggests that the figure of Eugene Landray is multiply coded. He is at once the conscience-less Lothario who uses women to gratify his libidinous desires and the artist who, though constrained by the forces of modernity, envisions the triumph of art from out of modernity's ruins. He is the "good one" of his first name and the barren soil or "dry land" of his last name (translated through pig latin), upon which his artistic seeds cannot take root.[20] Could it be that Eugene is an ambivalent alter ego, through whom Rice reassessed his Hollywood past? That is, that he represents both the Rice who prostituted his artistic abilities to the commercial interests of film and the Rice who was able to predict and transcend its artistic depredations? Without insisting upon an unambiguous link between Rice and his character Eugene, I want to suggest that the play's concern with the movies does provide evidence for reading *The Subway* as yet another affective autobiography.

Consider, for example, Sophie and Eugene's date in scene five, where they go to the movie theatre. Here, as in scene two of *The Adding Machine*, Rice interperses his characters' thoughts with their speech, juxtaposing their uncensored desires against their performance of expected social roles. But, besides giving voice to her conflicted feelings, Sophie additionally speaks the intertitles out loud. These three types of discourse must be represented by three vocal styles, requiring both actors to utilize their voices in markedly different ways. As Eugene holds Sophie's hand, she admonishes herself disapprovingly, saying, "I oughtn't to let him."

EUGENE: What's happening to me? It's incredible . . . A little shop-girl.
SOPHIE: "Suspecting nothing, Kathleen walks into the trap set for her by Lord Orville." . . . His knee . . . I oughtn't to let him.
EUGENE: Why don't I stop? Why don't I stop?
SOPHIE: What's the matter with me? I'm getting dizzy. Oh, why doesn't the music stop?
EUGENE: I must go on with it – go on with it – go on with it!
SOPHIE: "Hurry, Mr. Masters, hurry – before it's too late." . . . I'm afraid!
EUGENE: God, why doesn't she respond?
SOPHIE: Oh, he's hurting me – he's hurting me! He'll break my fingers.
EUGENE: Now! Now! At last!
SOPHIE: "You're a beast, Lord Orville – a vile beast." . . . I can feel his nails. They're digging into me. Go on! Hurt me some more.
EUGENE: I mustn't lose my head . . . A child . . . A woman . . . What has she done to me?

SOPHIE: "Your title means nothing to an American citizen, Lord Orville. It's man to man between us, now." . . . Let me go . . . Let me go . . . Squeeze me tighter! [*Eugene suddenly releases her hand and, throwing his arm about her, draws her close to him.*]

SOPHIE: [*Faintly*]: Don't! Don't!

EUGENE: [*Hoarsely*]: Sophie! [*He draws her closer. Their heads touch.*]

Part of the effect of this passage and, indeed, of the entire scene comes from the way that the on-screen drama is layered on top of the young lovers' drama, as Hogan and others have noted (40). As Sophie recites the film's intertitles, we hear her and Eugene each confess feelings of sexual arousal, while admonishing themselves to adhere to the codes of social propriety. We thus hear the story of Kathleen and Lord Orville woven into the story of Sophie and Eugene such that when they leave halfway through the movie, we already know how their story will end. Here, as in *The Adding Machine*, Rice seems to be suggesting that movies provide not only diversion but pitifully unoriginal scripts for living one's life. Sophie, like Daisy, is a Mademoiselle Bovary of the movies, aroused by their titillation, but punished by the morality they preach.

Although Sophie ultimately defies society's norms by giving in to her sexual desires, she is clearly no *Übermensch*, willing to define her own moral code. Rather, she is punished for both her defiance and her shame. In scene eight, we see Sophie suffer from that shame, tossing and turning in her sleep as she is awakened by the disapproving voices she has internalized. Her mother's voice scolds, her sister's voice disapproves, her father's voice recites moral pieties. Throughout it all, Eugene's voice is heard, affirming a romantic vision of love. But it recedes and, in the end, as a minister's voice proselytizes, and a chorus of boys and girls mock her bastard baby, a host of accusing fingers emerge from the darkness to the chant of "That's her! That's her! That's her! That's her!" (135).

Yet, even had she abided by society's norms, she would have been punished for that, too. Rice is unambiguous on this point, showing us the drab, lifeless existence of her very conventional family in scene three. While Sophie's mother irons clothes, her sister Annie pedals a sewing machine, her brother Tom chainsmokes, and her father reads the newspaper headlines in a droning voice. All of their actions, Rice tells us, are "mechanized and rhythmic" (36), pulling Sophie into their vortex by the end of the scene, but not before she attempts to find an escape. In a pantomime that closes the scene, Sophie tries to leave her house, tracing a straight trajectory downstage toward the audience, much like the bird in the cuckoo-clock on the back wall. But, like the cuckoo, she is drawn back into her regulated life, as

> *A curtain, consisting of broad, vertical stripes, corresponding to the wall-paper pattern, is lowered, between Sophie and the audience. She looks out, between the strips, as though she were in a cage. Then she turns slowly away, takes an apron from behind the door, puts it on and begins mechanically picking up the newspapers, which Tom and Mr. Smith have discarded.* (45)

Clearly, there is no way out for the Sophies of this world. Rice's vision of humanity here is as cynical as in *The Adding Machine*. Yet, unlike Zero, Sophie does achieve a conditional transcendence in Eugene's apocalyptic narrative. What are we to make of this possibility of hope? I suggested above that, in imagining Eugene the artist, Rice may have created an alter ego for his playwright-self. But Sophie, too, may be seen to function as an alter ego, a surrogate for the spirit of his art. Insofar as the play tells the story of how a Romantic conception of art was seduced and betrayed by commerce, it is a *Bildungsroman* of Rice's coming of age in Hollywood. But it is also the story of how art, once compromised by commerce and crushed by the forces of mass production, is able to rise from the ashes of modernity to resume its purest, untainted form. This accords with Rice's own professed views on the status of the theatre in the age of mechanical reproduction. Speaking of film's impact upon the theatre, Rice once remarked that, because it was more popular, film was able to entertain audiences with the "bald melodramas, simple-minded farce-comedies and treacly romances" that once dominated the stage. "Consequently[,] the movies siphoned off from the theatre that part of the audience whose preference was for the trite, the obvious and the conventional, making possible the development of a more adult drama" (*Living Theatre* 119). In this way, he suggests, the theatre was able to rise like a phoenix from the ashes of a modernity that had ignited its own conflagration.

Although never explicitly named, the expressive culture movement appears to have exerted a strong influence on Rice's dramatic technique. As we've seen, he clearly draws upon Curry's theory of expression to represent the spiritual disharmony of Mr. Zero and Sophie Smith. Their worlds, communicated to us through pantomimic images, disarticulated sounds, and punning word play, are worlds of chaos and spiritual degradation. Thus, the formal evidence in his plays suggests that the expressive culture movement, rather than German expressionism, is the probable source of his expressionistic style.

Circumstantial evidence exists as well. Rice's rhetoric reveals that he often thought of the artistic process in Romantic terms that evoke Curry's theory of expression. In a review of Sergei Eisenstein's *Film Sense* (1947), for example, Rice dismisses the possibility that film could ever be an artistic medium since

> The nature of the medium itself defeats the primary condition of creative art: a spontaneous impulse of the individual soul to give objective form to some deeply-felt or deeply-perceived universal truth. It seems highly improbable that the motion-picture, synthetic in its construction and heavily dependent upon technological paraphernalia for its production, will ever make manifest that human breath and those human thumb-prints, which characterize all great works of art. ("Scripts . . .")

Film, in other words, is not an expressive medium; it does not allow "the individual soul to give objective form to some deeply-felt or deeply-perceived universal truth." Unable to generate a Benjaminian "aura" due to its mechanical reproduction, it stands as a symptom of, rather than an antidote to, modernity. Similarly, in *The Living Theatre*, his 1959 study of the modern stage, Rice again invokes this understanding of the artistic process, describing the urge to create as an internal feeling that seeks release: "If [the artist] cannot get his trouble off his mind or off his chest by direct action, he must rid himself of it by symbolically externalizing it. Thus, literally, he presses it out, or expresses it" (1). Although he strips the idea of its mystical overlay, substituting the more respectable language of psychoanalysis instead, he maintains that expression is the outward projection of an internal feeling or idea. Such statements suggest that Rice was, indeed, familiar with Curry's theory of expression. Whether it was simply "in the air" for him, as it was for Santayana, or was a conscious subject of study we may never know.[21]

He appears to have known at least enough of it to have ironized it as expressionism. But even this may have come to him second-hand. In a letter to Harris written two months before beginning work on *The Adding Machine*, Rice reports that he had recently seen O'Neill's *The Hairy Ape*.[22] Offering his assessment, he writes that "O'Neill's ideas are good but he lacks the imaginative power to carry them through. Only one scene stirred me emotionally – the mannikin scene [i.e., scene five]. That was a flash of real insight – a vivid illumination of the unbridgeable psychic gulf between man and man" (letter 6/23/22).[23] Clearly, Rice was impressed with what he saw. Remarking specifically on the dramatic effectiveness of scene five, he appears to have adopted a similar technique for representing in his own plays "the unbridgeable psychic gulf between man and man." This would suggest that, however Rice learned of Curry's theory of expression, he was schooled in its ironization by O'Neill.

Whatever its source, Rice's expressionistic style is important not for what it tells us about aesthetic developments in the theatre, but for how it allows us to understand the imaginative worlds of his plays. Giving voice to a range of oedipal and professional anxieties, Rice's plays express a profoundly personal vision. If they continue to entertain audiences and intrigue critics to this day, it is because they manage to transcend the limitations of the personal by inviting us to experience the issues that they raise in visually and aurally imaginative ways.

6

"I love a parade!": John Howard Lawson's minstrel burlesque of the American Dream

Unlike o'neill and rice, john howard lawson never explicitly disavowed any German influence on the writing of his expressionist plays. But, given the American vocabularies at work in his expressionist play *Processional*, subtitled "*A Jazz Symphony of American Life*" (1924; 1925), he didn't have to. "'Processional' is America," Heywood Broun declared in his 22 February 1925 column in the *New York World*. "It is the first genuine view of America that I have ever seen on the stage."[1] Most critics agreed. Even the stodgy Drama League praised the play for "the superabundant vitality of contemporary American life [that is] pictured here with immense gusto and by a method that smacks rather of vaudeville and revue than of the 'legitimate'" (*Playlist* 1/26, JHLP "Clippings"). When reviewers mentioned German expressionism at all, they tended either to fault the production for not borrowing enough from the form or to hail Lawson for "turning it to his own uses."[2] That the play was fundamentally American in style was never really in question.

Lawson himself helped to propagate this understanding of the play's formal origins. In his opening notes to the published version of the play, he boasts that he has "endeavored to create a method which shall express the American scene in native idiom, a method as far removed from the older realism as from the facile mood of Expressionism" (Lawson, *Processional* v). Presumably referring to the German movement, Lawson downplays expressionism, considering it to be too allegorical and thus, like the static realism of the legitimate stage, unable to express the rich texture and dynamism of American life. Instead, he says, he has created a "new technique [that] is essentially vaudevillesque in character – a development, a moulding to my own uses, of the rich vitality of the two-a-day and the musical extravaganza," noting that "It is only in the fields of vaudeville and revue that a native craftsmanship exists. Here at least a shining if somewhat distorted mirror is held up to our American nature. Here the national consciousness finds at least a partial reflection of itself in the mammy melody, the song and dance act and the curtain of real pearls" (v–vi).

Critics have generally followed Lawson's lead, assuming the play's unmistakeable "vaudevillesque" style to be American in origin. And, indeed, as we shall see, it is. But, at the risk of seeming to take the contrarian's position simply for its own sake, I also want to argue that it was inspired by, if not exactly modeled upon, a European source. For, despite Lawson's claim of having originated it himself, I shall demonstrate that the play's popular style in fact derives from the modernist ballet *Parade* (1917). As we'll see, Lawson drew his inspiration from Jean Cocteau, Erik Satie, Pablo Picasso, and Léonide Massine, whose collaborative work offered him an odd reflection of "America" as refracted through the lens of a European avant-garde. This is not to deny Lawson's own creativity or imagination, however. As I shall also demonstrate, Lawson did in fact turn his European sources to his own dramatic ends. For, while he borrows the general thematic conceit of *Parade* and its formal vocabulary drawn from popular art, he does so to tell a quintessentially American story in *Processional*, one of labor disputes, racial strife, and capitalist corruption that derives its theatrical effectiveness from its ironic appropriation of S. S. Curry's theory of expression. Like O'Neill and Rice before him, Lawson counterpoints bodies, voices, and words to represent the alienation and social dislocations of his age, all to the syncopated rhythm of a jazz band.

The parade begins

Having served in the ambulance corps in France during World War I, Lawson, like many expatriate artists and writers, returned to Paris immediately after the war with the hope of being able to write freely, away from the commercial demands of Broadway. In Europe, Lawson was exposed to all sorts of new trends in modern art. Upon visiting friends in Rome, for example, he saw several short Futurist plays, and, in Vienna, he witnessed "some Middle European expressionist plays" (JHLP "Autobiography" 73B). Such experiments, however, left him cold: "The avant garde plays were unsatisfactory," he concluded, "because they seemed so remote from the savage reality of the streets" (73B). Back in Paris, he attended productions of Lenormand's *Les Ratés* and Stravinsky's *Le Sacre du Printemps*, and enjoyed both immensely, noting that, while Lenormand's play bore an affinity with German expressionism, it was less bleak and far more sympathetic toward

its characters (82A). Because it dealt with the problem of the artist in bourgeois society, an issue Lawson was wrestling with at the time, *Les Rates*
made a vivid impression on the young playwright.

But, as influential as *Les Rates* was, nothing had a more profound impact
upon Lawson's conception of modern stage possibilities than *Parade*, the
experimental ballet written by Cocteau, orchestrated by Satie, designed by
Picasso, choreographed by Massine, and performed by Diaghilev's Ballets
Russes in May 1917. Indeed, Lawson acknowledged that *Parade*, with its
ironic use of mechanical sounds and jazz rhythms, was very much in his
thoughts when he began work on *Processional* in 1918 (JHLP "Autobiography" 93B). Years later in a draft of his autobiography, Lawson noted his
admiration for the way *Parade'* s collaborators "spoof petit bourgeois foibles
with aimiable [*sic*] good will," adding that "They were largely responsible
for my interest in vaudeville, burlesque and jazz" (93B). Thus, the distinctly
"native idiom" Lawson drew upon for his "jazz symphony of American life,"
while certainly referencing American popular art forms, was inspired by a
French avant-garde production.

In conceptualizing the ballet, Cocteau took as his starting point the
definition of "parade" that appears in the Larousse French dictionary: "a
comic act, put on at the entrance of a travelling theatre to attract a crowd"
(quoted in Goldberg 77). Accordingly, notes art historian Roselee Goldberg,
the ballet's narrative "revolves around the idea of a travelling troupe whose
'parade' is mistaken by the crowd for the real circus act. Despite desperate
appeals from the performers, the crowd never enters the circus tent" (77).
Cultural historian Roger Shattuck describes the avant-garde ballet as "a
serious-humorous exploitation of popular elements in art, a turning to jazz
and music hall and to all the paraphernalia of modern life, not in a spirit
of realism, but with a sense of exhilaration in the absurd" (154–5). Indeed,
its ability to "épater" its initial Paris audience delighted its creators, landing
Satie in court after he sent a Wildean riposte to a critic who had written a
scathing review of the production. Although Cocteau mounted an eloquent
defense of the composer/slanderer, he, too, was arrested for insulting the
prosecuting attorney (R. Shattuck 153). Ironically, the ballet itself served
as a teaser for the real attraction – the artists' performance of their own
scandalous celebrity selves.

But to war-weary Paris, the ballet was supposed to be the main attraction.
Perhaps that is why audiences were so outraged: it mocked their expectations
of the balletic form. Not only did the music incorporate irreverent sound
effects such as an airplane engine, a whistle, and the clacking of typewriter

keys, but the oversized costumes obscured the dancers' movements, and the story was little more than a trivial conceit. Indeed, Cocteau's "book" barely featured a narrative at all, but rather a series of episodes in which the managers of the traveling show attempt to solicit paying customers by offering a preview of several attractions. The first manager, for example, introduces a "Chinese Prestidigitator" (played by Massine); the second manager showcases a "Little American Girl" who performs a "Steamship Rag"; and the third manager (who was supposed to appear on horseback but, because of staging difficulties, was represented simply as a horse) presents two tumbling acrobats. The ballet ends with the three managers desperately trying to woo the crowd inside but failing, the crowd having been so swept up in the parade that they mistake it for the main attraction.

As even this brief summary suggests, Cocteau's narrative is a cynical indictment of modern mass culture, where individual skills are commodified into saleable units, where those skills – the property of the performers – are sold by a separate managerial class, and where the sales pitch they use dazzles an audience incapable of discerning the advertisement from the real thing. If, on the one hand, *Parade* levels the distinction between high and popular art forms by combining them into a single dynamic mixture, on the other, it mocks the very culture that is capable of producing such a mélange for the ways in which it immediately commodifies artistic forms. That that culture is to some extent explicitly coded as "American" is worth noting; the second manager, after all, wears a skyscraper, the symbol of American industrial modernity. He introduces the "Little American Girl," the spirit of the new century, whose ragtime dance marks the syncopated tempo of the modern era. That all three managers are ultimately unable to control the actions of the audience and the effects that their attractions have on them suggests that, despite the logic of commodification, the new century will be one of delightful anarchy and chaos.

Lawson, in attendance at this landmark event in the history of modern art, was inspired to revisit this theme and incorporate popular elements in *Processional*. Not only did he tip his hat to Satie's jubilant celebration of popular music in scripting a major role for his jazz band, but he structured his play's narrative around Cocteau's conceit of the parade, translating it into the more American "processional."

Generally used to refer to any music used to accompany individuals processing into a formal ceremony, the term "processional" also had a more colloquial (though now lost) meaning in 1920s American popular culture. According to Virginia Meyers Callahan, it specifically referred to the tradition by which a troupe of blackface performers announced their arrival in each town of their touring circuit by giving an impromptu musical performance down the main street. Like the tradition of the "parade" referenced by the ballet, the processional was meant to act as an advertisement for a more extensive performance for which tickets could be purchased. Unlike the parade, however, this type of processional advertised the comic tradition of blackface minstrelsy. Callahan notes that, though her husband, comedian Chuck Callahan, was primarily a "burlesque doctor," responsible for writing gags and tightening up jokes, he, too, was expected to join the processional, despite the fact that he could not read music, remarking that "it was everybody's duty to parade through the town and sort of announce that there was going to be a show at a local meeting place" (Callahan 12). Handed a tuba and a crib sheet with fingering positions numbered so that he could play along, Callahan blacked-up with the rest of his troupe and dutifully marched down the street, his musical talents (or lack thereof) clearly not posing any impediment to the tradition (12).

In *Processional*, Lawson refers to this tradition when he has his jazz band process down the main aisle of the auditorium toward the stage at the beginning of the play. As coal miners, their faces are blackened by soot instead of burnt cork, but the reference is clear all the same; like the blackface musicians with whom Callahan performed, this band of coal miners offers us a promise of what is to come. But, as in the ballet, the gathering crowd of citizens in Lawson's play are less interested in the main attraction of what the band represents − a multi-ethnic coalition of labor − than in what it presents − the sound of jazz modernity.

Although many critics have focused on the importance of jazz as an organizing motif in Lawson's play, none has noted the minstrel context in which it is presented. Consequently, most critics have tended to read the play's use of the jazz trope as an uncomplicated figure of freedom or democracy. But, by the mid-twenties when Lawson wrote the final version of his play, the cultural meanings of jazz were hotly contested. As Ryan Jerving has shown, jazz in the 1920s was just as likely to be discussed as the sound of the machine age as of primitive authenticity (70). One reason for this was because of the way jazz was packaged and mass marketed to white audiences. Although first performed for white audiences by black musicians in blackface, jazz was stripped of its minstrel origins both by white bandleaders such as Paul Whiteman, whose smooth stylings popularized the musical form among white audiences, and by the recording industry which, by virtue

Figure 10. Act 1 from The Theatre Guild's 1925 production of John Howard Lawson's *Processional: A Jazz Symphony of American Life*. Sadie Cohen and the town's coal miners are "jazzin' up the big strike." Close inspection of this photograph reveals that many members of the jazz band have coal-blackened faces.

of its technology, was able to de-couple the music from the racially marked bodies of its performers. As disembodied sound, jazz became characterized either by its syncopated rhythms, suggesting the discombobulation of industrial modernity, or by its multivocality and accommodation of improvisatory solos within a single musical score, representing the plurality of voices within American democratic culture.

Jerving suggests that Lawson was among those who identified jazz with the sound of industrial modernity, arguing that *Processional* "articulate[s] both jazz and the futurist discourse through which it was imagined to left-identified ends" (78). Jazz, he suggests, is represented as "a revolutionary force, a counter-capital machine that, if only switched on and run in the right direction, might bring about a millenium [*sic*] of labor" (78). On the one hand, Jerving is right to read the play's use of jazz as a trope of industrial modernity rather than an uncomplicated figure of freedom. Its muted horns, ragged melodies, and jangled rhythms were taken by many to suggest the dislocations of the modern age, suggesting the spiritual disharmony theorized by S. S. Curry and other "expressionists." Nonetheless, in understanding the play to celebrate jazz, regardless of what it is taken to represent, Jerving persists in the critical tradition of reading the play as a straightforward romantic comedy in which the jazz wedding resolves the play's conflicts on a note of hope. As I suggest below, however, jazz occupies a much more complicated place within the play's structure of meaning.[3] Performed by coal-miner musicians in blackface who introduce the jazz motif in their processional, jazz is visually situated within the material conditions of its historical production – blackface minstrelsy – a practice that can hardly be read by a 1920s left-leaning audience as a model of freedom. Thus, when the characters invoke a rhetoric of freedom when they speak of jazz, we are asked to hear them with ears attuned to irony. Insofar as the play does associate jazz with industrial modernity through its coal-miner musicians, it does so not to celebrate jazz or the possible future of industrial labor, but to mock the rhetoric of freedom when used to mask the conditions of industrial servitude. Lawson's coal-miner characters, in other words, are so enraptured by the sound of freedom that, like *Parade*'s gathering crowd, they cannot tell the difference between it and the actual conditions of freedom it is supposed to represent. Understanding Lawson's use of jazz as an *illusion* of freedom, then, we may begin to unlock the symbolic structure of Lawson's play.

Jazzin' up the big *Parade*

Subtitled "*A Jazz Symphony of American Life*," *Processional* uses jazz both as a central organizing structure and as a thematic device by which to critique a patriotic rhetoric that masks the unfree conditions of labor. Set in a West Virginia coal-mining town on the fourth of July, *Processional* is about a group of striking coal miners and their struggle for freedom from the controlling interests of capital. It begins with a newsboy, Boob, entering through the audience, calling "Extry! Extry! Trouble in West Virginia! Charleston paper! Jazzin' up the big strike!" (Lawson, *Processional* 4). Like a jazz performance in which one soloist passes off to another, Lawson shifts our attention from Boob to the Jewish merchant, Cohen, as a transaction is made between them and from Cohen to his daughter, Sadie. Hoping to recreate "the color and movement of the American processional as it streams about us," Lawson denotes that the play's "rhythm is staccato, burlesque, carried out by a formalized arrangement of jazz music" (ix). Thus the play unfolds much like a jazz performance as our attention is directed from one character to another as the ensemble of townspeople move on and off the stage.

Perhaps because of the play's initial focus on the various people in the town rather than on any individual protagonist, *Processional* feels as if it starts and stops, as if its pace is syncopated. But once the audience forsakes its conventional expectations and adapts to the play's syncopated pacing, the dramatic action gets underway. For, though Act I initially seems to function as an extended exposition, introducing the town and all of its inhabitants, it actually sets up the play's central conflict between an entrenched establishment and the forces of resistance which seek to displace it.

These two sides of the conflict are represented in the play by two basic character groupings. On the one hand are the interests of the establishment, represented by Capital (the Man in Silk Hat), the State (Sheriff Connor and his soldiers, Bill and McCarthy), and their base of support in the petty bourgeoisie (Cohen) and the Press (Phillpots, "a George M. Cohan sort of newspaper man"). On the other hand are the forces of resistance, represented by Jake Psinski, the Polish union organizer, and his band of "jazz miners": Rastus Jolly, a "Negro"; Dago Joe, an Italian; Wayne Whifflehagen, a German; Smith, a Yank; and three or four of the unwashed masses ("Slop"; "Soiled Man"; Felix, "a little middle-aged anemic man"; and Alexander Gore, "a man of the hayseed type"). Psinski spends much of the play trying to organize not just this group but the entire town into a workers' collective – including Dynamite Jim Flimmins, the anarchist, his mother Mrs. Flimmins, a prostitute, and even the soldiers, proletariat of the state.[4]

When Dynamite Jim escapes from jail, both sides attempt to contain him in one way or another. The Sheriff seeks to rearrest him and remove him from the social order while Psinski wants to recruit him for the workers' cause. But as an anarchist, he cannot be contained by either side: "I'm the guy stands alone against everybuddy . . . me myself, understan'!" (164). Pure unbridled and undirected energy, even he cannot control himself or his own desires. In Act III, we see Jim flee from the law and the arms of his family, taking refuge in and advantage of Sadie's confused admiration of him, before finally being caught on an iron bar, where he hangs by the seat of his pants, like a "flag of defeat" (172). In Act IV we learn that Dynamite Jim has once again escaped. Tension mounts as the establishment redoubles its efforts to rein in anarchy by backing up the militia with the moral and ideological troops of the Ku Klux Klan. The Klan closes in, persecuting

Sadie, left pregnant by Jim, and Mrs. Flimmins for their fallen virtue. In order to reestablish the moral order, Sadie must be married. Enter Jim, who functions as her *deus ex machina*. Literally and figuratively blinded, Jim is unable to see the ways in which he has been conscripted back into the dominant ideology. But Jim is not the only one who is blind – so, too, are the jazz miners who accept the Man in Silk Hat's duplicitous concessions. And as klansmen metamorphose into "the shining faces of loyal workmen!" (211), Psinski is forced to admit defeat. "Go on, make a joke a' me," he says drunkenly, "it's all hopeless" (208). But hopelessness turns to forced happiness as resistance weds the daughter of commerce in an impromptu jazz wedding which spills out into the audience and recesses down the aisle.

The resolution of the play is not, as some critics have claimed, falsely "contrived."[5] Rather, it is ironic and shows the failure of forced resolution whereby conflicts are absorbed back into a dominant structure which remains in place and unchanged. The jazz wedding, then, does not conclude the play's action but functions as an ironic coda to Psinski's announcement that "it's all hopeless." For once resistance accommodates itself to the ideological structure of the establishment (as represented by the marriage), it ceases to be resistant. Thus the jazz wedding – or jazz more generally – becomes a way for Lawson to represent the false consciousness of freedom as a specifically American trait.

As we have seen, jazz has often been taken to represent the ideals of freedom and democracy insofar as it is produced by an ensemble of instrumentalists who are able to maintain their individuality (as demonstrated by their improvisatory solos) even while contributing to the musical whole. In his play, Lawson draws upon this idea, using jazz to orchestrate the relationships among his characters to suggest that American culture is like a jazz symphony which asserts the multivocality of its individual instruments even as they perform ensemble. But, rather than celebrate this notion of multiplicity-in-oneness as did Israel Zangwell in his ubiquitous metaphor of "the melting pot," Lawson suggests that we take a more skeptical view of how oneness is produced, of how structure is imposed upon the richness and diversity of sound to create harmony, of how some sounds are subordinated to others in order to assert a melodic line.

Recognizing the disparity between the way jazz was produced as a marketable myth and the historical conditions of its production on the minstrel stage, Lawson uses it as a metaphor not of freedom but of the illusion of freedom. This symbolism was far more evident in the structure of an earlier draft of the play where Lawson juxtaposed jazz against "The Internationale," the song of the international workers' union, a song which, for Lawson, represented a truer sense of freedom since it was a freedom that was not contingent upon a false sense of national unity. As the following dialogue from this draft illustrates, Lawson had initially included this symbolic battle of the bands. Asked if he is an American, Psinski responds,

> "Ain't we citizens of the world. Ain't there sunlight for all? There's a song says tomorrow there won't be any nations." He whispers the name of the song, "The Internationale," and hums the tune. As he waves the axe, gently, the others listen, frightened. Mrs. Flimmins screams, "Get out of here. I don't need your money. No freak borders now. No anarchist borders. I got my son to work for me. My son that don't sing ghost-like songs. He sings jazz like a man". (quoted in L. Robinson 97)

Lawson suggests far more explicitly here than in the final version that Mrs. Flimmins, for one, is trapped within American ideology which links the idea of freedom to American nationalism. She is, therefore, unable to understand freedom as an abstract concept which transcends national interests. Frightened by the strains of "The Internationale," she champions jazz as the music of American manhood, as a music which is linked to a specifically American sense of freedom. But of course, given the conditions of its production on the minstrel stage, jazz can only *represent* freedom since its Black originators were effectively denied the freedom of self-representation. Thus, within the symbolic schema of Lawson's play, jazz functions as a motif of false consciousness.

Because the commercial interests of a white capitalist recording industry stood to profit from the labor of mostly Black jazz musicians, Lawson saw their relationship as one best represented by minstrelsy. That is, white capitalist interests were behind Black jazz musicians in the same way that white performers were behind the mask of a black face on the minstrel stage. Thus, for Lawson, jazz represented the exploitation of Black labor by white capitalist interests which appropriated jazz as their own even as they denied the labor involved to produce it. On the minstrel stage, Black jazz musicians were obliged to perform their "blackness" along with their music, allowing white audiences attending the minstrel shows (or even jazz clubs and Harlem cabarets in which they performed) to perceive them as having spontaneous or natural abilities which required little or no labor at all. This link between jazz and effortlessness was important because the freedom that jazz came to represent was not only a freedom from the supposed social and moral constraints of a white-defined "civilization," but a freedom from the demands of an increasingly industrialized workplace. Thus, "blackness" became a mark of "natural" – that is, unalienated – labor.

Though such stereotypes persisted, the reality of the 1910s and 1920s was that, with the Great Migration of Southern Blacks to urban industrialized centers in the North, African Americans were entering the industrial work-force in greater and greater numbers. The huge influx of Blacks into the ranks of labor in Northern cities during this period shifted the color composition of the working class, creating tension among working-class whites and leading to the race riots of 1919. Writing in 1920, Lawson was well aware of the blackening of labor within the working class. As a burgeoning inter-nationalist, he was also aware of the need to create multi-ethnic collectives. Up to that time, most efforts to unionize white and Black workers had been met with failure – most, but not all, as demonstrated by the West Virginia coal miners' strike of 1920.

Significantly, Lawson chose to set the final version of his play in a West Virginia coal-mining town instead of a Northeastern canning factory which was the setting of the play in an earlier draft. In fact, as LeRoy Robinson documents, Lawson had been inspired to write the final version of his play after reading newspaper accounts of the West Virginia coal miners' strike of 1920.[6] The subject of John Sayles's film *Matewan*, the West Virginia coal miners' strike is important to American labor history because it was the first time that white ethnic workers (mostly Polish and Italian immi-grants) joined together with Black workers (originally replacement miners) to form what many on the Left hailed as a true workers' collective. Seen as a promise of cross-cultural alliance, the West Virginia miners' strike chal-lenged the notion that efforts to unionize Black and white workers into a single collective would always be doomed to fail. Although the strike itself was a success, it ended violently when federal troops were called in to restore order.

Unsurprisingly, Lawson treats this historical episode with tongue in cheek. Like the West Virginia strikers, his coal-miner characters are a multi-ethnic collective. But, unlike their real-life counterparts, Lawson's characters are never able to recognize themselves *as* a multi-ethnic col-lective and thus as a source of their own power. That they participate in Klan violence[7] and that they celebrate the union of resistance and com-merce as figured in the jazz wedding is, as noted above, a point of profound irony.

Blackened faces, mammy melodies, and vaudeville puns

If, as I have been arguing, *Processional* is highly ironic in its treatment of the American Dream, a tone and a perspective inspired by *Parade*, then why have so many critics failed to perceive the irony which undergirds its structure of meaning?[8] Almost as if in anticipation of this problem, Lawson offers us an answer to this question in his preface, when he rejects not only the "facile mood" of German Expressionism but what Nietzsche referred to as the "socratism" of the realist stage, where "a play might just as well be phrased in terms of a sonnet sequence or a grammar of Esperanto" if "color and movement are weeded out in the interests of a realism which has nothing remotely to do with reality" (*Processional* vi). Believing that "The reality of America spiritually and materially, is a movement, a rhythm of which the inner meaning has not been found," Lawson insists that the "Blood and bones of a living stage must be the blood and bones of the actuality stirring around us" (viii). Meaning, that is, resides just as much in the play's physical realization on stage as in its language, leading Anne Fletcher to refer to Lawson's work in general as "production-dependent."

Considering that *Processional*'s meaning lies in its staging, then, I would like to suggest that we examine its "expressionistic" form. For it is in its juxtaposition of bodies, voices, and words that the play's irony is most effectively deployed. As we'll see, Lawson uses the conventions of blackface minstrelsy, the sounds of jazz modernity, and vaudevillian puns to disrupt his seemingly straightforward narrative in order to invite his audience to understand the play ironically. Ultimately, I shall argue that, though the play may have been inspired by a European avant-garde ballet, its expressionistic form is primarily American in origin. For, like O'Neill, Rice, and – as we shall see – Treadwell, Lawson ironizes Curry's theory of expression, counterpointing his characters' thoughts, feelings, and lives in order to represent a loss of spiritual harmony within the industrial jazz age.

Take, for example, the presentation of his actors' bodies on stage. Smeared with coal dust, Lawson's characters appear in blackface, singing versions of "Yankee Doodle Blues" and "Runnin' Wild" in a minstrel parody of the sentiments expressed by the characters. Dynamite Jim repeatedly refers to his mother in good minstrel style as his "mammy." After killing a soldier, he says, "I want my mammy's arms 'cause I done a black thing, oh mammy help me now!" (99). Later he remarks that the soldiers are "coming for me, comin' to take me from my mammy's arms" (106). And in Act III, after finding out that his mother has been selling herself, Jim exclaims, "Every guy's had my mammy's arms!" (148), calling for "my mammy's arms" himself again in Act IV (197). In each of these instances, Lawson ironically juxtaposes the sentimentality of the line against the situation in which it is expressed. For example, when Jim calls for his mammy after having killed a soldier, his plaintive wail is set off against the "drunken laughter" of his mother entertaining the soldiers in the Labor Temple. And when Jim promises to fulfill his masculine duty by vowing to kill every guy who calls his mammy a bad name, his mother gently dissuades him with her practical wisdom, pointing out that her prostitution has earned them enough money to leave their indentured servitude to the coal mines and move to New York, where they can start a better life. Jim's sentimental rhetoric about the ideology of motherhood sounds absurd when framed against the actual circumstances in which his mother is forced to live; such rhetoric and the ideology it reinforces is yet one more example of the "parade" that keeps citizens from recognizing the true conditions of their lives.

But why minstrelsy? If Lawson is simply trying to create an alienation effect that would emphasize the gap between what is said and how it means, then why does he draw specifically upon minstrel conventions? To answer this question, we must look at how blackness is used symbolically in the play. As we've seen, "blackness" was often taken to be a mark of unalienated labor within the culture at large, at least when performed for white audiences by Black musicians in blackface. Within the context of the play's strike, this connotation of blackness becomes a mark of great irony: Lawson's striking coal miners are not unalienated; to the contrary, they are so alienated as to be unable to recognize the conditions of their alienation.

By thus portraying his coal-miner characters in blackface, Lawson would also seem to be using blackness as a way of coding the marginality and powerlessness of the working class. But, rather than critique how the dominant culture structures power relations based upon the notion of race, Lawson simply borrows the equation between blackness and marginality. He does not question the historical relationship between blackness and marginality itself. This means that the play has the unfortunate effect of reinscribing notions of Black inferiority even as it seeks to expose how hegemony creates and manipulates positions of marginality in order to remain in power.

For this reason, Lawson's symbolic use of blackness is often troublesome. For instance, Phillpots, the newspaper man, calls Sadie "Desdemona" at the end of the play when she is pregnant with Jim's child, saying that she bears the burden of "the black monster's hand" (204). Jim responds that he's not so black, suggesting the ancient link between blackness and evil. But Phillpots explains that by "the black monster" he means "coal" (204). Lawson's point would seem to be that Sadie bears in her womb a miner for the coal mines of tomorrow, pointing to the fact that the struggle for workers' rights is not limited to the here and now but will remain a struggle for generations to come. Nonetheless, the joke produced from Jim's confusion over how Phillpots uses the term "black" reinforces the equation between blackness and evil which, given the play's use of minstrel conventions, is transposed onto the category of race.

Lawson's portrayal of a Black man in the character of Rastus Jolly is another instance of his problematic use of race. When we first meet Rastus, he is described as "lazily twanging banjo" (9). He is later shown to be superstitious and easily frightened (63–70, 80). For instance, when Dynamite Jim seeks to make his escape from jail in a coffin which Psinski and Rastus are to carry, Rastus "trembles and goes down on his knees," wailing, "I'm a good nigger an' I done no wrong, I paid ma dues an' I done no wrong, I kilt ma mother-in-law but I done no wrong . . . " (63). Again, Lawson appears to be calling for such lines to be delivered with humor and irony, but the racist caricature is left intact.[9] Perhaps most confusing is when Rastus is revealed to be a Ku Klux "goblin" – he is so scared that his "eyes pop out of his head" (193). By having Rastus exposed as a member of the Ku Klux Klan, Lawson may be suggesting that African Americans, too, could be blindfolded by the ideology of a dominant, white-defined culture (as is indicated by Psinski's comment to Rastus that "You ain't fit to associate with class-conscious workmen" [193]), but the symbolic potential of the scene must be severely undercut by a sensitive audience's knowledge of the horrors that were committed against African Americans by the Ku Klux Klan.

A less-than-sensitive audience, however, may have realized what Lawson was up to insofar as they would have been familiar with the popular minstrel skit to which Lawson appears to be alluding. In *The World's Best Book of Minstrelsy*, published in 1926 for the production of amateur minstrel shows, Herbert Preston Powell collected a number of successful and well-known minstrel sketches including one entitled "The Radio Jazz Hounds." In it, blackface performers appear as members of a jazz band, playing a variety of musical numbers which are interspersed with typical minstrel jokes and puns. Toward the conclusion of the skit, after a number of "marriage-is-hell" jokes, the band decides to play a wedding march. "Catt Gutz," described in the list of characters as a "violin virtuososilly" is instructed to distribute a piece of music to each musician, and under his direction they play Chopin's Funeral March. Business of surprise after the first few bars are played. [Kant B.] BEET [the drummer] glares at his music with dwindling ferocity, his temper gradually melting into tears, and his sobs become so intense that GUTZ stops the band.

GUTZ. Doggone, dat's de funniest Wedding March I ever played.
[Sharpzan] FLATT [the pianist]. If dat's a Wedding March, I'se de Kleagle of de Ku Klux Klan.
[Ivor] PAYNE ["saxophone sobbist"] (who has been turning his music upside down, and back again). Why look huh, boy, we done been playin' dis music upside down. (130)

Several parallels between this skit and Lawson's play are worth noting. First, Flatt remarks upon the impossibility of the funeral dirge being a wedding march by concluding his conditional statement with the assertion that he is the Kleagle of the Ku Klux Klan. At the very least, this demonstrates that such travesties were a regular part of minstrel entertainment. Thus Lawson's decision to have Rastus appear as a Ku Klux goblin might have been received as part of this tradition of travesty. Secondly, the inverted wedding march turns out to be a funeral dirge. Significant within the scope of the minstrel skit only because it refers back to the sexist banter which immediately precedes it, the wedding march/funeral dirge inversion is relevant to Lawson's play because it suggests that his jazz wedding signals the death of the workers' resistance movement.

Sound – or, more specifically, music – also serves as an ironic counterpoint to the action depicted and sentiments expressed throughout Lawson's play.[10] Early in Act I, for example, when we first meet the Sheriff, we see him swagger back and forth across the stage *trying to intimidate the audience* (32), only to shift into a servile posture when the Man in Silk Hat appears, suggesting the state's subservience to the interests of capital. When the Man in Silk Hat commands him to keep an eye on "loose women" because "People take advantage of these periods of disorder to commit nuisances," Lawson's stage directions indicate that "Off stage the distant echo of the Jazz Band is heard again like a derisive echo" (33). "Derisive" music is heard again later in Act II, when the police scout the Labor Temple, looking for the escaped Dynamite Jim (76). When the Sheriff proclaims "We'll get him dead or alive," we hear from offstage the "distant blowing of discordant horns" (65).

Such "discord" suggests a lack of harmony that is not only acoustical but metaphorical, especially if we remember that harmonic balance was Curry's favorite metaphor for spiritual wholeness. Thus when Old Maggie, Jim's grandmother, ends Act I with her ominous prediction that "There's a black time comin'," the "single blare of discordant music" that punctuates her pronouncement would seem to suggest that it will be a time of confusion and spiritual malaise (48). Here, again, blackness is associated with evil, but it is also acoustically identified with jazz, suggesting that jazz for Lawson was the appropriate soundtrack for such troubled times.

Clearly, jazz serves as either an ironic counterpoint or an ominous accompaniment to the characters' lines of dialogue. What is worth noting is that, in each of these instances, it is sounded from off-stage, disembodied from its source. Only at the end of the play do we see the coal miners' jazz band reappear on stage, heralded by their own "raucous" introduction (207). Once on stage, they perform "violently" with many members carrying weapons in addition to their instruments. But, when the Man in Silk Hat offers them concessions, they lay down their weapons and play a lively accompaniment to Jim and Sadie's jazz wedding, before recessing down the aisle. Once again, jazz is used ironically since we are made to know that the Man in Silk Hat's offer is a ruse. Although he publicly concedes that the strike has been devastating in terms of morale and publicity, the Man in Silk Hat quietly instructs the Sheriff to "Make a list of the marked men and we'll get them in their beds tonight!" (212). Jazz, the sound of freedom – so appealing and infectious – is, alas, ultimately a sound masking conditions that are unfree.

Music is not the only off-stage sound we hear. Voices, too, are disembodied. Although their disembodiment is usually explained diegetically by the darkness of night, there is one scene in which we hear a voice – if not exactly disarticulated – oddly mediated from its source. In what has been described as one of the most "expressionistic" scenes in the play – the manhunt – Lawson has the Man in Silk Hat use a megaphone to announce the progress of Jim's escape and eventual capture as if it were a sporting event (171). Throughout his narration, we see the events depicted, as Jim "crosses from left to right, his arms gesticulating wildly" (171), and again from right to left. This gives the scene a Brechtian flavor, serving to defamiliarize the play's action in order to induce the audience to assume a critical perspective on what is represented. That the Man in Silk Hat narrates the events we see, and that he does so from an upper box suggests that ultimately he and what he represents commands the action of the play. Although we might root for the underdog, the force of anarchy in the play, Lawson wishes us to know that the action is ultimately scripted by the powers that be. The megaphone simply underscores that point by literally enlarging the voice of the one who gets to make the call.

Further disrupting our sense of the play's narrative action is Lawson's use of corny puns and vaudeville humor. Poor old Pop Pratt, for example, isn't allowed to join the procession because, as Wayne Whifflehagen points out, "he ain't a member a' the Union" (12). Punning on "union," Lawson has Pop appear in his blue Civil War uniform – he *is* a member of the Union army – but he isn't a member of the labor union. Another vaudevillian joke appears when Cohen acknowledges band-member Smith as a *real* American, unlike the others who are foreign-born. Smith refuses to shake Cohen's hand so Cohen shakes his own (18). Cohen himself is a standard vaudeville joke: as a Jew, he is "the vaudeville type of Yiddish figure" as demonstrated by his pecunious nature, his lisp, and his desire for upward mobility (4). For instance, Cohen brags to Phillpots about Sadie's respectable upbringing, telling him that he's saving money to send her to correspondence school (31). Cohen's bourgeois affectations are further revealed to be baseless when Phillpots asks of Sadie, "Are you one of the debutantes here?" Sadie replies, "No Sir, I'm a good girl" (29).

Not one to shirk from the vaudeville stock-in-trade of scatological humor, Lawson has Pop Pratt ask if the "proletariat" is something for the bowels (137). Fortunately, Lawson spares us some of the more sophomoric humor which appeared in earlier drafts. For instance, in the second draft of the play, he has a character, Mac, drop his trousers in order to show Pop Pratt a bayonet wound. "Old Pop shakes his head sadly: 'Poisonous gas, you say?'" (quoted in L. Robinson 88.) Slapstick, nonetheless, remains as when Boob throws firecrackers under Pop Pratt (*Processional* 22), and the Sheriff's chair breaks from under him, suggestively toppling authority (117).

More jokes center on unsettling the authority of establishment figures. For example, after Boob is seen swallowing money he took from Cohen's store, he declares that he'll be elected to the US Senate because "that's where a guy goes that can swaller coin!" (122). And when Phillpots holds up a copy of the newspaper he works for, the soldiers salute, substituting the press for a symbol of national unity, undercutting the integrity of both (36). In the same vein, Lawson has the soldier McCarthy ask the Sheriff, "What's this white house here?" to which the Sheriff answers, "That's no White House, that's the Labor Temple" (75). Hardly needing explication, this joke suggests that the interests of the executive branch and those of labor are not to be confused. But this Labor Temple, built as a tribute "To the Spirit of American Industry," is shown to be a sham, for engraved underneath is an explanation of what is meant by "industry:" "Coal . . . Steel . . . Oil . . ." (74).

Like Rice, then, Lawson draws upon the vaudeville tradition of "point-ing" on key words and phrases to demonstrate the instability and unre-liability of language. But, where Rice seemed to want to highlight the insufficiency of any significatory mode that is made to stand on its own, Lawson appears to direct his skepticism primarily at language, especially when aimed toward ideological ends. Consider, for example, the character of Phillpots. Representing the fourth estate, he inspires Psinski to entreat the others to "treat him good," explaining, "he owns us all, the guy that holds the wires . . . he laughs, he makes death, he telegraphs – ," to which Phillpots merrily replies, "that's me, Hiram the History Kid" (27).

The only "outsider" represented in the play, Phillpots would seem to offer an objective perspective on the strike. Yet, his perspective, too, is one that we are asked to place in doubt. When Psinski asks if he's looking for trouble, Phillpots responds, "If I don't find it, I'll make it" (31), suggesting that his brand of journalism is yellow. "What do I care for guns!" he continues, "I'm going to raise the lid off this strike, make it a national issue, put it on the front page, put it before Congress, put it – " (31). But his boast is interrupted by the appearance of the Sheriff, which sends the other characters diving for cover. Although the Sheriff is initially skeptical of Phillpots, threatening to subject him to a strip search, Phillpots wins his favor by handing over his flask of bourbon. With one swig, the Sheriff is momentarily appeased. Although he is still uncertain about Phillpots's intentions, asking about his "picture machine," the Sheriff is won over by Phillpots's sycophantic offer to "do you a big service, put your physiognomy on the front page in fourteen cities, badge and all," upon which Phillpots "takes out a handkerchief and polishes the Sheriff's badge" (36). The press, it would seem, is only as bold as the state will allow.

Yet, at the end of the play, even Phillpots is willing to question the integrity of the press that he represents. Buying all of Boob's newspapers, he tears them up, showering the newlywed couple with confetti, remarking that "there's where the news belongs!" (218). With the character of Phillpots, then, Lawson suggests that language – the stuff of print – necessarily bears the ideological imprint of the powers that be. But perhaps no more so than any other form of representation. After all, Lawson is equally suspicious of jazz and, indeed, the theatre itself as he mockingly appropriates the conventions of blackface minstrelsy. Disarticulating bodies, voices, and words, Lawson implores us to be suspicious of any form of representation that is meant to distract us from the actual subject at hand.

Native expressions

Although I have been arguing that, in its overall conceit, Lawson's *Processional* is, in effect, an Americanized version of *Parade*, I would also like to suggest that, in both its formal and thematic design, Lawson's play is primarily American in origin. Its disarticulation and contrapuntal arrangement of bodies, voices, and words ironically reappropriate S. S. Curry's theory of expression, as we have seen. This suggests that Lawson was, in fact, familiar with Curry's theory of expression. Indeed, while a student at the prestigious Cutler School, he won an elocutionary contest for his recitation of Wells's "The Intrepid Bee" (JHLP "Scrapbook"). Turning Curry's theory inside out, Lawson depicts the spiritual alienation of his coal-miner characters and thus creates the play's expressionistic form.

In terms of its thematic design, *Processional*, like the other plays discussed in this book, features a character who functions as its playwright's alter ego, reflecting Lawson's concerns about the theatre in an age of mechanical reproduction. Unlike these other plays, though, *Processional*'s concern with technology is considerably more muted. Using jazz as the sound of industrial modernity – or, in Curry's terms, the sound of spiritual disharmony – Lawson only implicitly references the structures of technology by which it is produced. Yet, in the jazz sounds that ironically punctuate the characters' dialogue from off-stage, there is the suggestion of a recording technology that disembodies the music from the material conditions of its source. Foregrounding those material conditions in his use of blackface conventions, Lawson reminds his audience of the bodies whose labor is erased, whether it be the labor of creating music or of mining the power that generates society's wealth.

Through his use of jazz, Lawson implicitly evokes industrial capitalism, situating the recording industry as both a synecdoche and a metaphor for capitalism itself. Insofar as it is one of many industries by which artistic production is turned into a commodity, it stands in a synecdochic relationship; insofar as its technology literally disembodies the commodity from its material source of production, it stands in a metaphoric relationship, representing the capitalist "machine." Although largely invisible like the jazz band that plays off-stage, capitalism and its effects resound throughout the culture at large.

As a playwright and artist, Lawson was concerned about his ability to write freely, away from the commercial demands of Broadway. That is why he fled to France in 1917. Having successfully placed his first play, *Standards*, with Cohan and Harris in 1915, Lawson had found it difficult to sell his next property, *Servant–Master–Lover*, later remarking that the experience had taught him "that the market was cruel and merciless; but more poignant was the knowledge that it was mad: the merchants were incapable of judging the wares they bought or sold. The system was venal, but it was also massively wasteful and incompetent" (JHLP "Autobiography" 39). Thus was his state of mind when he witnessed the cynical *Parade* and the equally affecting *Les Rates*. "Its importance for me," he later remarked of Lenormand's play, "relates to its more general importance as an early statement of the view that the artist is submerged in the bourgeois environment. He seeks another reality within himself, but he finds only despair, because his soul is a mirror of the society he hates" (JHLP "Autobiography" 84). Perhaps recognizing the struggle he himself was having with the "bourgeois society" he had left, Lawson explores the theme of the disaffected artist in *Processional*.

But who is the disaffected artist figure in the play? On the one hand, we might find it in the character of Dynamite Jim Flimmins. A murderer and a rapist, he is at once destructive and creative, representing the anarchic spirit of art which seeks to defy containment. On the other hand, we might read this figure in the character of Jake Psinski, the union organizer who, alone among Lawson's coal-miner characters, understands the larger forces which structure their lives. An organic intellectual, Psinski seeks to create order out of chaos by educating his fellow workmen and organizing them to work on their own behalf. Of course, both characters are defeated in the end: Jim, as we have seen, is literally and figuratively blinded before being conscripted back into the social order, while Psinski, maintaining his critical perspective from the margins, nonetheless stands his ground a little less firmly, having taken to drink. Such an ending suggests that Lawson himself despaired – not only about the future of labor but about the future of his art. Insofar as the play may be read as an affective autobiography, then, it suggests that Lawson feared that he would be instantly conscripted back into the commercial logic of Broadway, despite his critical misgivings about the commodification of art.

Even so, he found that he had to return to the United States. For like one of the original characters in the play – a French woman, representing "old-world wisdom," who was based upon his landlady – Lawson realized that "Felicite had no more place in West Virginia than I did in Paris" (JHLP "Autobiography" 72). Upon returning home, Lawson finished his play, placing it with the explicitly non-commercial Theatre Guild. Lawson's return was a homecoming in other ways as well. For, though he may have been inspired by a French avant-garde ballet to draw upon popular forms of art, Lawson looked only to those sources that could provide him with a distinctly "native idiom." The result was *Processional*'s "expressionistic" style.

However influential *Parade, Les Rates*, and other European avant-garde theatrical productions were on Lawson's thinking and composition, *Processional*'s expressionistic style appears to have been homegrown. Lawson's own statements certainly suggest that this was the case, even if he was not especially enthusiastic about the term itself. For example, in an article appearing in *The World* shortly after the play's premiere, Lawson expressed his disdain for the way "expressionism" was used to affect a pretense of European artistry:

> I am frequently accused of expressionism. It astonishes me to find myself tagged with this convenient but inappropriate label, because I believe that I am traveling in the exactly opposite direction. In fact, one of the chief objects of my study – and the source of my method – has been the work of that distinguished American expressionist, Mr. George M. Cohan.
>
> This expressionist trademark has come to be bandied about so indiscriminately that it ceases to have a meaning at all. Apply it, for instance, to the greatest American comedian, Al Jolson, in "Big Boy." Tell the world that his black-face characterization symbolizes the upward struggle of the Negro, ending in a great horse race in which the color line is passed. Label it written by Eugenius Hasenpfeffer and you have the great expressionist play. This might cause the members of the Ladies' Aid to Higher Culture to flock to the Winter Garden in vast numbers. But if you tell the majority of his admirers that Al Jolson is our foremost expressionist, I think they will shrug their collective shoulders and reply, "So is your old man!" (JHLP "A Few Plain Words . . ." in "Clippings")

Acknowledging an affinity between what he means by "expressionism" and the work of native performers George M. Cohan and Al Jolson, Lawson is quick to dismiss those who insist upon its German origins, as seen in his mocking reference to "Eugenius Hasenpfeffer."

Indeed, in an undated document in the Lawson papers entitled "Material for lecture publicity," the author (probably Lawson himself) elaborates upon the particular Americanness of the expressionistic form:

> It is often claimed that expressionism is merely an off-shoot of the great European movements which flowered in the work of Reinhardt and Gordon Craig, and later in the constructivism of Meyerhold in Russia and Piscator in Germany.
>
> But it is Lawson's own feeling, and the thesis of his lectures, that the American modernists are creating something definitely national in their art, that they are using this new technique to find an expression of the American language and the American soil. (JHLP "Material for lecture publicity")

Given that, throughout Lawson's papers, he is quick to acknowledge his artistic debts – to sources both foreign and domestic – there is little reason to doubt his sincerity in these statements. Clearly, he believed that there was something distinctly American about this particular manifestation of the expressionistic form.

Many who witnessed the play concurred. Fanny Hurst, for one, enthused:

> I consider "Processional" one of the most interpretive plays that have come out of America. It expresses our vulgarity, our yearnings, our ideals, our gorgeous vitality, our youth and our puritanisms in just the jumble that we express it in our everyday lives. "Processional" is as mad as we are mad . . . It is plays like this that mark the beginning of a new dramatic self-consciousness in America. (quoted in Bloch 139)

And as a reporter from the Brooklyn *Daily Times* remarked, "to criticize and to express the spirit of America in a single play is an extremely gigantic ambition. To have tried and to have succeeded even in small measure is an achievement. It is not the story but the manner of its expression that is important" (quoted in Bloch 138).

Indeed, the "manner of its expression" was, perhaps, the most important aspect of the play. Unfortunately, many of Lawson's intentions were not realized by the Theatre Guild production. As Beverle Bloch reports, the Guild's board members objected to the jazz band entering through the aisles because they were afraid it would interfere with late seating. Instead, they arranged to have the jazz band enter from the orchestra pit (116). For the same reason, board members objected to the recession of the jazz wedding party at play's end since they were afraid it would get in the way of patrons rushing to catch the last trains (Bloch 116). In an attempt to persuade them of the importance of his stage directions, Lawson took Theresa Helburn to a burlesque performance at Minsky's in order to illustrate the free exchange between performer and audience that he was after. According to Bloch, "Helburn enjoyed the burlesque show, and considered Lawson's 'running commentary in extremely highbrow terms about what he meant by burlesque technique and how it should be analyzed,' part of the fun" (Bloch 116). Nonetheless, the board won out, preventing Lawson from fully dismantling realism's fourth wall.[11]

Given the difficulties Lawson encountered in trying to realize the expressionistic manner of the play, he felt that he would have to find a new theatre-producing organization. Thus, two years after the Guild's production of *Processional*, Lawson joined with Mike Gold, John Dos Passos, Em Jo Basshe, and Francis Farragoh to found the New Playwrights Theatre in order to offer an alternative to the realism of Broadway and the bourgeois values of art theatres like The Theatre Guild. Although short-lived, it made a tremendous impact upon the American theatre, anticipating if not explicitly laying the groundwork for the experimental work associated with the Federal Theatre Project's "expressionist" Living Newspapers, and quite possibly, as Mardi Valgemae surmises, the Theatre of the Absurd (Valgemae, "Civil War" 10).

7

Sophie Treadwell's "pretty hands"

EIGHT MONTHS BEFORE GRADUATING FROM THE UNIVERSITY OF California at Berkeley in 1906, Sophie Treadwell took a leave of absence due to nervous exhaustion (Dickey, "Expressionist" 67). The reasons why are unclear. Perhaps her ministrations to victims of the San Francisco earthquake had simply taken their toll. Perhaps the prospect of graduation – and the uncertainties that loomed ahead – proved overwhelming to a woman who had thoroughly enjoyed her college career. Perhaps a love affair had ended badly. What we do know is that Treadwell retreated to the mountains of California, eventually finding work as a schoolteacher at a camp called Yankee Jim's.[1] Over the next several years, Treadwell held a series of odd jobs, working as a governess for two girls on a cattle ranch, an actor in a vaudeville play, and an amanuensis for the actor Helena Modjeska, all the while trying to find time to write her own plays. Financial uncertainties, however, constantly threatened to undermine her independence and her health; suffering another nervous breakdown in September 1909, Treadwell retired again to Yankee Jim's "to find peace" (Wynn 33). Although little evidence survives from this period in her life,[2] a few letters between Treadwell and her mother, Nettie, survive. They indicate that exacerbating – if not causing – Treadwell's condition was the relationship she had with her mother, an emotionally needy woman who relied upon her daughter's support after her marriage to Treadwell's father failed.[3] Why, her mother asks, does she not come home? Why, after leaving Yankee Jim's, does she repair to her aunt Josephine's house instead of coming home? Doesn't she realize what a humiliation it is for her own daughter to abandon her like this? And then, in a letter dated only "Tuesday morning," a chastened Nettie offers her daughter an olive branch, bearing congratulations for her first full-time job as a newspaper reporter (Treadwell, "Letters to mother"). The story that emerges from between the lines of these few letters is that Treadwell's adult independence had been hard won.

That that independence was won at the keys of a typewriter is worth noting. For, in providing her with a living wage and steady employment, Treadwell's job at the *San Francisco Bulletin* not only freed her from her mother's control, but – as the young Berkeley feminist was well aware – it granted her a freedom that women like her mother had never had. Determined never to be dependent upon a man the way her mother had been on her father, Treadwell saw journalism as a career that offered both intellectual satisfaction and financial independence. Indeed, she seems to have identified the typewriter itself with liberation, figuring it as such in a story she wrote for the *Bulletin*, entitled "How I Got My Husband and How I Lost Him, the Story of Jean Traig." In this serial, Treadwell tells the story of a neglected wife whose husband spent them into bankruptcy (presumably buying gifts for other women). With the promise that she can help him with his work, Jean begs him to buy her a typewriter and quickly teaches herself how to type. "I practiced on that typewriter day by day," Treadwell – as Traig – writes, "because I didn't know what else to do. It was 'something'" ("Jean Traig"). Something, Treadwell knew from her own experience, that could liberate her from the bonds of her dependency. Sure enough, Jean types her way out of this loveless marriage and into a job that gives her both financial independence and self-respect ("Jean Traig").

Sounding a theme that runs throughout Treadwell's writing, this story details the desperation that women feel when they are financially dependent upon men they do not love. Indeed, the stifling effects of such dependence is a theme that appears in both her reportage and her plays. As a journalist, she covered the sensational trials of Leah Alexander, a milliner who shot her married lover after he broke off their affair, and Elizabeth Blair Mohr, a wealthy physician's wife who hired her household servants to murder her husband and disfigure his mistress ("Her book, 1909–1914"). As a playwright, she often wrote about women seeking to free themselves from unhappy marriages, depicting a discontented wife who takes a lover in *Ladies Leave* (1929), and a neurasthenic woman who flirts with death in order to escape the boredom of her marriage in *For Saxophone* (1934). Most famous, of course, is *Machinal* (1928), a play that drew upon Treadwell's journalistic experience. Loosely based upon the trial of Ruth Snyder, who, along with her lover Judd Gray, was convicted of murdering Snyder's husband, *Machinal* portrays in episodic action the circumstances that might have led an "ordinary young woman" to murder her husband.

By the time she wrote *Machinal*, however, Treadwell appears to have begun to rethink the typewriter's significance. As the play's theme of mechanization suggests, such machines do not necessarily liberate women so much as subject them to further regulations on their lives. Eventually, Treadwell must have recognized that, while the typewriter had given her the means by which to support herself in a career, it was not able to alter the structure of patriarchal relations that continued to assign women to subordinate roles. For all her youthful optimism about the typewriter's ability to provide women with financial independence, Treadwell appears to have become newly ambivalent about the liberatory potential offered by such machines.

Reading *Machinal* as a meditation on these issues, I argue that the skills Treadwell learned as a journalist – specifically, the ability to imbue or disarticulate the performative attributes of her subjects from the words they spoke – were skills she drew upon in *Machinal*. Utilizing "characters in the background heard, but unseen" and "characters in the background seen, not heard" (496), Treadwell counterpoints the play's verbal, vocal, and pantomimic languages to express the spiritual disharmony that leads her central character to murder her husband. But what is more, I argue, Treadwell "points" on her character's "pretty hands" to comment not only on the commodification of women's bodies in the sex–gender system of traditional patriarchy, but on the anonymity of the female typewriter whose "pretty hand" inscribes the page.

Machinal and the reproduction of women's roles

The play begins in an office where a "Young Woman" works as a secretary for her boss, Mr. Jones. Oppressed by her job, she – along with her co-workers – speaks in a telegraphic style, having internalized the alienating rhythms of her work. Like Rice's Mr. Zero, she is a working drudge who has no life outside of her work; unlike him, she is the object of her boss's affections. Although she is physically disgusted by him, he offers her the only hope of escape available – marriage, complete with a promise to provide for her mother. Confused about her decision, the Young Woman consults her mother, who proves to be of little help. She, too, is unaware of the Young Woman's true desires, haranguing her with her own selfish needs as the strains of a "sentimental Mother song" ironically punctuate her advice. The Young Woman finds herself entering into marriage as if into legal prostitution, skittishly allowing herself to be pawed by her husband's "fat

Figure 11. Episode 1, "To Business," from Arthur Hopkins's 1928 production of Sophie Treadwell's *Machinal*. In this Taylorized hell, office workers perform their jobs with the precision of automata, eager to please their boss, who looks on with characteristic self-satisfaction.

hands." No longer Mr. Jones's secretary, she becomes Mr. Jones's wife but her job as wife and mother is no less alienating. When we see her in the recovery room after having given birth to a baby she will not nurse, the sound of jackhammers outside the hospital window symbolically describe her life as "machinal." In order to free herself from the industrial rhythms which order her life and sound its limitations, she takes a lover – a romantic outlaw who entertains her with stories of freedom and adventure in Mexico. Compared to his freedom, her married life becomes unbearable, and we see her driven first to distraction and then to murder. Tried and convicted, she is placed in prison but no more so, Treadwell seems to suggest, than she had been all the rest of her life. Calling out for "somebody, something" as she awaits her execution, the Young Woman begs for release from a life that has never truly been her own.

Thematically, *Machinal* illustrates how gender roles are produced and reproduced through a mechanistic process. Almost as if she had anticipated Judith Butler's theory of performativity, Treadwell suggests that gender is a performance that is made to appear natural through the enforced repetition of authorized codes of behavior. Only, in *Machinal*, it does not appear to be natural; the Young Woman's tragedy lies in her inability to perform that role with emotional conviction. Described in the preface as "an ordinary young woman, any woman" (Treadwell, *Machinal* 496), Treadwell's primary character appears as an allegorical "everywoman." A woman made, not born, she is defined by the structures all around her – work, family, law – a subject of their interpellating codes. The other characters who populate her world are similarly designated as types: a telephone girl, a stenographer, a filing clerk, an adding clerk, mother, husband, bellboy, nurse, doctor, young man, girl, man, boy, waiter, judge, lawyer, reporter, bailiff, jailer, matron, and priest. They exist to define her in relation to them and the interpellating structures they represent.[4] She is, for example, a secretary to her boss, a daughter to her mother, a wife to her husband, a patient to her doctor, a lover to her lover, a murderess to reporters, a criminal to the court, and a lost soul to the priest. Yet she is also always something more, as Treadwell indicates in the stage directions of her original manuscript:

> Of the characters, only the Young Woman is to be played as a straight, realistic performance[.] (She is any ordinary young woman. In age, any- where from eighteen to thirty, but probably twenty four)[.] All the other characters are to be played as "personifications" of what they represent (genuinely, type actors, giving type performances). Their make up (dress and facial) should be the "expression" of the kind of people they rep- resent, and once found should remain fixed (so as to become clear and established in the imagination of the audience). Gestures should not be quite automatic but simple and repetitious (as the make-up, – constantly declarative of what the characters are). (*Machinal* [typescript])

Thus, the actor playing the Young Woman must represent her alienation from the roles she is forced to play.

Indeed, her alienation from these roles is underscored throughout the play. In the first episode, for example, the Young Woman arrives late, sits idly in front of her broken typewriter, and "is preoccupied with herself" (497). Compared to her co-workers, who sort, file, add, subtract, answer, patch, transcribe, and type with hurried efficiency, she is the antithesis of a

Taylorized employee. Where she idly indulges a horrific fantasy about marrying her boss, they have accommodated themselves easily into their jobs: the telephone girl dexterously scorns a lover on one line while patching calls through on the others; the stenographer simultaneously composes letters and gossips about the Young Woman's marital prospects; the adding clerk cynically calculates the boss's worth while settling his accounts; to all of which the emasculated filing clerk responds "hot dog!" At once a source for their entertainment and a rival for their advancement, the Young Woman stands outside this office community. Alone, apart, she does not fit the role she has been assigned.

We see this alienation resurface in episode two, yet in a different form, as the Young Woman struggles to understand her duties as a daughter and a wife. Announcing to her mother that "There's a man wants to marry me" (502), she seeks her mother's advice. She doesn't love this man, she explains, but feels compelled to get married: "All women get married, don't they?" (502), she asks in earnest. "I suppose I got to marry somebody – all girls do – " (504). "Nonsense," her mother replies, disdaining the idea of love even as she insists upon her own material needs. The boss is a "decent" man, she coldly reasons, simply by virtue of his position as vice-president; the Young Woman would be "crazy" not to marry him and assure both of them a secure future (503–4). To the charge of "crazy," however, the Young Woman breaks down, accusing her mother of not listening, of not having any pity, of taking her labors for granted. "I'll kill you!" she shouts in an exasperated (and ominous) fury, finally softening when she sees her mother cry. As the strains of a "sentimental Mother song" come on the radio, she apologizes, telling her mother to sit and rest while she cleans up. But, as she puts on her rubber gloves to do the dishes, her mother lashes out in scorn: "I've been washing dishes for forty years and I never wore gloves! But my lady's hands! My lady's hands!" (504). "It's my hands got me a husband" (504), the Young Woman explains, announcing both her resolve and her recognition of how the sex–gender system works. The traditional patriarch being absent, she has become the currency of exchange between the households of her mother and her boss.

Again, in episode three, the Young Woman is alienated from her role, this time as wife to her husband. Barely able to tolerate being in the same room with him, she paces around their honeymoon suite "as though looking for a way out" (505). He, meanwhile, is oblivious to her discomfort, holding her on his lap and pawing her with his "fat hands" while regaling her with ribald jokes. Finally, in resignation, she retires to the bathroom to get undressed, returning stoically – and, then, hysterically – to her fate. That fate becomes evident in episode four, where the Young Woman lies in a hospital bed after having given birth to a baby girl. Physically and emotionally exhausted, she literally has no voice, shaking her head "no" to wanting the baby, "no" to nursing it, "no" to closing the window, and "no" to her husband's insistence that he knows exactly how she feels. Finally, feeling that she has "submitted to enough," she recovers her voice to shout "no" to the doctor's order that the baby be brought to nurse, begging simply to be "let alone – let alone" (508). Although the nurse tries to intervene on her behalf, telling the doctor that "she's behaved very badly every time" (508), the doctor asserts his authority and reissues his directive, proving that any resistance to her assigned role will be disciplined with force.

The mother's demands, the husband's advances, the doctor's orders – all reveal how the Young Woman's life is propelled by forces beyond her control. Indeed, her life is not so much propelled as *com*pelled by such forces, suggesting that it is not her own but the by-product, as Butler would have it, of social structures reproducing themselves through the compulsory actions of their subjects. Like Butler, Treadwell takes a rather bleak view of the defining power that social institutions have over women's lives. She depicts the ideological apparatus of the family, in particular, as a binding force upon women's freedoms. Within its constraints, women must perform the emotional work of filial, erotic, and maternal love, often without regard for their own feelings and needs. Yet, without a way to satisfy those feelings and fulfill those needs within the family structure, women are prohibited from going outside of it, being subject to moral codes regulating female sexuality. "Prohibited" is significantly the title of episode five, where the Young Woman begins a tryst with a handsome adventurer upon the urging of the telephone girl and her lover. The scene is a speakeasy, the liminality of which is represented not only by the free-flowing libations, but by the other couples who seek refuge for unsanctioned acts of love. At one table is a "middle-aged fairy" seducing an "untouched" youth with Amontillado and his affection. At another is an "ordinary" man and woman whose Hemingwayesque indirection reveals an unwanted pregnancy. Episode six finds the Young Woman and her lover in his apartment, luxuriating in the afterglow of their affair. However proscribed their union is morally, Treadwell establishes it as good and just. We see this in the way the Young Woman – now denominated "Woman" – speaks, moves, and acts. Having spent most of her life disciplined into observing what a young Herbert Marcuse referred to as the "performance principle," she finally has experienced pleasure by "desublimating" her repressed sexual desires.⁵ No longer is she alienated from the role she plays; as a "lover" she loves and loves well.

Back at home, however, she is beset again by the role she must play for her husband. Goaded into asking him about his business success, she plays her part "by rote"

> YOUNG WOMAN: Did you put it over?
> HUSBAND: Sure I put it over.
> YOUNG WOMAN: Did you swing it?
> HUSBAND: Sure I swung it.
> YOUNG WOMAN: Did they come through?
> HUSBAND: Sure they came through.
> YOUNG WOMAN: Did they sign?
> HUSBAND: I'll say they signed.
> YOUNG WOMAN: On the dotted line?
> HUSBAND: On the dotted line.
> YOUNG WOMAN: The property's yours?
> HUSBAND: The property's mine.   (517)

With self-satisfaction, the husband goes on to explain how he'll finalize the deal, turning the line of questioning around by asking "Happy?" to which his wife responds "Happy" – again "by rote." So oppressive is her life in this home that the Young Woman can only imaginatively break free, identifying with stories she reads in the newspaper about women who commit suicide, women who leave for love, women who disappear. A headline about a revolution in Mexico, however, prompts her to remember her lover's story about killing a man to be free. And the freedom she confines to her imagination soon erupts into her reality with force.

Episode eight opens on a courtroom in which the Young Woman is being tried for the murder of her husband. Although she tries to play the role of innocent bystander, claiming two men murdered her husband as she slept beside him, her performance on the stand is no more convincing than any of her previous turns. Innocent victim is yet another role she does not fit. No matter, though; a corrupt press is there to interpellate her into the ready-made roles of its scandal sheets. Treadwell dramatizes this through a chorus of newspaper reporters whose commentary upon the courtroom action as it unfolds reveals the gap between the reality we see and its representation in print. The Young Woman is said to tell a story that is at once "straightforward" yet "rambling, disconnected" (522); she is

SOPHIE TREADWELL   219

said to be at once "pale and trembling" yet "flushed but calm" (525). Unable
to account for the complicating circumstances of her life, the newspaper
reporters sensationalize the confession she is compelled to make, casting
her as a cold-blooded "murderess" or a betrayed lover whose "paramour
brings confession" (526). Even in the hallowed halls of justice, her story is
not her own (167).

A criminal, a convict, an outcast from society, the Young Woman paradoxically finds in jail a role that she can accept in episode nine. Identifying
with a Negro spiritual sung by an off-stage janitor, she stops the priest and
matron from silencing him, explaining "He helps me . . . I understand him.
He is condemned. I understand him" (527). Although Treadwell problemat-
ically conflates gender and racial oppression in this passage, she suggests that
the only freedom available to the Young Woman is outside the dominant
structures of society. The murder, as Barbara Bywaters argues, has made her
free: "When I did what I did I was free" (528).[6] Because her act was authen-
tically her own, she will accept her new role as criminal. But, if that role
places her outside the structure of oppressive gender norms, it also places
her back into the interpellating structure of the law. This is the ultimate
irony, Treadwell suggests: there is no freedom from the gender-prescribed
roles that society imposes upon women.

Treadwell powerfully illustrates the impossibility of escaping from such
roles through her use of stage space. As she notes at the beginning of her
play, the stage set remains consistent throughout. Although windows open
onto different scenes and doors lead to different places, the placement of
those windows and doors never changes. What does change is the way that
space is used to contextualize the social relationships of the characters who
occupy it. Thus, while the various roles the Young Woman plays over the
course of her life appear to change, they are, in fact, as unchanging as the
set itself. Treadwell specifies:

> Scenically this play is planned to be handled in two basic sets (or in one
> set with two backs).
>   The first division – (The first Four Episodes) – needs an entrance at
> one side, and a back having a door and a large window. The door gives,
> in
>
> Episode   1 – to Vice President's office.
>   "   2 – " hall.
>   "   3 – " bathroom.
>   "   4 – " corridor.

And the window shows, in

  '' 1 – An opposite office.
  '' 2 – An inner apartment court.
  '' 3 – Window of a dance casino opposite.
  '' 4 – Steel girders.   (496)

With the shift from the play's first to its second half, however, the back door is removed and the window is barred, suggesting a further limitation of the space in which the Young Woman is allowed to move, both literally and figuratively:

> The second division – (the last Five Episodes) – has the same side entrance, but the back has only one opening – for a small window (barred).
>
> Episode 5 – window is masked by electric piano.
>   '' 6 – '' disclosed (sidewalk outside).
>   '' 7 – '' curtained.
>   '' 8 – '' masked by Judge's bench.
>   '' 9 – '' disclosed (sky outside).
>   (496)

Only in episodes six ("Intimate") and nine ("A Machine") is the window "disclosed." Significantly, these are the episodes in which the Young Woman experiences the greatest freedom, first through a love affair and then through her suggested death. That these experiences take place in front of an open window is notable, given the Young Woman's desperate plea for fresh air in episodes three ("Honeymoon"), four ("Maternal"), and seven ("Domestic"). The window seems to figure the possibility of freedom from the roles she is forced to play, and – insofar as those roles are gendered – from the body itself. The stage, then, is not only the space in which the body performs, but the space of the body.

But how are we to interpret the Young Woman's execution at the end of episode nine? Is it a moment of transcendence, in which she is liberated from the constraints placed upon her female body? Or is it an ironic commentary upon the possibility of such a freedom? Jerry Dickey suggests that Treadwell herself might have been ambivalent about the resolution of her play, detecting a note of ambivalence in *For Saxophone* as well. "While creating works that depict women as subjects of the drama, Treadwell cannot yet envision them completely empowered or victorious," Dickey observes, noting however that "she refuses to allow her audiences to feel comfortable

with their defeat" ("The 'Real Lives'" 182). Given the way that Treadwell
represents the Young Woman's execution, it would seem that, if she does
experience freedom through death, it is at best an ironic freedom. For, even
as she is led to her death, she is violated once again. Her physical body,
represented by her hair, is stripped from her as the barber shaves her head.
Her personality, represented by the words she wishes to tell her daughter, is
denied. Led off to her execution, the Young Woman calls for "Somebody!"
to help. But when she calls again from the margins of the darkened stage,
"her voice is cut off" (529), effecting her total annihilation. She herself has
become a disembodied voice and, in death, a mute presence.

Female "typewriters" and "pretty hands"

When *Machinal* was first produced, many reviewers saw it as a straightforward dramatization of the events which led Ruth Snyder to murder her
husband. Some dismissed it on those grounds, presuming it to be a further
exploitation of the already infamous trial, made trendy by its expressionistic
style (often misattributed to Arthur Hopkins, the play's producer). Upon
its recovery by feminist scholars in the 1980s, however, *Machinal* was finally
given serious literary-critical attention. Insisting upon making a distinction between the trial that undoubtedly inspired it and the thematic and
formal elements that made it a play, many of these early feminist critics
interpreted the play as a powerful indictment of the patriarchal institution
of marriage. More recently, critics have begun to recontextualize the play
within the history of the Snyder trial not to dismiss Treadwell's achievement
but to better assess its feminist contribution. Jennifer Jones, for example,
carefully examines the play against the details of the trial in order to argue
that,

> *Machinal* is the testimony, disallowed by the court of law, that Treadwell
> wished to introduce into the court of public opinion. She sets forth her
> argument in a drama, not to prove Snyder's innocence, but to ask if perhaps
> there is another way of looking at the case, one that an all-male jury and
> predominantly male press corps did not understand. (486)[7]

Similarly, Ginger Strand convincingly argues that, in its focus on the media,
Machinal "outlines the process by which the reality of Ruth Snyder's story
was transformed into narrative – the process by which any woman's story is
reconfigured, retold, and absorbed into an ideology not her own" (167).

While I am in general agreement with these critics, reading the play as a feminist critique of the dependent roles into which patriarchal institutions interpellate women, I am not quite satisfied with an interpretation that accounts only for the play's narrative development and not its expressionistic style. For, while Treadwell most certainly seeks to critique patriarchy, the manner in which she does so invites further consideration of the meanings deployed by her play. The Young Woman's alienation is represented not only in the ill-fitting roles she is forced to play, after all, but in the play's disarticulation of bodies, voices, and words, suggesting that hers is the sort of modernist alienation described by S. S. Curry and his followers. Indeed, the recurrent motif of machines and mechanization to represent her dis-ease seems to identify the expressive culture movement as a probable source of the play's expressionistic form. As a young woman growing up at the turn of the twentieth century, Treadwell certainly would have known of Curry's theory of expression and its popularization through the expressive culture movement. As a drama student at Berkeley, she was probably trained in its methods. Like O'Neill, Rice, and Lawson, then, Treadwell appears to have developed her expressionistic style by ironizing Curry's theory of expression. Like them, she features an alienated central character; like them, she represents her character's spiritual disharmony by counterpointing – rather than coordinating – her play's verbal, vocal, and pantomimic languages. If, as we've seen, these expressionistic techniques also functioned as an affective allegory for their playwrights' own professional and artistic concerns, then it seems not unlikely that Treadwell's may, too. Unfortunately, few details about Treadwell's personal life are known. Those that are, however, suggest that, where her play diverges from the facts of the Snyder trial, her own life may have been a source to fill those gaps.

As Jones has documented, several details in the play suggest that the Young Woman was directly modeled on Ruth Synder: her dreamy state of mind, her habit of smoothing her hair, her tendency to faint (e.g., on the subway), her transition from a secretary to the wife of a man much older than she, her decision to marry for financial security, her apprehension of consummating the marriage on her wedding night, her general unhappiness in the marriage, her extra-marital affair, and her attraction to a lover whose travels represented freedom to her (490–1). Yet, there are differences, too.[8] Aside from the specific facts of the trial that Jones identifies are aspects of the Young Woman's life that resonate with Treadwell's own. When Treadwell was a young woman, after all, she – like her central character – was responsible for supporting her mother. That Treadwell found the situation burdensome, that it drove her "crazy," and that it threatened her own independence, we have already seen. Although it would be too easy to presume that episode two is directly autobiographical, the conflict between societal expectations to marry and the desire to pursue a career appears in several of Treadwell's early plays, suggesting that there is something about the affective tenor of this scene that rings true.[9]

When she married William O. McGeehan, a noted sportswriter, in 1910, for example, Treadwell found herself capitulating to the expectation that, as a wife, she should resign her position at the *Bulletin* in order to assume the domestic duties of the home. Six months after her marriage, however, she suffered yet another bout of nervous exhaustion and was sent to a sanitarium to recuperate (Dickey, *Research* 8). Upon her recovery, she began writing weekly book reviews (Ross 584), returning to her newspaper career full time in 1914. Although "Details about Treadwell's marriage to McGeehan are difficult to reconstruct," Dickey cautiously observes, "a short parable entitled 'The Gift,' apparently written by Treadwell at this time, suggests that McGeehan may have had difficulty living with Treadwell's increasing fame and independence" (*Research* 8–9). While she followed him from San Francisco to New York, they maintained separate residences off and on (*Research* 9).

Clearly, Treadwell harbored doubts about the institution of marriage. However much she may have loved McGeehan, she appears to have distrusted the dependent role that marriage assigned to women, having witnessed the devastating effects of her parents' marriage upon her mother. Perhaps this is why Ruth Snyder's story struck her as especially resonant. In it, she may have found both a template for thinking through the implications of marital restrictions on a woman's life and a point of her own affective identification. But, while this is a recurrent theme that appears in much of Treadwell's writing, its treatment in *Machinal* is unique. For, where Treadwell had once figured the typewriter as a means of liberation from a restrictive marriage, here the typewriter appears as a broken promise, in idle disrepair on the Young Woman's desk (*Machinal* 500). Sometime between 1914 and 1928, it seems, Treadwell came to realize that, while the typewriter offered women the means of self-authorization, the machine itself was not liberatory, especially when it was in the service of a patriarchal regime.

This was undoubtedly a lesson that Treadwell, herself, had learned the hard way. According to Ishbel Ross, Treadwell had to work her way up the masculine ranks of the San Francisco *Bulletin*, from the position of secretary, in which her duties were to "answer the telephone and type a little," to drama critic and eventually crime reporter, but only after receiving several lucky breaks (Ross 584). Later, as a special correspondent for *Harper's Weekly* during World War I, Treadwell again found herself having to overcome gender bias when, as a woman, she was not allowed to go to the front lines (Ross 377). Retreating to the army hospitals in Paris, Treadwell reported on the courageous civilians who celebrated life in the face of destruction, only to have her editors refuse to publish her dispatches, dismissing them as "the merest rubbish" ("War Correspondence," MS 318, Box 10). Even in her playwriting career, Treadwell encountered gender bias. Upon the advice of her mentor, Helena Modjeska, she submitted her first play manuscript under the name of "S. Treadwell," using a first initial to guarantee a fair reading – and a fair price.[10] Several years later, she again had to challenge the presumption of feminine weakness, threatening a lawsuit against John Barrymore when he purloined her play manuscript on the life of Edgar Allan Poe and attributed it to his wife. Although the typewriter gave her a means of self-authorization, it could not guarantee her that her work would be read without bias or even credited as her own. These experiences must have made her feel that her words and her identity had been erased.[11]

In *Machinal*, the Young Woman's words and identity are likewise erased. Sitting at her desk, in front of the broken typewriter, she free-associates about the horrid prospect of entering into a loveless marriage when it is clear she has no other choice. With no means of self-authorization before her, it is as if she has no self. Treadwell thematizes the erasure of selfhood in the dialogue that begins her play. All of the office employees engage ceaselessly in their automated work routines while simultaneously living out their own lives. Typing, adding, filing, patching, all are routinized mechanical skills, devoid of any personal expression. Treadwell draws our attention to this with a bit of patter in which the dim-witted filing clerk wonders aloud why folder Q is empty. The telephone girl explains that it's not "popular," to which the adding clerk quips, "Has it personality?" – a pun the stenographer and telephone girl play out, asking whether it's got halitosis or has "it," that indescribable quality of personality possessed by "it" girl, Clara Bow (497). Besides representing the utter inanity of the Young Woman's office companions, this dialogue helps establish the theme of emptiness that suffuses the Young Woman's life. Like folder Q, she has no personality to express; she is empty but must be filed in accordance with the laws of order.

As we've seen in chapter 2, the term "personality" had a special resonance in the early twentieth century, deriving from the specificity of its use in the expressive culture movement. Meaning that which is unique and unreproducible within any one individual, it described an essential quality that exceeded Delsarte's anatomization of gesture and expression. Without machine technology, of course, there would have been no need for such a concept. But, with the implementation of machines such as the typewriter, personality came to describe that which was unreproducible by machine. Handwriting, for example, came to be viewed as revealing something unique about the person whose hand inscribed the page. "Graphology," as the new science of handwriting analysis was deemed, dates to 1875, when Jean-Hippolyte Michon first theorized a connection between *how* one rendered one's characters and one's *own* character (Sonnemann 4). Like Delsarte's system of expression upon which it was based, Michon's "système de graphologie" proved foundational if ultimately untenable in the hands of unskilled followers, prompting Ludwig Klages to develop a more rigorous "scientific" approach.[12] Examining the pressure, width, size, and slant of the letters, as well as the harmony of movement, Klages claimed to be able to determine the dominant presence of reason, sentiment, or will within the writer's personality. Thus, graphology, like Delsarte's system of expression, was based upon a moral-psychological understanding of personality. It defined handwriting as "a rhythmic movement condition, in which each single movement reflects the entire personality, the sum total of the writer's intellectual, emotional, and physical tendencies" (Nevo 9).

Where graphology encouraged the cultivation of a "pretty hand," the better to reveal one's personality, typescript became valued for other reasons. The uniformity of its letters, the regularity of its spacing, and the ease of its comprehension made it a preferred mode of writing for business correspondence. Accordingly, secretarial work began to change. As handwriting was replaced by typescript, so were male clerks replaced by female "typewriters," leading to the feminization of the profession. Indeed, the gender demographics of secretarial work radically changed at the turn of the twentieth century. Between 1880 and 1890, the percentage of men to women working as stenographers or typists reversed itself: where, in 1880, 60 percent of these positions were held by men, 63.8 percent were occupied by women only ten years later. By 1920, women held 91.8 percent of such positions (US Bureau of the Census, quoted in Kittler 184). Friedrich Kittler suggests that the typewriter itself was largely responsible for this shift in gender dynamics.

For in 1881, the marketing strategists of Wyckoff, Seamans, and Benedict made a discovery: they recognized the fascination their unmarketable machine held for the battalions of unemployed women. When Lillian Sholes, as "presumably" the "first type-writer" in history, sat and posed in front of her father's prototype in 1872, female typists came into existence for purposes of demonstration, but as a profession and career, the stenotypist had yet to come. That was changed by the central branch of the Young Woman's Christian Association in New York City, which trained eight young women in 1881 to become typists and immediately received hundreds of inquiries (at $10 a week) from the corporate world. A feedback loop was created connecting recruitment, training, supply, demand, new recruitment, and so on – first in the United States, and shortly thereafter through Christian women's associations in Europe.

Thus evolved the exponential function of female secretaries and the bell curve of male secretaries. Ironically enough, the clerks, office helpers, and poet-apprentices of the nineteenth century, who were exclusively male, had invested so much pride in their laboriously trained handwriting as to overlook Remington's innovation for seven years. The continuous and coherent flow of ink, that material substrate of in-dividuals and indivisibilities, made them blind to a historical chance. (Kittler 193)

While the typewriter created new jobs for women to fill, it also assigned a lower value to the type of work they did. This was in large part due to the mechanical process of transcription. For, as Andreas Huyssen has noted with regard to mass culture generally, the association between biological reproduction and technologies of mass reproduction led to its feminization (and derogation) within the cultural imaginary. Undoubtedly, this same logic was at work in resymbolizing the gender of secretarial work.

In being marketed for use by female employees, the typewriter not only feminized a formerly respectable white-collar profession for men but, in doing so, relegated that profession to a more subordinate position within the office, replicating the patriarchal structure of marriage. The roles assigned to women in the office were not unlike those assigned to them at home. Indeed, Ruth Snyder – like the Young Woman and many women – worked as a secretary for her husband before marrying him. What is more, the typewriter symbolically erased the secretary's "personality," perhaps suggesting to Treadwell an analogy between the standardized forms of typescript and the standardized roles that women were assigned under patrarichy. Thus, rather than open doors to women by offering financial independence and a means of self-authorization, the typewriter appears to have become for Treadwell by 1928 a symbol of the patriarchal "machine" that subjects women to its interpellative logic.

Whether and to what extent Treadwell was using the typewriter to figure marriage as a mode of inscription – one that erases the woman's personality by replacing her identity with the characters of the man's name – is debatable. But running throughout her play is the motif of the Young Woman's "pretty hands." In her stage directions, Treadwell tells us that the Young Woman has "well kept hands" (497); the Young Woman herself remarks upon her boss's request to "hold [her] pretty little hands" (501); "It's my hands got me a husband," she tells her mother (504); her lover likewise compliments her "mighty pretty hands" (514); and, with his words ringing in her ears, she resumes her habit of wearing rubber gloves at night to protect and soften her hands – despite her husband's dislike of the gloves – providing the prosecution with a damning piece of evidence to introduce at her trial (523). Her husband's hands, by contrast, are "fat": "George H. Jones – Fat hands – flabby hands – don't touch me – please – fat hands are never weary," she free-associates at her desk (501); "When he puts a hand on me, my blood turns cold," she tells her mother, "his hands are fat – and they sort of press – and they're fat – don't you see?" (503). She even wonders what kind of hands God must have: "God is love – even if he's bad they got to love him – even if he's got fat hands – fat hands – no no – he wouldn't be God – His hands make you well – He lays on his hands" (508–9). Whether pretty, fat, or healing, hands are important to the overall meaning of Treadwell's play. They represent both the materiality of existence and the essence of the personality that they express.

In the case of the Young Woman, her hands serve to instantiate her existence, functioning much like a "point" where text and performance meet. But instead of a device that actors used to realize the meanings of the playwright's text, here the "point" functions as a device by which to inscribe the actor's body into the playwright's text. Unlike O'Neill, however, who inscribed his actors' bodies in order to ironize their characters' agency, Treadwell seems to use the "point" to assert her character's agency (if only provisionally) and disrupt the textual constraints upon her life. Her "pretty hands," in other words, erupt into the patriarchal narratives that attempt to define her life. Each time they do, we are made to see how poorly she fits the roles that they assign to her. But, because her hands function as a sign of her corporeal existence, they also represent her inability to transcend its limits. It is almost as if she is only a body, with no personality to express.

This focus on personality provides further evidence that Treadwell was influenced by the expressive culture movement. The Young Woman's alienation – her lack of personality – is, after all, a result not only of her enforced submission to patriarchy, as feminist critics have long maintained, but of the machines that inscribe her into a patriarchal logic. Thus, if Treadwell figures patriarchy as a narrative, as Strand persuasively argues, and if the play's use of machines is meant to suggest the Young Woman's inscription into that narrative, then perhaps the motif of her character's "pretty hands" is meant to suggest a point (so to speak) of resistance to such narratives. Treadwell emphasizes her character's "pretty hands," in other words, in order to reinsert the body back into the text and back into the writing processes that deny it.

Pretty hands, a nice voice, and a hell of a word

In creating her expressionistic technique, Treadwell does more than just inscribe the Young Woman's body into her text. She also counterpoints bodies, voices, and words. Whether she was directly inspired by the expressionistic plays of O'Neill, Rice, and Lawson, we cannot know, though Rice strongly believed that she had been influenced by *The Subway*.[13] What we do know is that Treadwell spent a summer studying with Richard Boleslavsky at his American Laboratory Theatre in 1923. And, as Dickey has suggested, that experience may very well have provided her with her ideas for the play's experimental form.[14] For among the lessons that Boleslavsky taught was one concerning rhythm.[15] In his *Acting, The First Six Lessons*, Boleslavsky writes, for example, that "the first level of Rhythm [is] consciousness. The second level arrives when outside forces impose their Rhythm on you" (119). Identifying some of those outside forces as "Rivets, horns, bells, grind of gears and high-pitched groans of breaks, whistles, gongs and sirens," he observes that they

> all seem to yell in a steady rhythm, "Go to work – right away. Go to work – right away." It is like two-fourths time in music repeated endlessly – with ever increasing volume. We are part of that rhythm. We walk faster. We breathe faster. Whatever words you say to me, you flash like radio signals. I answer you with speed. (109–10)

In making a distinction between conscious and external rhythms, and in associating the latter with mechanization and modernity, Boleslavsky clearly echoes Curry and his followers in the expressive culture movement.

Unlike Curry, however, he seems less concerned with countering these rhythms than with learning how to use them to represent various states of a character's existence.[16] Although he does not name Delsarte directly, Boleslavsky appears to refer to his method when identifying the twenty-six hand positions in Leonardo da Vinci's *The Last Supper*, describing the "orderly and measurable changes" between them as an illustration of the principle of rhythm (113–14). Citing Emile Jaques-Dalcroze, Isadora Duncan, and Angna Enters specifically, Boleslavsky suggests that he is, indeed, indebted to Delsarte and his legacy in turn-of-the-century expressive culture (111–14). Thus, if Treadwell were prompted to revisit Curry's theory of expression, she may have seen the spectrum of dramatic possibilities it offered from its refraction through Boleslavsky's prism.

Whatever its immediate source, Treadwell's expressionistic style clearly seems to involve a contrapuntal layering of bodies, voices, and words. This formal arrangement is immediately made evident in the stage directions to her play. As they indicate, her primary character's physical presence is constantly juxtaposed against voiceless presences and disembodied voices from off-stage. Along with her list of dramatis personae, for example, she specifically delineates the roles of "Characters in the Background Heard, but Unseen" – such as a janitor, a baby, a boy and girl, a husband and wife, a radio announcer, and a "Negro" singer – and "Characters in the Background Seen, Not Heard" – couples of men and women dancing, a woman in a bathrobe, a woman in a wheelchair, a nurse with a covered basin, a nurse with a tray, the feet of men and women passing in the street. She also calls for a variety of "mechanical offstage sounds" that are "chosen primarily for their inherent emotional effect" (496). These include: office machines (typewriters, telephones, adding machines, etc.), a radio, a small jazz band, steel riveting, an electric piano, a hand organ, telegraph instruments, and an airplane engine.[17] Together, these mute bodies and disarticulated sounds (both human and mechanical) combine to create a spatial and aural landscape of alienation in which the Young Woman lives.

Sound, in particular, is used to represent the Young Woman's spiritual disharmony. In episode two, for example, the Young Woman attempts to break free from society's expectation that she will become a wife and mother by rejecting her own mother's selfish logic, but the voices of a boy and girl sneaking out to see each other, the voice of a wife coyly resisting her husband's "silly kiss," and the "sentimental Mother song" on the radio all conscript her back into the ranks of patriarchal order. In episode four, a phallic jackhammer pounds unceasingly into the concrete outside her hospital room. Although it is explained diegetically by the nurse who remarks upon the new hospital wing that is being built, its effect is expressionistic in suggesting that the very ground of the Young Woman's existence is being ripped up from underneath her feet. Episode seven features the non-diegetic sounds of a barrel organ, her lover's voice, and accusatory voices that ring inside the Young Woman's head. Recalling the freedom to be herself that she experienced in his arms, these sounds echo within the lonely house that is her prison. This theme of freedom is sounded again in episode nine, when the Young Woman hears an airplane engine buzzing outside the window of her jail cell. As the priest proclaims "God in His Heaven," the Young Woman refuses his interpretation and the orthodoxy of obedience he preaches, insisting that the man with wings "is not an angel! . . . He has wings – but he isn't free! I've been free, Father! For one moment – down here on earth – I have been free! When I did what I did I was free!" (528). The airplane, then, functions as a sort of ironic *deus ex machina*; although it, like the electric chair to come, would seem to promise the Young Woman a kind of deliverance, Treadwell suggests that it is a deliverance bought at the cost of her soul in that it is a machine representing the regulatory forces of oppression.

Treadwell similarly uses silent images to represent a world apart from the one in which the Young Woman lives. In episode three, she looks out the window of the honeymoon suite she shares with her new husband, expecting a view of the ocean. What she sees instead is the image of dancers "going round and round in couples" to the accompaniment of a small jazz band (505). Almost as if they were projections on a movie screen, the dancing couples present a vision of idealized love and romance – something notably absent from the honeymoon scene before us. Hoping for an oceanic feeling of freedom from the life she had lived with her mother,[18] the Young Woman must content herself with a mass-produced image of happiness that substitutes for the real thing. Much like the false ideal of this image is that represented in the background of episode four. Here, the Young Woman's voiceless protestations against motherhood and nursing are implicitly denied by the dutiful nurses and docile patients that pass silently down the hall. Although she ultimately submits to the doctor's will, the Young Woman's submission has already been prefigured in these mute and passive images. In episode six, however, the silent background image makes a different statement. As she and her lover take refuge in his garden apartment, the rest of the world goes by, represented by "the feet of men and women passing in the street" (497).[19] It is as if Treadwell were suggesting that the freedom this Young Woman – any woman – wants poses no threat to the rest of the world. If it were in fact granted, life would be sure to go on. Such an appeal is made all the more powerful by the way Treadwell presents this idea. Because we can recognize it as a palpable possibility, if not yet a fully integrated part of the reality depicted on stage, we can imagine such freedoms into actual existence.

Treadwell's use of sounds and images – to represent both freedom and its negation – suggests that they have a greater power of expression than do words. This may seem strange for a woman who, in her early career, represented a woman's freedom as lying in the power to authorize her own words. Yet, as we have seen, Treadwell's initial enthusiasm for writing was tempered by her realization that language bore other significations than those denoted in its words. Insofar as it was marked as "women's writing" it could be disparaged, disqualified, dismissed. Thus, for women to obtain a meaningful freedom from gender oppression, they would have to challenge the institutions that enforce a gender divide. This, I believe, is what Treadwell is seeking to do here in her play. Through her use of sound and image, she is critiqueing the ways in which language is used to uphold male institutions of power. The meaningless clichés spoken by her colleagues, her mother, her husband, the nurse, the newspaper reporters, the judge, the priest all indicate the bankruptcy of language if it is isolated from other forms of meaning.

We see this, for example, in episode one, where the telegraphically terse dialogue of the Young Woman's office companions is spoken in "the monotonous voice of [their] monotonous thoughts" (497). Stripped of all extra-verbal levels of meaning – e.g., inflection, intonation, acuity, force, pitch – their words are reduced to their functional significance. Almost as if these workers are themselves machines, they are unable to impart any humanity into their communication. Nor, for that matter, is their boss, the Young Woman's husband. But, as a salesman, he is not subject to the industrial rhythm of machines; presumably, his work requires the human touch. The telephone, however, appears to have altered his rhythms of speech. For, as we see in episode seven, the only style of speech he knows is the unctuous patter of salesmanship which he chatters even at home. The Young Woman, by contrast, seeks to speak meaningfully throughout the play of her own hopes, desires, and dreams. But, in a world of uncomprehending ears, her voice often gives out. In episode four, as we've seen, she signs "no" with a shake of her head to the nurse's ministrations, her husband's solicitations, and the doctor's orders. Again, at the end of episodes seven and eight, the

Young Woman loses her voice. Her fantasia of murderous freedom ends in a cry of terror at the recognition of what she must do. The confession extracted from her at her trial similarly resolves in a moan of protracted grief. The "Young Woman begins to moan – suddenly – as though the realization of her enormity and her isolation had just come upon her. It is a sound of desolation, of agony, of human woe" (526). It is a sound whose humanity resonates against the "routine – mechanical" words and actions of the other characters in the courtroom (519).

While these scenes illustrate the power of non-verbal forms of communication to make meaning (e.g., the pantomime of a shaking head, the vocality of a cry or moan), they do not necessarily *critique* verbal significance itself. Yet Treadwell does just this in episode six of her play. Here, three groups of couples meet in a space where they can "speak easy," if not freely, of their desires that transgress social norms. One couple talks about an abortion, of their mixed feelings about it, and of the financial demands that make it necessary. Another talks about a homosexual encounter, of drinking Amontillado, and of the pleasures of the flesh. At the third table are two couples – the telephone girl and her married lover, the Young Woman and "Richard Roe" – who talk about adulterous love. Significantly, none of these couples actually says what they mean. "Abortion" is nowhere mentioned at the first table, "homosexuality" at the second, "adultery" at the third. Yet, it is clear from their circumlocutions what it is exactly that they mean. That these words are absent from their speech,while their meanings are made otherwise present, suggests that, contrary to Eliot, meaning does not reside in words alone. It resides as much in the pauses between them; in the context which defines them; in the gestures, nods, and expressions that straighten the path of indirection. Treadwell thus makes a canny critique of Eliotic modernism's assumptions about how language means. But, in case we missed the significance of this episode, she repeats the lesson by means of negation where, in the play's final scene, the priest ministers to the Young Woman's spiritual needs by chanting to her in Latin.

In both of these episodes, Treadwell demonstrates how meaning is either facilitated or restricted by the social structures which define the context of enunciation. The speakeasy, as a liminal space, is outside the dominant structures of discourse. While the characters who enter it speak the language into which they've been interpellated by society, they are nonetheless freed by this space to reinvent the rules of the language game they play. The jail, by contrast, reinforces literally the discursive structures from which the Young Woman has strayed. Although she seeks spiritual freedom by identifying with the Negro's song, she is disciplined back into her position of subjection by the priest. While the difference between these two spaces is not specifically gendered, Treadwell suggests throughout the play that the discursive structures in which the Young Woman is trapped are. That is, she seems to anticipate many of the insights made by French post-structuralist feminist theorists who identify dominant structures of language use with patriarchal authority.[20]

Where she differs from French post-structuralist feminism, however, lies in where she locates the gendered divide. Rather than distinguish between a feminine chora and a masculine thetic subject, Treadwell addresses the gender implications of the text/performance split, identifying verbal signification with masculine authority and performative modes of expression with women. Such an association was not unique to Treadwell. As Elizabeth Bell has discussed, the growing visibility of women in the expressive culture movement at the turn of the twentieth century was one of the main reasons it fell into intellectual disfavor (362). Indeed, much of the rhetoric in the debates surrounding the text/performance split derogated performance as a specifically feminine practice. Nancy Lee Chalfa Ruyter notes that

> The most striking difference between the men and the women associated with American Delsartism is in the scope of their expressional endeavors. All were involved in performance genres in which the spoken word was primary: recitations of stories or poems, dramatic readings, play productions, and oratory. In addition, at least 25 percent of the women, but only a few of the men, also taught and presented dance or quasi-dance pieces such as statue posing, tableaux mouvants, pantomime, Delsartean attitudes, and drills in their recitals. Most male Delsarteans limited their presentations to mainly verbal material, using bodily expression for enhancement of a text rather than as an end in itself. (59)

Contemporary calls for a more "literary" drama, then, were in fact calls for a remasculinization of the genre. But, while this was no problem for O'Neill or Rice, who sought to elevate the theatre above the mass cultural forms of melodrama and film, or even Lawson, whose critique of representation bore a masculinist bias, it was a problem for female playwrights such as Treadwell. Although she similarly ironizes Curry's theory of expression in order to lament the plight of the artist in the age of mechanical reproduction, she does so not to assert the importance of verbal signification over performative modes of expression (as did O'Neill), but to critique the grounds upon which such an assertion was made. Counterpointing bodies, voices, and

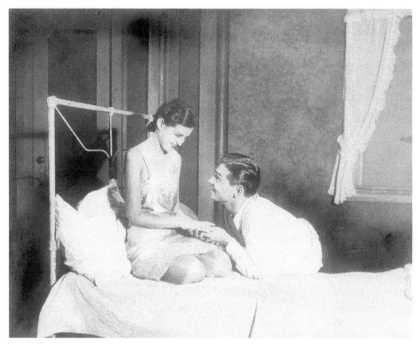

Figure 12. Episode 6, "Intimate," from Sophie Treadwell's *Machinal.* Zita Johann as the Young Woman is transformed by her illicit love affair with Clark Gable's Richard Roe. Now designated "Woman," she experiences a spiritual harmony that is seen in her bodily movements, singing voice, and self-authorized words.

words, Treadwell simultaneously demonstrates the meaningfulness of voice and gesture, while revealing the limitations of words.

The one scene in which Treadwell perfectly coordinates these three languages is episode six, where the Young Woman and her lover take refuge from the outside world in his apartment. With feet passing by the window, they literally *understand.* Which is to say that they experience the full integration of reason, emotion, and will, as reflected in their dialogue and actions. In a presumably post-coital moment, the woman lights a cigarette for the man. He compliments her on her "mighty pretty hands," repeating a few lines later "you got awful pretty hands" (514). When she gets dressed, fastening the waistband of her skirt as she steps into the light, he remarks "you look in good shape, kid," having also told her that she "looked like an angel" earlier (514–16). When she begins singing to the music played by the organ grinder outside, he tells her "you got a nice voice, honey."[21]

And, when she speaks giddily of their happiness together, remarking "Look at us!" and "We belong together!," he sanctions her use of the first person plural, laughing, "everything's us to you, kid – ain't it?" Acknowledging the agency that lies in her body, her voice, and her words, he recognizes her to be the whole person that she is. And she is, for a moment at least. Treadwell instructs the actor playing her central character to "turn th[e] episode of her dressing into a personification, an idealization of a woman clothing herself. All her gestures must be unconscious, innocent, relaxed, sure and full of natural grace" (516). Moreover, she asks her actor to strike a statuesque pose as the man kisses her goodbye: "she looks toward him, then throws her head slowly back, lifts her right arm – this gesture that is in so many statues of women [Volupte]" (516). In Treadwell's stage directions, she indicates that "the sound of her voice is beautiful" (514). And, in her dialogue, she gives her character a command over the language she speaks:

> WOMAN: I never knew anything like this way! I never knew that I could feel like this! So, so – purified! Don't laugh at me!
> MAN: I ain't laughing, honey.
> WOMAN: Purified.
> MAN: It's a hell of a word – but I know what you mean. That's the way it is – sometimes. (516)

By giving her central character control over the way her body moves, the way her voice sounds, and the way she authorizes her thoughts in language, Treadwell emphasizes that, along with the man, the woman herself is able to recognize her full potential. The freedom she experiences, if only for a moment, is not impossible. But it is a freedom that can only be found when women are allowed to experience embodied subjectivities – through their bodies, their voices, and their words.

Although *Machinal* was generally well received, many of its reviewers assumed that, like the plays of O'Neill, Rice, and, to a lesser extent, Lawson, its expressionistic style was derived from the German movement. Alison Smith in the *New York World*, for example, remarked that Treadwell's "method follows the pattern that the modernists set and called 'expressionistic' – that perilous form of distorted lights and brief vignettes and harsh, staccato utterances. It burst on to our Broadway stage with Kaiser's 'From Morn to Midnight,' and not since that unforgettable production has its value been so completely realized" (13). Similarly, J. Brooks Atkinson noted in the *New York Times* that the play was not particularly

original – either in terms of its subject matter or its design. Like many critics, he assumed the plot to have been transparently lifted from the Snyder
murder trial: "The news columns have chronicled that tawdry yarn before."
Yet, he qualifies, "They have never disclosed it, as 'Machinal' does, in terms
of an impersonal exposition of character in conflict with environment. In
the ten scenes of this play all the emotions well up, but crisp and austere –
like intellectual images of what we are usually asked to feel." For Atkinson,
the play's success lay in its expressionistic style. But, here again, it offered
nothing particularly new: "the episodic treatment of the story, the skele-
tonized settings, the descriptions of the dull routine of office life through
the medium of adding machines, filing cabinets and typewriters and dog-
matic tatters of office conversation, recall 'The Adding Machine,' 'From
Morn to Midnight' and the whole mad tumble of expressionistic drama."
Nonetheless, he is forced to conclude, "from all these factual resemblances,
'Machinal' emerges as a triumph of individual distinction, gleaming with
intangible beauty." Robert Littell in *Theatre Arts Monthly* agreed, praising
Treadwell for the "flexibility" and economy with which she used expressionistic techniques to tell her story, yet finding nothing in her method that was
wholly new:

> The past ten years have given us many plays, and parts of many other plays,
> in which the imprisoned sameness of American life has been satirized with
> mechanical effects, with automatons in verbal masks, repeating the deadly
> formulas of standardization. Miss Treadwell, in her opening episode, has
> a go at the same thing but where others failed or didn't even try, she has
> succeeded in showing the heart as well as the lid that oppresses it.

Among those features singled out for praise were the off-stage sounds
and mute presences that Treadwell scripts into her play. Littell, for example,
noted approvingly that "All sorts of things that do not strictly belong to
the play, things that would be excluded by other playwrights, stray into
Machinal and sink out of sight again, giving us overtones and glimpses and
other dimensions which the ordinary self-contained play is too 'well-made'
ever to tolerate." Nonetheless, he – like Atkinson – tends to credit Arthur
Hopkins with their dramatic effectiveness, implying that Hopkins, as much
as Treadwell, was the creative force behind the play:

> I think that *Machinal*, though I find that it reads very well, might have
> been ruined, underlined, made affected and unnatural by a commonplace
> performance. Arthur Hopkins has understood and reimagined it so well,
> and grasped it with so firm and light a hand, that anyone interested in the

almost invisible art of direction would do well to see *Machinal* a second
time and try to find out just where is the dividing line between what the
playwright, the actor and the director bring to a performance.

Without quite denying Treadwell's creative authority, Atkinson also
reserves much of his praise for Hopkins's direction as well as Robert Edmond
Jones's scenic design. For, while he feels that expressionism has a tendency to
mar the development of plot and character, he sees such narrative problems
overcome by Hopkins's and Jones's visual contributions:

> Whatever doubts there may have been about this truncated technique of
> story-telling Mr. Hopkins has quite dispelled by the discerning beauty
> of his production. The ten scenes record this Young Woman's tragic
> tale like a well-composed frieze that repeats the same motive in variant
> forms. Robert Edmond Jones's suggestive backgrounds may seem cryptic
> by comparison with the customary representational frame settings; but
> they are vividly alive and splendidly lighted. Matching the style of Miss
> Treadwell's drama, they have lopped off every superfluous detail; they
> are electric and vital. And in staging the play generally Mr. Hopkins
> has surpassed himself. Nothing sours the harmony of the illusion he has
> drawn from his materials; even the off-stage sounds, which usually rasp
> against the ear, float gently in and out of the action like the airplane that
> zooms across the last scene but one.

Clearly, Treadwell's technique – and it *was* hers, after all – proved to be
a large part of the play's success. Yet its originality and authorship were
frequently denied her.

O'Neill and Rice, as we've seen, were similarly denied credit for the originality of their expressionistic form. Yet, they were never denied authorship of
their own plays. That Treadwell was is noteworthy, especially in light of the
way that written and performative modes of signification were being gendered by the text/performance split. However annoyed Treadwell may have
been by such a reception, she surely must have expected it as well. For, as I've
argued in this chapter, *Machinal* not only thematically critiques patriarchal
structures of oppression, but formally functions as an affective autobiography, encoding Treadwell's frustrations as a woman struggling to authorize
a role for herself within the masculine world of work. Here, as in her earlier
work, the typewriter functions as a symbol of self-authorization (even as it
lies broken on the Young Woman's desk). Yet, it also exists in a synecdochal
relationship to the other machines regulating the Young Woman's life in
the play. As such, it represents the machine of patriarchal oppression more

generally, erasing the embodied subjectivity of the female "typewriter" who sits in front of its keys. The symbol is thus somewhat ambiguous, suggesting both the freedom of self-authorization and the erasure of female specificity from any self so authorized. To enter into the symbolic realm of language, in other words, is to enter it as a man. Treadwell seeks to resist the masculinization of language and meaning in the expressionistic form of her play. Through her use of bodies, voices, and words, she not only exposes the limitations of verbal signification alone, but affirms the meaningfulness of voice and gesture – those embodied forms of communication that do not deny the specificity of a gendered experience of the world. What's more, she "points" upon her character's "pretty hands" to disrupt the textual constraints of her play. In doing so, she reinserts her own body into the text, drawing our attention to the "pretty hand" that inscribes the page.

Epilogue: "modern times"

I N HIS 1936 FILM *MODERN TIMES*, CHARLIE CHAPLIN TRACES THE picaresque adventures[1] of his Little Tramp, out of work after his job at a widget factory proves too much for his nerves. In the hilarious opening scene, we see the Little Tramp working on the assembly line, adjusting sprockets with a wrench in each hand. The rhythms of sprocket adjustment have so taken over his own natural rhythms, however, that, when he goes to take a break, he finds he cannot walk straight and moves in a jerky manner, adjusting imaginary sprockets in the air. Back on the assembly line, the Little Tramp is distracted by the company secretary when she bends over to tie her shoe. Thinking the buttons on her skirt are sprockets to be adjusted, he accosts her, chasing her through the factory before wandering out into the street. As a buxom woman with well-placed buttons on her dress walks down the sidewalk, the Little Tramp moves toward her, threatening to adjust her sprockets, before a police officer intercepts him and hauls him away. Several months later, the Little Tramp is released from a mental hospital with the advice to avoid excitement and overstimulation. Apparently, we are led to infer, the Little Tramp suffers from a neurasthenic condition brought on by modern times.

Clearly, the rhythms of industry have so recalibrated his body's natural rhythms that the Little Tramp is unable to function normally in the world. But, while his condition establishes the premise for the rest of the film's comic action, it was likely an all too familiar concern for much of the film's original audience. As we've seen, cultural fears about the impact of modernity and modernization were widespread at the turn of the twentieth century. Though vague for the most part, suffusing many aspects of American culture and in a myriad of ways, such fears took on a definite shape within the expressive culture movement, which sought to counter the effects of technologies that fractured the act of communication. When telegraphs translated ideas into a series of dots and dashes, when typewriters erased the "personality" of the person authorizing its words, when telephone relays, phonograph recordings, and radio broadcasts rendered disembodied voices from wooden boxes and tin horns, when silent film projected moving images of mute bodies on the screen, the very human act of communication no longer seemed to be so human. It was thus to mitigate the de-humanizing impact of such technologies that leading figures in the expressive culture movement designed their program of de-alienation. As we've seen, they drew upon the work of speech educator S. S. Curry – itself derived from the work of French vocal instructor, François Delsarte – to teach students how to speak and move in harmony with the spiritual forces of the universe. For, where technology had fractured the once integrated act of communication into discrete bodies, voices, and words, Curry held that students must learn to recoordinate their three natural languages – verbal, vocal, and pantomimic. In this way, expressive culture enthusiasts maintained, students could overcome the alienating conditions of modernity and return to a natural state of existence, in harmony with the spiritual forces of the universe.

While Curry taught students to recoordinate languages that had been fragmented by modernity, many artists ironized his theory, disarticulating verbal, vocal, and pantomimic modes of signification in order to represent the alienating conditions of modern life. The four playwrights discussed in this book – Eugene O'Neill, Elmer Rice, John Howard Lawson, and Sophie Treadwell – for example, all used this strategy to represent an alienated anti-hero unable to adjust to the industrial rhythms of modern life. So, too, does Charlie Chaplin in *Modern Times*. For, though it was made in 1936, well into the era of sound film, Chaplin draws upon a silent film aesthetic to tell the story of the Little Tramp's modernist alienation. Nowhere in the film do we hear the Little Tramp speak. We see him move and gesture, but we never hear him speak. Nor, for that matter, do we hear the other characters speak; when necessary, we read the intertitles on which their words appear. When we do hear voices, they are mediated by machines. The supervisor of the factory in which the Little Tramp works instructs his foreman in telegraphic diction "section 5, give her speed," but his voice is joined to his image only on the television monitor mounted to the wall. Similarly, the "Billows feeding machine," designed to maximize workers' productivity by dispensing with the lunch hour, is explained by a voice on a phonograph record while an efficiency expert silently points out its features, which are demonstrated on the hapless Little Tramp. Finally, a radio announcer reads the day's news as the Little Tramp and a gastritic woman sit waiting for the mayor. Through the news broadcast, we learn that the mayor has commuted the Little Tramp's jail sentence in recognition of his inadvertent coke-induced bravery in stopping a prison break. These are the only three instances in the film in which we hear words vocalized. Together they trace a trajectory of increasing de-humanization: from the synchronized sound and image of the television screen to the disarticulated recording accompanied by explanatory pantomime to the disembodied voice on the radio. Although bodies are represented as still capable of producing sounds – the gastritic woman's stomach rumbles and her dog barks, for example – the sounds they make are less and less related to the realm of language. Yet, without language, these bodies are no less expressive. Indeed, as film critic Ira S. Jaffe observes, words are presented "as largely hostile to human life" (27), while "the most life-giving moments of *Modern Times* stem from the unleashed force of the tramp's non-verbal art" (29). For example, the Little Tramp gets a job as a singing waiter in a cabaret with the help of the Gamine, his companion of the streets. Of course, he is comically inept as a waiter, causing havoc in the kitchen and getting waylaid by a dancing crowd. Thus, when he prepares to sing his song, we don't expect him to succeed. Not only does he fail to memorize the words to the song, but he loses his cuff on which the Gamine has written the lyrics for him. Taking the stage, he improvises and is a huge success. We hear him sing – but not in English; the lyrics are in French. If we understand them without understanding the French language, it is because of the expressivity of the Little Tramp's pantomime and tone of voice.

Like O'Neill, Rice, Lawson, and Treadwell, then, Chaplin appears to ironize Curry's theory of expression in order to represent the alienation of modern times. Like them, too, he seems to be suggesting that technology threatens the integrity of the embodied act of communication. Unlike them, however, he works in a technological medium – film. But, while he tells his story in a mediated form, he also seems to lament the passing of the silent era. This would suggest that the technology he fears is not one that disarticulates bodies, voices, and words; it is one that, in resynchronizing these communicative elements, makes us accommodate ourselves all that more easily to the technological landscape of what we now call the "posthuman." As the film ends, the Little Tramp and the Gamine walk down the road toward an uncertain utopia, beyond the boundary of the modern city. The sun rises over the horizon of a pre-industrial past.

This was Chaplin's last film to feature the Little Tramp. Although it drew upon a silent film aesthetic, it was a product of its own modern times. Significantly, the end of the silent era also marks the end of the era of expressionism in the American theatre. For, though the techniques developed by these playwrights continued to have lasting influence well into the twentieth century, the obsessive concern with alienation as a result of modern technology seemed to abate. One reason may have been that each of these new technological media proved to be less of a threat to theatrical artistry than a means of further popularizing it. Another may have been that the introduction of sound film created new opportunities for playwrights who wished to be more than plot scenarists. Indeed, the call for a more "literary" drama was soon sounded for film, prompting many playwrights – including Lawson – to bolt Broadway for Hollywood.

If *Modern Times* serves as a fitting epilogue to this era, Chaplin himself serves as a fitting epilogue to this book. Born into a troupe of music hall performers in England, Chaplin brought his comedic talents to the United States. There, he thoroughly transformed the new medium of film, before being barred from re-entering the country for his political beliefs. Exiling himself to Switzerland for the remaining twenty-five years of his life, Chaplin continued to exert a tremendous influence on the art of the twentieth century, receiving numerous awards. Because of his transatlantic migrations, Chaplin is a perfect figure by which to represent the cross-currents of artistic exchange. Like the performance practices that Joseph Roach traces in *Cities of the Dead*, Chaplin's performance style draws from one culture, is infused by the cultural traditions of another, and extends its meanings and influences into other cultures still. Considered thus as a circumatlantic performer, Chaplin represents a challenge to the one-directional model of artistic influence that, prior to Roach, dominated studies of theatre history.

Traditional critical narratives of the modern American theatre's development, for example, typically assumed the importation of European techniques and a relatively faithful implementation by American theatre practitioners. Sheldon Cheney, Kenneth Macgowan, and Oliver Sayler were among the first critics to propagate this narrative, describing a "new movement" in the theatre which was sweeping across Europe and only beginning to appear in the United States. In 1914, for example, Sheldon Cheney claimed that "the new movement in America is hardly more than a promise, but that in England and on the Continent it is both a promise and a vital, lasting achievement" (*New Movement* 42). Three years later, he urged American theatre practitioners to realize this promise and develop their own art theatre, one that "must grow out of American conditions" (*Art Theater* 37). Although he affirmed that "it is neither necessary nor wise to copy outright European models," he noted nonetheless that "not one of the pioneers of the progressive theater movement in this country has failed to know and to find inspiration in the art theaters of Europe" (37). Similarly, Kenneth Macgowan insisted in 1921 that the promise of the American theatre lay in the movement that "has swept the playhouses of Germany and Russia, touched lightly the French and British stages, and in the last seven years risen to dominance in the serious theatre of America" (13). Oliver Sayler likewise understood the "new movement" to have originated in Europe, but insisted that its American manifestation was bound to be unique. Writing in 1923, he remarked that

> A movement largely foreign in its sources and its inspiration is in process of becoming thoroughly and honestly American. Its imitative period is passing with the development of original native ideas, with the increasing assurance of hands apprenticed abroad, with the growing freedom and expanding numbers of independent groups and individual artists, and with the tolerance and even welcome which the established theatre extends to new ideas. (10)

Thus, an initial wave of critics presumed American theatrical modernism to be of European origin. Succeeding generations of critics have tended to follow their lead,[2] cementing this narrative into place such that it appears to be commonsense.

Without wishing to deny the fact or the importance of European influence upon American theatre practitioners in the modern era, I believe that this dominant critical narrative is flawed for assuming a unidirectional model of influence and a blank slate of American theatrical practice. As I hope to have demonstrated in this book, American theatrical modernism was, in fact, produced by a rich exchange of ideas and artistic influences. Like Chaplin's comic art, its roots may have been in Europe, but its transplantation to the United States yielded a hybrid whose seeds were themselves disseminated throughout Europe. Specifically, I speak of François Delsarte's expressive method. Brought back to the United States by Steele MacKaye, it was given a uniquely American inflection, its basis in the Catholic Trinity replaced by the universal pantheism of American Transcendentalism. From there, it was theorized in relation to modernity by S. S. Curry, whose theory of "expression" (so named) was quickly appropriated by expressive culture enthusiasts as part of their program of de-alienation. Under the umbrella of the expressive culture movement, it was given a large popular audience – not only within the United States, but in Europe as well, with writers such as Genevieve Stebbins and Emily Bishop, lecturers such as Edmund Russell and Henrietta Hovey, dancers such as Ruth St. Denis, Ted Shawn, and Martha Graham exporting American expressionism to Europe.

As Nancy Lee Chalfa Ruyter observes, American expressionism – or American Delsartism, as she refers to it – made a tremendous impact upon Europe:

> It is unclear how American Delsartism first came to the attention of European physical culturists. Perhaps it was by means of its specialized and numerous publications. As early as 1899, an advertisement for Emily M. Bishop's 1892 *Americanized Delsarte Culture* includes a testimonial from a Harriet Davis Güssbacker of Berlin. She states that she is introducing the Delsarte system into Germany where "the people have never heard of aesthetic gymnastics nor of influencing the mind at the same time with the body." Presumably, Bishop's text would serve as her source. Evidence that the Delsarte system was known in Finland through the works of Stebbins is provided by Saga Ambegaokar in her thesis on the Finnish modern dance pioneer Maggie Gripenberg. Moreover in 1913, a Russian treatise on the Delsarte system by Prince Sergei Mikhailovich Volkonsky was published and listed 23 Delsarte texts in French, German, and English, including Stebbins' four books and 12 other works by American Delsartians. Clearly, American Delsartean literature was known in Europe. (67)

What's more, the lesssons it contained were often transported directly by Europeans who had studied in the United States. Ruyter notes, for example, that both Hade Kallmeyer and Bess Mensendieck – important figures in the physical culture movement in Germany – studied with Stebbins in New York before publishing their own books and opening training centers in Germany, Austria, the Netherlands, Denmark, and Czechoslovakia (67–70). Of course, as Ruyter points out,

> the genealogy of the American Delsartean contribution to German physical culture and dance is complicated by the fact that all sorts of influences were co-mingling at the same time: Delsarte, Dalcroze, Bode, Laban,

the Elizabeth Duncan School, and others. It is not possible to separate the strands, but one can establish that[,] through the work of Kallmeyer and Mensendieck, the American Delsartean principles and practices were [well] known. (70)

Indeed, if American expression was well received in Europe, it was undoubtedly because of the way European audiences had been prepared for it by their own tutorials in the Delsarte method. For, at the same time that MacKaye was translating Delsarte for an American audience, Delsarte's French disciples were disseminating their own interpretations of the master's system throughout Europe. And, just as in the United States, each exponent had his or her own unique interpretation which in turn inspired students to develop their own theories and practices.

Expression, in all of its manifestations, began to radiate outward from Paris to the United States and the rest of Europe, beginning around 1871, the year of Delsarte's death. Which suggests yet another reason to revise the traditional critical narrative of American theatrical modernism. For if, indeed, Delsarte's course of applied aesthetics is the root of modernist performance, then we must date the inception of theatrical modernism much earlier than critics such as Cheney, Macgowan, and Sayler do. Macgowan, for example, wrote in 1921 that "The thing that has been called the new movement in the theatre is a quarter of a century old" (13). Pushing back the date of theatrical modernism to the last quarter of the nineteenth century, then, would mean recontextualizing it within a slightly earlier historical milieu – one marked by the emergence of technologies of mass communication. The typewriter, after all, was in mass production by 1874; the telegraph became wireless in 1896; the telephone first appeared in 1876, eventually connecting the East and West coasts by 1915; the phonograph was patented in 1877, with sound recordings in mass production by 1893; the kinetoscope was invented in 1889, before being displaced by the cinematographe in 1895; and the radio made it first broadcast in 1906. Much like Delsarte's principles of expression, these technologies of mass communication exerted a tremendous influence that radiated outward from the initial site of their transmission, emitting wavelengths that have yet to be measured by history. Yet it would seem that, somewhere between Delsarte's salon in Paris and Edison's laboratory in Orange, New Jersey, their wavelengths refracted against one another to sound the beginnings of American theatrical modernism. What I have tried to argue in this book is that these technologies did more than simply serve as a backdrop for the historical emergence of modernism on the American stage; rather, I want to suggest, they informed the very shape of its unfolding. Radically altering the experience of communication itself, this revolution in communications technology threw into question the role of the human, the place of meaning, and the function of the artist. And though its impact was felt throughout American culture and beyond, it was felt most strongly in the theatre – that art form most dependent upon bodies, voices, and words.

Notes

Part I   Introduction

1. See, for example, Stephen Kern.
2. Indeed, anti-German sentiment may have been a contributing factor in Rice's decision to anglicize his name from the paternal "Reizenstein." But, considering that both O'Neill and Rice persisted in denying German influence throughout their lifetimes – which, in Rice's case, was well into the 1960s, long after anti-German sentiment had subsided – such a possibility is circumstantial and must remain at the level of conjecture.
3. Although the corpus of American expressionist plays is considerably larger, I have limited my study to these plays in particular because they specifically address the theme of technology. Other American expressionist plays include: Alice Gerstenberg's *Overtones* (1915), Susan Glaspell's *The Verge* (1921), Jean Toomer's *Natalie Mann* (1922) and *The Sacred Factory* (n.d.), Rachel Crothers's *Expressing Willie* (1924), and George S. Kaufman and Marc Connelly's *Beggar on Horseback* (1924), among others. I touch briefly on Crothers's and Kaufman and Connelly's plays in my introduction to part II.

1   Bodies: actors and artistic agency on the nineteenth-century stage

1. Although I trace the terminology of "points" to the eighteenth-century elocutionary reform movement, its appearance in Act v, scene i of Shakespeare's *A Midsummer Night's Dream*, where Theseus uses the term to critique Quince's performance as Prologue in the mechanicals' presentation of "Pyramus and Thisbe," suggests a much earlier usage. The institutionalization of theatrical criticism, however, does appear to date to the mid eighteenth century. For an extensive discussion of complaints made by Dr. Johnson, John Hill, and Thomas Davies (among others) about artificial habits of speech, see Alan Downer, "Nature" 1024–5.
2. According to Paul Edwards, Leland Roloff sees "the sudden interest in delivery – 'elocution' – in the eighteenth century, [as] not the revival of an ancient art[, but] the response to a profound mind–body dissociation, a sounding of alarms in our first crisis of the book" (Edwards 30).

3. I have modernized the orthography of these eighteenth-century texts throughout. Where, for example, Sheridan wrote "*eſſential*," I have transcribed "essential," hoping that such changes will make these passages easier for modern readers to read.

4. Jay Fliegelman notes that when the Declaration of Independence was first set in type, the printer included Jefferson's diacritical marks – meant to mark the "points" of his own delivery – which appeared to riddle the document with errant punctuation (7).

5. West's focus on the culture of connoisseurship as the fertile ground out of which dramatic criticism grew is important in helping us understand the context and function of the dramatic review. She suggests that the institution of dramatic criticism – with its "hierarchy, standard, and differentiation" – may very well have created differences in acting styles by providing a language which called fine "points" of differentiation into being (7–8). Nonetheless, it may also have provided a language with which to describe variations in acting practices already in use, especially since many of the critical treatises discussed here appear to codify aspects of Garrick's performance style (see discussion below). If so, this would call into question West's claim that actors were incapable of the erudition that reviewers often attributed to their performances. Thus, rather than invert the relations of causality, it may be more useful to consider the relationship between acting and criticism as dialectical, with each practice giving shape to the other – especially when evidence exists to suggest that actors did, indeed, engage in a concentrated study of the dramatic text so as to render their parts meaningfully.

6. For many writers of the Romantic period, this was cause for alarm. Responding to David Garrick's unprecedented popularity, Charles Lamb, for instance, expressed concern that growing interest in the art of dramatic interpretation would elevate the actor over the dramatic poet (Wood 24). And Lamb, as Gillen Wood points out, was not alone: "Coleridge mourn[ed] the passing of an Elizabethan golden age in which poetic 'recitation' rather than dramatic action was paramount. Likewise Shelley declared that 'the corruption which has been imputed to the drama begins when the poetry employed in its constitution ends' " (19).

7. Although most critics follow Thomas Davies in crediting Garrick with reforming the English stage, Downer suggests Macklin preceded him in inaugurating the change to a more "natural" style of delivery ("Nature" 1024–5). Similarly, Downer identifies Barton Booth as having preceded Garrick in introducing the meaningful pause, although he notes that the significance of this technique is in its departure from the declamatory tradition (1008). Despite Downer's attempt to complicate our understanding of the origins of the shift from a declamatory to a Romantic style of acting, evidence overwhelmingly suggests that it was Garrick who most thoroughly effected this transformation in the minds of his contemporaries.

8. Paul Edwards cites two elocutionists, in particular, who explicitly quoted from Garrick's performances: John Rice (see below) and William Cockin, who dedicated his *Art of Delivering Written Language* (1775) to Garrick. John Walker, too, mentions Garrick as a "great actor and excellent citizen" whose speeches would have been exemplified in his manual had Garrick not died before it was completed (xii–xiii).

9. P. Edwards cites Burgh on "fear" with regard to this scene; I see it as what Burgh would refer to as a "mixed" passion of "wonder" and "fear."

10. Placing him within the broader context of Romantic visual culture that included lithographs, panoramas, exhibitions, and photography, Wood argues that Garrick's emphasis upon his "legible" face helped shift the theatre away from being a primarily aural medium for the declamation of poetic verse to an increasingly visual medium for the presentation of dramatic spectacle.

11. Sheridan thought inflectional variation, for example, was the result of a haphazard and uneven development of spoken language. According to him, "barbarous nations" give unrestrained voice to their passions as nature dictates (133), but civilized nations (e.g., the English), whose language has become steady in expression and more even in tone, introduce random variations of cadence and inflection to make their speech more pleasing to the ear. Because this gives rise to numerous dialects, however, there appears a need for standardization and reform. Citing the Scottish brogue as an especially "discordant" example, Sheridan argues that it should be reformed according to the dialect spoken at court (where he seems to mean, quite literally, the Queen's English) (112–13).

12. Where Alfred Bernheim cites a $40 to $400 per week figure (41), Lawrence Barrett provides a $28 to $40 figure as well as the $200 per night figure Forrest accepted for a limited 80-day engagement during the 1827–8 season (39).

13. As Bigsby observes, the nineteenth-century theatre was "a literal platform for a posturing which was not unconnected with the celebration of bourgeois individualism" (1).

14. Jürgen Wolter identifies three phases of dramatic criticism in the US, tracing the beginnings of the first phase to 1746, when writings challenging the anti-theatrical prejudice of religious groups begin to appear, arguing on behalf of the theatre as an institution of moral instruction. The second phase, which he identifies as a shift from a moral to a social discourse in which the theatre is discussed as a specifically American institution, he dates from 1790 to 1860. It is this second phase with which I am primarily concerned here.

15. Miller cites William Dunlap's *A History of the American Theatre* (1832) which discusses one such group of professional-men-as-cultural-curators: John Wells, Elias Hicks, Samuel Jones, William Cutting, Peter Irving, and Charles Adams (2–3).

16. McConachie maintains that, in this early period of the American theatre, elite male spectators felt it their prerogative to correct actors on their interpretations of their roles. For an actor to contest such a judgment was an affront to such spectators' authority. "When an actor in the Virginia Company expressed his resentment at being hissed during a performance in 1769," McConachie notes, "he was reprimanded in newspaper print. The writer, shocked by the actor's 'sovereign contempt' for his superiors, cut him down for this 'violation of decorum'" ("American Theatre in Context" 124). Although fifty years separate this incident and Pemberton's letter, I believe both illustrate how the American stage was becoming a contested site for representing models of citizenship and how the American actor was emerging as an important figure of self-determination. This accords with McConachie's research on the changing demographic of audiences during this period in which many came to regard the stage as "a legitimate arena for the clash of political factions" ("American Theatre in Context" 132).

17. Evidently, "Thespis" was not the only one to need schooling in the actor's use of "points." Macready once complained of a prompter who, "in every pause I made in a scene where the pauses are *effects* kept shouting 'the word' to me till I was ready to go and knock him down" (1, 218).

18. Although the letter is signed only "T.C.R.P.," John Jacob Weisert identifies the writer as Pemberton, a member of Samuel Drake's troupe.

19. As is well known, tensions between the two actors were running high well before this incident, beginning with the suspiciously unfavorable reviews Forrest received from a London newspaper whose editor was a close friend of Macready's. The rivalry would be stoked by members of the press on both sides of the Atlantic. For a full historical account of the events surrounding the Astor Place Riots, see Richard Moody.

20. The full passage is as follows: "Although Kean's acting is full of what are termed points, (a term and system to which we are very averse,) yet, unlike many other actors, his points possess 'With the flash of the gem its solidity too' " (*New York Mirror* 4.18 [25 November 1826]: 143).

21. Macready, for example, often referred to "the vast *benefit* derived from keeping vehemence and effort out of passion" (1, 85) and chastised himself when he felt himself "relapsing into my old habitual sin of striving for effect by dint of muscular exertion" (1, 132).

22. As even William Alger (one of Forrest's laudatory biographers) conceded, his tendency to overindulge in physical exuberance was his one "defect": "There was often too much volition in his play, causing a muscular friction and an organic expense which made the sensitive shrink, and which only the robust could afford" (198).

23. From at least the early part of the century, however, a distinction was made between equestrian shows (a forerunner of the circus) and standard theatrical offerings, a distinction due perhaps in part to the fact that hippodromes and theatres were different types of spaces which cultivated different types of experiences for their audiences.

24. Historian Faye Dudden, however, argues persuasively that this process of specialization was due less to the pressures of consumption than to the pressures of production, demonstrating that it had begun well before the Astor Place Riots. Focusing on entrepreneurial theatre managers such as Thomas Hamblin, she shows how they adopted a "niche marketing" strategy by multiplying and diversifying their theatrical offerings in order to attract larger audiences and thus maximize their profits (79). Although she concedes that "[c]lass divisions in the city were in effect making it harder to achieve a common culture," she insists that this process of specialization "was accelerated or exacerbated by the logic of market segmentation, according to which there was no incentive to achieve one entertainment for all" (108).

25. Of course, characterization was augmented by costume and properties well before realism, but under realism – the aesthetic movement that arose from and gave expression to commodity culture – character came to be practically constituted by them. This tendency eventually expanded to include the entire stage set. As Bigsby notes, "Where stage sets had originally been either simple backdrops for bravura acting or spectacular enterprises offered as marvels of technical accomplishments and substitutes for subtlety of dramatic construction and character,

they now [at the turn of the twentieth century] assumed a defining power, a conventionalised significance, which became a shorthand for character and moral enquiry" (4).

26. Even the notoriously skeptical British press was moved to exclaim: "Mr. Forrest's Lear is, from beginning to end, a very masterly, intelligent, and powerful performance, giving evidence of the most careful and attentive study of the author's meaning, steering clear, at the same time, of all fine-drawn subtleties and tricky point-making, and affording a well-grasped and evenly-sustained impersonation of that magnificent and soul-stirring creation" (quoted in Alger 395).

27. As Herbert Blau remarks, what is generally taken for "naturalness in acting moves ideologically through a whole spectrum of computable appearances that synchronize the acceptable behavior of an actor with the price inscribed on a ticket or, in certain experimental quarters at certain times, the seeming absence of a price" (49).

28. No one challenged this narrative as it was being cast more forcefully than Forrest's friend and biographer, James Rees. In his laudatory biography of Forrest, Rees wrote:

Many actors of the modern school are idealists; that is, they are unable to draw the line of distinction between a bodiless substance, and objects which are the immediate emanations of the mind. These are called ideas which give form and figure to shapeless matter.

Mr. Forrest's conception and rendition of Hamlet were those of a close student and a finished artist. It was a triumphant refutation of the sneers of those who called him a mere physical actor. (190)

29. When Logan's comments, first delivered to the Women's Suffrage Convention in New York, were misinterpreted as an attack upon the theatre – and against female actors in particular – Logan took the opportunity to set the record straight in her book, *Apropos of Women and Theatres*. In it, she makes clear that the target of her attack is the burlesque, which she sees as exploitative of women. Coming from a theatrical family, Logan knew all too well the charges of exhibitionism directed against any and all types of theatrical performance. She also knew that such charges made female actors vulnerable to questions regarding their morality. Thus, her attempt to redefine acting was as much a feminist campaign as it was a concern with class. See Robert Allen's discussion of the Lydia Thomson burlesque troupe which motivated Logan's comments.

30. As taught by MacKaye, the Delsarte method had a profound influence on actor training in the United States. Beginning in March of 1871, MacKaye lectured widely, eventually establishing several short-lived acting schools, beginning with the St. James Theatre School later that same year, the School of Expression in 1877, and the Lyceum Theatre School in 1884, which developed out of a training program begun at the Madison Square Theatre in 1880 (McTeague 27). The last of these ventures was effectively co-founded with Franklin Sargent, whose steady guidance and pragmatic approach to the business of running a school provided a firm grounding for MacKaye's vision. Under Sargent's direction, the school – renamed the American Academy of Dramatic Arts in 1892 – proved a huge success. However temporary were MacKaye's own institutional affiliations, his teachings had positive and lasting results.

31. According to Lavater,

> The animal life, the lowest and most earthly, would discover itself from the rim of the belly to the organs of generation, which would become its central or focal point. The middle or moral life would be seated in the breast, and the heart would be its central point. The intellectual life, which of the three is supreme, would reside in the head, and have the eye for its centre. (quoted in Taylor and Shuttleworth 9)

While some of Delsarte's followers understood his expressive model to correspond exactly to Lavater's, dividing the torso into upper and lower regions with the arms and legs governed by moral and vital faculties respectively, others tended to ascribe morality to the torso and vitality to the limbs. According to this understanding, the head was the seat of reason, the torso the locus of sentiment, and the limbs the agents of will.

  Angelique Arnaud explicitly links Delsarte's thought to the moral philosophy of Pierre Leroux, who identified "sensation, sentiment, and consciousness" as the fundamental components of human behavior (Arnaud in Delsarte 172).

32. Claude Shaver identifies normal movement as vital, eccentric as mental, and concentric as moral (205), but this differs from most sources which list them as I have them here (see, for example, Giraudet in Shawn 108).

33. Taken to its logical conclusion, of course, Delsarte's method allows for the exponential potential of even more expressions than this. Marion Lowell, a student of MacKaye's, lists 405 expressive possibilities for the eye alone (214–90), while Alfred Giraudet, one of Delsarte's most distinguished French pupils, calculated 729 different whole body phenomena (Shawn 96)! Beginning with the three "Genera," Giraudet goes on to apply a terminology to the various elaborations of gesture within Delsarte's schema that approaches the scientific classification system of Carolus Linnaeus: "From the nine Species he arrives at the 27 Varieties, the 81 Sub-Varieties, the 243 Types and the 729 Phenomena" (Shawn 108).

34. Angélique Arnaud similarly insists upon understanding the Delsarte method as a science (Arnaud in Delsarte 173).

35. Duchenne, for example, used electrical stimulation to isolate and identify those parts of the human musculatory system which were involved in physiognomic expression. Charles Darwin drew upon Duchenne's research in *The Expression of Emotions in Man and Animals* (1872), in which he extended Duchenne's insights to the animal kingdom in order to suggest further evidence for his theory of evolution. Although published a year after Delsarte's death, Darwin's book proved popular among his followers, helping to stimulate further interest in expression, especially as it developed into the "expressive culture movement" (see discussion below and in chapter 2).

36. Ironically, phrenology initially appeared as a radical critique of physiognomy when Franz Joseph Gall opposed its "materialist" analysis of the brain to Lavater's idealist conjectures about a self that was little more than a secularized soul (Taylor and Shuttleworth 25).

37. The extent to which Delsarte was indebted to this moral-psychological medley is illustrated by his catalogue of "thermometers." Believing that the body was the truest

indicator of one's thoughts and feelings, Delsarte was fond of saying that, if you wish to know what someone means, attend not to what is said so much as to what the body is doing. For example, the shoulder is the thermometer of the soul and expresses love or sensuality; while the face tells you *which* passion is being expressed, the shoulder reveals the intensity of that passion (Delsarte 430–9). Similarly, the eyebrow is the thermometer of the mind. Accenting the eye, it reveals the mental attitude taken toward that which is in the eye's focus. The nose, meanwhile, is a moral thermometer, expressing approval or displeasure with the expansion or contraction of its nostrils. Such insights had begun with a trip to the morgue where Delsarte had observed that, in life, the thumb extends outward while in death it retracts back toward the palm of the hand, prompting him to identify the thumb as the thermometer of life (Delsarte 404). Extrapolating from this principle, he determined that the elbow is a thermometer of pride or humility, depending on its relation to the rest of the arm and torso (Delsarte 527–38).

38. Referring to the head, for example, Lavater explains:

If we take the countenance as the representative and epitome of the three divisions, then will the forehead, to the eyebrows, be the mirror or image, of the understanding; the nose and cheeks the image of the moral and sensitive life; and the mouth and chin the image of animal life; while the eye will be to the whole as its summary and centre . . . It cannot, however, too often be repeated that these three lives, by their intimate connexion with each other, are all, and each, expressed in every part of the body. (quoted in Taylor and Shuttleworth 9)

This corresponds almost exactly to Delsarte's analysis of the head as an expressive medium, though here, as elsewhere, minor variations were introduced.

39. See also McArthur, who discusses this emphasis on "personality" in relation to urbanization. He notes that

urban life fostered a sense of continual performance. The obsession with personality and the image one projected betrayed anxiety not only about acceptance by others, but also about self-identity. Mass society threatened to overwhelm the individual, to destroy personal identity. Consequently, the new imperative was to distinguish oneself from the mass, a task accomplished through the conscious creation of a distinctive personality. (188)

Thus, he sees the shift on stage from "points" to personality as a reflection of changing attitudes, needs, and experiences within American culture (187).

40. See also Moses True Brown 49; 70–4. For him, personality is revealed through bearings, attitudes, and inflections.

41. Not unique to MacKaye, this class bias appears in Delsarte's writings, too. Noting a difference in the use of the shoulder between the upper and lower classes, for example, "Delsarte goes on to state that people of higher classes have a gamut of expression subtler than those of the lower . . . There must be a difference between 'the swift and flexible movements of an elegant organism and those evolutions clumsily executed by the torpid limbs hardened by constant labor'" (Delsarte quoted in Stebbins 48). And, even where stances may appear to be the same, Stebbins notes that many factors bear upon their significance. Referring to the example of "legs strong and wide apart; standing in breadths, knees straight," she remarks that such a posture

may signify a condition (e.g., fatigue, vertigo, or intoxication) or a sentiment (e.g., familiarity or vulgar boorishness) (66). Context, however, is also important, as she goes on to explain: "A gentleman, in the privacy of his own household, might permit himself to stand, his hands under his coat-tails, his back to the fire in [this] attitude. He would be a vulgar boor if he assumed the same position in society" (67). All of these examples suggest that the Delsarte method functioned to naturalize social hierarchies by correlating class-specific habits of gesticulation to stages of moral development.

42. There also appears to be an implicit gender bias in the method, though it is far less pronounced. A diagram of head positions, for example, uses a woman's head to indicate various attitudes combining predominantly moral and vital dispositions, but shifts to a man's head to indicate attitudes with predominantly mental dispositions (Stebbins 135). Similarly, race/nationality appears to be a factor (albeit understood in class terms). Moses True Brown, for example, compares the physical movement involved in the labor performed by "the plantation slave or the Mexican peon," to that performed by "the slave or serf emancipated" and to that of the more highly evolved soldier (45–6).

43. Here, I disagree with Dudden's critique of Robert Allen: while female burlesque performers may have had *limited* agency, given the gender politics of theatrical management, on the stage they *did* have agency insofar as they acted on "points." Of course, these were not the "points" of Forrest or Macready earlier in the century. For, where they used their bodies to realize a word or image in the dramatic text, female burlesque performers used bawdy puns to highlight their physiques, inverting the "point" in a burlesque of it. However differently they deployed their "points," the fact that female burlesque performers stood on "points" meant that their audiences most certainly understood them to have interpretive authority.

44. Pearson herself questions her identification of Delsarte with histrionism, asking:

Why equate Delsartism with the histrionic code? Delsartism thrived at the end of the nineteenth century, by which time histrionically coded performance had all but vanished from most stages. Moreover, Delsarte and some of his more faithful disciples professed to follow nature, a practice that was anathema to many of those championing histrionically coded performance. Delsarte, it would seem, desired to challenge the hegemony of the histrionic code, but the wholesale acceptance of Delsartism perverted its founder's intentions. His system, in its debased form, became emblematic of histrionically coded performances. (22)

While she is probably right to suggest that perversions of Delsartism do, indeed, inform the histrionic code, those perversions are likely the result of actors who *conflate* Delsartean gestures with melodramatic posing.

45. Kuleshov once belonged to a group of theatre artists devoted to the Volkonsky–Delsarte–Dalcroze system, though he claimed later to have broken with them over their "scholastic Delsartism" (Yampolsky 51).

46. Yampolsky persuasively argues that Eisenstein's theory of montage is a combination of Delsarte's anatomization of the body with Emile Jaques-Dalcroze's system of eurythmics. As he points out, however, Eisenstein was not the first to use Delsarte's insights to experiment with montage. See his discussion of the

Volkonsky–Delsarte–Dalcroze system in pre-Soviet Russian theatre and its importation into film through the work of Vladimir Gardin (49–56).

47. See McArthur for a discussion of actors' ambivalent feelings about early film. As he
points out, many actors were lured by film's promise of a reliable income, especially
given the stock theatre's decline. Its debased reputation, however, led some to hide
their involvement by wearing disguises before the camera. As for the movie studios,
this desire for anonymity posed no problem; they began to list screen credits only
after 1910, when they realized the commercial advantages of the star system (193–5).

2 Voices: oratory, expression, and the text/performance split

1. Donald K. Smith notes that the general trend among universities was to absorb
oratory into departments of English. He adds, however, that several universities
founded separate departments or even schools of oratory, many of which went on to
become quite influential, including Northwestern in 1878, Michigan in 1892, Ohio
Wesleyan in 1894, and the University of Southern California in 1895 (461).

2. For example, the projective agent (the lungs) expressed life, the vibrative agent
(the larynx) was moral, and the reverberative agent (the mouth) revealed mind.
Each agent was further characterized by three defining features of its sound-making
capacity. The lungs controlled intensities, shades, and respirations; the larynx produced prolations, pathetic effects, and registers; and the mouth controlled emissions,
articulations, and vowels (Delsarte 491). In keeping with the law of the "ninefold
accord," the three variations within each vocal agent gave expression to the principles
governing the other two, revealing the one within the many. The mouth, for example, gave voice to the mental principle, but, according to the Abbé Delaumosne,
one of Delsarte's French followers, vowels were essentially moral while consonants,
requiring the "gesture" of the tongue, were vital, expressing life (Delsarte 125).

3. Delsarte writes, for example, that

Under the influence of *sentiment* the smallest and most insignificant things that
we may wish to represent proportion themselves to the degree of acuteness of
the sounds, which become softened in proportion as they rise.
   Under the influence of *passion*, on the contrary, the voice rises with a corresponding brilliancy, in proportion to the magnitude of the thing it would express,
and becomes lowered to express smallness or meanness. (Delsarte 420–1)

Here again we see Delsarte's classist and gendered bias clearly at work when he
notes: "Vulgar and uncultured people, as well as children, seem to act in regard to
an ascensional vocal progression in an inverse sense to the well-educated, or, at any
rate, affectionate persons, such as mothers, fond nurses, etc." (Delsarte 419).

4. Believing with Pythagoras that every sound is a tonic chord that contains its own
fifth and third, Delsarte went on to theorize that the three form the perfect harmony
of life, mind, and soul. Whenever a dissonant note is sounded, it creates a desire in
its audience to go "home" to its tonic base. "Sound is the reflection of the Divine
image," whereby the tonic expresses the principle of the Father, the dominant (fifth)
expresses the Son, and the mediant (third) expresses the Holy Ghost (Delsarte 484).

5. John Walker's rule xv states: "Prepositions and conjunctions are more united with the words they precede than with those they follow; and, consequently, if it be necessary to pause, the preposition and the conjunction ought to be classed with the succeeding words, and not with the preceding" (Walker 1, 100).

6. See Johannes Fehr. Attempting to situate Saussure's work within its cultural-historical context, Fehr has suggested that Saussure's structuralist analysis of the signier–signified relationship developed as a scientific corrective to the popular (Delsartean?) belief that there was a mystical correspondence between signs and their meanings. (See discussion below.) It is worth noting that, on the banks of Lac Leman, across the river from the Uni-Bastion where Saussure was delivering his famous lectures, Emile Jaques-Dalcroze was staging civic pageants with performers trained in "eurhythmics," his program of physical movement derived from Delsarte's teachings.

7. See, for example, Shaver (205). The extent to which Delsarte's method was founded upon specific religious principles, however, is a matter of debate. Among those who insisted upon the importance of the Holy Trinity to an understanding of it was the Abbé de Delaumosne, a student of Delsarte who was also the curé of the Church St. Genevieve in Nanterre, with whom Genevieve Stebbins studied. Stebbins's book, *The Delsarte System of Dramatic Expression* – a bestseller, published in six editions from 1885 to 1902 – helped to popularize Delaumosne's Catholi-cized version of the Delsarte method in the United States. On the other side of the debate was Angélique Arnaud, also a student of Delsarte, who emphasized the scientific and philosophical aspects of his method instead. Although she acknowl-edged that Delsarte fell short of developing his method into a comprehensive system due to his tendency toward mysticism (Delsarte 197–8), she challenged the idea that Delsarte's method was based upon Catholic principles, calling it a "heresy" to suggest that it was based upon any specific religious tenets whatsoever (Delsarte 211). "Profound passion, lofty style, art itself, these are not learned from any cat-echism," she exhorts. "If religion was blended with [Delsarte's method], it was that which speaks directly to the heart of all beings endowed with poetry, to those who are capable of vowing their love to the worship of sublime things" (quoted in Delsarte 309).

8. Although Monroe is credited with having wed Delsarte's system to the theories of American Transcendentalism, it is quite likely that such an engagement was first proposed by Steele MacKaye, from whom Monroe first learned of Delsarte's work. MacKaye, as we've seen, was the first American to study with Delsarte and the first to generate interest in Delsarte's teachings in the United States. Given the ease with which he learned the Delsarte method, it is quite possible that a familiarity with Transcendentalism facilitated his understanding of the quasi-mystical under-pinnings of Delsarte's system. (See Percy MacKaye, *Epoch* 1, 77; 230; 289; *Epoch* 11, 212.) MacKaye most likely translated Delsarte through an Emersonian lexicon, and Monroe made more systematic correlations between their respective grammars of thought.

9. Speech historian Edyth Renshaw describes it as a "watered-down transcendentalism" (321).

---

10. In marking this break, Curry was not alone. Solomon Henry Clark at the University of Chicago referred to his somewhat similar method of instruction as the "new elocution," while Genevieve Stebbins and Mary S. Thompson referred to theirs as "interpretation" (P. Edwards 64). "Expression" and "interpretation" were used somewhat interchangeably throughout the first quarter of the twentieth century.

11. Mary Margaret Robb further notes that several of Curry's students "were leaders in the reinstatement of speech in the college and university curriculum in the early part of the twentieth century" ("Elocutionary" 193). (See discussion below.)

12. For Curry's method of reading figurative language, see *Imagination* 112; for his elucidation of meter and the significance of line length, see *Foundations* 234. For a critical account of Curry's "think-the-thought" method, see Robb, "Elocutionary" 193–6.

13. The expressive culture movement was especially influential on the development of modern dance. See, for example, Ted Shawn's discussion of Delsarte's influence on dance in *Every Little Movement*.

14. Referring to these decomposing exercises, Genevieve Stebbins describes how she lets her body go limp, from fingers to hand, to forearm, entire arm, waist, spine, hips, knees, ankles, toes, jaw, and eyelids, finally allowing herself to fall by withdrawing her "vital force" into the reservoir of the brain (Stebbins 11).

15. Many of them bought into the medicalization of this malaise, however, referring to the decomposing and recomposing exercises as "nerve gymnastics" (P. Edwards 54).

16. Of course, moveable type had separated the act of sending and receiving verbal communication for centuries, but however familiar the printed word had since become, these new communication technologies could only be perceived, in this moment, as strange.

17. For a discussion of the Chautauqua phenomenon, see Lynes 9–12.

18. Famous for his formulation of "tone-color," Clark attempted to define it in the following way:

> One might say that tone-color is the avenue along which the emotion passes in its progress from within outward or from the poet to the hearer. The mere fact is expressed by the words; the emotion is expressed by the various qualities of the voice, and these qualities of the voice may be more surely and easily manifested on certain elements than on others. (quoted in Robb, *Oral* 176)

See also my discussion of Vachel Lindsay's use of the technique below.

19. D. Edwards notes that "It was on Harriet Monroe's advice, at the time of the publication of *General William Booth Enters Into Heaven*, that Lindsay first indicated tone color effects by marginal notes" (189).

20. Another source, of course, was Richard Wagner, whose *The Artwork of the Future* (1849) postulates an explicit link between the aural features of prosody and their emotional effects.

21. Although Joel Porte is not wrong to identify debates about the relationship between science and religion as part of the intellectual context shaping Santayana's thought, I believe the context to which Santayana refers in this rather elliptical comment is in

fact the expressive culture movement. Summarizing Santayana's position on these debates, Porte writes:

> Science, for example, is like a bridge that allows thought to arch from fact to fact but always returns us to real experience. Theology and metaphysics, however, are "in the air after the fashion of a captive balloon," bound to earth at one point only, and thus "essentially a kind of poetry" . . . It is when the balloon "gets loose altogether," he goes on, that "our fictions become absolutely vapid and without value of any sort" – empty symbols symbolic of nothing real. (xxiv)

This suggests to me that, given its penchant for mystification, the expressive culture movement is Santayana's untethered balloon.

22. Santayana's term recalls the "correlate objects" of German phenomenologist Edmund Husserl, for whom consciousness is always a consciousness of something in the world. Shifting the terms of philosophical discourse away from the idea that thought was a hermetic internal process distinct from the external objects of its contemplation, Husserl posited two types of knowledge – primary or sensuous knowledge (which is perceptual) and psychic or categorial knowledge (which is abstract) – both of which pertain to internal processes and external relations in the world. For example, sensuous knowledge could present itself to the imagination (e.g., a pink elephant) and categorial knowledge could apply to one's experience of the world (e.g., the passage of time). The proper distinction between types of understanding, then, was not one of internal/external but of one's relationship to the object of his/her knowledge, whether that object was abstract or concrete (Rée 342). Thus, a "correlate object" for Husserl was one that pertained to the sort of thought one had about it.

    In "The Elements and Function of Poetry," Santayana seems to invoke this understanding when he speaks of the poet's need to find "correlative objects" adequate to the emotion he/she wishes to express:

    > The substance of poetry is, after all, emotion . . . The various forms of love and hate are only possible in society, and to imagine occasions in which these feelings may manifest all their inward vitality is the poet's function, – one in which he follows the fancy of every child, who puffs himself out in his day-dreams into an endless variety of heroes and lovers. The thrilling adventures which he craves demand an appropriate theatre; the glorious emotions with which he bubbles over must at all hazards find or feign their correlative objects. (165)

23. Since the first appearance of "Hamlet and His Problems" in the *Athenaeum*, Eliot's phrase "objective correlative" has prompted many critics to debate its origin and significance. J. C. Maxwell, for instance, was the first to cite Santayana as a probable source, while R. W. Stallman locates the first English language use of the phrase in Washington Allston's *Lectures on Art, and Poems* (1850). F. N. Lees was the first to note the link between Eliot and Nietzsche (see discussion below), but, while David J. DeLaura concedes that "this may be the germ of Eliot's application of the term to Hamlet" (427), he defers to Eliot's claim that he coined the phrase himself, arguing that he did so in order to describe the artistic precision necessary to protect a work of art from the pathetic fallacy committed by critics like Walter Pater. Pasquale Di

Pasquale, meanwhile, suggests that Eliot's phrase may also owe a debt to Samuel Taylor Coleridge's "framework of objectivity."

24. The full passage in Oscar Levy's translation reads as follows:

> The history of the rise of Greek tragedy now tells us with luminous precision that the tragic art of the Greeks was really born of the spirit of music: with which conception we believe we have done justice for the first time to the original and most astonishing significance of the chorus. At the same time, however, we must admit that the import of tragic myth as set forth above never became transparent with sufficient lucidity to the Greek poets, let alone the Greek philosophers; their heroes speak, as it were, more superficially than they act; the myth does not at all find its adequate objectification in the spoken word. The structure of the scenes and the conspicuous images reveal a deeper wisdom than the poet himself can put into words and concepts: the same being also observed in Shakespeare, whose Hamlet, for instance, in an analogous manner talks more superficially than he acts, so that the previously mentioned lesson of Hamlet is to be gathered not from his words, but from a more profound contemplation and survey of the whole. (129)

Evidently, Nietzsche's notion of an "adequate objectification" itself comes from Richard Wagner's theory of tone-speech, as expressive culture enthusiast Florence Holden aptly noted. In her article "The Fine Art of Poetry," appearing in an 1897 issue of *Werner's Magazine*, she quotes the following passage from Wagner's "The Art-Work of the Future," where he speaks of how feelings must struggle for an external object through which to become expressed:

> In pure tone-speech, with its tale of the received impression, the feeling gave only itself to be understood . . . To denote and distinguish between outer objects and themselves, however, the feeling must cast about it for something answering to and embodying the impression of the object, for a distinctive garment wherewith to clothe the open tone; and this it borrowed from the impression, and through it from the object itself. (16)

25. Evidence that Curry might, indeed, have served as Eliot's lightning rod exists in *The Province of Expression* (1891), where he writes:

> There are many things which the tone of the voice can say better than words. A motion of the hand, an action of the eye or of the face, can supply an ellipsis which the essayist or novelist must give in words.
> One of the most familiar illustrations of this is the difference between the drama and the novel. All probably agree that the amount of thought is as great in Hamlet as in a great novel – as for example, in David Copperfield, though Hamlet covers only a few pages and David Copperfield takes several volumes. This difference is due to the fact that the drama is to be presented through the living languages of man and be both seen and heard, while the novel is only intended to be read in an easy-chair. (*Province* 42)

26. As many scholars have noted, 1927 was an important year for Eliot, marking his conversion to Anglicanism, his assumption of British citizenship, and his turn to conservative politics. As Jed Esty argues, it is also the year that marked a significant

shift in Eliot's aesthetic style. Where Eliot's earlier work focused on the representation of an individual consciousness in isolation from the modern world, his later work takes what Esty refers to as a more "anthropological turn," searching for new ways to represent social experience in a moment when "England" was feeling less like the seat of a sprawling empire and more like a single nation defined by the common heritage of its people. Given that his experiments in drama date to this later period, we might see Eliot's renewed interest in drama and performance as part of this anthropological turn.

27. Thus, Eliot, with his insistence upon regulating theatricality, would be an example of what Puchner refers to as a "diegetic" dramatist.

28. Reading the Imagist manifesto (1913; 1915) in light of the expressive culture movement, we see that their call for the "*exact* word, not the nearly-exact, nor the merely decorative word" evokes the same imperative that Eliot would make several years later in "Hamlet and His Problems." Thus, it would appear that a whole new generation of poets developed their craft in response to disciplinary debates between oral and textual interpretation at the turn of the century. And, it would appear that, in doing so, they, too, helped define literary high modernism in anti-performative terms. See Pound's "Preface to Some Imagist Poets" in Kolocotroni 268–9.

29. See Rarig and Greaves 499. They recount the events leading up to the meeting on 28 November 1914. See also D. Smith, who notes that the impulse to form this new association was felt a year earlier when discontented members passed a resolution calling for the separation of Public Speaking from English departments at a regional meeting in New England (455).

30. Writing in 1954, Paul Kozelka notes,

> The slow process of establishing accredited courses in theatre arts began in 1915 and, of course, has not ended yet. In 1917 a notice in the *English Journal* asked members of the association to urge their principals to give credits in English for dramatics. By 1915 thirty-five schools in southern California were offering from one-half to four credits for dramatic classes, and colleges and universities had begun to give entrance credit for courses in dramatics which included certain stipulated material. (603–4)

> By 1921, "Professor Frederick Koch reported to the convention of the Drama League of America that 398 courses in dramatics representing 998 academic hours were being given in 164 institutions of higher learning" (608).

3   Words: copyright and the creation of the performance "text"

1. Although acknowledging the lower court's distinction beween high and low art, the Supreme Court did not find the distinction itself grounds for restricting copyright protection. Indeed, in expanding the definition of "useful" to include commercial applications, it effectively relaxed the distinction between "high" and "low" art to shift the dominant terms of aesthetic value. Where art was once judged in moral terms (e.g., its ennobling effect upon the viewer and thus society), it would now be judged in formal terms (e.g., its ability to fulfill its own "use").

2. Mark Rose imports the significance of the *Bleistein* decision backwards, seeing the concept of personality at work as early as 1769 in *Millar v. Taylor* (137). He argues that the court's finding of a common-law right precedent to the act of printing was based on John Locke's definition of personal property whereby one "removes materials from the state of nature and mixes his labor with them, thereby producing an item of personal property." Rose concludes that, as applied to Thomson's poem *The Seasons* (the subject of the *Millar* case), this idea allowed for the protection of one's *personality* as expressed in a work of literature (114). As my discussions of this term in chapters 1 and 2 undoubtedly make clear, I strongly disagree. While I follow Benjamin Kaplan in hearing an "echo" of "the Romantic gospel" of original genius in the concept of "personality" (35), I want to insist upon the historical specificity of the term as it comes out of the expressive culture movement at the turn of the twentieth century. The 1903 *Bleistein* decision, then, is historically important for introducing this understanding of "personality" into the law.

3. Rose traces the emergence of the notion of intellectual property to the early eighteenth century, when authors tactically analogized their books to estates in an effort to extend their legal rights (56). Siva Vaidhyanathan, however, notes that the term itself does not appear until 1976, when the United Nations' World Intellectual Property Organization first convened (11–12).

4. See Judge Learned Hand's decision in *Nichols v. Universal Pictures Corp.* (1931) in which the plaintiff claimed the defendant infringed upon her play, *Abie's Irish Rose*, when it made a film, *The Cohens and the Kellys*, using similar characters and incidents. The plaintiff, hoping to invoke the precedent of *Daly v. Palmer* (see discussion below), was disappointed with Hand's ruling in which he held that "the defendant had taken, at most, the plaintiff's 'ideas' but not her 'expression': the plot at a generalized level, the characters only as general types. These 'ideas' the plaintiff's copyright could not cover, for so to 'generalize' her copyright would tend to bar subsequent writers from too large a precinct" (Kaplan 47).

5. The full passage is revealing. Hand writes:

> If *Twelfth Night* were copyrighted, it is quite possible that a second comer might so closely imitate Sir Toby Belch or Malvolio as to infringe, but it would not be enough that for one of his characters he cast a riotous knight who kept wassail to the discomfort of his household, or a vain and foppish steward who became amorous of his mistress. These would be no more than Shakespeare's 'ideas' in the play . . . It follows that the less developed the characters, the less they can be copyrighted; that is the penalty an author must bear for marking them too indistinctly. (quoted in Kaplan 50)

6. For an excellent discussion of the emergence of the Office of the Revels, see Richard Dutton, who recounts that the origin of the office dates to the reign of Edward VI when, in 1549, a decree was issued to ban entertainments on the grounds that they might inflame religious tensions between Catholics and Protestants. Eventually, this ban was modified to allow private performances sponsored by aristocratic patrons and, later, under Elizabeth, performances licensed by the magistracies of individual cities and towns. 1574 marks the date when Leicester's Men received a royal patent from Elizabeth herself, ensuring their right to perform not only in the city of London

but throughout the kingdom, provided that their entertainment was approved first by Elizabeth's Master of the Revels, who was responsible for making sure that it was fit for her to see (17–40).

7. The details of their financial dispute are fairly complicated, with neither playwright nor actor clearly in the right. According to Quinn, Bird and Forrest had an oral agreement that Bird would be paid $1,000 for *The Gladiator*, with another $2,000 following if the play were a success. Assuming that this agreement held for the other plays he wrote for Forrest, Bird accepted $1,000 each for *Oralloossa* and *The Broker of Bogota* (both of which were successful), but received no payment for *Pelopidas* (which Forrest never produced) nor his revision of Stone's *Metamora*. Thus, Bird believed he was due $6,000 plus payment on the two unproduced plays. In the meantime, however, he had borrowed $2,000 from Forrest for personal expenses. When Forrest asked that the loan be repaid, Bird demurred, believing he had a right to subtract it from the royalties he felt he was due. Forrest felt otherwise. Perhaps believing Bird to have mistakenly presumed a royalty agreement for *Oralloossa* and *Broker*, he refused to pay anything more. But, since he didn't sue Bird for the unpaid note, it would appear he was willing to count the $2,000 royalty on *Gladiator* against the loan. In any event, the dispute ended there, with no further collaboration between the two. Quinn concludes that "there can be no question that [Forrest] treated the playwright unfairly," noting that "Even on the old benefit system of 'third nights' Bird should have received at least $5,000 apiece" (245). Ethically, of course, he is right. But, because Bird fell between the old patronage and the new market systems of exchange, and because the law had not yet developed to protect playwrights under these new terms, Forrest had done nothing *legally* wrong. Had it come before the courts, Forrest would have had the clear advantage.

8. See Stephens for a discussion of the 1842 law that finally regulated the adaptation of non-dramatic works for the British stage (97–8). In the US, specific protection for theatrical adaptations of non-dramatic works does not appear in the law until the general revision of 1870 (Kaplan 32).

9. See McConachie, "Out of the Kitchen" 5–28.

10. As Quinn observes, the law required only that the title of a play be registered. Nonetheless he – along with other scholars who have cited him – is wrong to conclude therefore that only the title and not the text was protected (Quinn 369).

11. In the short story, however, there is no second character. Captain Tom, lying unconscious on the track, comes to, just as the train swooshes by on an adjacent track.

12. See Stephens for an in-depth discussion of this practice and its history. He notes that it unofficially began in 1861, when Boucicault decided to stage a token first performance in Britain before any US run, after a British court found that he had "dedicated" *The Colleen Bawn* to the public by allowing it to be performed in the US before securing copyright at home (105–6). Stephens further notes that, though it was never formally adopted into British law, the practice of stage-righting was unofficially recognized as a means of securing ownership in a dramatic property.

13. Even at that, entanglements continued. The case of *Ferris v. Frohman* (1912) reveals the convolutions the courts had to go through in the wake of the international agreement in order to recognize the copyright provisions of the two countries – Britain and the US – and arrive at a fair and equitable solution.

14. The Berne Convention includes the following provision: "It is understood that the manufacture and sale of instruments serving to reproduce mechanically the airs of music borrowed from the private domain are not considered as constituting musical infringement" (quoted in *White-Smith v. Apollo Co.* decision).

15. Consider, for example, a 1906 memorandum before the US Congress pertaining to the player piano. Acknowledging the difficulty of distinguishing between the respective purviews of patent and copyright law, the House committee on patents urged Congress to restrict the use of such devices on the grounds that they did away with the "personal performer and at the same time with the sheet music which is required by the performer to guide him in striking the proper notes." Clearly there is some confusion here as to what it is exactly that these machines reproduced. Did they copy the composition in a manner analogous to that of the printing press, the object of existing copyright regulation? Or did they copy the performer in interpreting that composition? In supplying a demand that otherwise would be filled by the sale of sheet music, these inventions, the report continued, are "doing away with the laborious studying and tiresome practicing that are necessary to master the instruments played by hand from written or printed scores" (United States Congress House Report [59-2] 7083, part 2, 1–2, 4).

16. Justice Day notes that the plaintiff (the appellant in the case) did not claim an infringement of his performance rights as embedded in the copyrighted composition, nor did he explicitly cite the 1856 law. Had he done so, the case may have been decided differently, necessitating a distinction between a violation committed by a performer and one committed by a machine. Because the plaintiff invoked copyright specifically, framing the question as to whether or not perforated rolls were "copies," the court found that the law did not apply.

Part II Introduction

1. See Stephens's discussion of how, in the 1890s, publishers began to convert acting editions, with their elaborate stage directions, into reading editions, with significantly streamlined authors' notes (132). "On the assumption that the older form inhibited public demand," he explains, "the new reading editions were an attempt to educate a novel-buying public into the purchase of plays" (132). Playwrights such as Oscar Wilde and George Bernard Shaw assisted in this development by taking direct control over the publication of their plays. Shaw, for example, had very specific ideas about how stage directions should appear in reading editions. As Stephens notes, "His rule was 'never to mention the stage, proscenium or spectators; to discard all technical expressions and insert plenty of descriptive matter; to give sufficient guidance to the theatre management and information to the actor of *what* but not *how* to act – without spoiling anything for the reader'" (141).

2. Although considered one of the leading playwrights of the first half of the twentieth century, Crothers has "consistently been undervalued by drama historians and literary critics," as Brenda Murphy reminds us (82).

3. Crothers studied elocution (and probably expression) at the New England School of Dramatic Instruction in Boston in 1892 before becoming an instructor at the Stanhope-Wheatcroft School, where she was allowed to present her own plays at

the Madison Square Theatre (Lindroth 3–4). See McTeague for an account of the Stanhope-Wheatcroft School.

4. In his preface to the 1924 published version, Alexander Woollcott notes that the play is loosely based on *Hans Sonnenstoessers Hohlenfahrt* by Paul Apel. Although Kaufman and Connelly borrow the idea for a dream sequence from Apel, Woollcott claims that its stylization is completely their own, even if it does invite a comparison to "that undigested lump in dramatic criticism called 'Expressionism.' Such experiments in that kind of staging as one encountered in 'The Hairy Ape,' 'The Adding Machine,' and 'Beggar on Horseback,'" he wryly observes, "are invariably attributed to the German influence on the American theater, an attribution which does not matter much, although it must wring a wry smile from Arthur Hopkins, who employed precisely this technique for a kindred play called 'Poor Little Rich Girl,' which he produced a dozen years ago" (15).

4 The "unconscious autobiography" of Eugene O'Neill

1. The citations from the Gelbs' biography that follow refer to the 1962 original *O'Neill*; references to *O'Neill, Life with Monte Cristo* (2002), the first of their three-volume revision-in-process, are specifically noted.

2. See, for example, Mardi Valgemae and William Elwood, who suggest that O'Neill was influenced by the German film *The Cabinet of Dr. Caligari*. See also Ronald Wainscott, who argues that O'Neill came by his knowledge of German Expressionism from scenic artists who imported European staging techniques to the American Art Theatre as the New Stagecraft (*Emergence* 93), while the Gelbs suggest that Susan Glaspell may have told O'Neill about her encounters with German Expressionism while traveling in Europe in 1908 (*Life* 575). Travis Bogard follows Clara Blackburn and Virginia Floyd in claiming that O'Neill derived his expressionistic technique from a reading knowledge of August Strindberg's and Georg Kaiser's plays, adding books on the burgeoning art theatre movement by Sheldon Cheney and Kenneth Macgowan to his reading list (172–5). He even goes so far as to argue that *The Hairy Ape* was written with Macgowan's specifications for an art theatre in mind, despite the fact that O'Neill had finished drafting the play before he had read Macgowan's *The Theatre of Tomorrow*. Bogard hypothesizes somewhat unconvincingly that, "Evidently he and Macgowan had discussed its contents and he had read some of it in draft," concluding that "*The Hairy Ape*, for all its seeming originality of style and substance, is perhaps the most derivative" (242–4).

Among O'Neill's critics, there are two notable exceptions to the "derivative" camp. Egil Tornqvist sees O'Neill as an artistic free agent, always searching for a style of his own. He argues that "O'Neill's proneness to experiment with dramatic form – especially during his formative years he often refers to his plays as 'experiments' – follows logically from the assumption that just as every play has its own subject matter, so it must also have its own form" (29). What's more, he challenges the view that *The Emperor Jones* and *The Hairy Ape* are anomalous, seeing elements of what he refers to as their "super-naturalism" in many of O'Neill's plays. Timo Tiusanen has also resisted the inevitability of this critical narrative, noting a key difference between the "socio-expressionism" of German playwrights and the "psycho-expressionism" of O'Neill (98–101).

3. The Gelbs claim that Jones's line, "Dey's some tings I ain't got to be tole. I kin see 'em in folks' eyes," was a direct quotation from Smith. Sheaffer suggests that Jones's remark about laying his Jesus on the shelf came directly from Scott.

4. In *O'Neill, Life with Monte Cristo*, Arthur and Barbara Gelb claim that "O'Neill had, in fact, been writing disguised versions of his family mythology since the beginning of a career that began off Broadway in 1916" (5). Most critics who take a psychobiographical approach to O'Neill's work, however, tend to focus primarily on *Long Day's Journey Into Night* (1939–41; 1956) and other late plays. While they acknowledge the presence of incidental autobiographical details in O'Neill's early work, they tend to assume that he did not explore the psychodynamics of his family life until later in his career. Travis Bogard, for example, dates the beginning of such a turn in O'Neill's writing to 1922, the period after his mother's death (xii). Frederic Carpenter takes a similar position, though is more forceful in dismissing the relevance of the early plays, claiming that O'Neill "emphatically lacked th[e] insight" to write autobiographically in his early career. "[T]he major autobiographical plays were all written toward the end of his career; for in his early life, his best plays were not autobiographical: *The Emperor Jones*, for instance, is one of the least autobiographical plays in literature" (42).

5. I use "African-American" here to refer to the experiences of Africans in the new world (i.e., in the Americas). Further historical and cultural details include: O'Neill's claim that the idea of the drum came from a book about religious feasts in the Congo, Travis Bogard's suggestion that Charles Sheeler's book of documentary photographs of African sculpture was another important source (Bogard, 135), the Gelbs' hypothesis that another source for Jones may have been Henri Cristophe, the one-time slave who became king of Haiti in 1811 and who, upon becoming ill, shot himself in the head (439), and Sheaffer's suggestion that Toussaint L'Ouverture may have also served as a model (29). See also Joel Pfister, who suggests a link between images of Marcus Garvey in his uniform and racist constructions of Africa that appeared in American popular culture during the 1910s and 1920s (132–133). See, too, Philip J. Hanson and Peter Saiz, both of whom situate the play within the larger history of colonialism in the new world.

6. In fact, the Gelbs note that James confided as much to a Cincinnati reporter when on a final tour there in 1911 (181). What is important for me here is that Eugene understood his father to have had this realization only on his deathbed and to have made this confession only to him, as if it were a moment of tragic anagnorisis.

7. Like many critics, Frederic Carpenter interprets this episode (as represented in *Long Day's Journey Into Night*) as a simple case of James having given up serious acting in exchange for financial success, as if it were a conscious choice (20). My point here is that it wasn't a conscious choice; it was the result of historical forces which James was too blind to see, making him a tragic figure in his son's mind.

8. In arguing that O'Neill sought to atone for such feelings in writing *The Emperor Jones*, I agree with Lisa Schwerdt, who is alone among critics in noting that "the element of guilt seen in [*Long Day's Journey Into Night*] is present as early as *The Emperor Jones*" (73).

9. In support of my supposition that Jones is a figure for James, Robert Conklin suggests that both Jones and Yank, in *The Hairy Ape*, are nineteenth-century character types, forced to adjust to the theme of alienation on the twentieth-century stage (104). Although he goes on to argue that these characters are ill-suited to the play's expressionistic treatment (105), I maintain that, in fact, the tension between these nineteenth-century character types and the twentieth-century milieu in which they're trapped is perfectly suited to the play's expressionistic style.

10. Speaking of his father's enduring physical strength which only prolonged his illness, O'Neill wrote to a friend that "his grand old constitution kept him going and forced him to drain the cup of agony to the last bitter drop" (quoted in Gelb 430).

11. Evidently, James's imperiousness was not limited to his on-stage impersonation. When on tour with *The Count of Monte Cristo*, James ran a tight ship, insisting that cast members be punctual and professsional at all times. Despite his leniency toward Jamie's antics, James was respected by the actors in his combination troupe and was commonly referred to as the "Governor" (Gelb 107).

12. Besides Szwed, Roediger, and Flynn, discussed below, see Noel Ignatiev and Michael Rogin.

13. For more on Torrence, see John Clum.

14. Sheaffer notes that, "As an undergraduate at Princeton, O'Neill was noted for his ability to recite poetry from memory," suggesting to me that, like most Americans of his generation, O'Neill was well versed in Curry's theory of expression (120).

15. The fact that the play experientially aligns the audience with its central character may explain why so many critics persist in reading Jones as a universal figure. Thus, despite the undeniably racist assumptions that surface in O'Neill's description of Jones, the play's formal design would seem to suggest a more complicated attitude toward race.

16. Evidently, O'Neill had a cinematic technique specifically in mind. In a letter to George Tyler, he wrote that, in this play, he sought to combine "the scope of the [silent] movies with all that is best of the spoken drama" (quoted in Wainscott, *Staging* 53).

17. "The forest scenes might be only six representative tableaux selected and shown to the audience out of innumerable shots of pictures stored in Jones's psyche," Sohn observes. But "If these tableaux are connected in a sequence, they might look like a long motion picture put in reverse time order" (1086).

18. Murray points out that the year O'Neill began writing plays – 1912 – was the same year that his father made a silent film version of *The Count of Monte Cristo* for Jesse Lasky's "Famous Players in Famous Plays" series (16). Implicitly suggesting that O'Neill experienced a vexed relationship between these two media, Murray quotes Louis Sheaffer, who observed that O'Neill "always wrote for the screen on a typewriter but for the theater by hand." Sheaffer explained that "Behind the dual practice were most likely his different attitudes toward the two mediums: for the movies he was writing off the top of his head, concocting stories simply for money, whereas he was trying to get something of himself into plays" (Sheaffer, quoted in Murray 17). I would like to offer another possible explanation: the mechanism of the typewriter may have seemed better suited to the mechanism of film while

the embodiedness of handwriting was better suited to the embodied art form of the theatre. (See my discussion of the typewriter and its erasure of "personality" in chapter 7.)

19. Given that this type of primitivist thinking appears in the Transcendentalist beliefs of the expressive culture movement, even the play's seemingly racialized atavism may be more "universal" than critics have previously thought.

20. As Jameson points out, the aesthetic resolution offered by a fantasy master narrative is never completely satisfactory (180).

21. While O'Neill's short story was destroyed, the response it received from Carl Hovey, managing editor of *Metropolitan* magazine, survives. As Peter Egri has uncovered, Hovey's comments suggest that the reason the manuscript was rejected was because the story's resolution – Yank becoming a member of the I. W. W. – was too simple (93). This was one of three possible endings that O'Neill considered in composing the play. Egri notes that another was to have Yank return to his buddies on the ship a grimmer, less boastful man, while the third was to conclude the play – as he did – with Yank's death (94).

22. The Gelbs report that, in a 1945 letter, O'Neill revealed "that both *The Emperor Jones* and *The Hairy Ape* had been written in ten days. In the case of the former, he said, 'no scenario, just a few notes in preparation.' As for *The Hairy Ape*, it had been 'dashed off too, without much preparation.' Both, he added, were 'easy' plays: 'They just came to me'" (*Life* 466).

23. Wainscott reports that O'Neill's professional ambitions led to the final rift between him and Cook. By the time *The Hairy Ape* went into production, O'Neill had already contacted Arthur Hopkins to produce it, accusing Cook of being a "'rotten producer' and claiming that his plays now needed 'more competent direction'" (*Staging* 107).

24. Insofar as the Irish Paddy (pater?) is the father figure in this oedipal dynamic, we might expect Yank to be Irish, too. In fact, O'Neill had intended to make Yank Irish, but, as he mentioned in a letter to Kenneth Macgowan, the American-born O'Neill thought it more fitting to make Yank an American instead (Bogard 241). Indeed, the character's Americanness is reflected in his very name, "Yank," a generic term O'Neill undoubtedly heard used by the international sailors with whom he worked to refer to Americans such as he. Even Yank's given name – Robert Smith – underscores his Americanness, its Anglo-Saxon specificity suggesting the ethnic privileges of a "native-born" son. Although native-born himself, O'Neill would have savored the strange and delicious irony of being accorded such privileges by foreign-born shipmates who regarded this son of an Irish immigrant with an Irish-sounding last name simply as a "yank."

25. As "Robert Smith," Yank's given name suggests that he is related to "Smitty" from the earlier sea plays. Pfister makes just such a link between the two characters, hearing an echo of Smitty's quasi-philosophical ruminations in Yank's existential laments (119).

26. Both Hughes and Kehl note that the parishioners speak of "rehabilitating the veil of the temple," a reference to the veil in the Temple's Holy of Holies which was rent by Christ's death, opening the way of man to God. They also note that "dear Doctor Caiaphas," whose sermon the parishioners speak of having just heard, is an

allusion to the high priest who, in sacrificing Jesus to avoid political unrest, represents expediency over justice.

27. Where Massa's analysis of Yank's dialogue is illuminating, Egri's examination of the prosody of O'Neill's stage directions seems to me to be severely misguided. Unlike the dialogue, such words are not sounded by an actor's voice; they are written for the reader's comprehension only and contribute nothing to the vocal dynamics of the play in performance.

28. Bogard argues that

> The Rodin sculpture held for O'Neill an evolutionary significance appropriate to the play – brutish man attempting to puzzle out the truth of his existence and perhaps to better it, mind triumphing over brute force. Rodin's bronze, however, is far from pessimistic, and considering the course Yank is to follow, question may be raised as to the appropriateness of its ironic use here. (246–7)

29. As Jean Chothia notes, "the [stage] directions are unusually full, even for an O'Neill play" (32). See Kurt Eisen for a discussion of O'Neill's novelization of the drama.

30. Although the relationship between "manner" and "matter" was a constant subject of debate within modernist circles, these terms seem to bear some specificity to Curry's theory of expression. For example, in defending the intellectual integrity of oral interpretation in his widely taught book *The Province of Expression* (1891), Curry refuted the criticism made by textual critics that oral interpretation was concerned solely with the manner of speaking, claiming that such an idea reduces the speaker to a mere imitator when, in fact, he or she must imaginatively recreate the thoughts and feelings which originally motivated the written text. "Supposing for the sake of argument," he reasons,

> we grant that vocal and pantomimic expression have simply to do with manner, and that verbal expression has to do with the matter of speech, then, as has been shown, the manner has power to reverse the matter, and oratorical truthfulness absolutely requires the two to be consistent with each other. Both are absolutely necessary to a complete and adequate manifestation of the thought and soul of the man. (44)

Thus, it would seem that O'Neill has Curry specifically in mind here when he answers his critics. Although Curry always insisted that all three languages must be perfectly coordinated, and O'Neill counterposed them to illustrate his characters' spiritual disharmony, both agreed that there was an integral relationship between the manner and matter of speaking. O'Neill, in his characteristic way, simply ironized Curry's teachings to achieve an "oratorical truthfulness" of his own.

5   Elmer Rice and the cinematic imagination

1. This and all subsequent citations to Rice's correspondence with Frank Harris will be indicated by date only. Please refer to the bibliography for the appropriate catalogue number. Other miscellaneous correspondence will be noted separately. N. B. much of this letter is reprinted in *Minority Report* (190).

2. As a boy, Rice tells us, he was physically repulsed by his father's cadaverous figure and blackened teeth, shrinking from his proffered hugs and kisses – much to his father's enduring resentment (*Minority Report* 22). "We were seldom in open conflict," Rice remarks of their relationship, "but there was always an undercurrent of hostility" (25). As he grew older, Rice transferred the oedipal drama onto a social platform, defining his values against those of his father. Where his father was "always fulminating against the niggers and the dirty dagoes," and directing "his most vitriolic comments . . . against the kikes" (despite his own German-Jewish ethnic heritage), Rice discriminated against no one and actively worked on causes of social justice (63). The oedipal conflict finally came to a close at the end of his father's life. Exploding in violent fits caused by dementia, Jacob Reizenstein had to be institutionalized in a public hospital for the insane on Ward's Island, just across the East River from upper Manhattan (163). The guilt and sadness Rice surely felt for having had to consent to this decision was only further compounded by an exchange Rice had with his father while on a final visit. "Why did you send me to a place like this?" his father asked piteously in a rare moment of lucidity. "I can still see the reproach in his eyes," Rice confesses in his autobiography, more than forty years after the fact (163).

3. The Theatre Guild's prompt copy not only cuts Joe's part considerably, but gives Zero the last line, allowing the play to end on a much less cynical note.

4. Durham argues that, with the murder in scene two, Zero "gains a stature he has never had before and will never achieve again. For one moment he is not an automaton; he is a madman. But he is a man" (43). Valgemae, however, points out that the murder itself occurs off-stage; we see only the events leading up to it, suggesting that it is not meant to be read as a moment of triumph (*Accelerated Grimace* 65). I agree with Durham that, in committing this act of passion, Zero momentarily transcends his slave status, but acknowledge Valgemae's point that, because Rice leaves the act undramatized, we are not meant to read it as such. This points to an unintended ambiguity in Zero's character that Rice tried to shut down. Although Zero is clearly capable of asserting a Nietzschean will (and is rewarded for having done so with a free pass to heaven), he must, in terms of the story, remain a perpetual slave. Thus, Rice has Zero disavow his act in scene four, in order to reaffirm his slave status.

5. This scene was deleted from the Theatre Guild production and its original publication of the play. Rice tried repeatedly to have the scene restored, urging a representative at Samuel French, Inc. to do so upon the Phoenix Theatre's succesful revival of the full play in 1956. The representative, however, demurred on having the play republished, noting that copies of the scene could always be sent to anyone expressing interest in producing the play. See 22 February 1956 letter to Mr. Van Nostrand and Van Nostrand's 5 March 1956 reply in "Business Correspondence, *The Adding Machine*."

6. This unoriginality may be seen in the titles of actual films released in the late 1910s and early 1920s that are similar to the fictional titles mentioned in Rice's play:

For Love or Money (1920)
For Love of Service (1922)
For His Sake (1922)

A Mother's Secret (1918)
A Mother's Sin (1918)
Mother's Darling (1921)

The Price of Innocence (1919)
The Price of Redemption (1920)
The Price of Silence (1920, 1921)
The Price of Possession (1921)
The Price of Youth (1922)

The Devil's Wheel (1918)
The Devil's Trail (1919)
The Devil's Claim (1920)
The Devil's Garden (1920)
The Devil's Passkey (1920)
The Devil's Riddle (1920)
The Devil's Angel (1922)
The Devil's Bowl (1923)
The Devil's Confession (1921)
The Devil's Dooryard (1923)
The Devil's Ghost (1922)
The Devil's Match (1923)
The Devil's Needle (1923)
The Devil's Partner (1923).

7. Although Jules Chametzky follows Rice in claiming there was no significance to the fact that he changed his name from Reizenstein to Rice in January 1921 (74), I want to suggest that there was. Having just been released from his contract with Goldwyn to pursue his own playwriting career, Rice undoubtedly wanted to make a break with his former life and, perhaps, his former self. Although he remained in Hollywood for financial reasons for another seven months, working as a freelance for Jesse Lasky, Rice – as "Rice" – was able nonetheless to direct his thoughts to the future – a future in the theatre, a future in New York – where he could be his own free agent. Thus, while there may be no *cultural* significance to the name change, in that he was not attempting to hide his Jewish or German heritage, there may very well have been great *personal* significance to the act.

8. Rice's letter of 26 September 1919 indicates that he had authorized his agent to enlist Zoë Akins to make any necessary revisions.

9. The city of Los Angeles also helped quash labor activity, so effectively breaking strikes in the late 1910s and early 1920s that the labor unions were unable to establish a meaningful presence in Hollywood until the 1930s (May 187; 239).

10. In *Minority Report*, Rice tells us that he dropped the case after Jordan tearfully begged him not to send him to prison. Gratefully, Jordon promised to repay him in full, but – as Rice wryly notes – never did (193).

11. As Christopher Wixon argues with regard to *Counsellor-at-Law*, this culturally acceptable standard of success often appears as a theme in Rice's plays, and is almost always figured specifically as a white ethnic privilege. Indeed, the racist epithets

shouted by the men in scene three suggest this to be true for *The Adding Machine*, too.

12. Lary May notes that

    sound films were possible long before 1927. In fact, Edison's first demonstration in 1889 included sound. Film makers chose to keep the movies silent. The reasons are obscure, but it is likely that producers knew that silent movies could appeal to an audience of immigrants who spoke many languages. The result was an emotional communication through the universality of pictures. (39)

13. The original manuscript also differs from the published version in the way it orchestrates the men's and women's movements. In the manuscript, Rice calls for them to engage in a sort of square dance while clapping hands as in a children's game.

14. Ironically, this may have led to his neglect by literary critics, as Hogan argues in his introduction (9–14). Rice's refusal to valorize language at the expense of vocal and pantomimic modes of signification appears to be the source of both his plays' exceptional theatricality and his critical neglect.

15. See 29 September 1953 letter from Jean Collette, Chairman of Dramatics at the University of Idaho. See "*The Adding Machine*, miscellaneous."

16. See "Business Correspondence, *The Subway*." Sheldon Cheney of The Actors' Theatre evidently considered producing *The Subway* in January 1925, going so far as to enlist Mordecai Gorelik to design the production. Unfortunately and for reasons unknown, Cheney's plans did not materialize. Palmieri convincingly suggests that the cancelation was due to the group's financial problems; it folded a few months after backing out of its agreement to produce Rice's play (77). Rice then sold his production rights to Irma Kraft of The International Playhouse, but, according to Harris, that group had no money or backing for the play – only Kraft's enthusiasm. He thus recommended that Rice negotiate with Charles Hopkins of The Punch & Judy Theatre. Although Rice had his doubts about Hopkins, Harris urged him to pursue this course since The Theatre Guild had already turned the play down and few other possibilities existed. Finally, in 1929, the play was performed by the Lenox Hill Players (Palmieri 12).

17. Hogan sees *The Subway* as an "equally deft but more affirmative satire" than *The Adding Machine* (36); like it, it is full of "sound, movement, and color," requiring "excellent staging" for "its full theatrical effect" (37). Durham sees it as considerably more flawed, arguing that it "suffers from a heavy-handed obviousness, a failure of taste" (72). Palmieri agrees, extending Durham's insight to argue that the play lacks cohesion: on the one hand, it is about the crushing force of the subway and what it represents; on the other, it is about the sexual predation of Sophie (85).

18. Durham, for example, applauds Rice's use of "sound effects and lights – the thunderous rumble of the train hurtling through the darkness, the tooting of the whistle, the grinding noise of a flat wheel, the rhythmic flashing of lights" (70), while Palmieri approvingly describes the dialogue as empty yet full of meaning; George and Hurst speak in advertising clichés, he points out, as if modern man is not allowed to think for himself (79).

19. Hogan, for example, argues that Sophie's leap to death, as the subway train approaches, "superbly makes Rice's point about the ultimate rape of humanity and the mechanization of human feeling in the modern world" (41). Mardi Valgemae, however, points out that this is not a rape – "the language is clearly that of willing submission"; Sophie throws herself before the train as she would a lover. See Valgemae, "Rice's *The Subway*."

20. It is tempting to read "Eugene" as a barely coded figure for Rice's playwriting rival, Eugene O'Neill. As discussed below, Rice admired O'Neill's ideas but felt that he "lack[ed] the imaginative power to carry them through." He also may have been critical, as O'Neill himself apparently was, of O'Neill's readiness to reap Broadway's profits when he had achieved an artistic success. But this, of course, is mere speculation. We might just as easily be tempted to read "Sophie" as a figure for Sophie Treadwell, though it is extremely unlikely that Rice knew who she was until *Machinal* premiered in 1928, when he accused her of plagiarizing this 1923 play. See Rice's letter to Arthur Hopkins (11/22/28) in "Business Correspondence, *The Subway*" where he expresses concern over perceived similarities between *The Subway* and *Machinal*. His play, he notes, was written five years previous and was in constant circulation:

    It has been in almost every producer's office in New York. I do not know Miss Treadwell, but I do know that she is a professional play reader. I do not wish to imply that she deliberately borrowed from *The Subway*, but I do feel that the conclusion that she read the play and was influenced by it – consciously or unconsciously – is an inescapable one.

21. As Rice relates in his autobiography, his formal education was irregular. Although his mother made sure that he went to a good elementary school, he eventually went on to the High School of Commerce, where he prepared to enter a business trade. Economic necessity, however, compelled him to leave early. Later, as a law clerk, Rice earned his high school degree and entered New York Law School, graduating cum laude in 1912. Trained to enter into business and law, Rice may not have had much formal exposure to literature and oral expression, but he appears to have had enough to know what and how to teach himself. While working as a law clerk in his uncle's office, for example, he took to memorizing as many poems as he could – many of which he could still recite in his later years (*Minority Report* 92).

22. Palmieri speaks of O'Neill's influence on Rice as "rather nebulous," but admits that "it seems unlikely that he would not have known of these experimental plays [i.e., *The Emperor Jones* and *The Hairy Ape*] and perhaps been inspired by them" (11). In fact, as we have seen, he makes reference to *The Emperor Jones* in a 1923 letter to Marc Connelly (see discussion above) and refers here to having seen *The Hairy Ape*.

23. Despite his claim to the contrary, Rice appears to have admired more than just O'Neill's expressionistic technique in scene 5. Lines from *The Adding Machine* echo lines from *The Hairy Ape*, as when Lt. Charles tells Zero that he's a "waste-product. A slave to a contraption of steel and iron. The animal's instincts but not his strength and skill. The animal's appetite but not his unashamed indulgence of them" (138).

6 "I love a parade!": John Howard Lawson's minstrel burlesque

1. See "Clippings" file, "John Howard Lawson Papers," Special Collections, Morris Library, Southern Illinois University. All future citations to this collection will be abbreviated JHLP.
2. See Osborn, *Evening World* 1/12/25, and anonymous, *The Stage* 1/29/25; JHLP 16-4-5.
3. In his notes to the play, Lawson acknowledges an intentional "double use of jazz," whereby it is to be used "as absurdity and truth, as cheap popular music and as a genuine folk form" (JHLP "Yankee Doodle Blues" 227).
4. After talking to Psinski, for instance, soldier Bill says that he doesn't want to be a "pack-horse" anymore, he wants to be a man! (86).
5. This is the claim made for example by Mardi Valgemae, who writes, "In the last act the mutilated hero marries Sadie, who carries his child, in a jazz wedding. Like Edmund Wilson's *The Crime in the Whistler Room*, Lawson's early plays conclude on a note of hope, reminiscent of a number of German expressionist dramas that proclaimed the coming of the utopian New Man" (*Accelerated Grimace* 78).
6. LeRoy Robinson documents that Lawson wrote *Processional* after having read about the coal miners' strike in July and August 1920 (115). He quotes a section of Lawson's unpublished autobiography which refers to the coal miners' strike: "I did not want to write a documentary study of these events. But the strike gave me the setting for a ritual of primitive fury: the proud mountain people who had been in this area for more than a century were projected into an alliance with Negro and foreign-born workers. This gave the play a historical texture" (115).
7. Despite Sayles's hagiography of the West Virginia strikers, many white workers were less than enlightened on the subject of multi-ethnic solidarity. Among Lawson's papers is a clipping entitled "West Virginia Mine Fight Started by Fiery Cross" – dateline Morgantown, June 19 – which details the events of a strike at the Brady Warner Coal Corporation in which a group of presumably white miners known as "the regulators" burned a cross on a hillside. That Lawson clipped this article provides evidence for my contention that he assumed an ironic relationship to his coal-miner characters; like the Brady Warner strikers, Lawson's jazz miners are unable to see the actual conditions of their own situation, and thus are unable to direct their anger at its proper source ("Notes for *Processional*" 16-65-3).
8. That the play is meant to be ironic, Lawson's papers leave little doubt. Among them is "A Plot Outline," in which he sets up the play's action as follows:

   I.   Labor in agony of a strike. People go laughing, singing (?) as if nothing had happened – a man escapes – He knows nothing about the strike – caught among gigantic forces, feeling [fleeing?] away in clouds of coal smoke. He escapes in the confusion.
   II. Everything turns to ruins around the man – he learns the truth – vague revolt stirs in him – he goes out carelessly to die – irony of events saves him again, but a woman traps him.
   III. The same irony of the individual's case turns the whole industrial dispute to an absurd farce – after we cometh a builder. (JHLP "Notes for *Processional*")

9. Lawson later came to regret such stereotypes, thinking they were not ironized enough.

> *Processional* is too naive, too eager for shortcuts in the means it employs. The cartoon, the comic strip, the stereotype, are used for themselves, rather than as the starting point of a deeper exploration. The leading characters break through the stereotypes in moments of emotion. But these people, driven by violence and a tragic sense of life, are not fully realized as persons. (quoted in L. Robinson 64)

Bloch notes that, in the 1960s, Lawson refused to allow *Processional* to be included in an anthology, explaining to its editor that

> I have come to the conclusion that it is better not to include it. I have thought about it a great deal, because it is a play of great and neglected significance, but the vaudeville or cartoon method I use includes caricatures of Negro and Jewish personalities: this is presented as part of the raw crudity and violence of American life in the middle twenties, but it is so exaggerated that it has a very different and possible unfortunate meaning in our world of the middle sixties. I feel I cannot publish a work which suggests racist stereotypes. (quoted in Bloch 154–5)

10. In his notes for the play, for example, Lawson considers using the song "I Want a Girl Just Like the Girl that Married Dear Old Dad" in the context of Sadie's out-of-wedlock pregnancy "for ironical use" (JHLP "Notes for *Processional*").

11. Ten years later, Clifford Odets's *Waiting for Lefty* would get to dismantle realism's fourth wall. Had the Theatre Guild yielded to Lawson's request, *Processional* might have been the first to win this place of honor in the history of American drama.

7 Sophie Treadwell's "pretty hands"

1. During this time, Treadwell wrote a fictionalized account of her early life entitled, "The Story of Muh Life by One Who Has None" ("College papers and stories, 1902–06"). Dickey dates this manuscript to 1908, but, given its autobiographical nature and lack of dramatic form, I believe it is probably her first attempt at playwriting, composed during her first stay at Yankee Jim's in 1906–7.

2. According to Nancy Wynn, Treadwell recuperated from her first nervous breakdown at her mother's family's ranch in Stockton, California for about three months, finding work at Yankee Jim's in October, 1906 (16). There, she began work on her first full-length play, *Le Grand Prix*, and wrote an article for the *San Francisco Sunday Chronicle* about the camp's history as a gold mine (21). From June through October 1907, she served as a governess for two girls, living on their family's cattle ranch in Modoc County (22) – an experience which provided her with the setting for her play, *The Right Man*. From October to December 1907, she scrapped around Los Angeles with her mother, looking for work on the vaudeville stage. Although she eventually landed a small part in a religious play, she was soon disgusted by the working conditions most actors had to face (22–7). Destitute and on the verge of another nervous breakdown, Treadwell and her mother parted, with her mother returning to her family's ranch. Treadwell, meanwhile, continued

to look for work. With $16 to her name, she wrote her father for financial assistance, but her letter received no response (27–8). Picking up small typing jobs here and there, Treadwell finally secured work as an amanuensis for retired actor Helena Modjeska in February 1908, typing – and probably ghostwriting – much of Modjeska's 571-page memoir (28). When her mother fell ill in July, she returned to San Francisco, but did not live with her, residing instead at a boarding house nearby. The letters I cite appear to date from this period, for, within a year, Treadwell had again suffered another nervous breakdown, retiring to Yankee Jim's in September 1909, to recuperate (33). It was also during this year that she began work as a journalist at the *San Francisco Bulletin*.

3. Dickey observes that Treadwell "frequently experienced embarrassment and humiliation over her mother's persistent attempts to follow and reunite with Alfred," her father ("Expressionist" 66). Nancy Wynn reports that Nettie eventually filed divorce papers, but lost her courage at the last minute when she was unable to enter the courtroom to finalize the process. Although Alfred agreed to set up another home for them, his support was sporadic at best (5).

4. As the qualification "young" suggests, Treadwell's primary character assumes a subordinate position in all of the various binary relationships of which she is a part. Only in the episodes with her lover is she able to free herself from the imbalance of power inherent in all of her other relationships. In the scenes with him, she is simply indicated as "Woman."

5. In his 1955 book *Eros and Civilization*, Marcuse weds the theories of Karl Marx and Sigmund Freud to argue that contemporary civilization has reached a stage of "surplus repression." Where earlier epochs of human history required the gratification of the pleasure principle to be deferred in order for basic human needs to be met, modern civilization has reached a point where that is no longer necessary. In a culture characterized by the production of excess goods, the compulsion to obey the reality principle (which Marcuse redubs the "performance principle") becomes in fact oppressive. Marcuse argues that, in the face of such "surplus repression," humanity needs to "desublimate" its repressed desires and integrate the pleasure principle back into daily life. Marcuse would later retheorize the liberatory potential of "desublimation," recognizing capitalism's ability to reabsorb such energies back into a form of "repressive desublimation," but his belief in the compulsory nature of the "performance principle" is worth revisiting, I believe, given its apparent legacy in Butler's thought.

6. Nancy Nester, however, disagrees, arguing that critics are wrong to identify murder and madness as tropes of freedom in women's writing since they propose a withdrawal from society rather than a transformation of it. "One might ask Bywaters: How does murder as problem resolution represent this type of freedom for women when the last image in Treadwell's play situates Jones [*sic*] in prison, about to be executed by males, according to the laws of males, alienated physically and spiritually from the other females in her life?" (8).

7. Many scholars have rightly observed a similarity between Susan Glaspell's *Trifles* and Treadwell's *Machinal*. In them, both playwrights drew from their experience as journalists to dramatize the reasons a woman would choose to murder her husband. For an excellent discussion of the Margaret Hossack murder case dramatized in Glaspell's play, see Linda Ben-Zvi.

8. Jones observes that, where Snyder and Gray were both found guilty, the Young Woman, alone, is held responsible for her husband's murder; and that, where Snyder's last words were to ask that her executioners be forgiven, the Young Woman's last words are to offer her daughter advice (492–3).

9. See, for example, *Le Grand Prix* (1906–7), *The Right Man* (1908).

10. A letter from Modjeska to Treadwell, dated 7/23/08, responds to Treadwell's request for advice on how much to ask for production rights to her play. Modjeska notes that the going rate for young authors at this time is usually $100 plus $2\frac{1}{2}$ percent of gross proceeds. But, she continues, "Do not forget that you are a man or he will like to get the play for nothing. Women authors are usually considered vain fools who write for the sake of writing. When your play is a success you may put 'Sophie' before your name" ("Modjeska, correspondence").

11. Although she similarly received no credit for ghostwriting Helena Modjeska's memoirs, Treadwell apparently held no grudge, esteeming the actor highly, faithfully following her professional advice, and characterizing her and her husband in an unfinished sketch for a play.

12. Klages's work dates to the nineteen-teens, with *The Problems of Graphology* (1910), *Handwriting and Character* (1917), *Expressive Movements and Creativity* (1923), *The Foundations of Characterology* (1928), and *Graphological Exercises* (1930). In mentioning it, I make no claim that Treadwell necessarily knew it or Michon's work. Rather, I wish to suggest that handwriting analysis was yet another area in which Delsarte's theory of expression was influential. That Michon was French and Klages German suggests that expression circulated widely – and in many different contexts – throughout Europe during these years. See my epilogue for a fuller discussion of the cross-cultural currents of expression.

13. See chapter 5, note 20.

14. "Perhaps," Dickey conjectures, "the seeds of Treadwell's best play, *Machinal*, were sown years before its creation as she sat in the Princess Theatre listening to Boleslavsky's lectures. In one lecture, Boleslavsky spoke of his vision for the experimental use of sound in the theatre, a vision which may have prompted Treadwell's expressionistic use of patterned sounds and offstage voices in *Machinal*" (Dickey, "Sophie Treadwell's Summer" 13).

15. Amy Koritz has recently focused on the use of rhythm in several of the expressionist plays I discuss in this book. Noting a structural opposition between "moments of narrative stasis" and a repetitive rhythm that prompts their central characters to act (553), she reads these plays against the background of what Jackson Lears refers to as the "therapeutic ethos" of American individualism, arguing that they articulate a middle-class anxiety about individual self-fulfillment in a moment when industrial work rhythms were being imposed onto white-collar professions. While Koritz usefully identifies an inherent tension between "natural" and "mechanical" rhythms in these plays, and while she is right to see that tension as a symptom of changing patterns in professional and managerial work, she lacks the fuller context of the expressive culture movement to account for this perceived tension and its cultural meanings. As we've seen in chapter 2, proponents of expressive culture believed that the industrial rhythms of modernization had thrown the body's natural rhythms out of alignment, and that, only by learning to recoordinate the three languages of the

body, could one overcome the spiritual alienation caused by modernity. An interest in rhythm develops out of these concerns, being most fully explored by Emile Jaques-Dalcroze and his system of eurhythmics.

16. Although scholars are right to associate Boleslavsky's method of actor training with that of Stanislavsky (Dickey, *Research* 10), his focus on body positions and transitions between them suggests an affinity not only with Delsarte but with Meyerhold, whose constructivist program of biomechanics itself may have been influenced by Delsarte's course of applied aesthetics. See Yampolsky, though much more research on Delsarte's influence on Russian theatre practice needs to be done.

17. The radio isn't actually listed in these opening stage directions, but Treadwell calls for a radio in episode two.

18. The ocean as a figure of freedom appears again in episode six, where Treadwell's central character remembers holding a seashell up to her ear to hear the sound of the sea when she was a little girl (514).

19. These are the stage directions that open the play; those that introduce episode six suggest a darkened stage with the sound of footbeats passing by (514).

20. Here I follow Marcia Noe, who suggests that Susan Glaspell similarly anticipates many of the insights of French feminist theory in her experimental play, *The Verge*.

21. Referring to reviews of the original 1928 production, Jennifer Parent notes that "Much praise was lavished on the quality of the acting, especially the honest intensity, power and beautiful vocal quality of Zita Johann as the Young Woman" (88).

Epilogue: "modern times"

1. For an excellent discussion of the film as a picaresque and of the picaresque as a modern form, see Geoffrey Guevara-Geer.

2. See, for example, Gassner's introduction to Treadwell's *Machinal*.

Works cited

Abel, Richard, ed. *Silent Film*. New Brunswick: Rutgers University Press, 1996.

Abrams, Howard B. "The Historic Foundation of American Copyright Law: Exploding the Myth of Common Law Copyright." *Wayne Law Review* 29.3 (spring 1983): 1120–91.

Alger, William Rounseville. *Life of Edwin Forrest, the American Tragedian*, vol. I. Philadelphia: Lippincott & Co., 1877.

Allen, Robert. *Horrible Prettiness: Burlesque and American Culture*. Chapel Hill: University of North Carolina Press, 1991.

"An Act supplemental to an Act entitled 'An Act to amend the several acts respecting copyright . . .'" "American Memory Project." United States Congressional Documents and Debates, 1774–1873. US Stat., 34th Congress, 1st Session. <http://memory.loc.gov/cgi-bin/ampage> 138–9.

"An Act to revise, consolidate, and amend the Statutes relating to Patents and Copyrights." "American Memory Project." United States Congressional Documents and Debates, 1774–1873. US Stat., 41st Congress, 2nd Session. <http://memory.loc.gov/cgi-bin/ampage>.

Anonymous. "Mr. E. Forrest." *New York Mirror* 4.42 (12 May 1827): 335.

Applebee, Arthur N. *Tradition and Reform in the Teaching of English : A History*. Urbana IL: National Council of Teachers of English, 1974.

Archer, William. *The Old Drama and the New, an Essay in Re-valuation* Boston: Small, Maynard and Company, 1923.

Atkinson, J. Brooks. "Against the City Clatter." *New York Times* 6 September 1928.

Atlas, Marilyn J. "Innovation in Chicago: Alice Gerstenberg's Psychological Drama." *Midwestern Miscellany* 10 (1982): 59–68.

Ayres, Alfred. *Acting and Actors, Elocution and Elocutionists: A Book About Theater Folk and Theater Art*. New York: D. Appleton & Co., 1894.

Barrett, Lawrence. "Edwin Forrest." *Actors and Actresses of Great Britain and the United States: From the Days of David Garrick to the Present Time*. Vol. IV. Ed. Brander Matthews and Laurence Hutton. New York: Cassell & Co. Ltd., 1886. 33–67.

Beckerman, Bernard. "The University Accepts the Theatre: 1800–1925." *American Theatre: A Sum of its Parts; A Collection of the Distinguished Addresses Prepared Expressly for the Symposium "The American Theatre – A Cultural Process" at the First*

American College Theatre Festival, Washington DC, 1969. New York: Samuel French, Inc., 1971.

Bell, Elizabeth. "Performance Studies as Women's Work: Historical Sights/ Sites/Citations from the Margins." *Text & Performance Quarterly* 13 (1993): 350–74.

Benjamin, Walter. "The Work of Art in the Age of Mechanical Reproduction." *Illuminations.* Trans. Harry Zohn. Ed. Hannah Arendt. New York: Schocken Books, 1969. 217–51.

Ben-Zvi, Linda. "'Murder, She Wrote': The Genesis of Susan Glaspell's Trifles." *Susan Glaspell: Essays on Her Theater and Fiction.* Ed. Linda Ben-Zvi. Ann Arbor: University of Michigan Press, 1995. 19–48.

Bernheim, Alfred. *The Business of the Theatre: An Economic History of the American Theatre, 1750–1932.* 1932. New York: Benjamin Blom, 1964.

Bigsby, C. W. E. *A Critical Introduction to Twentieth Century American Drama.* Vol. 1. Cambridge: Cambridge University Press, 1982.

Bigsby, C. W. E. and Don B. Wilmeth. "Introduction." *The Cambridge History of American Theatre.* Vol. 1. Eds. Don B. Wilmeth and Christopher Bigsby. Cambridge and New York: Cambridge University Press, 1998. 1–19.

Black, Stephen. *Eugene O'Neill: Beyond Mourning and Tragedy.* New Haven: Yale University Press, 1999.

Blackburn, Clara. "Continental Influences on Eugene O'Neill's Expressionistic Dramas." *American Literature: A Journal of Literary History, Criticism, and Bibliography* 13.2 (May 1941): 109–33.

Blanchard, Fred C. "Professional Theatre Schools in the Early Twentieth Century." *The History of Speech Education in America.* Ed. Karl Wallace. New York: Appleton-Century-Crofts, Inc., 1954. 617–40.

Blau, Herbert. *To All Appearances: Ideology and Performance.* New York: Routledge, 1992.

Bleistein v. Donaldson Lithographing Co. No. 117. Supreme Court of the US. 2 February 1903.

Bloch, Beverle. "John Howard Lawson's 'Processional': Modernism in American Theatre in the Twenties." PhD dissertation, University of Denver, 1988.

Blumin, Stuart. "The Hypothesis of Middle-Class Formation in Nineteenth-Century America: A Critique and Some Proposals." *American Historical Review* 90 (April 1985): 299–338.

Bogard, Travis. *Contour In Time: The Plays of Eugene O'Neill.* New York: Oxford University Press, 1972, repr. 1988.

Bogard, Travis and Jackson R. Bryer, eds. *Selected Letters of Eugene O'Neill.* New Haven: Yale University Press, 1988.

Boleslavsky, Richard. *Acting, The First Six Lessons.* 1933. New York: Theatre Arts Book, 1965.

Bourdieu, Pierre. *The Field of Cultural Production: Essays on Art and Literature.* Ed. Randal Johnson. New York: Columbia University Press, 1993.

Bowles, Patrick. "*The Hairy Ape* as Existential Allegory." *The Eugene O'Neill Newsletter* 3.1 (1979): 2–3.

Brooks, Cleanth. *The Well Wrought Urn.* New York: Harcourt, Brace, 1947.

Brooks, Cleanth and Robert Heilman. *Understanding Drama*. New York: Henry Holt & Co., 1945.

Brown, Moses True. *The Synthetic Philosophy of Expression as Applied to the Arts of Reading, Oratory, and Personation*. Boston, New York and Chicago: Houghton Mifflin and Co., 1886.

Bryer, Jackson, ed. *"The Theatre We Worked For": The Letters of Eugene O'Neill to Kenneth Macgowan*. New Haven: Yale University Press, 1974.

Buckley, Peter. "To The Opera House: Culture and Society in New York City, 1800–1860." PhD dissertation, State University of New York-Stony Brook, 1984.

Bürger, Peter. *Theory of the Avant Garde*. Trans. Michael Shaw. 1984. Minneapolis: University of Minnesota Press, 1996.

Burgh, James. *The Art of Speaking*. 7th ed. London: T. Longman & J. Buckland, T. Field, and C. Dilly, 1787.

Burrow-Giles Lithographic Co. v. Sarony. Supreme Court of the US. 17 March 1884.

Bywaters, Barbara. "Marriage, Madness, and Murder in Sophie Treadwell's Machinal." *Modern American Drama: The Female Canon*. Ed. June Schlueter. London and Toronto: Associated University Presses, 1990. 97–110.

Callahan, Virginia Meyers. "Biography." Chuck Callahan Archive. Players' Club, New York City.

Carpenter, Frederic. *Eugene O'Neill*. Boston: Twayne Publishers, 1979.

Chametzky, Jules. "Elmer Rice, Liberation, and the Great Ethnic Question." *From Hester Street to Hollywood: The Jewish-American State and Screen*. Ed. Sarah Blacher Cohen. Bloomington: Indiana University Press, 1983. 71–84.

Cheney, Sheldon. *The Art Theater*. New York: Knopf Publishers, 1917.
The New Movement in the Theatre. New York: Mitchell Kennerly, 1914.

Chothia, Jean. "Theatre Language: Word and Image in The Hairy Ape." *Eugene O'Neill and the Emergence of American Drama*. Ed. Marc Maufort. Costerus New Series Vol. 75. Amsterdam and Atlanta: Rodopi, 1989. 31–46.

Cima, Gay Gibson. "Discovering Signs: The Emergence of the Critical Actor in Ibsen." *Theatre Journal* 35 (1983): 5–22.

Clark, Barrett H. *Eugene O'Neill, The Man and His Plays*. New York: Dover Publications, 1926; rev. 1947.

Clark, Solomon Henry. *Interpretation of the Printed Page*. Chicago and New York: Row, Peterson and Company, 1915.

Clum, John. *Ridgely Torrence*. New York: Twayne, 1972.

Cmiel, Kenneth. *Democratic Eloquence: The Fight Over Popular Speech in Nineteenth-Century America*. Berkeley: University of California Press, 1990.

Colakis, Marianthe. "Eugene O'Neill's *The Emperor Jones* as Senecan Tragedy." *Journal of Dramatic Theory and Criticism* 10.2 (winter 1990): 153–9.

Cole, Toby and Helen Krich Chinoy. *Actors on Acting: The Theories, Techniques, and Practices of the Great Actors of All Times as Told in Their Own Words*. New York: Crown Publishers, 1970.

Conklin, Robert. "The Expression of Character in O'Neill's *The Emperor Jones* and *The Hairy Ape*." *West Virginia University Philological Papers* 39 (1993): 101–7.

Cooley, John R. "*The Emperor Jones* and the Harlem Renaissance." *Studies in the Literary Imagination* 7.2 (1974): 73–83.

Crothers, Rachel. "Expressing Willie." *Three Plays by Rachel Crothers*. New York: Brentano's Publishers, 1924.

Cunningham, Frank. "Romantic Elements in Early O'Neill." *Critical Essays on Eugene O'Neill*. Ed. James Martine. Boston: G. K. Hall & Co., 1984. 65–72.

Curry, S. S. *Foundations of Expression*. Boston: The Expression Co., 1907.

Imagination and the Dramatic Instinct. Boston: The Expression Company, 1896.

The Province of Expression. Boston: The School of Expression, 1891.

Daly v. Palmer. No. 3552. Circuit Court of New York. December 1868.

Dawley, Herbert and Tony Sarg. *The Original Movie*. *Treasures from American Film Archives*. National Film Preservation Foundation, 2000.

DeLaura, David J. "Pater and Eliot: The Origin of the 'Objective Correlative.'" *Modern Language Quarterly* 26 (1965): 426–31.

Delsarte, François *et al*. *Delsarte System of Oratory*. 4th ed. New York: Edgar S. Werner, 1893.

Di Pasquale, Jr., Pasquale. "Coleridge's Framework of Objectivity and Eliot's Objective Correlative." *Journal of Aesthetics and Art Criticism* 26.4 (summer 1968): 489–500.

Dickey, Jerry. "The Expressionist Moment: Sophie Treadwell." *Cambridge Companion to American Women Playwrights*. Ed. Brenda Murphy. New York: Cambridge University Press, 1999. 66–81.

"The 'Real Lives' of Sophie Treadwell: Expressionism and the Feminist Aesthetic in *Machinal* and *For Saxophone*." *Speaking the Other Self: American Women Writers*. Ed. Jeanne Campbell Reesman. Athens: University of Georgia Press, 1997. 176–84.

Sophie Treadwell: A Research and Production Sourcebook. Westport CT: Greenwood Press, 1997.

"Sophie Treadwell's Summer with Boleslavsky and Lectures for the American Laboratory Theatre." Paper presented at "Art, Glitter and Glitz: The Theatre of the 1920s Celebrates American Diversity." Hofstra University, 3 November 1994.

Downer, Alan S. *Fifty Years of the American Drama: 1900–1950*. Chicago: Henry Regnery Co., 1951.

"Nature to Advantage Dressed: Eighteenth-Century Acting," *PMLA* 58 (1943): 1002–37.

"Players and Painted Stage: Nineteenth-Century Acting," *PMLA* 61 (1946): 522–76.

Dudden, Faye. *Women in the American Theatre: Actresses and Audiences, 1790–1870*. New Haven: Yale University Press, 1994.

Durham, Frank. *Elmer Rice*. New York: Twayne Publishers, 1970.

Durivage, Francis. "Delsarte." *The Atlantic Monthly*, vol. 27. Boston: James R. Osgood & Co., 1871, 618–9.

Dutton, Richard. *Mastering the Revels: The Regulation and Censorship of English Renaissance Drama*. Iowa City: University of Iowa Press, 1991.

Edwards, Davis. "The Real Source of Vachel Lindsay's Poetic Technique." *The Quarterly Journal of Speech* 33 (April 1947): 182–95.

Edwards, Paul. "Unstoried: Teaching Literature in the Age of Performance Studies." *Theatre Annual* 52 (1999). 1–147.

Egri, Peter. "'Belonging' Lost: Alienation and Dramatic Form in Eugene O'Neill's *The Hairy Ape*." *Critical Essays on Eugene O'Neill*. Ed. James Martine. Boston: G. K. Hall & Co., 1984. 77–111.

Eisen, Kurt. *The Inner Strength of Opposites: O'Neill's Novelistic Drama and the Melodramatic Imagination*. Athens: University of Georgia Press, 1994.

Eliot, T. S. "Hamlet and His Problems." *The Sacred Wood: Essays on Poetry and Criticism*. New York: Alfred A. Knopf, 1930.

Selected Essays, 1917–1932. New York: Harcourt Brace and Co., 1932.

Elwood, William R. "An Interview with Elmer Rice on Expressionism." *Educational Theatre Journal* 20 (1968): 1–7.

Emerson, Ralph Waldo. "Nature." 1836. *Selected Essays*. Ed. Larzer Ziff. New York: Penguin Books, 1982. 35–82.

Engel, Edwin. *The Haunted Heroes of Eugene O'Neill*. Cambridge, MA: Harvard University Press, 1953.

Esty, Jed. *A Shrinking Island: Modernism and National Culture in England*. Princeton: Princeton University Press, 2003.

Eysteinsson, Astradur. *The Concept of Modernism*. Ithaca: Cornell University Press, 1990.

Falk, Doris V. *Eugene O'Neill and the Tragic Tension, An Interpretive Study of the Plays*. New Brunswick: Rutgers University Press, 1958.

Fehr, Johannes. "Die Theorie des Zeichens bei Saussure und Derrida oder Jacques Derridas Saussure-Lektüre." *Cahiers Ferdinand de Saussure: Revue Suisse de Linguistique Générale* 44 (1992): 35–54.

Feltes, N. N. "International Copyright: Structuring 'the Condition of Modernity' in British Publishing." *Cardozo Arts & Entertainment Law Journal* 10.2 (1992): 535–44.

Fitzgerald, Percy. *The Art of Acting, In Connection with the Study of Character, The Spirit of Comedy and Stage Illusion*. London: Swan Sonnenschein & Co.; New York: Macmillan & Co., 1892.

Fletcher, Anne. "The Theory and Practice of Mordecai Gorelik (1925–1935): Emblem for the Changing American Theatre." PhD dissertation, Tufts University, 1992.

Flexner, Eleanor. *American Playwrights 1918–1938: The Theatre Retreats From Reality*, pref. John Gassner, pref. to 3rd ed. Eleanor Flexner. Freeport, New York: Books for Libraries Press, 1969; reprinted from 1938 original.

Fliegelman, Jay. *Declaring Independence: Jefferson, Natural Language, and the Culture of Performance*. Stanford: Stanford University Press, 1993.

Floyd, Virginia. "The Search for Self in *The Hairy Ape*: An Exercise in Futility?" *The Eugene O'Neill Newsletter* 1.3 (1978): 4–7.

Flynn, Joyce. "Melting Plots: Patterns of Racial and Ethnic Amalgamation in American Drama Before Eugene O'Neill." *American Quarterly* 38 (1986): 417–38.

Friedman, Sharon. "Feminism as Theme in Twentieth-Century American Women's Drama." *American Studies* 25.1 (1984): 69–89.

Gaines, Jane. *Contested Culture: The Image, the Voice and the Law*. Chapel Hill: University of North Carolina Press, 1991.

Geddes, Virgil. *The Melodramadness of Eugene O'Neill*. Brookfield, CT: Brookfield Players, Inc., 1934.

Gelb, Arthur and Barbara. *O'Neill*. 1962. New York: Harper & Row, 1973.

O'Neill: Life with Monte Cristo. New York: Applause Theatre & Cinema Books, 2000.

Gerstenberg, Alice. "Overtones." *Ten One-Act Plays*. New York: Brentano's Publishers, 1921.

Goldberg, Roselee. *Performance Art: From Futurism to the Present.* New York: H. N. Abrams, 1988.

Grimsted, David. *Melodrama Unveiled: American Theater and Culture 1800–1850.* Chicago: University of Chicago Press, 1968.

Guevara-Geer, Geoffrey W. "*Lazarillo de Tormes* and the Little Tramp of *Modern Times*: Two Modern *Picaros* Find Their Way." *Canadian Review of Comparative Literature* (June 1997): 235–45.

Halfmann, Ulrich. *Eugene O'Neill: Comments on the Drama and the Theater.* Tübingen: Gunter Narr Verlag, 1987.

Hamar, Clifford Eugene. "College and University Theatre Instruction in the Early Twentieth Century." *The History of Speech Education in America.* Ed. Karl Wallace. New York: Appleton-Century-Crofts, Inc., 1954. 572–94.

Hammerton, J. A. *The Actor's Art, Theatrical Reminiscences, Methods of Study and Advice to Aspirants.* London: George Redway, 1897.

Hanau, Stella and Helen Deutsch. *The Provincetown: A Story of the Theatre.* 1931. New York: Russell & Russell, 1972.

Hanson, Philip J. "*The Emperor Jones*: Naturalistic Tragedy in Hemispheric Perspective." *American Drama* 5.2 (spring 1996): 23–43.

Hay, Carla H. *James Burgh, Spokesman for Reform in Hanoverian England.* Washington: University Press of America, 1979.

Hecht, Stuart. "The Plays of Alice Gerstenberg: Cultural Hegemony in the American Little Theatre." *Journal of Popular Culture* 26.1 (summer 1992): 1–16.

Heck-Rabi, Louise. "Sophie Treadwell: Agent for Change." *Women in American Theater: Careers, Images, Movements.* Ed. Helen Krich Chinoy. New York: Crown Publishers, 1981. 157–62.

Hewitt, Barnard. *Theatre U.S.A.: 1668–1957.* New York: McGraw-Hill, 1959.

Hinden, Michael. "*The Emperor Jones*: O'Neill, Nietzsche, and the American Past." *The Eugene O'Neill Newsletter* 3.3 (1980): 2–4.

"Ironic Use of Myth in *The Hairy Ape*." *The Eugene O'Neill Newsletter* 1.3 (1978): 2–4.

Hodge, Francis. "The Private Theatre Schools in the Late Nineteenth Century." *The History of Speech Education in America.* Ed. Karl Wallace. New York: Appleton-Century-Crofts, Inc., 1954. 552–71.

Hogan, Robert. *The Independence of Elmer Rice.* Carbondale: Southern Illinois University Press, 1965.

Holden, Florence C. "The Fine Art of Poetry." *Werner's Magazine* 19.9 (September 1897): 3–19.

Hughes, Ann D. "Biblical Allusions in *The Hairy Ape*." *The Eugene O'Neill Newsletter* 1.3 (1978): 7–9.

Huyssen, Andreas. *After the Great Divide: Modernism, Mass Culture, Postmodernism.* Bloomington: Indiana University Press, 1986.

Ignatiev, Noel. *How the Irish Became White.* New York: Routledge, 1995.

Irving, Henry. "The Art of Acting." *The Drama Addresses.* 2d ed. London: William Heinemann, 1893. 35–69.

Jaffe, Ira S. "Fighting Words: *City Lights, Modern Times* and *The Great Dictator*." *The Journal of the University Film Association* 31.1 (winter 1979): 23–32.

Jameson, Fredric. *The Political Unconscious.* Ithaca: Cornell University Press, 1981.

Jaszi, Peter. "Toward a Theory of Copyright: The Metamorphoses of 'Authorship'." *Duke Law Journal* 2 (1991): 455–502.

Jefferson, Joseph. *The Autobiography of Joseph Jefferson.* 1889. Ed. Alan S. Downer. Cambridge, MA: The Belknap Press of Harvard University, 1964.

Jerving, Ryan. "Hep: Jazz Modernisms." PhD dissertation, University of Illinois at Urbana-Champaign, 2000.

Jones, Jennifer. "In Defense of the Woman: Sophie Treadwell's *Machinal.*" *Modern Drama* 37.3 (1994): 485–96.

Kagan, Norman. "The Return of *The Emperor Jones.*" *Negro History Bulletin* 34 (1971): 160–2.

Kaplan, Benjamin. *An Unhurried View of Copyright.* New York: Columbia University Press, 1967.

Kasson, John. *Rudeness and Civility, Manners in 19th-Century Urban America.* New York: Hill and Wang, 1990.

Kaufman, George S. and Marc Connelly. *Beggar on Horseback.* New York: Boni and Liveright Publishers, 1924.

Keat, Murray. "O'Neill's 'The Hairy Ape' and Rodin's 'The Thinker.'" *Journal of Evolutionary Psychology* 19.1–2 (March 1998): 108–15.

Keene v. Kimball. Supreme Court of MA. Suffolk. November 1860.

Keene v. Wheatley. No. 7644. Circuit Court of PA. 1861.

Kehl, D. G. "The 'Big Subject' in *The Hairy Ape*: A New Look at Scene Five." *The Eugene O'Neill Review* 17.1–2 (spring–fall 1993): 39–43.

Kern, Stephen. *The Culture of Time and Space: 1880–1918.* Cambridge, MA: Harvard University Press, 1983.

King, Barry. "Articulating Stardom." *Screen* 26.5 (September–October 1985): 27–50.

Kirby, E. T. "The Delsarte Method: 3 Frontiers of Acting Training." *The Drama Review* 16.1 [T-53] (March 1972): 55–69.

Kittler, Friedrich. *Gramophone, Film, Typewriter.* Trans. Geoffrey Winthrop-Young and Michael Wutz. Stanford: Stanford University Press, 1999.

Kobler, John. *The Trial of Ruth Snyder and Judd Gray.* Garden City and New York: Doubleday, Doran & Co., 1938.

Kolocotroni, Vassiliki, Jane Goldman, and Olga Taxidou, eds. *Modernism, An Anthology of Sources and Documents.* Chicago: University of Chicago Press, 1998.

Koritz, Amy. "Drama and the Rhythm of Work in the 1920s." *Theatre Journal* 53.4 (2001): 551–67.

Kozelka, Paul. "Dramatics in the High Schools, 1900–1925." *The History of Speech Education in America.* Ed. Karl Wallace. New York: Appleton-Century-Crofts, 1954. 595–616.

Lawson, John Howard. "Autobiography," 16-93-1; 16-93-2. "John Howard Lawson Papers, 1905–1969." Special Collections, Morris Library, Southern Illinois University at Carbondale.

"Clippings file for *Processional*," 16-4-4 to 16-4-5. "John Howard Lawson Papers, 1905–1969." Special Collections, Morris Library, Southern Illinois University at Carbondale.

"Material for lecture publicity," 16-5-2. "John Howard Lawson Papers, 1905–1969." Special Collections, Morris Library, Southern Illinois University at Carbondale.

"Notes for *Processional*," 16-65-3. "John Howard Lawson Papers, 1905–1969." Special Collections, Morris Library, Southern Illinois University at Carbondale.

Processional: A Jazz Symphony of American Life. New York: Thomas Selzer, 1925.

"Scrapbook," 16-1-5. "John Howard Lawson Papers, 1905–1969." Special Collections, Morris Library, Southern Illinois University at Carbondale.

"Yankee Doodle Blues," 16-94-5. "John Howard Lawson Papers, 1905–1969." Special Collections, Morris Library, Southern Illinois University at Carbondale.

Lears, T. J. Jackson. *No Place of Grace: Antimodernism and the Transformation of American Culture, 1880–1920*. New York: Pantheon Books, 1981.

Lees, F. N. "T. S. Eliot and Nietzsche." *Notes and Queries* 11 (1964): 386–7.

Levine, Lawrence. *Highbrow/Lowbrow: The Emergence of Cultural Hierarchy in America*. Cambridge, MA: Harvard University Press, 1988.

Lewis, Barbara. "Movement and Music Education: An Historian's Perspective." *Philosophy of Music Education Review* 6.2 (fall 1998): 113–23.

Lindroth, Colette and James. *Rachel Crothers: A Research and Production Sourcebook*. Westport, CT: Greenwood Press, 1995.

Littell, Robert. "Chiefly About *Machinal*: Broadway in Review." *Theatre Arts Monthly* 11 (November 1928): 774–782.

Logan, Olive. *Apropos of Women and Theatres*. New York: Carleton Publisher, 1869.

Lott, Eric. *Love and Theft*. New York: Oxford University Press, 1993.

Lowell, Marion, ed., *Harmonic Gymnastics and Pantomimic Expression*. Boston: Marion Lowell, 1895.

Lowenstein, Joseph. "The Script in the Marketplace." *Representations* 12 (fall 1985): 101–14.

Lukács, Georg. "The Sociology of Modern Drama." Ed. Eric Bentley. *The Theory of the Modern Stage*. New York: Penguin Books, 1968; repr. 1979. 425–50.

Lynes, Russell. *The Lively Audience: A Social History of the Visual and Performing Arts in American, 1890–1950*. New York: Harper & Row, 1985.

Macgowan, Kenneth. *The Theatre of Tomorrow*. New York: Boni and Liveright, 1921.

MacKaye, Percy. *Epoch: The Life of Steele MacKaye, Genius of the Theater, in Relation to His Times and Contemporaries, a Memoir by His Son*. 2 vols. New York: Boni & Liveright, 1927.

MacKaye, Steele. "Expression in Nature and Expression in Art." *The Voice* 6 (June 1887): 82–3.

MacKaye, Mrs. Steele. "Steele MacKaye and François Delsarte, A Letter Outlining Their Personal and Professional Relations." *Werner's Voice Magazine* 7 (July 1892): 188.

Macready, William Charles. *The Diaries of William Charles Macready 1833–1851*. Vols. I and II. Ed. William Toynbee. London: Chapman and Hall, 1912.

Maddock, Mary. "Alice Gerstenberg's Overtones: The Demon in the Doll." *Modern Drama* 37.3 (1994): 474–83.

Marcuse, Herbert. *Eros and Civilization: A Philosophical Inquiry into Freud*. Boston: Beacon Press, 1955.

Martin, Randy. *Performance as a Political Act: The Embodied Self.* Westport, CT: Bergin & Garvey Publishers, 1990.

Massa, Ann. "Intention and Effect in *The Hairy Ape*." *Modern Drama* 31.1 (March 1988): 41–51.

―――. *Vachel Lindsay: Fieldworker for the American Dream.* Bloomington: Indiana University Press, 1970.

Matthews, Brander and Laurence Hutton. *The Life and Art of Edwin Booth and His Contemporaries.* 1886. Boston: L. C. Page & Co., 1906.

Matthews, Fred. "The New Psychology and American Drama." *1915, The Cultural Moment.* Eds. Adele Heller and Lois Rudnick. New Brunswick, NJ: Rutgers University Press, 1991. 146–56.

May, Lary. *Screening Out the Past: The Birth of Mass Culture and the Motion Picture Industry.* New York: Oxford University Press, 1980.

McArthur, Benjamin. *Actors and American Culture, 1880–1920.* Philadelphia: Temple University Press, 1984.

McConachie, Bruce. "American Theatre in Context, from the Beginnings to 1870." *The Cambridge History of American Theatre.* Vol. 1. Eds. Don B. Wilmeth and Christopher Bigsby. Cambridge and New York: Cambridge University Press, 1998. 111–81.

―――. "Historicizing the Relations of Theatrical Production." *Critical Theory and Performance.* Eds. Janelle G. Reinelt and Joseph Roach. Ann Arbor: University of Michigan Press, 1992. 168–78.

―――. *Melodramatic Formations: American Theatre and Society, 1820–1870.* Iowa City: University of Iowa Press, 1992.

―――. "Out of the Kitchen and into the Marketplace: Normalizing *Uncle Tom's Cabin* for the Antebellum Stage." *Journal of American Drama and Theatre* 3 (winter 1991). 5–28.

McTeague, James H. *Before Stanislavsky: American Professional Acting Schools and Acting Theory, 1875–1925.* Metuchen, NJ: The Scarecrow Press, Inc., 1993.

Miller, Tice L. *Bohemians and Critics: American Theatre Criticism in the Nineteenth Century.* Metuchen, NJ: The Scarecrow Press, Inc., 1981.

Moody, Richard. *The Astor Place Riot.* Bloomington: Indiana University Press, 1958.

Morgan, Anna. *An Hour with Delsarte.* 1889. Boston: Lee and Shephard Publishers, 1890.

Moses, Montrose. *The Fabulous Forrest: The Record of an American Actor.* Boston: Little, Brown, and Co., 1929.

Moses, Montrose and John Mason Brown, eds., *The American Theatre as Seen by Its Critics, 1752–1934.* New York: Cooper Square Publishers, Inc., 1967.

Murphy, Brenda. "Feminism and the Marketplace: The Career of Rachel Crothers." *The Cambridge Companion to American Women Playwrights.* Ed. Brenda Murphy. Cambridge: Cambridge University Press, 1999. 82–97.

Murray, Edward. *The Cinematic Imagination: Writers and the Motion Pictures.* New York: Frederick Ungar, 1972.

Musser, Charles. "The Changing Status of the Film Actor." *Before Hollywood: Turn-of-the-Century Film from American Archives.* New York: American Federation of Arts, 1986. 57–62.

Nelson, Cary. *Repression and Recovery: Modern American Poetry and the Politics of Cultural Memory, 1910–1945.* Madison: University of Wisconsin Press, 1989.

Nester, Nancy. "The Agoraphobic Imagination: The Protagonist Who Murders and the Critics Who Praise Her." *American Drama* 6.2 (1997): 1–24.

Nevo, Baruch, ed. *Scientific Aspects of Graphology.* Springfield, IL: Charles C. Thomas Publisher, 1986.

Nickel, John. "Racial Degeneration and *The Hairy Ape.*" *The Eugene O'Neill Review* 22.1–2 (spring–fall 1998): 33–40.

Nietzsche, Friedrich. *The Complete Works, The First Complete and Authorised English Translation.* Vol. 1, *The Birth of Tragedy or Hellenism and Pessimism.* Ed. Oscar Levy. Trans. Wm. A. Haussman, Ph.D. Edinburgh & London: T. N. Foulis, 1910.

Noe, Marcia. "*The Verge*: L'Ecriture Feminine at the Provincetown." *Susan Glaspell: Essays on Her Theater and Fiction.* Ed. Linda Ben-Zvi. Ann Arbor: University of Michigan Press, 1995. 129–42.

Nolan, Patrick J. "*The Emperor Jones*: A Jungian View of the Origin of Fear in the Black Race." *The Eugene O'Neill Newsletter* 4.1 (1980): 6–9.

O'Neill, Eugene. *Complete Plays.* Ed. Travis Bogard. New York: The Library of America, 1988.

Palmieri, Anthony F. R. *Elmer Rice: A Playwright's Vision of America.* Rutherford, NJ: Associated University Presses, Inc., 1980.

Parent, Jennifer. "Arthur Hopkins' Production of Sophie Treadwell's *Machinal.*" *The Drama Review* [T93] 26.1 (spring 1982): 88–100.

Patterson, Lyman Ray. *Copyright in Historical Perspective.* Nashville: Vanderbilt University Press, 1968.

Pearson, Roberta. *Eloquent Gestures: The Transformation of Performance Style in the Griffith Biograph Films.* Berkeley: University of California Press, 1992.

Pemberton, T. C. R. "To Thespis." *Louisville Public Advertiser* 21 May 1823.

Pfister, Joel. *Staging Depth: Eugene O'Neill and The Politics of Psychological Discourse.* Chapel Hill: University of North Carolina Press, 1995.

Poole, Gabriele. "'Blarsted Niggers!' *The Emperor Jones* and Modernism's Encounter with Africa." *The Eugene O'Neill Review* 18.1–2 (spring–fall 1994): 21–37.

Porte, Joel. "Introduction." *Interpretations of Poetry and Religion.* George Santayana. 1900. Cambridge, MA: Massachusetts Institute of Technology, 1989. xiii–xxxi.

Powell, Herbert Preston. *The World's Best Book of Minstrelsy.* Philadelphia: The Penn Publishing Co., 1926.

Puchner, Martin. *Stage Fright: Modernism, Anti-theatricality, and the Drama.* Baltimore: Johns Hopkins University Press, 2002.

Quinn, Arthur Hobson. *A History of the American Drama, From the Beginning to the Civil War.* New York: Harper & Brothers, 1923.

Rarig, Frank M. and Halbert S. Greaves. "National Speech Organizations and Speech Education." *The History of Speech Education in America.* Ed. Karl Wallace. New York: Appleton-Century-Crofts, Inc., 1954. 490–522.

Rée, Jonathan. *I See a Voice: Deafness, Language and the Senses – A Philosophical History.* New York: Metropolitan Books, Henry Holt & Co., 1999.

Rees, James. *Colley Cibber's Life of Edwin Forrest*. Philadelphia: T. B. Peterson & Brothers, 1874.

Renshaw, Edyth. "Five Private Schools of Speech." *The History of Speech Education in America*. Ed. Karl Wallace. New York: Appleton-Century-Crofts, Inc., 1954. 301–25.

Rice, Elmer. *The Adding Machine*. 1922. New York: Samuel French Publishers, 1956.

   "*The Adding Machine*, miscellaneous." F-76-543 to F 77-694. Harry Ransom Humanities Research Center. University of Texas.

   "Business Correspondence, *The Adding Machine*." B47-24 to B47-191. Harry Ransom Humanities Research Center. University of Texas.

   "Business Correspondence *The Subway*." B58-654 to B58-718. Harry Ransom Humanities Research Center. University of Texas.

   Letters to Frank Harris. G87-20 to G87-54 "Rice, Elmer/Harris, Frank, n.d.–1919/Letters." Harry Ransom Humanities Research Center. University of Texas.

   Letters to Frank Harris. G87-55 to G87-77 "Rice, Elmer/Harris, Frank, 1920/Letters." Harry Ransom Humanities Research Center. University of Texas.

   Letters to Frank Harris. G87-78 to G87-110 "Rice, Elmer/Harris, Frank, 1921–1925/Letters." Harry Ransom Humanities Research Center. University of Texas.

   Letter to Marc (Connelly?) 4/18/23. F-76-543 to F-77-694 "*Adding Machine*, Miscellaneous." Harry Ransom Humanities Research Center. University of Texas.

   The Living Theatre. New York: Harper & Bros., 1959.

   Minority Report: An Autobiography. New York: Simon and Schuster, 1963.

   "Scripts, published articles, stories, letters, speeches, radio, etc." F-75-1 to F-75-76. Harry Ransom Humanities Research Center. University of Texas.

   The Subway. New York: Samuel French, 1929.

Richardson, Gary A. "Plays and Playwrights: 1800–1865." *The Cambridge History of American Theatre*. Vol. 1. Eds. Don B. Wilmeth and Christopher Bigsby. Cambridge and New York: Cambridge University Press, 1998. 250–302.

Roach, Joseph. *Cities of the Dead: Circumatlantic Performance*. New York: Columbia University Press, 1996.

   "The Emergence of the American Actor." *The Cambridge History of American Theatre*. Vol. 1. Eds. Don B. Wilmeth and Christopher Bigsby. Cambridge and New York: Cambridge University Press, 1998. 338–72.

   The Player's Passion: Studies in the Science of Acting. 1985. Ann Arbor: University of Michigan Press, 1993.

Robb, Mary Margaret. "The Elocutionary Movement and Its Chief Figures." *The History of Speech Education in America*. Ed. Karl Wallace. New York: Appleton-Century-Crofts, 1954: 178–201.

   Oral Interpretation of Literature in American Colleges and Universities. New York: The H. W. Wilson Co., 1941.

Robinson, James A. "The Masculine Primitive and *The Hairy Ape*." *The Eugene O'Neill Review* 19.1–2 (spring–fall 1995): 95–109.

Robinson, LeRoy. "John Howard Lawson's Second Draft of *Processional*, 1921." *Bulletin of the Faculty of Liberal Arts*. Nagasaki University 21.1 (August 1980): 85–116.

Roediger, David. *The Wages of Whiteness: Race and the Making of the American Working Class*. New York: Verso Press, 1991.

Rogin, Michael. *Blackface, White Noise: Jewish Immigrants in the Hollywood Melting Pot*. Berkeley: University of California Press, 1996.

Rose, Mark. *Authors and Owners: The Invention of Copyright*. Cambridge, MA: Harvard University Press, 1993.

Ross, Ishbel. *Ladies of the Press: The Story of Women in Journalism by an Insider*. New York: Harper Brothers, 1936.

Roy, Emil. "Eugene O'Neill's *The Emperor Jones* and *The Hairy Ape* as Mirror Plays." *Comparative Drama* 2 (1968): 21–31.

Ruyter, Nancy Lee Chalfa. *The Cultivation of Body and Mind in Nineteenth-Century American Delsartism*. Westport, CT: Greenwood Press, 1999.

Saiz, Peter R. "The Colonial Story in *The Emperor Jones*." *The Eugene O'Neill Review* 17.1–2 (spring–fall 1993): 31–8.

Santayana, George. *Interpretations of Poetry and Religion*. 1900. Cambridge, MA: Massachusetts Institute of Technology, 1989.

Sarony v. Burrow-Giles Lithographic Co. Circuit Court of Southern District New York. April 1883.

Sayler, Oliver. *Our American Theatre*. New York: Brentano's Publishers, 1923.

Schwerdt, Lisa. "Blueprint for the Future: *The Emperor Jones*." *Critical Essays on Eugene O'Neill*. Ed. James Martine. Boston: G. K. Hall & Co., 1984. 72–7.

Segel, Harold B. *Body Ascendant: Modernism and the Physical Imperative*. Baltimore: Johns Hopkins University Press, 1998.

Shattuck, Charles H. *The Hamlet of Edwin Booth*. Urbana: University of Illinois Press, 1969.

Shattuck, Roger. *The Banquet Years: The Origins of the Avant-Garde in France, 1885 to World War I*. New York: Vintage Books, 1955; rev. 1968.

Shaver, Claude. "Steele MacKaye and the Delsartian Tradition." *The History of Speech Education in America*. Ed. Karl Wallace. New York: Appleton-Century-Crofts, Inc., 1954. 202–18.

Shawn, Ted. *Every Little Movement: A Book about François Delsarte*. 2d ed. 1954. New York: Ted Shawn, 1963.

Sheaffer, Louis. *O'Neill: Son and Artist*. Boston: Little, Brown & Co., 1973.

Sheridan, Thomas, A. M., *Lectures on the Art of Reading*. London: J. Dodsley, J. Wilkie, E. and C. Dily, T. Davies, 1775. Volumes I, *On the Art of Reading Prose* and II, *On the Art of Reading Verse*.

Sievers, W. David. *Freud on Broadway: A History of Psychoanalysis and the American Drama*. New York: Hermitage House, 1955.

Smith, Alison. "The New Play: Mills of the Gods." *New York World* 10 September 1928: 13.

Smith, Donald K. "Origin and Development of Departments of Speech." *The History of Speech Education in America*. Ed. Karl Wallace. New York: Appleton-Century-Crofts, Inc., 1954. 447–70.

Smith, Susan Harris. *American Drama: the Bastard Art*. New York: Cambridge University Press, 1997.

Sohn, Dong-Ho. "*The Emperor Jones*: Cinematic Imagination and Modern Spatiality." *Journal of English Language and Literature* 41.4 (1995): 1083–98.

Sonnemann, Ulrich. *Handwriting Analysis as a Psychodiagnostic Tool*. New York: Grune & Stratton, 1950.

Stebbins, Genevieve. *The Delsarte System of Dramatic Expression*. New York: Edgar S. Werner, 1886; copyright 1885.

Steen, Shannon. "Melancholy Bodies: Racial Subjectivity and Whiteness in O'Neill's *The Emperor Jones*." *Theatre Journal* 52.3 (2000): 339–59.

Stephens, John Russell. *The Profession of the Playwright, British Theatre 1800–1900*. Cambridge: Cambridge University Press, 1992.

Strand, Ginger. "Treadwell's Neologism: *Machinal*." *Theatre Journal* 44.2 (May 1992): 163–75.

Susman, Warren. "'Personality' and the Making of Twentieth-Century Culture." *New Directions in American Intellectual History*. Eds. John Higham and Paul K. Conkin. Baltimore: Johns Hopkins University Press, 1979. 212–26.

Sutherland, Cynthia. "American Women Playwrights as Mediators of the 'Woman Problem.'" *Modern Drama* 21.3 (1978): 319–36.

Szwed, John. "Race and the Embodiment of Culture," *Ethnicity* 2 (March 1975), 253–70.

Taylor, Jenny Bourne and Sally Shuttleworth. *Embodied Selves: An Anthology of Psychological Texts, 1830–1890*. Oxford: Clarendon Press, 1998.

Tiusanen, Timo. *O'Neill's Scenic Images*. Princeton, NJ: Princeton University Press, 1968.

Tornqvist, Egil. *A Drama of Souls: Studies in O'Neill's Super-naturalistic Technique*. New Haven: Yale University Press, 1969.

Treadwell, Sophie. "College papers and stories, 1902–06." MS 318, box 20, folder 7. University of Arizona Manuscript Collection.

"Her book." Scrapbook, 1909–14. MS 318, box 8, folders 1–2. University of Arizona Manuscript Collection.

"How I Got My Husband and How I Lost Him, the Story of Jean Traig." Scrapbook, 1914–15. MS 318, box 9. University of Arizona Manuscript Collection.

"Letters to mother." MS 318, box 6, folder 12. University of Arizona Manuscript Collection.

Machinal (typescript). MS 318, box 17, folder 6. University of Arizona Manuscript Collection.

Machinal. Twenty-Five Best Plays of the Modern American Theatre. Ed. John Gassner. 1928. New York: Crown Publishers, 1949.

"Modjeska, correspondence." MS 318, box 5, folder 22. University of Arizona Manuscript Collection.

"War Correspondence." MS 318, box 10. University of Arizona Manuscript Collection.

United States Congress. House Report (50-1) 1875, 21 April 1888.

House Report (51-1) 2401, 10 June 1890.

House Report (53-2) 1191, 29 June 1894.

House Report (59-2) 7083, 30 January 1907.

House Report (60-2) 2222, 22 February 1909.

United States Senate Report (59-2) 6187, pt. 2, 5 February 1907.

Vaidhyanathan, Siva. *Copyrights and Copywrongs: The Rise of Intellectual Property and How It Threatens Creativity.* New York: New York University Press, 2001.

Valgemae, Mardi. *Accelerated Grimace: Expressionism in the American Drama of the 1920s.* Carbondale: Southern Illinois University Press, 1972.

"Civil War Among the Expressionists: John Howard Lawson and the *Pinwheel* Controversy." *Educational Theatre Journal* 20: 10.

"Rice's *The Subway.*" *Explicator* 25.7 (March 1967): 62.

Vanden Heuvel, Michael. *Elmer Rice: A Research and Production Sourcebook.* Westport, CT: Greenwood Press, 1996.

Vardac, A. Nicholas. *From Stage to Screen: Theatrical Method from Garrick to Griffith.* Cambridge, MA: Harvard University Press, 1949.

Wainscott, Ronald. *The Emergence of the Modern American Theater, 1914–1929.* New Haven: Yale University Press, 1997.

Staging O'Neill: The Experimental Years, 1920–1934. New Haven: Yale University Press, 1988.

Walker, John. *Elements of Elocution.* Vols. I and II. 1781. Ed. R. C. Alston. Menston, England: The Scolar Press Limited, 1969.

Walker, Julia. "Why Performance? Why Now? Textuality and the Rearticulation of Human Presence." *The Yale Journal of Criticism* 16.1 (spring 2003): 149–75.

Watermeier, Daniel J., ed. *Edwin Booth's Performances: The Mary Isabella Stone Commentaries.* Ann Arbor: UMI Research Press, 1990.

Weisert, John Jacob. "The First Decade at Sam Drake's Louisville Theatre." *Filson Club History Quarterly* 39 (October 1965): 287–310.

West, Shearer. *The Image of the Actor: Verbal and Visual Representation in the Age of Garrick and Kemble.* New York: St. Martin's Press, 1991.

White–Smith Music Publishing Company v. The Apollo Company. No. 8126; 8127. Circuit Court of NY. 21 June 1905.

White–Smith Music Publishing Company v. The Apollo Company. No. 110, 111. Supreme Court of US. 24 February 1908.

Wilson, Garff. *A History of American Acting.* 1966. Westport, CT: Greenwood Press, 1980.

Wister, Fanny Kemble, ed. *Fanny, The American Kemble: Her Journals and Unpublished Letters.* Tallahassee, FL: South Pass Press, 1972.

Wixon, Christopher. "Everyman and Superman: Assimilation, Ethnic Identity and Elmer Rice's *Counsellor-at-Law.*" *American Drama* 8.1 (fall 1998): 59–74.

Wolter, Jürgen. *The Dawning of American Drama, American Dramatic Criticism 1746–1915.* Westport, CT: Greenwood Press, 1993.

Wood, Gillen D'Arcy. *The Shock of the Real: Romanticism and Visual Culture, 1760–1860.* New York: Palgrave, 2001.

Woodmansee, Martha. "The Genius and the Copyright: Economic and Legal Conditions of the Emergence of the 'Author.'" *Eighteenth-Century Studies* 17.4 (summer 1984): 425–48.

Woods, Leigh. *Garrick Claims the Stage: Acting as Social Emblem in Eighteenth-Century England.* Westport, CT: Greenwood Press, 1984.

Woolbert, Charles. "Theories of Expression: Some Criticisms." *Quarterly Journal of Speech* 1 (July 1915): 127–43.

Wynn, Nancy Edith. *Sophie Treadwell: The Career of a Twentieth-Century American Feminist Playwright*. PhD dissertation, City University of New York, 1982.

Yampolsky, Mikhail. "Kuleshov's Experiments and the New Anthropology of the Actor." *Silent Film*. Ed. Richard Abel. New Brunswick: Rutgers University Press, 1996. 45–67.

Zapf, Hubert. "O'Neill's *Hairy Ape* and the Reversal of Hegelian Dialectics." *Modern Drama* 31.1 (March 1988): 3–40.

Index